NF

LABOUR MARKET AND ECONOMIC PERFORMANCE

Also by Toshiaki Tachibanaki

SAVINGS AND BEQUESTS

Labour Market and Economic Performance

Europe, Japan and the USA

Edited by

Toshiaki Tachibanaki
Professor of Economics
Kyoto University
Kyoto, Japan

St. Martin's Press

© Toshiaki Tachibanaki 1994

First published in Great Britain 1994 by
THE MACMILLAN PRESS LTD
Houndmills, Basingstoke, Hampshire RG21 2XS
and London
Companies and representatives
throughout the world

A catalogue record for this book is available
from the British Library.

ISBN 0–333–59905–5

Printed in Great Britain by
Ipswich Book Co Ltd
Ipswich, Suffolk

First published in the United States of America 1994 by
Scholarly and Reference Division,
ST. MARTIN'S PRESS, INC.,
175 Fifth Avenue,
New York, N.Y. 10010

ISBN 0–312–12273–X

Library of Congress Cataloging-in-Publication Data
Labour market and economic performance : Europe, Japan and the USA /
edited by Toshiaki Tachibanaki.
p. cm.
Includes index.
1. Labor market—Japan. 2. Labor market—Europe. 3. Labor
market—United States. I. Tachibanaki, Toshiaki, 1943– .
HD5827.A6L33 1994
331—dc20   94–24882
                                                    CIP

Contents

v

Preface

Preliminary versions of the papers included in this volume were presented at the Conference on 'Labour Market and Economic Performance' held in Osaka, Japan, in July 1992. The conference was organized by Toshiaki Tachibanaki, and financed by the Kansai Economic Research Centre. We are indebted to the Centre for its support.

The conference was the thirtieth memorial event. The conference was called 'Rokko Conference', and is now popularly called 'Biwako Conference', which assembled leading Japanese economists and econometricians. It has been held during the past thirty years, and it is known as one of the most prestigious conferences for economists in Japan. Financial support has always been provided by the Kansai Economic Research Centre. We are very grateful to the Centre for its continuous support.

The thirtieth memorial conference focused on a relatively narrow subject, namely 'Labour Market and Economic Performance', and invited several leading non-Japanese economists in order to hold an international conference. The editor believes that the outgrowth of the conference, this book, provides readers with many useful insights and understandings of the relationship between labour markets and economic performance in Europe, Japan and the US.

Finally, the editor would like to express his gratitude to the following individuals – Messrs Osamu Uno (the President of the Kansai Economic Research Centre), Shotaro Miyano (the Executive Director of the Kansai Economic Research Centre), Professors Chikashi Moriguchi (Osaka University) and Toshihisa Toyoda (Kobe University) – for their advice and support.

TOSHIAKI TACHIBANAKI

Notes on the Contributors

Charles Brown is Professor of Economics, and Research Scientist at the Institute for Social Research, at the University of Michigan. His research has focused on the reasons why firms adopt particular wage-setting arrangements, and the consequences of those choices for payroll costs, turnover, and worker quality. He has also studied differences between large and small employers more generally, work that is presented in *Employers Large and Small*. He has also taught at the University of Maryland, and served as senior economist for the US Minimum Wage Study Commission.

Per-Anders Edin is Associate Professor of Economics at Uppsala University, Sweden, and a Research Economist of the National Bureau of Economic Research, Cambridge. He has published a number of articles in labour economics on topics such as wage structure, evaluation of labour market programmes, and unemployment duration, but also on taxes and portfolio choice, exchange rates, and housing demand.

Yoshio Higuchi is Professor of Business and Commerce at Keio University and Invited Professor at the Institute of Economic Research of Hitotsubashi University. He is also a research adviser at the Japan Institute of Labour. His main fields of interest are the labour market, wage structure and job turnover. He has written numerous articles in academic journals and books including *Japanese Economy and Labour Supply Behavior*.

Bertil Holmlund is Professor of Economics at Uppsala University, Sweden. Previously he was a research associate at the Industrial Institute for Economic and Social Research (IUI) and at the Trade Union Institute for Economic Research (FIEF) in Stockholm. He has written extensively on labour economics, including books on labour mobility, trade union wage policies, and unemployment insurance. He has published a large number of theoretical and empirical journal articles covering a broad range of issues in labour economics and macroeconomics.

Tsuneo Ishikawa is Professor of Economics at the University of Tokyo. He has studied widely in the theories of personal income distribution and intergenerational transmission of wealth. His recent publication *Income and Wealth* (1991, in Japanese, English version in preparation) conducts an extensive theoretical survey on the development of the theories of personal income and wealth distribution. He is currently occupied with a large scale research project to assess the overall state and the changes of income distribution in Japan, whose outcome will be published shortly.

Richard Layard is Professor of Economics at the London School of Economics and Director of its Centre for Economic Performance. He has worked on understanding unemployment for the last ten years and in 1991 co-authored *Unemployment, Macroeconomic Performance and the Labour Market* with Stephen Nickell and Richard Jackman. He has also been active in the employment policy debate as founder of the Employment Institute in 1985. His most recent proposals are in *Stopping Unemployment* co-authored with John Philpott. For the last year he has been in Moscow as an adviser to the Russian Government.

Jonathan S. Leonard is Professor of Management of the University of California at Berkeley. He was formerly Senior Economist at the President's Council of Economic Advisers, and Co-editor of the journals *Industrial Relations* and *Journal of Human Resources*. He has served as a consultant to the OECD, the US Department of Labour, US Commission on Civil Rights, and US National Academy of Sciences. He is an expert on labour market issues, and a Research Associate of the National Bureau of Economic Research.

Hisakazu Matsushige is Associate Professor, Osaka School of International Public Policy, Osaka, Japan, where he has been teaching economic theory, econometrics and economic comparative studies. He has written several articles, mainly on skill formation, internal labour markets and wage determination in Japan and also in Australia.

Stephen Nickell is currently Professor of Economics at the University of Oxford, Director of the Oxford Institute of Economics and Statistics and Professorial Fellow of Nuffield College. He is a Fellow of the Econometric Society and a Council Member of both the Econometric Society and the Royal Economic Society. He is an Associate Editor of the *Economic Journal*. He has written widely on unemployment, wage and employment determination, investment and economic performance.

Isao Ohashi is Professor of Economics at Nagoya University. Previously he was Associate Professor of Economics at Nagoya City University and at Tsukuba University. He has written extensively on theoretical economics and labour economics. His publications include The *Theory of Labor Markets*.

Souichi Ohta is a graduate student at the London School of Economics. His main field of interest is labour economics, especially the internal labour market in the firm. He has written several articles on the field.

Fumio Ohtake is Associate Professor of Economics at Osaka University, Japan. He has published numerous articles on labour, social security and taxation, including two books, *Economic Analysis on Taxation and Social Security*, and *A Study Guide to Macroeconomics*, both in Japanese.

Hiroshi Osano is Associate Professor of Economics, Osaka School of International Public Policy, Osaka University. His main fields of interest are labour economics, banking and financial economics, and macroeconomics. He has written numerous articles in academic journals, mainly on theoretical and empirical studies of labour contract and banking contract theories, and business cycles.

Thomas Östros is a graduate student in Economics at Uppsala University. He is doing microeconometric research on the Swedish wage structure. He is also a member of the city council in Uppsala.

Toshio Serita is Assistant Professor of the Department of Economics at Konan University. His main fields of research are finance and international finance. He has written articles on asset prices and financial intermediation in academic journals.

Toshiaki Tachibanaki is Professor of Economics at Kyoto University, Japan. He has taught at several universities and had research positions in Europe and the US. He had various visiting positions at research institutions of the Japanese government and the Bank of Japan. He has written numerous articles on labour, public economics and finance in both English and Japanese, including the editorships of several books. Also, he is a member of the editorial boards of various academic journals.

Robert H. Topel is the Isidore Brown and Gladys J. Brown Professor in Urban and Labor Economics at the Graduate School of Business, University of Chicago. He is a Research Associate of the National Bureau of Economic Research, a founding member of the National Academy of Social Insurance, and an elected member of the Conference on Income and Wealth. He is the author of numerous articles related to labour markets. He is an Editor of the *Journal of Political Economy* and has served on the editorial boards of the *Journal of Labor Economics*, the *American Economic Review*, and the *Journal of Business Economics*.

Joseph S. Tracy is Associate Professor of Economics at Columbia University. He was an Ohlin fellow at the National Bureau of Economic Research. He has written extensively on unions and collective bargaining. A focus of much of this work has been on assessing the importance of informational problems as a cause of labour disputes.

1 Introduction: Labour Market and Economic Performance

Toshiaki Tachibanaki

1.1 MOTIVATION FOR THIS BOOK

This book examines the effect of labour markets on economic performance in an international perspective. Labour markets are an important determinant of the performance of both national economies and individual firms, as well as employee rewards, namely, wages and satisfaction levels. If we pay attention to national economies, the high level of unemployment is the most devastating problem in Europe among many problems related to labour. In Japan, the unemployment rate is relatively low, which indicates rather good performance of its labour market. Nevertheless, there may be hidden labour problems even in Japan. The US economy suffers from two major labour market related problems: low real income growth, primarily due to its low level of productivity growth; and widening wage dispersions among its workers. The purpose of this book is to examine the reasons why the Japanese labour market is so different from the European and the US labour markets, and why it appears to be so efficient.

Table 1.1 indicates very broadly the general features of the labour markets in Europe, Japan and the US to which the essays presented in this book seek to address. Of the nine features four refer to average levels, and five refer to the feature's variability.

Table 1.1 indicates that significant differences exist among the labour markets in these three regions. For example, the low rate of unemployment in Japan may make Europeans and Americans envious, while they are less likely to envy the longer average working hours in Japan. A second example concerns the high level of wage flexibility which may help to raise employment in Japan, while wage rigidity may be detrimental to employment in Europe. A third example concerns the rate of unionization, which is relatively low in Japan and the US, and high in Europe. The different rates of union participation are

1

Table 1.1   Several key features of the labour markets in Europe, Japan and the US

	Europe	*Japan*	*US*
Level			
Unemployment rate	High	Low	Average
Working hours	Short	Long	Average
Productivity growth	Low	High	Average
Unionization	High	Low	Low
Variability			
Unemployment rate	High	Low	High
Production	Average	High	High
Employment	Average	Low	High
Working hours	Average	High	Low
Real wages	Low	High	Low

likely to affect the relative efficiency of their labour markets.

The purpose of this book is to provide readers with several key features which are able to explain the cause of various differences in the performance of labour markets in Europe, Japan and the US. The book includes both theoretical and empirical studies of various countries undertaken by labour and macroeconomists.

Before proceeding, three points merit attention. First, we have to recognize that Europe is not a homogeneous region. There are substantial differences among European nations in various aspects of their labour markets. For example, in some countries wages are determined in a centrally negotiated bargaining process, while in other countries wages are determined in a decentralized process at the industry, factory or even individual worker level. As a second example, some countries emphasize, in determining their macroeconomic policies, a low rate of inflation (e.g., Germany), while other countries pursue different policy targets. Also, the growth rate of productivity differs from country to country in Europe. These examples suggest that European countries are fairly heterogeneous. This is in particular true if eastern European nations (i.e., the former socialist countries) are included.

Second, although the differences among Europe, Japan and the US are the primary concerns of this book, emphasis is also placed upon the differences between Euro-American nations and Japan, simply because these differences are quite large. The chapters in this book can be divided into those examining Euro-American countries and those examining Japan, but it should nevertheless be pointed out that there

Table 1.2   Labour market features: Japan and Euro-American countries

	Japan	Euro-American countries
(1) Labour mobility	Less mobile	More mobile
(2) Wages and promotion	Seniority	Free competition
(3) Union	Enterprise unionism	Crafts or industry unionism

is a school which proposes that Euro-American countries are also het-erogeneous. For example, Albert (1991) distinguishes between Anglo-Saxon (i.e., the UK and the US) capitalism and Rhenish or Alpine capitalism (Germany, Switzerland and Sweden). Japan, in fact, according to Albert, belongs to the latter group. Thus, Japan is in a anomalous position in the taxonomy of capitalism.

Third, similarities among Europe, Japan and the US should be ex-pected since these regions are industrialized, and exhibit relatively high *per capita* income and productivity. Also, they belong to market econ-omies, although the degree of market economies differs from country to country. Equal emphasis is therefore placed upon similarities in the labour market in these regions.

1.2   DIFFERENCES IN LABOUR MARKETS BETWEEN EURO-AMERICAN NATIONS AND JAPAN

It would be useful to give a brief survey of the differences between Euro-American nations (in particular Anglo-American or Anglo-Saxon nations) and Japan, regarding the feature of their labour markets. Tra-ditionally, there have been three primary labour market features which separate Japan from Euro-American countries (see Table 1.2).

The above distinctions require some explanation. Regarding labour mobility, Japanese workers tend to stay with one employer, and change employers less frequently than Anglo-American workers. Average job tenure in Japan is thus longer than that in the UK and the US. The expression 'life-long employment', which signifies that employees stay in one company until retirement, is often used to characterize the Japanese employment system. Regarding wages and promotion, employers in Japan pay wages and determine the promotion possibilities of employees largely by workers' seniority, i.e., job tenures and ages, while the wages and promotions for Anglo-American employees are determined mainly

on the basis of their productivity and performance. Regarding unionism, all unions in Japan are organized at the enterprise level, while the
organization of unions in Euro-American nations are based on workers'
occupation and/or the firm's industry.

Two caveats must be added with respect to the above three distinctions. First, in reality there does not exist a clear dichotomy between
Japan and Euro-American nations. For example, in Japan wages and
promotions are not based *only* on their seniority, as productivity or
contribution also plays a role. It would be impossible to promote every-
body to be president of a company, if the strict rule of seniority were
applied to all employees. Competition is required to select employees
for a limited number of superior positions. The same story holds for
the determination of wages in Japan. If the strict rule of seniority were
the only criterion for wage determination, workers who were capable
and productive would lose incentives, and possibly shirk. Similarly, in
Euro-American nations, decisions are not based only on productivity
and performance. Seniority is also important in determining the level
of wages, promotions and even 'who should be laid-off' in unionized
firms, as many studies on seniority in Europe and the US have showed.

As a second example, consider 'life-long employment'. In Japan,
only a small proportion of all employees possess 'life-long employment', as females and employees in smaller firms change their employers frequently. Several studies even in the US have demonstrated
that many employees stay in one company until retirement after having
experienced labour turnover during their younger years. These two
examples suggest that a clear dichotomy between Japanese and Euro-
American labour markets does not exist; differences are more a matter
of degree than of kind. It is preferable to say that seniority is taken
into consideration more strongly in Japan for the determination of wages
and promotions than in Euro-American nations, and labour mobility in
Japan is less frequent than in Euro-American nations.

The second caveat is as follows. The three distinctions do not provide us with causes or incentives, but merely indicate the empirical
evidence of the labour markets in Europe, Japan and the US. It is
certainly important and challenging to investigate and discuss the reasons why these distinctions have appeared, and what are their consequences for incentive mechanisms and labour market efficiency.

In addition to the traditional three features described above, two other
labour market and industrial relations characteristics merit discussion.
First, industrial relations is 'organization-oriented' in Japan rather than
'market-oriented' as it is in Europe and the US. This is emphasized by

Dore (1993). 'Organization' here implies a firm which determines workers' wages and promotions. Most economic decisions are made within a firm with the consent of its employees. Supply and demand forces thus play a less direct role in Japan in determining employment and wages. In Europe and the US the supply and demand forces are more direct, and thus a 'market-oriented' paradigm prevails. A by-product of being 'organization-oriented' is that Japanese employees feel loyalty to their firm. This loyalty affects employees' work ethic, how they react to the firm's incentive, and the probability of their changing firms after receiving training. Japanese firms are consequently more willing to pay the cost of training their employees than are firms in market-oriented systems. Chapter 6 by Higuchi in this volume examines training in Japan related to this issue.

The second additional characteristic concerns the observation that Japanese employees have wider careers, in the sense that they frequently change units or sections in offices or factories while working for the same firm. In other words, they experience various production units (blue-collar workers) and clerical sections (white-collar workers) during their careers. Further, Japanese employees are promoted to superior positions at relatively later stages of their careers. In other words, differentiation between promoted employees and unpromoted ones is determined when employees become older. This issue is examined carefully in chapter 5 Ohashi and Matsushige for Japan. In the UK and the US employees typically experience a less wide career than Japanese employees. Workers in the UK and the US also tend to specialize in particular jobs or tasks. At the same time, promotion is determined at a relatively early stage in their careers. In other words, 'high-flyer' managers are selected at an early stage. This distinction was emphasized by Koike (1975).

I have mentioned two features and three traditional distinctions for Japan. It would be worthwhile to note that these characteristics appear to be changing today. For example, Japanese labour markets have become somewhat less organization-oriented, and somewhat more market-oriented. Witness, for example, the recent increase in the degree of labour turnover in Japan. Employees change employers more frequently than previously. Another example is that much recent fieldwork proposes that many white-collar and some blue-collar Japanese employees are becoming more specialized in one job or task having narrower experiences in the firm. These examples suggest that industrial relations in Japan are changing. Industrial relations in Euro-American countries are also changing, and we have to watch these changes carefully.

Why did Japan exhibit the above features and characteristics? Japanese people tend to prefer long-term contractual relationships and commitments. This is true for Japanese firms, banks and employees because they believe that long-term relations are beneficial in the long run. The Anglo-Saxon tradition, however, emphasizes 'spot-market' relationships which are often short-term. They also like to keep many options open. Aoki (1988) elegantly analyzed the advantages of long-run contractual relations or commitments in Japan based on the modern theory of incentives. Williamson (1985) has also presented significant theoretical developments, such as that long-term relationships can minimize transaction costs and provide mutual reputations for trust. The latter theoretical property is now proposed as a common and universal merit in many standard microeconomics textbooks in the UK and the US. Following these arguments, one might predict that the Anglo-American economies will begin to emphasize increasingly long-term contracts in the future.

Why do both Japanese employers and employees prefer long-term relations to spot-market relations? Despite the recent development of microeconomics which verifies that long-term relations are more efficient, it is somewhat doubtful that both employers and employees in Japan *explicitly* recognized such economic efficiency. I would like to offer three alternative hypotheses which are sociological or psychological, rather than economic in their orientation.

The first hypothesis is that Japanese people are fairly risk-averse. They are not willing to take significant risks in their social and economic behaviour, and they seek economic security. Lower labour turnover among Japanese employees can be explained by this philosophy. Long-run contractual relationships between a parent firm and its subcontracting firms, as well as long-term 'main' bank relationships between banks and firms, which are examined by Osano and Serita in Chapter 11 in this volume, are also consistent with this hypothesis, although there should also be economic rationalities behind them. I can point to several other examples; the fact that Japan exhibits a very high personal saving rate is consistent with the Japanese being relatively risk-averse. It is noted that no economic theories have been capable of explaining appropriately the cause of this high saving rate in Japan, and a large part has thus been explained by a residual factor. I attribute this residual factor to the degree of risk preference. In other word, it might be necessary to rely on this psychological characteristic of the Japanese people, namely high risk aversion, to justify many social and economic behaviours in Japan. As a final example, in their portfolio choice decisions Japanese investors prefer time deposits and demand deposits, and do not emphasize riskier asset such as equities and bonds. Japanese life insurance holdings are also among the highest in the world. All these examples are consistent with the notion that Japanese individuals are relatively risk-averse.

The second hypothesis is that Japanese people enjoy belonging to a group, or a clan with shared interests, responsibilities, duties, and so on. This group may be a family, a firm, a school, a club, or any other institution. Members of a group feel as if they are sailing a boat. Leaving the boat implies ostracism, which is extremely unpleasant for Japanese people (see Okuno, 1984, who provided an economic analysis of 'ostracism'). Leaving a firm results in the similar feeling. A sinking boat signifies the death of all of its members, and thus they all try to rescue the boat at the expense of individual temporary losses. The boat's captain is not chosen quickly, but only after a long period of mutual monitoring and assessment by the group's members. This is similar to how firms select executives and senior managers. Members of a boat who have similar qualifications are treated fairly equally, and interpersonal competition is kept at a minimum. This is similar to how firms allow seniority to determine wage payment and promotion, so that employees are treated fairly equally.

The third hypothesis is that Japanese firms structure their incentive systems to motivate their less qualified and low ranking employees, while American firms structure their incentive systems to motivate their most qualified and high ranking employees. To raise average productivity levels, it appears that Japanese firms believe that it is important to focus on less qualified and low ranking employees, while American firms believe the opposite: American firms believe that strong leadership by qualified and high ranking employees is vital to raise average productivity. Consequently, the wage distribution in Japan is narrower than it is in the US, for example, on average the salary differential between a company president and an average employee is narrower in Japan that it is in the US.

Do qualified and high ranking employees in Japan work very hard and efficiently despite their relatively lower wages? Do less qualified and low ranking employees in the US work hard and not shirk despite their relatively lower wages? The answer to both questions should be 'no' according to the efficiency wage theory, which argues that the higher an employee's wage payment, the greater is his incentive to work. Two chapters in this volume, Chapter 7 by Ishikawa and Chapter 3 by Tachibanaki and Ohta, discuss the Japanese evidence regarding the above issue, while Chapter 8 by Brown gives evidence for the US.

I offered three hypotheses to explain why long-term relations were more common in Japan than in Anglo-Saxon economies. These hypotheses are intuitive to a certain extent, and largely sociological and psychological. Although quantitative evaluation of these hypotheses may be difficult, I believe that they are useful in helping us to understand the Japanese economy, in particular labour markets and industrial relations.

Before proceeding, I would like to examine one important reservation on Japan. Several features and characteristics which were attributed to Japanese firms are relevant only for large firms, and employees who work in these firms. Some of the features and characteristics of small firms are very different. The dual structure in terms of firm size differences, wider differences in wages, productivities, profit rates and others between large and small firms, is an important subject in Japan. Employees who work in small firms, account for over 50 percent of the total labour force in Japan, possibly over 70 percent, and they are recipients neither of 'life-long employment', nor of strong seniority in the determination of their payment and promotion. Further, most employees in small firms do not belong to a union. These conditions suggest that employment in small enterprises is considerably different from employment in large enterprises. It is possible that some sacrifices or costs are borne by small firms or employees in these firms, even if economic performance on average is excellent in Japan. Alternatively speaking, only economic performance in large firms is excellent, and small firms' performance may be quite low. Many Marxian economists in Japan called this the exploitation of small firms by large firms. I offered, in Tachibanaki (1987), several examples of these sacrifices and costs in the Japanese labour market, not only for the difference between small firms and large firms, but also for the unfavourable treatment of female workers, longer working hours, less appropriate public welfare systems, and so on. Ishikawa's Chapter 7 in this volume also examines the implication of the dual structure. In sum, it is quite misleading to believe that the labour market and industrial relations in Japan perform very well. A large number of hidden aspects, which are mostly dark and sometimes taboo, in reality remain.

Leaving Japan for a moment, unemployment in Europe is a disastrous problem, and thus is of great interest to both academic economists and public policy makers. Several countries in Europe have unemployment rates over 10 percent, and at the same time the mean duration of unemployment is considerable. This situation is not socially acceptable, and as a result many social and institutional arrangements such as unemployment compensation, or more broadly social welfare programmes have been developed. About half of the European nations are often referred to as welfare states. We cannot forget familial support for unemployed. Some economists and policy makers argue that these social programmes induce moral hazard or disincentive. Although I personally do not denounce social welfare programmes, we have to recognize that the unemployment benefit system both raises the rate of unemployment and prolongs the duration of unemployment, as Chapter 9 by Layard and Nickell in this volume clearly shows.

In addition to the issue of unemployment compensation, a large number of investigations have been presented to show the reasons for the higher unemployment observed in Europe, and to seek possible policy suggestions. For example, Layard, Nickell, and Jackman (1991), and Bean (1992) provide us with comprehensive analyses of these issues. Japan, the Scandinavian countries, and the US are frequently compared with Europe as countries which have relatively low rates of unemployment, and hence examining these countries is useful for understanding European unemployment. Nearly all the chapters in this volume that examine Japan, as well as the chapter on Sweden by Edin, Holmlund, and Östros (Chapter 2) contribute to this comparative perspective. At the same time, Chapter 10 by Leonard on the US is useful because it demonstrates the possibility that the growth of establishments, and the jobs they create, may be able to lower the number of unemployed. Thus, the Japanese, Swedish and US experiences may help us better to understand the situation in the rest of Europe.

Fortunately or unfortunately, high European unemployment has helped to enrich the quality of economic analyses in labour economics and macroeconomics. The wage gap theory, the implications of demand and supply shocks, the efficiency wage hypothesis, the hysterisis hypothesis, the insider–outsider approach, the implications of wage bargaining models, models with imperfect competition in both product and factor markets, and so on have all resulted. By employing these new developments in economics, Layard and Nickell in Chapter 9 in this volume undertake tests of unemployment in the OECD countries, including, of course, European countries.

It would be useful to assemble several key factors which are supposed to be important when examining European unemployment. Bean (1992) emphasizes demand for goods, the productivity slowdown, import prices and taxes, worker militancy, unemployment benefits, mismatch, and price mark-ups. Layard and Nickell add shocks which affect unemployment temporarily and/or persistently. Bean proposes the importance of institutional differences in labour markets for understanding the problem of unemployment. Some of the aspects such as productivity, wage determinations, worker militancy (i.e., union power), and unemployment benefits are analyzed in this book, emphasizing institutional differences in labour markets. For example, the effect of worker militancy (i.e., union power) is investigated by Ohtake and Tracy in Chapter 12 for both Japan and the US.

Finally, I would like to discuss several issues regarding the labour market in the US. Its most serious problems are (1) declining or stagnant real earnings over time, due primarily to declining or stagnant industrial productivity, and (2) increasing earnings inequalities. The first issue is very complex and discussing it is beyond the scope of this Introduction, because the issue includes not only labour economics or industrial relations but also many branches of economics such as finance, taxation, industrial policy, trade policy and so on. It may be useful, nevertheless, to refer to the MIT volume (1989) which advocates that the US adopt several practices which are common in Japan, such as just-in-time, team work, flexible job definitions, job security, intensified training, worker participation in decision making, and so on. These practices are all, directly or indirectly, related to labour markets or industrial relations. It therefore appears that improving the efficiency and performance of the US labour markets is crucial for obtaining better economic performance.

Let me add one reservation about differences in productivity between Japan and the US. Clearly, Japan possesses a relative comparative advantage in many industries over the US, for example, iron–steel, car making, consumer electronics, and so on. However, the US also possesses a relative comparative advantage in many industries, for example, chemical products, airplanes, computers, soft-ware, finances, services, and so on. The number of industries in which Japan is superior to the US in their productivity *levels* is fewer than that in which the US is superior to Japan. The relative positions based on their *growth rates* of productivity may be quite different.

The US labour market's second problem, namely increasing earnings inequalities, may be more serious than the first, partly because it may reduce future productivity growth because, as argued above, of its adverse impact on work incentives, and partly because higher earnings inequality violates equity, which is one of the most important policy goals. In any case, this problem is strictly related to the relationship between labour market and economic performance. While this book does not address this problem extensively, it does contain two chapters, Chapter 4 by Topel on regional wage inequality and local labour market performance, and Chapter 8 by Brown on pay and performance, that examine the problem for the US. Next, I shall briefly describe the issue of increasing earnings inequality in the US, and provide an outsider's conclusions.

Levy and Murnane's (1992) survey article on earnings levels and inequalities in the US provides several important findings. First, earnings inequalities were stable in the 1970s but increased rapidly in the 1980s. This trend has resulted in an important polarization with the number of both high pay and low pay jobs increasing, while the number of middle income jobs declined considerably. Secondly, earnings inequalities within groups defined by age, education and gender have grown steadily in the 1970s and 1980s. The male–female gap, however, narrowed in the 1980s. Possible explanations for the increasing within-group inequalities are (1) increasing returns to skill, (2) increasing wage inequalities among industries, and (3) increasing employer and plant specific wage differentials. Chapter 3 by Tachibanaki and Ohta in this volume provided evidence related to these issues for Japan.

The third important finding in Levy and Murnane (1992) is that both supply and demand shifts are crucial for explaining the increasing earnings inequality. For example, relatively well-educated baby boomers in the 1970s, and the deceleration in the 1980s of both the overall rate of labour force growth and the rate at which the educational attainments of the labour force were increasing, are the supply effect. A steady increase in the demand for skilled workers relative to unskilled workers is the demand effect. It is somewhat surprising to see many studies in the US which investigated and assessed the importance of these supply and demand effects for explaining increasing wage inequalities. This may reflect the preference of American economists, who are largely neoclassical, and emphasize market forces. In contrast, many European and Japanese economists emphasize the importance of institutional arrangements such as wage-setting institutions, the legal framework and other industrial relations and/or firm considerations. This difference in emphasis was noted earlier in this Introduction.

The above discussion provided some introductory remarks regarding the differences in the labour markets in Europe, Japan and the US, and it also discussed possible interactions between labour markets and economic performance in these regions. There are many issues which have not been discussed. The chapters in this volume examine many issues which are important for understanding the relationship between labour markets and economic performance. I thus now proceed to briefly introduce each chapter in this volume.

1.3   OVERVIEW OF THE VOLUME

This volume consists of four parts. Part I examines various wage issues. Part II discusses work and incentives, including the subject of worker satisfaction. Part III examines employment and unemployment. Part IV discusses unions. Each examines the relationship between the labour market and economic performance for various countries in Europe, Japan and the US, employing specific subjects in labour and industrial relations.

1.3.1   Wages

Part I consists of three chapters. Edin, Holmlund and Östros in Chapter 2 examine wage behaviour in Sweden. It is well-known that the Nordic countries' labour markets have considerably different features from labour markets in other European nations. First, the rate of unemployment is considerably lower. Secondly, they have centrally determined wage negotiation systems, while most other countries have decentralized wage determination systems. These features were examined by, for example, Calmfors (1990). One of the most important reasons for the lower unemployment rates in the Nordic countries, and in particular in Sweden, is the famous labour market programmes, which include both temporary public jobs (relief works) and training programmes. Some authors have argued that these programmes increase wage pressure, and thus crowd out current employment. Many time-series studies in Sweden have supported this argument.

Edin, Holmlund and Östros applied fruitful microdata, to avoid any simultaneous equation bias and identification problems in time-series data, to investigate the effect of labour market programmes. After finding a positive effect of these programmes on the reduction of unemployment, they present a theoretical model to examine the effect of temporary public employment on wages and equilibrium unemployment by employing a matching model of wage bargaining. The Nash bargaining solution depends on both the 'insider' (employed) and 'outsider' (unemployed) workers. Finally, they present an empirically testable equation, combining all behaviour of utility-maximizing workers and profit-maximizing firms.

Edin, Holmlund and Östros apply both OLS and GMM (generalized method of moments) for their final equation, by employing the engineering industries' cross-section data. Although the GMM estimation provided a somewhat less clear result than the OLS estimation, they conclude that labour market programmes contributed to wage moderation rather than wage pressure, unlike many time-series studies. They offer two reasons for their conclusion. First, the programmes are likely to reduce the tightness of the labour market. Secondly, unemployed people lose the programmes' benefits, if they are offered, and then reject places in programmes.

What policy implications can be proposed based on their study? First, they confirm the usefulness of Swedish-type labour market programmes in reducing unemployment. Second, the programmes can be implemented without a detrimental effect. Some reservations may be plausible. The Nordic labour market programmes cannot be applied easily to large countries and to countries with high tax burdens for labour market programmes because they are not politically accepted by the citizens.

Chapter 3 by Tachibanaki and Ohta presents evidence on wage determination in Japan. It is often argued that flexibility in wage determination helps to lower the rate of unemployment. This was verified by Japanese example, including both monthly wage and bonus payment flexibilities (see Tachibanaki, 1987, for example). Chapter 3 does not examine flexibility in wage payments, but investigates wage differentials, by both industry and firm size, emphasizing industrial differentials.

Tachibanaki and Ohta estimate the pure advantages and disadvantages of industrial effects on wage determination, after controlling for a large number of labour quality variables, by applying Wage Census data in Japan. Although they find considerably large spurious wage differentials by industries (or industrial rents) for raw data, they conclude that a large part of the wage differential is reduced after they control for labour quality. Therefore, pure industrial rents in Japan are not substantial. This is different from various other countries, but does not necessarily imply, however, that no industrial rents are observed. In fact, a significant part of the industrial rents remain. One interesting result is that the industries which have pure positive and negative industrial rents are not the same in Japan and the US; in fact, they are considerably different. This is again inconsistent with the view that the pattern of both positive and negative industrial rents is universal internationally as proposed by Dickens and Katz (1987), and Katz and Summers (1989).

What are the most important control variables which produced the spurious industrial rents? Tachibanaki and Ohta found that (1) education, (2) size of firm, and (3) job tenure, were the most important variables. It is therefore concluded that the most important variables for explaining wage differentials in Japan are these three variables. After the control variables have been employed, what are the most important variables for explaining the residual wage differentials by industries? Tachibanaki and Ohta found that they were the variables which indicate an 'ability to pay' and/or the rent-sharing of firms.

Finally, Tachibanaki and Ohta propose two interesting findings. First, wage differentials by the size of firm are very substantial. This is true even after employing labour quality controls, unlike the previous wage differentials by industries. Tachibanaki (1993) provided a comprehensive study of the employer size effect on wages. Second, the existence of compensating wage differences is not supported, at least by the Japanese data.

Summarizing Chapter 3, there are substantial differences between Japan and other countries with respect to wage differentials by both industry and the size of firm. This reflects several differences between Japan's and other countries' labour markets and industrial relations, as described earlier in the Introduction.

Chapter 4 by Topel examines wage inequalities and regional labour market performance in the US. It was noted earlier that earnings inequality in the US has been increasing. Many reasons have been suggested for this. Topel concentrates on wage inequality within geographic areas, and investigates the causes of the changing wage inequality. After briefly examining data on regional employment and wages, Topel presents a general equilibrium model which incorporates regional labour demand. The basic idea of his model is that local labour demand is driven by patterns of regional specialization. These patterns convey aggregate product demand and technology shocks into local market effects, and changes in relative supplies of factors of production.

Topel considers four factors which affect wage inequality. They are (1) changes in relative supplies of various skill groups, (2) changes in the composition of labour demand across industries for given supply patterns, (3) changing patterns of labour force participation by women, depending upon the degree of substitution possibility with men, and (4) industry specific patterns of technical change which shift the market demand for specific skill groups. Topel derives an equation which is capable of decomposing the total factor into the above four components, and then estimates these components by applying skilful econometric techniques. One element, which plays an important role in his model, is the elasticities of complementarity, which relate changes in market wages to changes in observed quantities and to technical change.

Topel concluded that differences in labour demand have had little effect on relative wages. The most important driven factor for regional differences in wage inequality is regional differences in labour supply, in particular among less skilled workers. It is also important to supplement the fact that technical change has favoured skilled workers, which raises the overall wage inequality. Topel also concluded that increased labour force participation by female workers has reduced the wages of unskilled male workers, and has raised the overall wage inequality. This conclusion presumes that unskilled men and women are reasonable substitutes. His overall conclusion suggests that technical change, labour supply, and female labour force participation are responsible for changes in regional wage inequality, and that the changing pattern of labour demand does not play an important role. This is different from the finding by many American economists that both supply and demand factors are important for explaining wage inequality at the national level. This probably reflects the difference between regional and national factors. The effect of regional immigration may be an important factor in this difference.

1.3.2 Work and Incentives

Part II, which investigates work and incentives, consists of four chapters. Chapter 5 by Ohashi and Matsushige investigates the relationship between a firm's growth rate and the promotion possibility of employees in Japan theoretically and empirically. The authors develop a model of a hierarchical firm to demonstrate that the growth rate of a firm (i.e., the growth rate of employment in a firm) is the most important firm objective. This is because it elevates workers' incentives by increasing their promotion possibilities, and because it decreases the average wage through changing the age composition of employees. Ohashi and Matsushige applied the model to automobile industry employees who work for Toyota and its subcontracting companies, and the top six companies in the electronic industry. These two industries show the highest growth rates, and are thus suitable for their model.

The model developed by Ohashi and Matsushige is an application of Aoki's equilibrium growth of hierarchical firms (1982), combined with an efficiency wage model as given by, for example, Lazear (1979). They apply the notion of incentives and shirking, and present two theoretical results: (1) the firm has an incentive to raise the promotion possibilities of all capable employees by expanding employment; and (2) the firm can lower the average wage of its employees by changing their age composition. The most important firm policy is, thus, to have a high growth rate. Here, a seniority system is assumed in determining wages and promotions, otherwise, their theoretical propositions are not sustainable. It is noted that the authors' second proposition is inconsistent with Weitzman's share economy (1984), which is often argued to be applicable to Japan, because employment growth reduces the average wage in a share economy. Which model best describes Japan is an important issue.

Ohashi and Matsushige apply two data sources in their empirical work. First, they regress the ratio of foremen (i.e., promoted employees) to ordinary workers on the firm's growth rate, the average age of its employees, and the total number of employees in the company. They find that promotion possibilities increase as a company is expanding its number of employees, and this is particularly true for younger employees. Second, they regress the actual average wage on the contracted wage, the rate of change in employment and the change in the average age of employees. They obtain a negatively significant coefficient for the effect of employment changes on the average wage, which supports their second proposition. In summarizing the above, they propose that Japan's excellent economic performance is explained by firm's expansion policies. Their empirical work supports their two theoretical propositions.

Chapter 5 raises two questions. First, how can we evaluate declining industries? If the growth of firms in declining industries is not foreseeable, the incentives of employees may not be observable. Second, the high growth of employment enjoyed by Japan in recent decades was feasible partly because Japan had a large number of young relative to older workers. The country is in an ageing trend, and the model by Ohashi and Matsushige may thus be less applicable to Japan in the future.

Higuchi in Chapter 6 investigates the relationship between job training, productivity growth and retention rate in Japan. It was pointed out earlier in this Introduction that company training is quite important through largely on-the-job training (OJT) in Japan. Firms can bear the cost of training provided that employees stay for long periods at firms, and thus a low separation rate of employees is essential. Higuchi believes that, while male employees typically satisfy this condition, the case for female employees is less clear. He investigates these issues for male and female employees separately, and finds significant differences between them.

Higuchi uses several steps. First, he examines the relationship between training and productivity growth rates by calculating correlation coefficients. While introductory basic training at the entry level into firms is not correlated with productivity growth, training at later stages of an employee's career is positively correlated with it. Second, he estimates the effect of various types of training on job retention rates, by applying survival analysis into the *Employment Structure Survey*. Third, the *Basic Wage Structure Survey* is analyzed in order to link information on wages in the *Wage Survey* to training and job retention rates.

Higuchi obtained the following three findings. First, firms that reinforce job training for males have a higher tenure–wage profile than those that do not. Second, there is a clear distinction between the impact of introductory training for developing general skills conducted shortly after recruitment and the impact of job training which improves knowledge and skills given at a later stage in the employee's career, because the latter shows a stronger positive effect on retention rates than the former. According to Higuchi these two findings suggest that human capital theory is useful for explaining the behaviour of males in Japan. Third, the situation for female employees is considerably different. Although female high school graduates appear to behave similarly to males, the result for female university graduates is considerably different, because the effect of job training on their retention rate is almost negligible. There are several factors which affect female job separation rates. These include flexible working hours, the childcare leave system, and so on. Higuchi concludes that special care must be given to female workers in order to utilize their human resources fully in view of the coming labour shortage. 'Who shares such cost?' is an important public and corporate policy question. Is it the government, firms, or employees (i.e., females only, or females and males together)? This problem has not been discussed extensively in Japan yet because only the private sector (i.e., firms and male employees) have been involved with this issue in the past.

Chapter 7 by Ishikawa investigates the degree of job satisfaction among individuals in Japan. Many studies, including several chapters in this volume, try to determine why the Japanese labour market and industrial relations system work so well. No serious effort, however, has been made to study whether or not Japanese employees are satisfied with their jobs or working conditions. High incentives and the hardworking ethic of Japanese people are famous (or notorious) in the world. 'Are they happy?' is the issue of Ishikawa's analysis. He addresses this subject as an economic analysis rather than as an issue of traditional industrial sociology and psychology, or labour management and control.

Ishikawa adopts several statistical techniques for investigating both the distribution of job satisfaction, and the factors which determine their current level of satisfaction by using the *Survey on the Accumulation of Assets and on Worker Life in Major Metropolitan Areas*. The survey asked many questions on organizational characteristics, workers' job characteristics and hierarchical positions, work attitudes, both pecuniary and non-pecuniary job rewards, and workers' level of satisfaction. Ishikawa cautions the reader regarding some sampling biases due to location (i.e., urban versus non-urban areas), industry and size of firms, and thus suggests some reservations when interpreting his findings.

After presenting preliminary investigations, Ishikawa evaluates job satisfaction levels, from intrinsic job interests (non-pecuniary) to pecuniary rewards (i.e., wages). One important result is that workers who are satisfied (dissatisfied) with the quality of their job are more likely to be simultaneously satisfied (dissatisfied) with their pecuniary rewards than the reverse. He then applies an ordered probit technique to determine the level of satisfaction, which is then regressed on several variables such as education, job tenure, occupation, size of firms, industry, hierarchical rank, and so on.

Ishikawa obtains the following conclusions. First, the effects of education and job tenure on satisfaction are very small. Second, the size of firm has a notable effect on the degree of satisfaction on both pecuniary and non-pecuniary dimensions. Employees in small firms are more disadvantaged. Third, blue-collar workers are clearly disadvantaged in both dimensions, while white-collars are advantaged. Fourth, workers in the manufacturing sector are less satisfied than those in the non-manufacturing sector. Ishikawa points out a paradox, namely, that the blue-collar workers who are responsible for Japan's internationally renowned productivity and excellent performance in the manufacturing sector exhibit relatively low levels of satisfaction. This is consistent with the work of Lincoln and Kalleberg (1990) which also found relatively low job satisfaction among Japanese employees. The paradox induces two comments. First, a large gap between expectations and reality may be responsible for their low level of satisfaction. Second, Japanese workers may be losing their hardworking ethic, and thus may not continue to be highly productive, if the low degree of satisfaction continues.

In Chapter 8 Brown provides a useful survey on the relationship between pay and performance. Here, 'performance' signifies a worker's performance in production activity, and 'pay' is monetary compensation (wages). The survey includes both theoretical works mostly related to incentive theory and effort of workers, and many US empirical studies. The first part of this Introduction discussed wage compression in Japan, and its implications for the incentives of employees. The US-oriented chapters by Brown provides us with an interesting comparison.

Brown raises two difficulties encountered when examining the relationship between pay and performance. First, a worker's output (or performance) is not easily observed, and often the cost of measuring (or monitoring) that output precisely is too high. Second, workers who are uncertain about the value of their marginal product, or more simply less productive workers, will prefer a more egalitarian wage distribution as insurance. Keeping these difficulties in mind, many interesting topics and concepts exist in this field such as (1) paying the conditional expectation of marginal product, (2) piece rate and time rate payments, (3) principal–agent models, (4) relative performance evaluation, (5) rank-order contests, (6) workers' concern for relative positions, (7) career concerns, and (8) discharges. Brown provides a concise explanation of each of these subjects.

Brown examines the difference between piece rates and time rates, and argues that piece rate workers should receive higher pay than those paid time rates within a given combination of occupation and industry. However, the cost of measuring output (or performance) discourages the use of piece rates. Group incentive pay, or bonus payment is sometimes used as an intermediary rule. These propositions are largely supported empirically. A large number of both case studies and econometric studies in the US suggest that wages vary less than proportionately with workers' output. This is called 'compression' of the wage distribution. Finally, Brown predicts that the compressed wage distribution will induce more voluntary turnover for higher rated employees and less voluntary turnover for lower rated employees. The evidence, however, tells us that the opposite occurs. Thus, employers should not worry about a loss of higher rated employees even in the US. However, involuntary turnover (i.e., layoffs or enforced discharges) is much more (negatively) related to rated performance.

Brown predicts that improvements in monitoring technology may induce a tighter pay–performance link, raising the wages of the most productive workers while reducing the wages of those who are less productive. Brown expects, of course, more effort from the most productive employees. This is, probably, the American philosophy that the most able and productive employees must be compensated very highly. This is in contrast to the Japanese philosophy, as was explained previously. This, however, is likely to increase the existing wage inequalities which were described earlier for the US. Finally, Brown suggests that it would be interesting to compare the degree of wage compression between Japan and the US, and to examine its effect on incentives.

1.3.3   Employment and Unemployment

Part III of this volume examines employment and unemployment issues, and consists of three chapters. Layard and Nickell in Chapter 9 present a theoretical model of unemployment which is able to explain both the difference in unemployment among the OECD countries, and the time-series changes in unemployment in each OECD country. This is a worthwhile attempt, because we can test whether a theoretical model, which incorporates an analysis of pricing, employment and wage determination at the firm level, is able to explain unemployment. There exist, of course, significant differences in institutional settings and economic behaviour among the OECD countries. These differences are taken into account in their empirical tests of the model, and it is quite successful in explaining the dramatic fluctuations in the unemployment rates in the OECD countries over time.

Layard and Nickell's theoretical macro model has strict micro foundations, as both firm behaviour and union–non-union worker behaviour are explicitly modelled. First, they consider the firm's pricing and employment decisions, which depend on both the quantity theory form for demand, and an Okun's law-type equation. Firms supply whatever quantity of output is demanded. Second, their wage determination model incorporates the following three factors, (1) a Nash bargaining framework for unions, where only wages are bargained, (2) job vacancies which affect the non-union wage determination, and (3) real wage resistance which occurs if workers resist falls in their living standard. Third, the equilibrium rate of unemployment is derived, which depends on wage pressures such as (1) union effects, (2) benefit effects and (3) real wage resistance. Then, they derive an unemployment–inflation tradeoff, which reveals the factors associated with a deviation of unemployment from equilibrium. Finally, they consider three types of shock, namely, (1) productivity, (2) money supply and (3) wages, to obtain an empirically testable equation for the OECD countries.

Layard and Nickell were successful in estimating their unemployment equation which has more than 14 parameters, plus 19 country dummies for a 33-year time period span. They reach the following empirical conclusions. First, levels of unemployment, the size of the unemployment response to shocks, and the persistence of unemployment all depend on the structure of the unemployment benefit system and on the wage determination system. Second, the degree of employment flexibility also affects unemployment levels. Third, the impact of nominal shocks is negatively related to both the degree of nominal flexibility in the wage bargaining process, and to the variance of nominal shocks over the sample period. They also obtained many useful empirical findings regarding unemployment.

Layard and Nickell make several policy suggestions, although some debate about their appropriateness remains. First, they suggest restricting the level of unemployment compensation, in particular the benefit duration. Second, the centralization of wage bargaining or cooperative wage determination is recommended (see the important work of Bruno and Sachs, 1985, and Newell and Symons, 1987, related to this subject). Third, coordination in wage bargaining among employers in unionized economies is helpful.

Chapter 10 by Leonard shows the pattern of growth and decline among establishments and firms for the US economy between 1978 and 1984, and also compares the US and Japanese experiences. The result is compared with Leonard (1987), which showed a useful and innovative analysis of Wisconsin establishments. The growth dynamics of establishments and firms is important not only for industrial organization issues but also for employment and unemployment issues, because it involves the creation and destruction of jobs.

Leonard examines the model, which shows that enterprise size is the sum of transient and cumulative innovations. The first difference of the logarithm of size is then equal to the growth rate, and is decomposed into the innovation in the random walk component of size, and the remaining part of a moving average component. By examining correlation matrices of both the logarithm of firm size and the growth rates, it is possible to provide various interpretations about the dynamic properties of establishments and firms. Leonard applies four

samples, namely, (1) single-establishment firms, (2) constituent establishments of multi-establishments firms, (3) firm level data for multi-
establishment firms, and (4) establishments. A simple time-series analysis
suggests that neither the pure random walk model nor models of chronic
success or failure (including partial adjustment and persistent stock
models) adequately characterize the time-series behaviour of any of
these samples. However, the growth rate of establishments follows a
mean reverting and error-correction process, although it neither exhibits persistence nor follows a random walk.

Leonard offers the following economic interpretations based on his
empirical results. First, establishments exhibit very heterogeneous growth
rates because the standard deviation of establishment growth rates is
about 0.3. This diversity is not reduced by focusing on specific industries, regions or years. Frictional unemployment arising from fluctuations in labour demand is therefore very important in the US. Second,
a persistent factor in the growth rate of establishments is not observed.
This implies that establishments attempt to make quick adjustments
that overshoot, rather than hoarding labour or smoothing our fluctuations. Third, small establishments appear surprisingly stable and insulated from cyclical pressures. Fourth, the most significant determinant
of establishment growth is the skill intensity of the workforce. Investment in skilled workers, in particular white-collar workers, is thus
desirable. Finally, Leonard notes that the US and Japan have considerably different degrees of employment stability. This difference reflects
differences in their industrial organization and firm behaviour.

Chapter 11 by Osano and Serita analyzes the relationship between
main bank relations and life-time employment contracts in Japan. The
'main' bank is defined as the bank which has a long-term financial
customer relation with the firm through the largest lending share among
private financial institutions that make loans to the firm. Osano and
Serita are interested in examining empirically the 'duality principle'
for large Japanese firms proposed by Aoki (1990), which emphasizes
the combination of life-time employment contracts (with deferred compensations) and main bank relations.

After showing how the combination of these two relations works in
Japan, Osano and Serita derive two competing hypotheses by incorporating the worker-incentive, or the risk-sharing model into the main
bank model. The first hypothesis supports the joint hypothesis of the
worker-incentive (or specific human capital) and main bank model,
while the second supports the joint hypothesis of the risk-sharing and
main bank model. Their empirical tests focus on the sign of the esti-

mated coefficient of MB, the strength of ties of the firm to its main bank, after estimating microdata for both manufacturing and non-manufacturing firms. Their theoretical model is based on those by Curme and Kahn (1990), and Hart and Moore (1988).

Osano and Serita examine their model using cross-section firm data. The dependent variable is the notional payment of retirement compensation, which is defined as the total amount of lump-sum compensation plus the present value of enterprise pensions at the time of the worker's retirement. One important explanatory variable is the firm's monitoring ability, and many other control variables for both the firm's financial structure and the worker's qualifications are used. Osano and Serita find the following four empirical results. First, stronger ties with the main bank reduce the probability that the firm goes bankrupt, or is taken over. Second, retirement compensation for male workers is used for risk-sharing purposes among the two competing hypotheses. Third, retirement compensation for female workers is not used for incentive-inducing. We recognise here that the male–female difference is important in Japan. Fourth, the hypothesis that employee stock ownership plans are used for insurance purposes is not supported empirically. Incidentally, the hypothesis that bonus compensation is used for incentive-inducing or insurance purposes is not supported, either. The fourth finding contradicts Ohashi (1989), and thus we need more work about this issue. To conclude, it appears that long-run relations, in both employment contracts and financial activities, are important in Japan, and that they work as complements.

1.3.4 Unions

Part IV of this volume investigates the role and effects of unions in both Japan and the US. Ohtake and Tracy in Chapter 12 estimate the determinants of disputes and strikes in Japan in comparison with the US, and evaluate several hypotheses to explain why there are fewer strikes in Japan. It is frequently suggested that unions in Japan are cooperative, while unions in Euro-American nations are non-cooperative, and that this affects the difference in economic performance between the two. This view is too simplistic since, for example, union members in Europe receive significant benefits along various dimensions, and because some positive effects from unions are suggested in the US, as shown by Freeman and Medoff (1984). The problem remains, probably, in the difference between union members and non-union members in these countries.

Ohtake and Tracy show empirical evidence on disputes and strikes
in Japan and the US. While the strike incidence is higher in the US
than in Japan, dispute incidence is higher in Japan than in the US.
Further, both strike and dispute durations are longer on average in the
US than in Japan. They then offer several reasons for the above difference, by examining collective bargaining processes in the two countries. First, they argue in favour of asymmetric information bargaining
models which examine the division of rent between firms and unions.
It is important to remember that (1) enterprise unionism is prevalent
in Japan, whereas crafts and industrial unions are prevalent in the US,
and that (2) life-long employment is more common in Japan than it is
in the US. Ohtake and Tracy also show the implications of information sharing through the Joint Consultation System (JCS) in Japan,
and several other differences in the institutional setting and the legal
structure between Japan and the US.

Ohtake and Tracy, finally, present their econometric evidence on
disputes and strikes in Japan, by applying the minimum logit chi-square
method and logistic transformations. They use the rate of unemployment, profit rates, inflation rates, and several other control variables
as independent variables, to obtain the following results. First, factors
of macro uncertainty such as inflation and profitability are more important than industry specific uncertainty in explaining strikes in Japan,
while strike activity is procyclical with respect to the aggregate unemployment rate in the US. According to Ohtake and Tracy the asymmetric information bargaining model may be less relevant to Japan
than to the US, and the JCS role may be more relevant to explain why
strikes are less common in Japan. Second, the data suggest that both
the long-term employment system and the profit-sharing *à la* Weitzman
(1984) are useful.

1.4   CONCLUDING REMARKS

Several important conclusions and implications based on the chapters
in this volume can now be presented. It is noted, however, that significant disagreements may remain among the contributors to this volume. Therefore, the conclusions and implications described here reflect
the editor's preferences, and should not be regarded as representing a
consensus achieved by the contributors.

First, wages are very important determinants of the level of employment and unemployment, incentives and productivity of workers, and

naturally earnings inequalities. Therefore, 'what kind of wage determination mechanism is considered?' is crucial for examining these issues. Important considerations related to wage determination include (1) is it a centralized or a decentralized process?, (2) are wages indexed to inflation or not? (3) are workers insiders (unions) or outsider (non-unions)?, (4) is compensation determined by piece rates or time rates?, (5) is a seniority-based system in place?, and so on. These considerations are important for the working of labour markets, the incentives and productivity of workers, earnings inequalities, and the level of satisfaction of workers, as many chapters in this volume have analyzed for various countries.

Second, wage determination systems are very different even in the advanced industrialized countries in Europe, Japan and the US, although there is a consensus that wages are important for various issues. Importantly, these different wage determination systems affect the working of labour markets differently. Two examples illustrate this point. First, centralized wage negotiations work relatively well in smaller countries like the Scandinavian countries, while decentralized wage negotiations work better in larger countries like Japan and the US. Second, piece rate wage determination may work well in competitive societies, while time rate wage determination may work better in less competitive societies. It is important to identify the wage determination system which is optimal for each country.

Third, recent advances in labour economics emphasize several key factors such as incentives, shirking, contracts, bargaining, renegotiation, learning, tournaments, promotion, career concerns, monitoring, agency costs, transaction costs, and so on. These key factors derive from microeconomic analysis of the relationship between employers and employees, and the relationship among employees in hierarchical ranks. Several key factors derive from game theoretic approaches. Several of the above key factors appear at various places in the volume. Thus, although this volume focuses on the relationship between labour economics and macroeconomics, recent developments in labour economics has been influenced by both microeconomics and game theory. Developing microeconomic foundations has provided us with many useful insights into the relationship between the labour market and economic performance.

Fourth, it is important to recall the fact that the work force is very heterogeneous. Age, sex, education, occupation, rank, seniority, union status, location of residence, family status, and many other factors, differentiate workers. For example, the rate of unemployment varies greatly among various demographic groups in all countries. Also, various characteristics of firms such as industry, size of firm, public firm versus private firms, location of firms, and many other factors, are important in differentiating employees. For example, firm size is an important determinant of wages in Japan. Differences in both workers' qualifications and firms' characteristics greatly affect the working of labour markets. Consequently, we have to be careful in determining 'What kind of employees and firms do we examine, or who are most affected by various policies and institutions?'.

Fifth, both public policies and institutional settings are influential in determining the effectiveness of policies and in achieving the desired goals. For example, consider the Swedish labour market programmes, and unemployment compensation systems in many countries. Training can be another example. It is necessary to identify the outcomes associated with various public policies and institutional arrangements, in particular whether implementing these policies and arrangements is desirable or detrimental for both efficiency and equity. The economist's task in evaluating various policies or changes in institutional settings is, probably, to identify those who will be affected favourably and those who will be affected badly, and to quantify the various benefits and costs. Several chapters in this volume provide examples of this type of evaluation.

Sixth, the view of workers must be taken into account when analyzing labour markets and industrial relations. Labour activity accompanies human involvement. It is thus crucial to recognize the degree to which workers are satisfied or not satisfied by their working activity. The Japanese case is interesting because, despite Japan's strong labour market performance, it appears that workers in Japan are not highly satisfied with their working activity. It may be necessary to modify labour market institutions and policies in Japan to raise the degree of satisfaction, even if this has a detrimental effect on economic performance.

Seventh, capital and financial markets are interrelated with labour markets, as the examination of the Japanese 'main bank system' showed. Given that capital and labour are the two factor inputs in the production process, it is reasonable to expect that the two markets will be highly interrelated. It is desirable to investigate the interrelationship between labour and capital markets further, and to keep in mind the effect of capital and financial markets when we analyze labour markets.

Eighth, there is a substantial difference in the degree to which the countries investigated in this volume rely on market forces in the functioning of their labour markets and industrial relations. For example, in some countries employers and employees and policy makers emphasize the merit of supply and demand relations, a highly competitive world, and market clearing forces, while in other countries they rely more on non-market forces. Several of the chapters in this volume showed such differences. The US economy is, probably, a representative example of the former, while Japan and Sweden are representative examples of the latter although Japan and Sweden are different in other ways. It should be emphasized, nevertheless, that the distinction between Japan and the US in their degree of reliance on market forces should not be overemphasized.

Each chapter contains discussions of a large number of interesting issues, and presents theoretical and empirical results which help us to understand the relationship between labour markets and economic performance in Europe, Japan and the US. Labour markets are important not only for the national economy's performance, but also individual firms' performance. Labour markets also affect individual welfare and satisfaction. The three regions examined in this volume share similar difficulties, which arise from being advanced industrialized economies. The three regions, however, also possess many differences. Each chapter in this volume examines these issues in an internationally comparative perspective. They offer many ideas, opinions, views and findings which, due to space limitation, have not been covered in this Introduction. The editor believes that readers will learn a great deal from a careful reading of each chapter, and that an understanding of the relationship between labour markets and economic performance will be greatly enhanced.

References

Albert, M. (1991) *Capitalisme contre Capitalisme*, Paris, Seuil.
Aoki, M. (1982) 'Equilibrium Growth of the Hierarchical Firm: Shareholder–Employee Cooperative Game Approach', *American Economic Review*, vol. 70, pp. 1087–1110.
———— (1988) *Information, Incentives, and Bargaining in the Japanese Economy*, Cambridge, Cambridge University Press.
———— (1990) 'Towards an Economic Model of the Japanese Firm', *Journal of Economic Literature*, vol. 28, pp. 1–27.
Bean, C. (1992) 'European Unemployment: A Survey', Centre for Economic Performance, *Discussion Paper*, no. 71, London School of Economics.
Bruno, M. and J.D. Sachs (1985), *Economics of World Wide Stagflation*, Oxford, Basil Blackwell.

Calmfors, L. (1990) (ed.) *Wage Formation and Macroeconomic Policy in the Nordic Countries*, Oxford, SNS and Oxford University Press.

Curme, M. and L.M. Kahn (1990) 'The Impact of the Threat of Bankruptcy on the Structure of Compensation', *Journal of Labor Economics*, vol. 8, pp. 419–47.

Dickens, W.D. and L.F. Katz (1987) 'Inter-Industry Wage Differentials and Industry Characteristics', in K. Lang and J. Leonard (eds), *Unemployment and the Structure of Labor Markets*, Oxford, Basil Blackwell.

Dore, R.A. (1993) 'Japanese Capitalism, Anglo-Saxon Capitalism: How will the Darwinian Contest Turn Out?' in F. Burton and N. Campbell (eds), *The Global Kaisha: Strategic and Organisational Issues*, London, Routledge.

Freeman, R.B. and J. Medoff (1984) *What Do Unions Do?*, New York, Basic Books.

Hart, O. and J. More (1988) 'Incomplete Contracts and Renegotiation', *Econometrica*, vol. 56, pp. 755–85.

Katz, L.F. and L.H. Summers (1989) 'Industrial Rents: Evidence and Implications', *Brookings Papers on Economic Activity, Microeconomics*, pp. 209–90.

Koike, K. (1975) *Labour Union and Participation at the Shopfloor*, Toyo-Keizai Shimpo Sha (in Japanese).

Layard, P.R., S. Nickell and R.A. Jackman (1991) *Unemployment: Macroeconomic Performance and The Labour Market*, Oxford, Oxford University Press.

Lazear, E.P. (1979) 'Why is There Mandatory Retirement?' *Journal of Political Economy*, vol. 87, December, pp. 1261–84.

Leonard, J.S. (1987) 'In the Wrong Place at the Wrong Time: The Extent of Frictional and Structural Employment', in K. Lang and J. Leonard (eds), *Unemployment and the Structure of the Labour Market*, Oxford, Basil Blackwell.

Levy, F. and R.J. Murnane (1992) 'U.S. Earnings Levels and Earnings Inequality: A Review of Recent Trends and Proposed Explanations', *Journal of Economic Literature*, vol. 30, pp. 1333–81.

Lincoln, J.R. and A.L. Kalleberg (1990) *Culture, Control, and Commitment: A Study of Work Organisation and Work Attitudes in the U.S. and Japan*, Cambridge, Cambridge University Press.

MIT (1989) *The Machine that Changed the World*, Cambridge, MA, MIT Press.

Newell, A. and J.S.V. Symons (1987) 'Corporatism, Laissez-Faire and the Rise in Unemployment', *European Economic Review*, vol. 31, pp. 567–601.

Ohashi, I. (1989) 'On the Determinants of Bonuses and Basic Wages in Large Japanese Firms', *Journal of the Japanese and International Economies*, vol. 3, pp. 451–79.

Okuno, M. (1984) 'Corporate Loyalty and Bonus Payment: An Analysis of Work Incentives in Japan', in M. Aoki (ed.), *The Economic Analysis of the Japanese Firm*, Amsterdam, North-Holland.

Tachibanaki, T. (1987) 'Labour Market Flexibility in Japan in Comparison with Europe and the U.S.', *European Economic Review*, vol. 31, pp. 647–84; reprinted (1992) in G. de Ménil and R.J. Gordon (eds), *International*

Volatility and Economic Growth, Amsterdam, North-Holland.

———— (1993) 'The Employer-Size Effect on Wage Differentials in Japan, Revived', Kyoto Institute of Economic Research, *Discussion Paper no. 377*.

Weitzman, M.L. (1984) *The Share Economy*, Cambridge, MA, Harvard University Press.

Williamson, O. (1985) *The Economic Institutions of Capitalism*, New York, Free Press.

Part I

Wages

2 Wage Behaviour and Labour Market Programmes in Sweden: Evidence from Microdata

Per-Anders Edin, Bertil Holmlund and Thomas Östros*

Sweden
J31
J44
J64
J68
R23

2.1 INTRODUCTION

A voluminous and primarily American literature has investigated the microeconomic effects of labour market programmes. This literature has often focused on how program participation influences individual earnings, which is taken as a measure of the productivity-augmenting effects of a programme. The literature has been econometrically innovative, but it has hardly produced much consensus regarding the effects of training programmes or other labour market interventions. Microeconometric evaluations of Swedish labour market programmes are few and have not produced very conclusive evidence on individual wage effects (Björklund, 1990).

The relationships between labour market programmes and wages have over the past few years also been scrutinized from a macroeconomic angle. This line of research has been particularly active in the Nordic countries, and Sweden in particular. The point of departure for this work is wage-setting relationships of the type suggested by Sargan (1964) and later developed by Layard, Nickell and others (see for example Layard, Nickell and Jackman, 1991). These models are typically based on bargaining theory and deliver wage-setting relationships where the wage in a firm is a function of 'insider' and 'outsider' factors; the firm's productivity belongs to the former category and unemployment − or some other measure of labour market pressure − belongs to the latter. Unemployment has a wage-reducing affect

33

because it reduces the value to the worker (or the union) of not accepting a wage agreement.

Labour market programmes may increase wage pressure in so far as they offer unemployed workers favourable alternatives to living on the dole. This is an undesirable possibility, since it suggests that the programmes may crowd out regular employment. A number of recent papers have exploited time-series data in order to examine how labour market programmes affect wage behaviour.[1] Two types of programmes have been in focus (although rarely separately studied), namely temporary public jobs ('relief works') and training programmes. A common finding is that labour market programmes contribute to wage pressure. The estimated responses vary across the different studies, but a frequent result is that unemployment depresses pay whereas programmes have no wage-reducing effect.

There are reasons to treat these results with caution, however. First, although there are several studies, there are rather few observations that deliver variation in the data on programmes. Data from the late 1960s to the late 1980s have primarily been used. Second, the time-series studies are potentially subject to problems of identification and simultaneous equations bias. An investigation of whether the results survive in analyses on micro data is therefore warranted. This is the main purpose of our chapter.

We examine variations in hourly earnings across individuals, with particular focus on the effects of labour market programmes, by using a large pooled cross-section and time-series dataset from the Swedish engineering industry for the period 1972–87. The effects of the programmes are here measured not as post-programme earnings for the trainees, but as wage responses arising from variations in the level of 'programme activity' in the worker's regional labour market. We find little evidence that labour market programmes increase wage pressure. In fact, manpower training programmes seem to *reduce* wage pressure.

The organization of the chapter is as follows. Section 2.2. presents a few basic facts about unemployment and labour market programmes in Sweden, and describes the dataset we are using in the empirical work. Section 2.3 outlines the theoretical framework, a matching model with wage bargaining augmented to account for labour market programmes. The framework delivers a wage equation at the micro level. The empirical analysis is contained in section 2.4, and section 2.5 offers a comparison with other studies. Section 2.6 concludes.

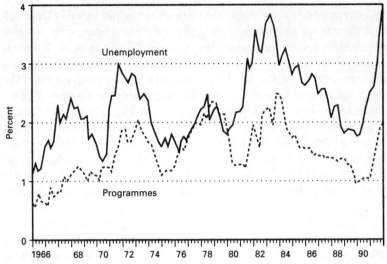

Figure 2.1   Unemployment and labour market programmes, 1965–91

Notes: The programmes (relief jobs, manpower training programmes and half of the number in youth teams) are measured as a percentage of the labour force. Figure 2.1 shows seasonally adjusted data. The unemployment rate is adjusted so that it conforms to the pre-1987 definition.

Sources: Statistics Sweden and the Swedish Labour Market Board.

2.2   SOME FACTS

2.2.1   Unemployment and Labour Market Programmes

Sweden has over the past three decades practised very ambitious countercyclical labour market policies. Two of the main instruments have been temporary public employment and manpower training programmes. The total number of participants in the two main labour market programmes has varied between 1 and 2 percent of the labour force for most of the period 1965–91 (Figure 2.1). There are marked counter-cyclical movements in the programmes, particularly in relief jobs. As is evident from Figure 2.1, the programmes have adjusted to changes in unemployment with rather short lags.

Unemployment in Sweden has increased sharply during 1991 and 1992. The unemployment rate by the end of 1992 was close to 5 percent, a level unprecedented in the postwar period. Concomitant with this development there has also been a sharp fall in inflation (from 10 to 2 percent on an annual basis) and a marked increase in the volume of labour market programmes. By the end of 1992 close to 4 percent of the labour force was engaged in relief jobs, manpower training programmes or subsidized on-the-job training schemes for youths.[2] The latter schemes were initiated in 1992 and accounted for over 12 percent of the youth labour force by the end of 1992.

Manpower training programmes and relief jobs typically last six months. Participants in training programmes receive a stipend corresponding to the unemployment benefit level, whereas workers in relief jobs are paid at the same rate as workers in regular jobs. Relief workers are supposed to be engaged in search for regular jobs, and the jobs can be abolished when the labour market improves.

The accommodative labour market policy is also strikingly visible in a regional dimension. The higher a region's unemployment rate, the higher is the fraction of the labour force engaged in relief jobs and training programmes. Figure 2.2 plots average programme participation in manpower training programmes and relief jobs against average unemployment rates for 24 regions (län). A percentage point higher unemployment rate in a region is associated with close to a percentage point higher programme participation rate.

Stockholm and Norrbotten (in the far north of Sweden) are the two regions with the lowest and highest unemployment rates. The unemployment rate in Stockholm has varied between 1 and 2 percent, whereas unemployment in Norrbotten has fluctuated between 4 and 7 percent (Figure 2.3). The differences in programme activity are of the same order of magnitude, as is clear from Figure 2.4. In fact, the fraction of the labour force outside regular employment has typically exceeded 10 percent in Norrbotten.

2.2.2   Data for the Engineering Industry

Our wage data are from the engineering industry (fabricated metal products, machinery and equipment, ISIC 38), which comprises almost half of employment and value added in the manufacturing industry. The source is the wage statistics collected by the employers' organization in the engineering industry, Sveriges Verkstadsförening. The population is blue-collar workers and the time period is 1970–87. The dataset is based on three random samples of 5000 workers pertaining to each of the fourth quarters of 1975, 1980 and 1985. Data for these workers were then collected for each fourth quarter in the period 1970–87. The

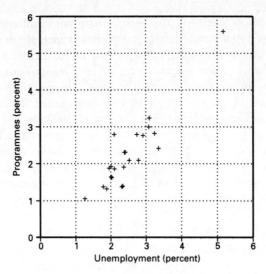

Figure 2.2   Unemployment and labour market programmes across regions, averages for 1970–89

Sources: Statistics Sweden and the Swedish Labour Market Board.

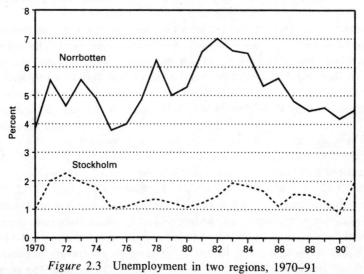

Figure 2.3   Unemployment in two regions, 1970–91

Note: The unemployment figures are not adjusted to the changes in measurement techniques introduced 1987.

Sources: Statistics Sweden and the Swedish Labour Market Board.

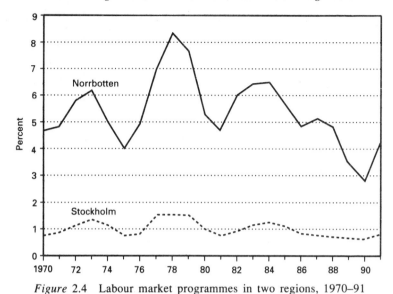

Figure 2.4   Labour market programmes in two regions, 1970–91

Sources: Statistics Sweden and the Swedish Labour Market Board.

resulting unbalanced panel data set thus involves at least one and at most 18 observations per individual. The dataset obtained through these procedures included 147,379 observations for 14,761 different workers. A few variables contained a large number of missing observations for the first two years of the panel. For the research reported in this chapter we have therefore always excluded observations for 1970 and 1971.

The wage data are based on the firms' reports on a worker's earnings and hours worked during a particular quarter. There are reasons to believe that the wage data in this sample is of a higher quality than data based on workers' own reports of earnings and hours. The data are rich concerning wages, including for example information on the type of compensation (piece rate versus hourly pay, holiday pay, etc.). The data also include information on industry, occupation and firm size, but is meagre when it comes to personal characteristics other than age and gender. There is, for example, no information on education. We do not consider this as a serious drawback for our purposes, however. The sample is confined to a relatively homogeneous group, blue-collar workers in the engineering industry, and by including occupation dummies we are likely to control for most of the individual differences that are related to education. The influence of time-invariant individual attributes can be eliminated by exploiting the longitudinal structure of the data.

The wage data have been merged with data on regional labour market characteristics, including regional wages, unemployment, vacancies and labour market programmes.[3] The region is the county (län), of which there are 24 in Sweden. The regional wage is the average blue-collar wage in mining and manufacturing, and the unemployment rate is taken from the labour force surveys (annual means). These regional unemployment series are likely to be measured with error because of small samples. We will therefore also make use of an alternative unemployment series, 'registered unemployment', which is based on the administrative records of the employment exchange offices. Vacancy data refer to unfilled vacancies notified to the employment exchange offices; notification behavior may vary across regions, but little is known about such regional differences. Data on labour market programmes are likely to be of high quality as they are based on administrative records on the total number of individuals in relief jobs and training programmes.

Table 2.1 presents sample statistics for some of the variables in the dataset. We note that the dispersion of individual log wages has decreased during the period, and this is also reflected in county wages. The mean nominal wage increase has been 9.8 percent per year among workers in the sample, which is very close to the increase in the corresponding county wages pertaining to mining and manufacturing as a whole.

2.3 THEORETICAL FRAMEWORK

Our theoretical framework is a matching model with wage bargaining. The model has been developed by Diamond (1981), Mortensen (1982) and Pissarides (1985, 1990). Holmlund and Lindén (1993) use this model to examine the effects of temporary public employment on wage determination and equilibrium unemployment; our exposition draws heavily on their analysis.

Consider an economy with trading frictions where the matching of workers to jobs is costly and time-consuming. The search process is summarized by an aggregate matching function which relates the flow of new hires (H) into regular jobs to the number of searchers (S) and the number of vacancies (V), i.e., $H = h\,(S, V)$. The matching function is increasing in both its arguments and exhibits constant returns

Table 2.1   Sample characteristics, means (standard deviations in parentheses)

	1975	1980	1985	1972–87
ln w	7.653	8.081	8.464	7.972
	(0.167)	(0.116)	(0.103)	(0.384)
Δ ln w				0.094
				(0.079)
age	36.0	37.8	38.8	39.2
	(12.81)	(12.91)	(12.86)	(12.40)
female	0.19	0.20	0.21	0.19
piece rate	57.2	54.3	57.5	56.8
	(46.0)	(46.4)	(46.6)	(46.3)
ln $\bar{w}$	7.818	8.303	8.696	8.163
(county wage)	(0.047)	(0.035)	(0.036)	(0.384)
Δ ln $\bar{w}$				0.092
				(0.028)
v	1.27	1.27	0.86	0.94
(vacancy rate)	(0.18)	(0.19)	(0.14)	(0.31)
u	1.61	2.04	2.86	2.40
(unemployment rate)	(0.58)	(0.56)	(0.79)	(0.91)
r	0.37	0.56	0.91	0.84
(relief jobs)	(0.25)	(0.30)	(0.44)	(0.50)
m	0.83	1.09	0.84	1.18
(manpower training)	(0.29)	(0.26)	(0.25)	(0.63)
# observations	9230	9159	8036	103 852

Notes: The hourly wage rate (w) is the sum of time rate and piece rate compensation. Female is a dummy variable, and v, u, r and m are measured as percent of the labour force. Half of the number of people in youth teams are included in r. The piece rate is measured as hours of work with piece rate compensation as a percent of total hours worked.

to scale. The number of searchers is given as the number of unemployed plus the effective number of job searchers in programmes, i.e., $S \equiv U + cP$, where U and P are the number of unemployed and programme participants, respectively. Search effectiveness is captured by the parameter c, where $c \geq 0$. Programme participants are either employed in full-time temporary public employment (relief jobs) or engaged in manpower training, so it is natural to think that they search less intensively than the unemployed; the limited available evidence supports this conjecture (Edin and Holmlund, 1991). If c is interpreted as the fraction of time devoted to search among programme participants, we can reasonably expect $0 \leq c \leq 1$. We assume that unemployed workers search full time, i.e., $c = 1$.

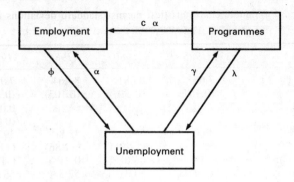

Figure 2.5   Labour market flows

There are L individuals in the exogenously given labour force, and the unemployment and vacancy rates are given as $u \equiv U/L$ and $v \equiv V/L$, respectively. We introduce a new variable, $\theta \equiv V/S$, to capture labour market tightness, and another variable, $q \equiv H/V$, to represent the rate at which vacant jobs are filled. By the constant returns assumption we have $q(\theta) \equiv h(S/V, 1) = h(1/\theta, 1)$, where $q'(\theta) < 0$. The flow of new hires into regular jobs is given as $H = \alpha S$, where $\alpha = (H/V)(V/S) = q(\theta)\theta$. It is clear that $\alpha'(\theta) > 0$ since $\alpha = \theta h(1/\theta, 1)$ and thus $\alpha = h(1, \theta)$, where $h(\cdot)$ is an increasing function.

Regular job offers arrive according to Poisson processes with arrival rates that are exogenous to the individual worker. The arrival rate for an unemployed worker is α and for a program participant $c\alpha$; the arrival rate is thus in general higher for unemployed searchers. Unemployed individuals may also exit to labour market programmes at the rate γ. There is an exogenously given rate ϕ at which regular jobs break up, and a government-determined rate λ at which programmes expire. Figure 2.5 illustrates the flows between the three states.

The flow equilibrium constraints for regular employment and labour market programmes, which together imply a flow equilibrium constraint for unemployment as well, are given as

$$[c\alpha(\theta) + \lambda]p = \gamma u, \qquad (1)$$

$$\phi(1-u-p) = \alpha(\theta)(u + cp), \qquad (2)$$

where $p \equiv P/L$. Condition (1) states that the flow out of programmes equals the inflow. Condition (2) gives the corresponding steady-state relationship for regular employment; the rate of separations equals the rate at which workers are hired from the unemployment pool and the pool of programme participants. (1) and (2) determine u and p, given θ. Note that (1) and (2) can be used to obtain a 'Beveridge curve', i.e., a relationship between the unemployment and vacancy rate. It is straightforward to show that an increase in γ (or a decrease in λ) produces an inward shift of the Beveridge curve, i.e., a reduction in unemployment at a given vacancy rate.

Firms maximize the present value of profits. Vacancies are costly to maintain and opened so long as they yield positive profits. An occupied job is associated with expected present value J_o and a vacant job yields expected present value J_v. Let δ denote the discount rate, y the constant marginal product, w the wage rate and k the cost of maintaining a vacancy. J_o and J_v satisfy the equations:

$$\delta J_o = y - w + \phi(J_v - J_o), \tag{3}$$

$$\delta J_v = -k + q(\theta)(J_o - J_v). \tag{4}$$

An occupied job yields a per period surplus of $y - w$ and is turned into a vacant job at the rate ϕ; worker separations are associated with a capital loss equal to $J_v - J_o$. Analogously, a vacancy yields a negative surplus per period of $-k$ and is turned into an occupied job at the rate $q(\theta)$, with an associated gain of $J_o - J_v$. In equilibrium we have $J_v = 0$ and the value of an occupied job is obtained from (3) as $J_o = (y - w)/(\delta + \phi)$. Substituting into (4) yields

$$\frac{y - w}{\delta + \phi} = \frac{k}{q(\theta)}. \tag{5}$$

This is the fundamental equilibrium condition for the firm. The left-hand side of (5) is the present value of profits per worker and the right-hand side is the expected present value of the firm's hiring cost. Labor market tightness influences decisions on vacancies by affecting hiring costs; the tighter the labour market, the more costly to hire because of longer duration of vacancies.

Let Λ_e, Λ_u and Λ_p denote expected discounted life-time income for workers in regular employment, unemployment and programmes, respectively. The value functions take the form

$$\delta \Lambda_{ei} = w_i + \phi(\Lambda_u - \Lambda_{ei}), \tag{6}$$

$$\delta\Lambda_u = b + \alpha(\Lambda_e - \Lambda_u) + \gamma(\Lambda_p - \Lambda_u), \tag{7}$$

$$\delta\Lambda_p = z + c\alpha(\Lambda_e - \Lambda_p) + \lambda(\Lambda_u - \Lambda_p), \tag{8}$$

where $\Lambda_e = (1/\delta)[w + \phi(\Lambda_u - \Lambda_e)]$ is the value of a job anywhere in the economy. A worker employed by firm i receives the wage rate w_i and is separated from the job at the rate θ. An unemployed worker receives unemployment benefits b and finds regular jobs at the rate α and programmes at the rate γ. A programme participant, finally, earns the wage z on the current job, finds regular jobs at the rate $c\alpha$ and is separated from the job at the rate λ.

We may think of b and z as inclusive of any non-pecuniary costs or benefits of being unemployed or a programme participant. The observed pecuniary compensation during unemployment does not exceed pecuniary compensation in programmes; we have already noted that relief workers receive the going wage in Sweden, whereas workers on training programmes receive a stipend that amounts to the unemployment benefit level. How *total* compensation – b and z – are related to each other is unclear, but note that z cannot be too low relative to b in a system based on voluntary worker decisions on programme acceptance. An unemployed individual would be willing to accept an offered place in a programme so long as $\Lambda_p \geq \Lambda_u$. This incentive compatibility condition places restrictions on z and b, among other parameters. Although $\Lambda_u > \Lambda_p$ seems implausible, it cannot be ruled out *a priori*. If the government practises as tough work test it may withdraw unemployment benefits for unemployed people who refuse to accept relief jobs and programmes. In that case $\Lambda_u > \Lambda_p$ may well be consistent with the observation that unemployed individuals prefer not to reject offered relief jobs or training programmes. We impose no restriction on the sign of $\Lambda_p - \Lambda_u$, but assume that $\Lambda_p \geq \Lambda_u^0$, where Λ_u^0 is the value of unemployment for an individual who has lost his eligibility for benefits.

Wage determination at the level of the firm is given by the solution to a Nash bargaining problem. The bargain maximizes the weighted product of the firm's and the worker's utility surplus relative to the parties' disagreement points. The firm's disagreement point is given by the value of a vacant job, and the worker's threat point is the worker's net worth when unemployed. The worker's threat point is the same irrespective of whether he has entered the bargain from unemployment or from a programme. This is the natural assumption in a model where continuous renegotiations between the firm and the worker are possible; once a programme participant has been employed by the firm he will be in exactly the same situation as a previously unemployed worker and cannot fall back on his income in a programme.

The Nash bargain thus solves

$$\max_{w_i} \; \Omega_i(w_i) \equiv [\Lambda_{ei}(w_i) - \Lambda_u]^\beta [J_{oi}(w_i) - J_v]^{1-\beta},$$

where $0 < \beta < 1$. The value of an occupied job at firm i is given, analogously to (3), as $J_{oi} = (1/\delta)[y_i - w_i + \phi \, (J_v - J_{oi})]$. The outcome of the Nash bargain is a wage equation of the form

$$w_i = \beta y_i + (1 - \beta)\delta\Lambda_u, \tag{9}$$

where the zero-profit condition on new vacancies is invoked ($J_v = 0$). The negotiated wage is thus given by a convex combination of firm specific (or 'insider') variables and general labour market (or 'outsider') variables). Any policy that raises the value of unemployment to the worker is bound to increase the negotiated wage. The value functions given by (6) – (8) can then be used to obtain an explicit expression for the value of unemployment. To simplify that expression we focus on the limiting case where the discount rate goes to zero and obtain:

$$\delta\Lambda_u = \frac{(c\alpha + \lambda)(\alpha w + \phi b) + \gamma(c\alpha w + \phi z)}{(\alpha + \gamma) \, c\alpha + \phi(\gamma + c\alpha) + \lambda(\alpha + \phi)} \equiv f(\cdot). \tag{10}$$

Noting that $\alpha = \alpha(\theta)$ we obtain $f_\theta > 0$, $f_w > 0$, $f_b > 0$, $f_z > 0$ and $f_\phi < 0$. The wage is increasing in labour market tightness, the outside wage, the benefit level, the wage received in programmes and decreasing in the rate of inflow into unemployment. An increase in search effectiveness among programme participants (c) will in general increase wage pressure, i.e., $f_c > 0$; this holds under the plausible assumption that the value of employment exceeds the value of programmes, $\Lambda_e - \Lambda_p > 0$. The reason for this effect is that an increase in search effectiveness makes unemployment more favorable relative to employment.

The effects of labour market programmes depend crucially on the utility difference between programmes and unemployment, i.e., $\Lambda_p - \Lambda_u$. We have $f_\gamma \gtrless 0$ so long as $\Lambda_p \gtrless \Lambda_u$, with the opposite sign if $\Lambda_p < \Lambda_u$; the effects of an increase in λ, the duration of programmes, are opposite in sign to f_γ. The intuition for these results is not difficult. The wage is increased by intensified hirings of unemployed workers into programmes so long as the value of a relief job exceeds the value of unemployment, the reason being that the policy makes unemployment more attractive relative to employment analogous to an increase in unemployment benefits. The increase in wage pressure can be made arbitrarily small (or negative) by paying programme participants sufficiently low compensation.

The upshot of this is a wage equation at the firm level of the form

$$w_i = \beta y_i + (1 - \beta)f(\overset{+}{\theta}, \overset{+}{w}, \overset{+}{b}, \overset{+}{z}, \overset{-}{\phi}, \overset{+}{c}, \overset{?}{\gamma}, \overset{?}{\lambda,}), \tag{11}$$

with the signs of the partial derivatives indicated. (11) is the theoretical relationship that guides our empirical analysis. Before proceeding to that analysis it is useful to briefly consider the general equilibrium of the model. A symmetric equilibrium involves wage equality across firms; the resulting wage equation can thus be obtained from (11) and written as

$$w = g(\theta; y, b, z, \phi, c, \gamma, \lambda), \tag{12}$$

where sign g_θ = sign f_θ, sign g_γ = sign f_γ, etc. The equilibrium of the model is now given by the flow equilibrium conditions, (1) and (2), the equilibrium condition for firms, (5), and the wage equation (12). (5) and (12) determine θ and w, and by substituting θ into the flow equilibrium conditions we obtain u and p. The effect of labour market programmes on equilibrium unemployment works through two routes. First, there is a fall in unemployment at a given level of tightness (or an inward shift of the Beveridge curve). Second, there is an effect on tightness induced by wage-setting behaviour. The wage effect tends to offset the reduction in unemployment so long as $\Lambda_p > \Lambda_u$, and reinforce the reduction if $\Lambda_p < \Lambda_u$.

Our empirical analysis is confined to wage responses at the micro level and does not provide quantitative information on the effects at the macro level. Still, the micro results are useful for assessing the macro outcomes. If we find no effect on wage pressure at the micro level we can reasonably expect that labour market programmes contribute to lower unemployment.

2.4   EMPIRICAL ANALYSIS

Several of the variables in (11) are unobservable, or at least not available in our data. We will estimate the model using time dummies, so the variables without regional variations are taken care of by these dummies; b and z are such variables. The inclusion of time dummies also effectively removes the influence from changes in contractual wage changes agreed upon at the industry level (to the extent that those are uniform across firms). This means that we focus primarily on the relationship between 'wage drift' and labour market conditions; wage drift has traditionally been defined as the difference between total wage increases and wage increases negotiated at the industry level.

The duration of the programmes, captured by λ, is taken to be constant. The key parameter of interest is then γ, the rate at which unemployed individuals are transferred into programmes. This parameter varies over time and regions, but is unobserved in the data. We can however invoke the flow equilibrium constraints, (1) and (2), and obtain $p = p(\theta, \gamma, \phi, c, \lambda)$. The inverse function of $p(\cdot)$ is $\gamma = h(\theta, p, \phi, c, \lambda)$, with $h_\theta > 0$ and $h_p > 0$ (at least if c is a sufficiently small number). The wage effect of an increase in p, given the vacancy rate and the unemployment rate, is then given as

$$\frac{dw_i}{dp} = (1 - \beta) \left[\frac{\partial f}{\partial \theta} \frac{\partial \theta}{\partial p} + \frac{\partial f}{\partial \gamma} \frac{d\gamma}{dp} \right], \tag{13}$$

where $d\gamma/dp = h_p + h_\theta \theta_p$. The first term within brackets in (13) is negative as long as c is positive, i.e., so long as programme participants to some extent engage in active search. The second term captures the effect operating via the higher probability of entering a programme. We have $f_\gamma > 0$ so long as the value of programmes exceeds the value of unemployment. The derivative $d\gamma/dp$ can take either sign so long as c is positive and hence θ_p is negative; a positive sign seems however much more plausible than a negative one.

Inflow into unemployment is driven by separations (ϕ) in our framework; in a more general model inflow would also be caused by new entrants into the labour market. There are also likely to be persistent regional differences in matching efficiency; there are for example substantial differences in the location of the Beveridge curve in different regions. These considerations motivate the inclusion of regional dummies. We can also to a large extent control for regional effects by estimating the model with individual fixed effects. Age, age squared and piece rate work, as well as dummies for year, industry, occupation, plant size and gender are always included in the basic equation. (The age and gender effects are not identified when we allow for fixed effects and time dummies.) No information on productivity at the level of the firm is available. We use value added series pertaining to the worker's three-digit industry level (log value added per hour), but these are obviously crude proxies. Unemployment and vacancies are always entered as separate variables without restrictions; other specifications such as the difference $v - u$, the v/u-ratio or the log v/u ratio were typically inferior in terms of the standard errors of the equations.

The unemployment series are plagued by (small sample) measurement errors, which are likely to produce a bias toward zero in the estimated coefficients. We have therefore also made use of an alternative unemployment series, 'registered' unemployment (u^r), based on administrative records of the number of unemployed searchers at the employment exchange offices. This alternative unemployment series is available from 1976 and onwards.[4] Labour force data from the labour force surveys are used to calculate unemployment *rates*.

In the estimations we allow for individual fixed effects. Table 2.2 displays results from estimations by means of OLS on deviations from individual means. All specifications allow for some dynamics; we include among the regressors the lagged wage level as well as differences and lagged levels of all labour market variables. The results are partly as expected, partly slightly surprising. The coefficients on the change and the level of vacancies are remarkably stable across all equations. An increase in the vacancy rate by 1 percentage point causes an increase in the wage by 1 percentage point in the short run and an increase in the wage level by close to 2 percent in the long run (holding the county wage constant). If we set $w = \bar{w}$ and solve for the long-run wage we obtain a long-run wage response of almost 3 percent in conjunction with an increase in the vacancy rate by 1 percentage point. The unemployment variables always appear with negative coefficients. The coefficients on registered unemployment are in general better determined and numerically larger, which is what we should expect if registered unemployment is less affected by measurement errors.

The surprising results pertain to the effects of labour market programmes. The estimated coefficients on the regional programme rate (p) and its first difference are always *negative* and almost always significantly so, suggesting that labour market programmes would *reduce* wage pressure. The same pattern typically emerges when we allow for separate effects of relief jobs (r) and manpower training programmes (m).

Table 2.2   Fixed-effects OLS estimates of the wage equation; dependent variable: ln w

	(1)	(2)	(3)	(4)	(5)	(6)
ln w_{-1}	0.401	0.401	0.401	0.401	0.401	0.401
	(228.5)	(228.6)	(228.6)	(228.6)	(228.6)	(228.6)
Δ ln $\bar{w}$	0.325	0.308	0.307	0.331	0.313	0.307
	(15.30)	(14.28)	(14.10)	(15.4)	(14.4)	(13.99)
ln $\bar{w}_{-1}$	0.171	0.152	0.155	0.180	0.161	0.162
	(8.15)	(7.09)	(7.19)	(8.54)	(7.46)	(7.48)
Δu	−0.191	−0.154	−0.163			
	(3.64)	(2.92)	(3.01)			
u_{-1}	−0.193	−0.101	−0.092			
	(3.05)	(1.55)	(1.34)			
Δu^r				−0.329	−0.311	−0.366
				(3.86)	(3.62)	(4.10)
u^r_{-1}				−0.366	−0.267	−0.289
				(5.25)	(3.68)	(3.47)
Δv	0.857	0.900	0.902	0.920	0.927	0.915
	(5.31)	(5.55)	(5.56)	(5.62)	(5.66)	(5.58)
v_{-1}	1.210	1.155	1.178	1.234	1.167	1.160
	(6.92)	(6.59)	(6.69)	(7.02)	(6.62)	(6.57)
Δp		−0.252			−0.228	
		(5.27)			(4.76)	
p_{-1}		−0.302			−0.275	
		(5.04)			(4.52)	
Δr			−0.099			0.060
			(0.72)			(0.42)
r_{-1}			−0.422			−0.254
			(3.33)			(1.78)
Δm			−0.268			−0.274
			(4.98)			(5.10)
m_{-1}			−0.270			−0.299
			(3.77)			(4.15)
SE	0.04445	0.04444	0.04444	0.04445	0.04444	0.04444

Notes: The estimations allow for individual fixed effects through deviations from individual means. Other variables on the right hand side are time dummies, age squared, proportion of working time in piece rate, 5 dummies for plant size, 8 dummies for occupation, 4 dummies for industry, and log industry value added per hour. All variables measuring unemployment, vacancies and labour market programmes are expressed as ratios relative to the regional labour force. The period of estimation is 1977–87, with 77,213 observations (at least two observations per individual). Absolute t-values in parentheses.

Among other results (not reported in the tables), we find higher wages for piece rate workers, and a slight tendency that large firms pay higher wages. The value added variable typically appears with negative (although very small) estimated coefficients. Earlier work on Swedish wage behaviour has not found much effect at all from firm or industry specific variables, so estimated coefficients close to zero do not come as a surprise.[5] Negative coefficients are of course difficult to interpret, but the variable used is clearly a very crude proxy.

It is well known that OLS estimations of dynamic fixed-effects models yield a bias of the order $1/T$, where T is the number of time periods in the dataset. Arellano and Bond (1988, 1991) have developed an instrumental variable procedure to estimate dynamic panel data models. Table 2.3 presents results of estimations using the generalized method of moments (GMM) technique, with the lagged dependent variable treated as endogenous.[6] The fixed effects are eliminated by means of first differencing. The error term in the differenced equation has an MA(1) structure under the assumption that the error in the level equation is white noise. Instruments dated $t - 2$ and backwards are valid under this assumption. Absence of second-order serial correlation in the differenced equation is implied by white noise in the error of the level equation.

The results in Table 2.4 differ somewhat from those displayed in Table 2.3. Negative signs on the estimated coefficients on programmes are now less frequent. Only one variable, Δm, enters with a marginally significant coefficient. These results indicate that the OLS estimates may have exaggerated the wage-reducing effects of the programmes. Other specifications, for example with individual effects replaced by regional fixed effects, show results largely similar to those set out in Table 2.2. Although the OLS estimates are biased, the bias is unlikely to be substantial given the reasonably large number of time periods.

2.5 COMPARISONS WITH OTHER STUDIES

How do our results from micro data square with earlier findings regarding wage responses to labour market programmes? Table 2.4 displays results from a number of earlier studies. These are based on aggregate time series for the private sector (Holmlund 1990; Calmfors and Forslund 1991; Calmfors and Nymoen 1990; Löfgren and Wikström 1992; Eriksson *et al.* 1990), time series for private-sector workers in mining and manufacturing disaggregated by age, gender and occupation

Table 2.3   Fixed-effects IV estimates of the wage equation, dependent variable: ln w

	(1)	(2)	(3)	(4)	(5)	(6)
ln w_{-1}	0.472	0.472	0.471	0.472	0.471	0.471
	(27.31)	(27.26)	(27.27)	(27.23)	(27.21)	(27.22)
Δ ln $\bar{w}$	0.205	0.206	0.203	0.198	0.199	0.195
	(5.44)	(5.37)	(5.24)	(5.15)	(5.06)	(4.95)
ln $\bar{w}_{-1}$	−0.024	−0.019	−0.014	−0.023	−0.019	−0.016
	(0.50)	(0.40)	(0.30)	(0.49)	(0.38)	(0.33)
Δu	−0.174	−0.169	−0.185			
	(2.60)	(2.53)	(2.80)			
u_{-1}	−0.123	−0.107	−0.125			
	(1.27)	(1.09)	(1.23)			
Δu^r				−0.216	−0.233	−0.268
				(1.26)	(1.40)	(1.72)
u^r_{-1}				−0.202	−0.182	−0.219
				(1.47)	(1.27)	(1.42)
Δv	1.239	1.220	1.220	1.181	1.143	1.135
	(5.65)	(5.55)	(5.52)	(4.99)	(4.80)	(4.78)
v_{-1}	1.482	1.454	1.434	1.374	1.326	1.291
	(5.38)	(5.26)	(5.10)	(4.67)	(4.48)	(4.39)
Δp		−0.072			−0.070	
		(0.96)			(0.91)	
p_{-1}		−0.038			−0.030	
		(0.41)			(0.31)	
Δr			0.124			0.132
			(0.52)			(0.53)
r_{-1}			−0.023			0.063
			(0.11)			(0.28)
Δm			−0.124			−0.126
			(1.65)			(1.69)
m_{-1}			−0.091			−0.099
			(0.81)			(0.89)
SE	0.04795	0.04794	0.04793	0.04795	0.04794	0.04794
Ser corr						
$N(0,1)$	1.198	1.195	1.193	1.197	1.195	1.193

Notes: The equations are estimated in first differences and include time dummies, age squared, proportion of working time in piece rate, 5 dummies for plant size, 8 dummies for occupation, 4 dummies for industry, and log industry value added per hour. The period of estimation is 1978–87, with 59,463 observations (at least five observations per individual). The lagged dependent variable is treated as endogenous; the instrument set includes ln w_{-2} and backwards. All variables measuring unemployment, vacancies and labour market programmes are expressed as ratios relative to the regional labour force. Ser. corr. is a test for second-order serial correlation in the differenced equation. Heteroscedasticity consistent absolute t-values in parentheses.

Table 2.4   Empirical studies of wage behaviour and labour market
programmes

Studies	Estimated effects
Eriksson, Suvanto and Vartia (1990)	+
Holmlund (1990)	0
Calmfors and Forslund (1991)	+
Calmfors and Nymoen (1990)	
Sweden	0
Norway	–
Finland	+
Denmark	+
Skedinger (1990)	+
Löfgren and Wikström (1992)	0
Forslund (1991)	+
Forslund (1992)	
Relief jobs	+
Manpower training	–

Notes: Table 2.4 is based on estimates of specifications of the form ln w = $f(u, p, Z)$, where Z captures other variables in the wage equation. The signs in Table 2.4 refer to the estimated coefficients on (p)rogrammes; zeros indicate that the estimates are not significantly different from zero. The paper by Eriksson *et al.* is based on Finnish data.

(Skedinger 1990), or pooled cross-section and time-series data for firms or industries (Forslund 1991, 1992). Labor market programmes are typically either manpower training plus relief jobs, or relief jobs only. Few studies attempt to distinguish between the effects from training programmes and relief jobs. It is important to note that virtually all Swedish studies have used aggregate data on programmes; this is also true for Forslund's studies of wage setting at the firm and industry level.[7] No previous study has exploited regional variations in programmes.

Few of the earlier studies have found that programmes actually reduce wage pressure, analogous to an increase in unemployment or a fall in the vacancy rate. Forslund (1992) is one exception; he finds that manpower training programmes reduce wage pressure whereas relief jobs have wage-increasing effects. Our results show some similarity with Forslund's findings, although we are unable to detect any significant wage hikes from relief jobs.

It is not clear why the different studies produce such variety of results. One might suspect that the time-series studies are more prone to simultaneous equations bias, which would induce a positive bias in the estimated coefficients on programmes. It should also be emphasized that the time-series studies do not always reject an hypothesis of equal coefficients on unemployment and programmes. Unemployment and programmes are highly correlated in aggregate data (cf. Figure 2.1 above), so precise estimates of effects of unemployment and programmes may be hard to obtain.

Our wage equations are likely to capture wage drift more than contractual wage changes. Despite recent research on the relationships between wage drift and negotiated wages we are still far from an understanding of how these relationships actually operate. The earlier studies listed in Table 2.4 have not addressed the question whether programmes may have different effects on wage drift and contractual wage increases. In fact, all of these studies assume, explicitly or implicitly, that wage formation takes place at the sectoral (possibly firm) level, and no distinction between wage drift and contractual wages is made. There is however an old stylized fact indicating that wage drift is more sensitive to labour market conditions than contractual wage increases, suggesting that the sensitivity of aggregate wages to labour market conditions is driven by wage drift. To the extent that participants in labour market programmes are active job searchers we should expect that programmes have a stronger downward pressure on wage drift than on contractual wages.

2.6   CONCLUDING REMARKS

We have offered a new study of the relationships between labour market programmes and wage pressure in Sweden, using a large micro dataset matched with regional labour market variables. The results do not support the view that programmes contribute to wage pressure, as has been found in several time-series studies. Taken at face values, our findings from micro data suggest that manpower training programmes may deliver wage moderation rather than wage hikes. If these results are interpreted within our theoretical framework it follows that training programmes may reduce equilibrium unemployment. The sensitivity of the results to estimation method suggests, however, that policy conclusions should be drawn with caution.

The mechanisms at work need to be further investigated. Our framework suggests that programmes may reduce wage pressure via two routes. First, the programmes may reduce tightness if programme participants behave as effective job searchers. The other possibility is that programmes are inferior to unemployment from the unemployed individual's point of view; wage pressure would be reduced by the programmes provided that people lose their benefits if they reject offered places in programmes (and hence are 'forced' to accept the places). The first possibility does not square with the (limited) evidence we have on search behaviour among the unemployed and programme participants (Edin and Holmlund 1991). The other possibility seems slightly implausible but cannot be ruled out without investigations of actual practices at the employment exchange offices.

Our focus on wage-setting has implied that we have ignored other potentially important effects of labour market programmes. For example, we have paid no attention to the possibility that programmes may influence geographical mobility, possibly reducing emigration from declining regions. We have also ignored the obvious skill-enhancing objectives of manpower training programmes. These linkages between labour market programmes and unemployment may well be at least as important as the mechanisms examined in this chapter.

Notes

* We have received useful comments from Hiroyuki Chuma, Yukinobu Kitamura, Andrew Newell, Nicholas Kiefer, Stephen Nickell and participants in conferences and workshops in Borgå, Osaka, Århus and Chelwood Gate. The chapter has in part been financed by The Bank of Sweden Tercentenary Foundation, Jan Wallander's and Tom Hedelius' Foundation and the European Unemployment Programme.
1. Recent work on wage behaviour and labour market programmes include Eriksson *et al.* (1990), Holmlund (1990), Calmfors and Forslund (1991), Calmfors and Nymoen (1990), Skedinger (1990), Forslund (1991, 1992), and Löfgren and Wikström (1992).
2. We express the number of programme participants as a percentage of the labour force despite the fact that people in training programmes do not belong to the labour force according to the conventional definition.
3. The regional data are obtained from a database put together by Jansson and Östros (1991).
4. We have estimated the model for different time periods, including the whole period 1972–87 (using unemployment series from the labour force surveys). The results with respect to the effects of labour market programme are in general very similar to those reported in Table 2.2.
5. See Holmlund and Zetterberg (1991) and Forslund (1991, 1992).
6. The Arellano–Bond procedure for dynamic panel data models is implemented by means of the Gauss program DPD. See Arellano and Bond (1988).
7. Skedinger also used relief jobs pertaining to particular age categories, but only the aggregate variables entered with significant coefficients.

54   Sweden: Wage Behaviour and Labour Market Programmes

References

Arellano, M. and S. Bond (1988) 'Dynamic Panel Data Estimation Using DPD – A Guide for Users', *Working Paper*, 88/15, Institute for Fiscal Studies.
——— (1991) 'Some Tests of Specification for Panel Data: Monte Carlo Evidence and an Application to Employment Equations', *Review of Economic Studies*, vol. 58, pp. 277–97.
Björklund, A. (1990) 'Evaluations of Swedish Labor Market Policy', *Finnish Economic Papers*, 3, 3–13.
Calmfors, L. and A. Forslund (1991) 'Real-Wage Determination and Labour Market Policies: The Swedish Experience', *Economic Journal*, 101, 1130–48.
Calmfors L. and R. Nymoen (1990) 'Real Wage Adjustment and Employment Policies in the Nordic Countries', *Economic Policy*, 11, 397–448.
Diamond P. (1981) 'Mobility Costs, Frictional Unemployment, and Efficiency', *Journal of Political Economy*, 89, 798–812.
Edin, P.A. and B. Holmlund (1991) 'Unemployment, Vacancies and Labour Market Programmes: Swedish Evidence', in F. Padoa Schioppa (ed.), *Mismatch and Labour Mobility*, Cambridge, Cambridge University Press.
Eriksson, T., A. Suvanto and P. Vartia (1990) 'Wage Formation in Finland', in L. Calmfors (ed.), *Wage Formation in the Nordic Countries*, Oxford, SNS and Oxford University Press.
Forslund, A. (1991) 'Wage Setting at the Firm Level – Insider versus Outsider Forces', Department of Economics, Uppsala University, mimeo.
——— (1992), *Arbetslöshet och arbetsmarknadspolitik* (Unemployment and Labor Market Policy), Stockholm, Allmänna Förlaget.
Holmlund, B. (1990) *Svensk lönebildning – teori, empiri, politik* (Wage Formation in Sweden – Theory, Evidence, Policies), Stockholm, Allmänna Förlaget.
Holmlund, B. and J. Lindén (1993) 'Job Matching, Temporary Public Employment, and Equilibrium Unemployment', *Journal of Public Economics*, vol. 57, pp. 329–43.
Holmlund, B. and J. Zetterberg (1991) 'Insider Effects in Wage Determination: Evidence from Five Countries', *European Economic Review*, 35, 1009–34.
Jansson, M. and T. Östros (1991) 'Regionala arbetsmarknadsdata. En databas på länsnivå' (Regional Labor Market Variables. A Database at the County Level), Department of Economics, Uppsala University.
Layard, R., Nickell, S. and R. Jackman (1991) *Unemployment: Macroeconomic Performance and the Labour Market*, Oxford, Oxford University Press.
Löfgren, K.G. and M. Wikström (1992) 'Lönebildning och arbetsmarknadspolitik' (Wage Formation and Labor Market Policy), Ds 1991:53, Arbetsmarknadsdepartementet (Swedish Ministry of Labour).
Mortensen, D. (1982) 'The Matching Process as a Noncooperative Bargaining Game', in J.J. McCall (ed.), *The Economics of Information and Uncertainty*, Chicago, University of Chicago Press.
Pissarides, C.A. (1985) 'Taxes, Subsidies and Equilibrium Unemployment', *Review of Economic Studies*, 52, 121–33.
——— (1990), *Equilibrium Unemployment Theory*, Oxford, Basil Blackwell.

Sargan, J.D. (1964)   'Wages and Prices in the United Kingdom: A Study in Econometric Methodology', in Sargan, J.D., *Econometric Analysis for National Economic Planning*, London, Butterworth.

Skedinger, P. (1990)   'Unemployment, Real Wages, and Labor Market Programs: A Disaggregative Analysis', *Working Paper*, 1990:15, Department of Economics, Uppsala University.

3 Wage Differentials by Industry and the Size of Firm, and Labour Market in Japan

Toshiaki Tachibanaki and Souichi Ohta*

3.1 INTRODUCTION

Wage differentials by industry is an old issue and now a revivified one. In the past it was fairly popular to investigate interindustry wage differentials. These studies used data which reported only the average wage figures for various groups of workers, and derived implications from these figures. Recently, individual survey data on wages and other personal characteristics have become available. Economists attempt to standardize individual wage figures by controlling various quality variables of individual employees such as education, sex, and many others. These works derive a pure effect of industrial differences on wage differentials, after controlling for the contribution of quality variables. Past studies (i.e., the old type) typically used average figures and it was not easy to derive a pure effect, while the new type typically use individual observations, and it is thus easy to derive a pure effect. This is a clear distinction between old and new studies.

Wage differentials by the size of firm has been a very popular subject in Japan (for the US see Brown and Medoff, 1989). This chapter touches on this issue in order to show results based on controlled wage figures. The arguments for wage differentials by industry can be applied also for employer-size wage differentials, because it is necessary to control various quality variables to derive a pure effect of the size of firm. Since the main purpose of this chapter is to present wage differentials by industry, the discussion on wage differentials by size of firm is very brief; for a fuller analysis refer to Tachibanaki (1993).

56

There are various studies on the interindustry wage structure in Japan. Sano (1969) and Mizuno (1973) belong to the old, while this chapter belongs to the new type. It will be useful to summarize studies on wage differentials in Japan very briefly as a rough introduction to the literature. Theoretically speaking, the human capital theory was the dominant and possibly the sole theory which attracted economists in Japan, according to Tachibanaki and Taki (1990). Mincer and Higuchi (1988) is an example of such a work. Empirically speaking, various studies such as Ono (1989) and Tachibanaki (1975, 1982) investigated the contribution of individual characteristics and firms' effect to wage differentials quantitatively, without necessarily relying on the human capital theory.

The neoclassical theory of wage determination suggests that the wage rate is equal to the marginal value product of labour under the ideal market, and thus employees who have common qualifications receive normally identical wages. In the real economy various wage levels are paid to individual employees. The above studies in Japan estimated the difference in wage payments caused by various qualifications, and found that the wage is not determined by the neoclassical economic theory. The present study examines another aspect of wage differentials, namely, the inter industry wage differentials, and the employer-size wage differentials.

In sum, the chapter examines interindustry wage differentials and derives a pure effect of industries after a comprehensive control for various factors and qualifications, and estimates the effect of economic factors which are responsible for explaining the pure difference in industrial wages. The pure effect of size of firm is also briefly examined. Section 3.2 presents the pure effect of industries on wage differentials, after controlling for qualifications, and the method of the control. Section 3.3 estimates dispersions of wage differentials by industries, and attempts to investigate the relative importance of various qualifications to such dispersions. Section 3.4 presents various economic factors which are able to explain the pure industry effect on wage differentials, and discusses them. Section 3.5 presents the result under the presumption that returns to various labour qualifications are not identical for all industries. Section 3.6 shows the result of wage differentials by the size of firm. Section 3.7 summarizes the result and implications for further studies.

The data used in this chapter are briefly explained in two Appendixes. The principal data source is the *Wage Structure Survey* (called popularly the *Census of Wages*) collected by the Ministry of Labour.

The survey contains an unbelievably large number of observations, for over 1 million employees. It includes wage figures of individual employees, working hours, personal characteristics such as sex, education, occupation, firm size, industry, region, and others. It is not an exaggeration to say that this is probably the most comprehensive survey on wages in the world. The present study uses individual observations of this survey. Since more than 1 million observations goes beyond the capacity of any computer, we use only about 35,000 observations which have been selected purely randomly.

3.2 ESTIMATION OF A PURE EFFECT OF INDUSTRY

Wages are differentiated by the characteristics and quality of both employees and employers. It is essential to eliminate these contributions in order to investigate interindustry wage differentials. In other words, it is necessary to estimate them under the condition of equal qualifications of employees and common firm specificities, after controlling for human capital variables and a variety of job characteristics. It is natural that an industry in which the majority of employees are male, educated, and longer-tenured and work at larger firms will pay a higher average wage than another industry in which the majority of employees are female, less well educated, and shorter-tenured and work at smaller firms. It is necessary to control for these effects in order to derive a pure effect of industry on wage differentials by industry; the interindustry wage differentials which are estimated without such controls may have a spurious industry effect. This pure effect may be called an industrial rent, which indicates a capability of paying higher wages in one industry even though qualities of employees and characteristics of firms in this industry are the same as in others.

The compensating wage differential is a popular theory among labour economists; these suggests that inferior work conditions such as longer working hours, dangerous and physically hard jobs have to be compensated to attract workers because otherwise firms find difficulty in employing them; a higher wage payment is a representative compensation. Conversely, an industry or a firm which provides superior work conditions may keep the wage level lower for this reason. It is interesting to examine whether this theory of compensating wage differential is supported in Japan because the confirmation of this theory induces a departure from neoclassical wage determination. A popular term '3K industries', specifying industries which have many Kitsui (physically hard), Kitanai (dirty), and Kiken (dangerous) jobs, implies that these industries are not preferred by people, in particular, by the youth in contemporary Japan. Thus, the examination of compensating wage differentials is worthwhile.

What kind of variables should be used for controls is the next consideration. Fortunately, we know quite a lot about the wage differentials by various factors in Japan, as given for example by Ono (1989), and Tachibanaki (1975, 1982). We thus adopt variables which are supposed to be influential on the determination of wages. The method of controls for such variables is performed through the estimation of the following wage function,

$$\ln(W_{ij}) = \text{constant} + (\text{industry dummies}) + (\text{various variables})$$

where W_{ij} stands for hourly fixed wage figures for jth employee in the ith industry, and industry dummies signify two kinds of industry classification. The first is the one-digit broad industry classification such as mining, manufacturing, construction, and others. There are a total of nine industries in this classification. The second is the two-digit industry classification, which consists of 55 industries. Bonuses are excluded in wage figures. Overtime hours are not taken into consideration.

The pure industry effect can be estimated by the following formulation,

$$p_i = \frac{W_i - W}{W}$$

where p_i is the ith industry's pure effect, W_i is the estimated average wage for the ith industry on the basis of the above wage function, and W is the overall average wage before the control.

We estimate the data for two years, 1978 and 1988, to study the time-series change in wage differentials. It would be possible to take into account the structural change during the 10 years, by introducing a dummy variable, for example. It was not attempted because we thought that there were no significant changes during the period. It is noted that the following categories of employees are eliminated from the sample: (1) public employees, (2) part-time employees, (3) employees whose working hours are zero, and (4) employees whose wages are zero. There are no strong reasons for eliminating the first two categories, but they were eliminated because their wage may be determined based on other grounds. The latter two categories of workers indicate the existence of non-active workers such as those suffering sickness, on temporary assignment in other firms, and others.

The adopted control variables are briefly explained. The Appendixes show a list of variables and their statistical sources. (1) Regular employee dummies; a regular permanent employee is unity, a fixed-duration employee is zero. This variable is an important variable in view of so-called implicit 'life-time employment' in Japan because employees with fixed-duration contracts are not guaranteed implicit 'lifetime employment'. (2) White-collar and blue-collar dummies; a white-collar worker is unity, a blue-collar worker is zero. (3) Six firm size dummy variables; the number of employees in a firm is classified by the following seven classes: (i) 5000 and more, (ii) 1000–4999, (iii) 500–999, (iv) 300–499 (v) 100–299, (vi) 30–99 and (vii) 10–29 in 1988. Classes (i)–(vi) take unity, and class (vii) takes zero for these dummies. In 1978, additional size, 15,000 and more is added. These dummies are crucial in view of the fact that the inter scale wage differentials have been believed to be important in Japan. (4) Establishment variable is scaled by the number of workers in one establishment. (5) Sex dummy; a male is unity, a female is zero. (6) Two regional dummies which are defined as follows; one group consists of the following prefectures which show the highest wages: Tokyo, Kanagawa, Saitama, Chiba, Osaka, Kyoto, Hyogo, and Aichi. The remaining prefectures are subdivided into two groups, one which shows higher wage payments and another which shows lower wage payments. (7) Fixed regular working hours. (8) Overtime hours. (9) Ages. (10) Job duration at the current employer. (11) Two education dummies; one dummy in which university graduate is unity, and another in which a senior high school graduate is unity, while a junior high school graduate is zero.

Several documents may be added with respect to the above explanatory variables. First, it may be somewhat redundant to include both firm size variables and establishment size variables because they may be slightly colinear. They were included, nevertheless, to meet our requirement such that we would like to take account of a large number of control variables. Incidentally, establishment variables were not included in Tachibanaki (1975, 1982), but Ono (1989) included them (see Brown and Medoff, 1989 for the treatment of firm size and establishment size for the US). Second, the inclusion of working hours, both fixed regular hours and overtime hours, may be somewhat strange in view of the fact that the dependent variable is already standardized by fixed regular hours. They were included for the purpose of examining compensating wage differentials related to working hours. A simple idea may be suggested as follows; jobs with longer working hours may be compensated by higher per-hour wages. Another reason is that in many cases wages in Japan are determined based on monthly rather than per-hour figures. Thus, with the inclusion of working hours as one independent variable we are able to investigate the effect of working hours on wages. Third, regional dummies are a new edition to the knowledge of past studies. Higher living expenses in urban areas are likely to induce an offer of higher wages in these areas. This variable was totally ignored in Japan. Fourth, we considered a square form for all continuous variables in addition to a linear form, and all possible interaction terms among independent variables. The consideration of squared variables and interactions is highly desirable because the effect of one variable is normally non-linear and also highly interacted with other variables. This is probably the most important contribution to the wage function estimated here because no other studies adopted such comprehensive square forms and interaction terms. In sum, the total number of control variables is 112 for one-digit industries, and 158 for two-digit industries, respectively. The controls are therefore nearly comprehensive and thorough, and thus a pure effect of industry is derived after the comprehensive control. Table 3.1 shows the estimated wage function for the one-digit industry level in 1988. Other estimated functions are not shown to save space.

It is impossible to interpret the empirical results of the estimated wage functions, partly because they have so many explanatory variables, and partly because our main concern is to derive a pure effect of industry after the controls. The estimated wage functions are considerably robust because of both the calculated R^2 (over 0.70) and the statistical significance of the majority of the estimated coefficients. We have rarely seen studies of individual wage functions whose R^2 are higher than 0.50. Thus, this function is fairly successful as a wage function. This is due largely to an extremely large number of explanatory variables. Moreover, it should be emphasized that the null hypothesis such that all industry dummy variables are equal to zero is rejected at the 1 percent significance level. Thus, we can safely estimate a pure effect of industry on wage differentials based on the estimated wage functions.

Table 3.2 shows the figures of industry effect before and after the controls. Figures in the first column are industrial advantages (and disadvantages) compared to the average wage of total observations, while figures in the second column are industrial advantages (and disadvantages) after the controls. The former may be called a spurious

Table 3.1   Estimated wage function, one-digit industry level in 1988

Dependent variable: lnW	Coefficient	Standard error
INTERCEPT	0.99779710**	0.09652899
PRO	−0.21296776**	0.02491041
PRO*T	−0.00082827**	0.00040450
PRO*A	−0.00167548**	0.00030556
PRO*ESZ	5.40994E–06	0.00000370
PRO*HR	0.00089407**	0.00012498
PRO*EHR	0.00159893**	0.00013922
SX	−0.22331547**	0.02356294
T*SX	−0.00469097**	0.00045526
A*SX	0.00976419**	0.00029726
ESZ*SX	−1.76474E–05**	0.00000488
HR*SX	0.00137010**	0.00011939
EHR*SX	−0.00152505**	0.00022685
PER	0.50553926**	0.06970156
T*PER	0.00855983**	0.00179829
A*PER	−0.00148486*	0.00084729
ESZ*PER	3.72223E–06	0.00002116
HR*PER	−0.00228296**	0.00032618
EHR*PER	0.00037447	0.00051403
PRF1	0.3868837	0.03266555
T*PRF1	0.00183436**	0.00054921
A*PRF1	−0.00094809**	0.00041935
ESZ*PRF1	6.90310E–05**	0.00001516
HR*PRF1	−0.00079056**	0.00015991
EHR*PRF1	7.39328E–05	0.00020239
PRF2	−0.04314644*	0.02207358
T*PRF2	−0.00185466**	0.00036469
A*PRF2	0.00255435**	0.00028875
ESZ*PRF2	−1.29766E–05**	0.00000305
HR*PRF2	0.00056130**	0.00011545
EHR*PRF2	−0.00069715**	0.00012977
T	0.02975502**	0.00260156
T*T	−0.00037258**	0.00002077
T*A	0.00029697**	0.00002664
A	0.04536628**	0.00178074
A*A	−0.00061161**	0.00001290
ED1	0.17357611**	0.02875426
T*ED1	0.00182208**	0.00039547
A*ED1	0.00042278	0.00034891
ESZ*ED1	−3.15111E–06	0.00000450
HR*ED1	−0.00067679**	0.00013422
EHR*ED1	−0.00114715**	0.00015326
ED2	0.11183046**	0.05021893
T*ED2	−0.00222366**	0.00098245

Table 3.1   continued

Dependent variable: lnW		
	Coefficient	*Standard error*
A*ED2	0.00753524**	0.00072208
ESZ*ED2	−1.50091E–05*	0.00000831
HR*ED2	−0.00100197**	0.00025162
EHR*ED2	−0.00129193**	0.00030981
ED3	0.34436756**	0.04145866
T*ED3	−0.00615863**	0.00071707
A*ED3	0.01456672**	0.00062797
ESZ*ED3	1.29507E–05**	0.00000631
HR*ED3	−0.00324393**	0.00019277
EHR*ED3	−0.00207503**	0.00023129
FSZ1	0.54613188**	0.04336746
T*FSZ1	0.00265162**	0.00075235
A*FSZ1	0.00341879**	0.00062618
ESZ*FSZ1	−0.00221116**	0.00055457
HR*FSZ1	−0.00267904**	0.00021200
EHR*FSZ1	−0.00024088	0.00026178
FSZ2	0.57553105	0.04443052
T*FSZ2	0.00507726**	0.00074619
A*FSZ2	−0.00028101	0.00059710
ESZ*FSZ2	−0.00219736**	0.00055458
HR*FSZ2	−0.00252868**	0.00022273
EHR*FSZ2	−0.00036608	0.00024701
FSZ3	0.63218921**	0.05062316
T*FSZ3	0.00493062**	0.00082557
A*FSZ3	−0.00135322**	0.00063817
ESZ*FSZ3	−0.00212980**	0.00055481
HR*FSZ3	−0.00286697**	0.00024865
EHR*FSZ3	−0.00046819**	0.00026955
FSZ4	0.56609994**	0.05076716
T*FSZ4	0.00393203**	0.00081251
A*FSZ4	−0.00051674	0.00060604
ESZ*FSZ4	−0.00212329**	0.00055548
HR*FSZ4	−0.00258134**	0.00024804
EHR*FSZ4	−0.00075563**	0.00028072
FSZ5	0.45087864**	0.03959155
T*FSZ5	0.00263093**	0.00061192
A*FSZ5	−0.00020054	0.00042434
ESZ*FSZ5	−0.00216124**	0.00055626
HR*FSZ5	−0.00197145**	0.00018396
EHR*FSZ5	−0.00035716**	0.00021202
FSZ6	0.19623953**	0.03645808
T*FSZ6	0.00214806**	0.00056488

Table continued on page 64

Table 3.1   continued

Dependent variable: lnW	Coefficient	Standard error
A*FSZ6	−0.00016766	0.00037472
ESZ*FSZ6	−0.00213152**	0.00056907
HR*FSZ6	−0.00067227**	0.00016231
EHR*FSZ6	−0.00059634**	0.00019486
ESZ	0.00232565**	0.00055552
T*ESZ	−2.56593E−07	0.00000041
A*ESZ	−14.6211E−07	0.00000038
ESZ*ESZ	−4.61942E−11	0.00000000
ESZ*HR	−5.23403E−07**	0.00000010
ESZ*EHR	−3.15792E−08	0.00000008
HR	−7.51269E−05	0.00053511
T*HR	−0.00012162**	0.00000724
A*HR	−3.01457E−07	0.00000529
HR*HR	9.74912E−07	0.00000096
HR*EHR	−2.56117E−05**	0.00000287
EHR	0.00600783**	0.00085630
A*EHR	−1.27197E−05*	0.00000743
T*EHR	−9.25798E−05**	0.00000922
EHR*EHR	1.74390E−05**	0.00000162
D1	−0.01944335	0.01285998
D2	−0.08428975**	0.01146452
D3	−0.02068015	0.01549764
D4	−0.14140039**	0.01229343
D5	−0.07262488**	0.01225233
D6	0.05398482**	0.01274532
D7	−0.02783857**	0.01640771
D8	−0.04132546**	0.01199761
R^2	0.764616	
Sample	35977	

Notes:
Explanation of the independent variables appears in Appendix 1.
** : 5% significant.
* : 10% significant.
* means cross-term.

advantage (or disadvantage) of an industry, while the latter may be called a pure advantage (or disadvantage) of an industry, or a pure industrial rent (or a pure negative rent).

Spurious advantages (or disadvantages) are discussed first (Table 3.2a). The highest wage payment is seen by electricity, gas, and water supply industries in 1988, and its advantage is very high, 42.3 percent

Table 3.2a Spurious and pure industrial advantages (or rents):
before-control and after-control for various qualifications in employees and
firms, one-digit industrial classification (%)

1988	Before-control	After-control	SE
Mining	0.23	6.89	0.0965
Construction	3.33	4.83	0.0129
Manufacturing	−0.75	−1.75	0.0115
Electricity, gas, heat supply and water	42.3	4.70	0.0155
Transport and communication	9.74	−7.21	0.0123
Wholesale and retail trade, eating and drinking places	−9.43	−0.60	0.0123
Finance and insurance	37.17	12.82	0.0127
Real estate	0.14	3.95	0.0164
Services	−2.92	2.56	0.0120

1978	Before-control	After-control	SE
Mining	6.58	7.79	0.0671
Construction	1.27	3.15	0.0120
Manufacturing	−4.88	−2.45	0.0104
Electricity, gas, heat supply and water	41.05	2.70	0.0148
Transport and communication	2.75	−3.06	0.0116
Wholesale and retail trade, eating and drinking places	−6.63	−1.14	0.0113
Finance and insurance	29.39	14.13	0.0118
Real estate	10.38	2.50	0.0163
Services	−3.75	1.39	0.0112

1988	R^2	0.765	1978	R^2	0.729
	Sample	35977		Sample	35952

Note:
SE: Standard error of the coefficient of the industry dummy variables (SE of
mining is that of the constant term).

above the average. The next highest wage is paid to finance and insurance industries, and its advantage is 37.1 percent. Conversely, the
lowest wage payment is wholesale, retail trade, and restaurant industries, and its disadvantage is 9.4 percent below the average. We observe so wide a difference in the wage payments by industries. This is
also true for 1978.

What happened to pure industrial advantages (or disadvantages), or
rents after the very comprehensive controls? Some authours use the
word 'industrial rent'. Since 'rents' must be defined fairly rigorously,

Table 3.2b   Pure industrial advantages: after-control for
various qualifications in employees and firms, two-digit industrial
classification (%)

	1988 After-control	SE	1978 After-control	SE
Mining	6.31	0.0966	7.73	0.0671
Construction works general	4.20	0.0136	3.21	0.0125
Construction works by occupation	10.47	0.0196	9.02	0.0256
Equipment installation works	2.00	0.0158	0.36	0.0152
Food	−4.88	0.0134	−4.95	0.0121
Beverage, feed, tobacco	2.47	0.0182	0.99	0.0215
Textile mill products	−8.13	0.0140	−9.56	0.0128
Apparel	−11.99	0.0145	−12.48	0.0135
Lumber and wood products	−7.45	0.0151	−7.48	0.0137
Furniture and fixtures	−4.52	0.0155	−4.44	0.0151
Pulp, paper and paper products	−1.10	0.0145	−3.02	0.0134
Publishing and printing	3.76	0.0140	0.58	0.0127
Chemical products	4.69	0.0133	2.80	0.0123
Plastic products	−1.31	0.0148	−4.02	0.0162
Rubber products	−3.69	0.0153	−1.98	0.0145
Ceramic, stone and clay products	−0.58	0.0136	0.14	0.0124
Iron and steel	0.69	0.0141	2.40	0.0135
Non-ferrous metal and products	−0.87	0.0149	−0.54	0.0142
Fabricated metal products	−0.04	0.0137	0.11	0.0130
General machinery	1.06	0.0132	0.55	0.0123
Electrical machinery	−3.87	0.0126	−5.30	0.0117
Transportation equipment	−2.77	0.0128	−1.63	0.0118
Precision instruments	0.18	0.0145	−0.82	0.0137
Electricity	4.95	0.0172	4.36	0.0164
Gas	4.76	0.0204	1.61	0.0197
Railways	−16.21	0.0142	−14.19	0.0165
Road passenger transport	−12.05	0.0137	−4.94	0.0128
Road freight transport	0.20	0.0138	−0.30	0.0131
Transport services	−1.98	0.0170	0.86	0.0163
Communication	−2.89	0.0156	0.88	0.0521
Wholesale trade	1.17	0.0129	1.75	0.0120
Retail trade general merchandise	−1.66	0.0156	−0.57	0.0145
Retail trade, dry goods, apparel and accessory stores	2.38	0.0207	−0.97	0.0211
Retail trade, food and beverage stores	−6.08	0.0174	−5.29	0.0176
Retail trade, motor vehicles, bicycles carts	−0.56	0.0161	−3.79	0.0162
Retail trade, furniture, stores fixture and household utensils	−0.98	0.0194	−3.87	0.0231
Miscellaneous retail trade	−0.86	0.0212	−3.14	0.0175

Table 3.2b   continued

	1988 After-control	SE	1978 After-control	SE
Eating and drinking places	0.40	0.0168	−5.00	0.0150
Banks and trust companies	21.91	0.0158	12.70	0.0137
Financial institutions for small-sized enterprises, etc.	2.79	0.0145	3.45	0.0138
Securities and commodity brokers, dealers and exchanges	23.55	0.0173	12.31	0.0166
Insurance trade	23.52	0.0157	33.19	0.0140
Real estate	4.36	0.0160	3.40	0.0158
Goods rental and leasing	11.64	0.0202	4.41	0.0420
Hotels, boarding houses and other lodging places	−0.08	0.0149	−5.62	0.0139
Laundry, beauty and bath services	−8.76	0.0189	−9.87	0.0163
Amusement and recreation services except movies	3.28	0.0160	−3.93	0.0152
Miscellaneous repair services	−3.88	0.0198	−2.73	0.0310
Cooperative associations	−9.01	0.0187	−6.00	0.0161
Information services, research and advertising	7.34	0.0152	7.96	0.0268
Miscellaneous business services	−13.79	0.0160	−12.35	0.0178
Professional services	4.34	0.0171	6.60	0.0207
Medical services	13.07	0.0138	21.22	0.0137
Education services	9.86	0.0147	11.44	0.0146
Social insurance and social welfare	9.51	0.0182	16.69	0.0234
1988 R^2	0.775	1978	R^2	0.743
Sample	34227		Sample	34072
WASD	0.078		WASD	0.076

Notes:
SE: Standard error of the coefficient of the industry dummy variables (SE of the mining is that of the constant term).
WASD: Weighted Adjusted Standard Deviation.

we use the word 'advantages' (or 'disadvantages') to avoid ambiguity. The pure advantage of electricity, gas, and water supply industries has reduced to 4.7 percent, and of finance and insurance industries to 12.8 percent. The highest industrial advantage is given to finance and insurance industries. The change is from 42.3 percent to 4.7 percent, and from 37.2 percent to 12.8 percent, respectively. These decreases are drastic. Incidentally, three effects, namely (1) more larger firms,

(2) more male employees, and (3) more longer-tenured workers, are responsible for the drastic decrease in advantages from before-control to after-control for gas, electricity, and water supply industries. A similar explanation is also possible for finance and insurance industries (see Tachibanaki, 1992 for more in detail). It is interesting to observe that the lowest spurious disadvantage for wholesale, retail trade, and restaurant industries disappears, while the lowest pure industrial disadvantage is observed for transportation and communication industries. Service industries turned out to show a pure positive advantage after the control, while they showed a disadvantage before the control. The above observations are largely applicable for 1978 as well.

We can derive three implications from the above results. First, it is very crucial to control for employees 'qualifications and firms' specificities to derive a pure industry effect on wage differentials by industries because spurious wage differentials by industries were reduced substantially. In other words, it is quite risky to argue the interindustry wage differentials based only on the wage figures before controls.

Second, the ranking of industries due to industrial advantages is subtly different before and after the controls, as explained previously. This again suggests the necessity of controls. We found that finance and insurance industries showed the highest advantage, namely 12.8 percent in 1988, and 14.1 percent in 1978, and that transportation and communication industries showed the highest negative advantage, namely 7.2 percent in 1988, and 3.1 percent in 1978, respectively. We need a subjective judgement to evaluate whether the pure advantage is too high, and/or the pure disadvantage is too low. The comparable figures for the US are about 22 percent advantage (mining) and 12 percent disadvantage (wholesale and retail trade) (see these numbers in Kruger and Summers, 1988). Kruger and Summers conclude that the difference is substantial. It is possible to conclude that the Japanese difference is considerably smaller than the US one.

Third, somewhat related to the above, there is a substantial difference between Japan and the US with respect to ranks of industries due to pure effects. Japan ranks as follows; (1) finance and insurance, (2) mining, (3) construction, (4) electricities, gas, and water supply, (5) real estate, (6) services, (7) wholesale, retail trade, and restaurant, (8) manufacturing, and (9) transportation and communication. The US ranks as follows; (1) mining, (2) transportation and public utilities, (3) construction, (4) manufacturing, (5) finance, insurance, and real estate, (6) services, and (7) wholesale and retail trade. Since one-digit level industrial classifications are not identical between the two countries, it is somewhat risky to draw a firm conclusion. It is obvious, nevertheless, that ranks are considerably different between them. This contradicts the proposition given by Katz and Summers (1989) which asserted a fairly similar pattern in spurious wage differentials by industry in the international context. When we use wage figures after controls, the inter industry wage differentials are different at least between Japan and the US for one-digit level industries. It may be too hasty to predict that all countries have the identical structure of industrial advantages. The examination of two-digit level industries between Japan and the US confirms it more rigorously, although it is not examined in detail here to save space.

Next, we examine the pure industrial effect of two-digit industries in 1978 and 1988 (Table 3.2b). The highest advantage was given to securities and commodity transactions industries, and insurance industries (23.6 and 23.5 percent advantages respectively) in 1988, and to insurance (33.2 percentage advantage) in 1978, while the highest negative advantage was given to railroad industries in 1988 (16.2 percent disadvantage) and 1978 (14.2 percent disadvantage). Within manufacturing industries the highest advantage was given to chemical industries in both 1988 and 1978, while in both years the highest negative advantage was to given to apparel and other textile industries. A similar pattern was observed also for the US, when we pay attention to the two extremes, namely highest positive and negative effects. The above results suggest a fairly stable interindustry wage structure across time. The very high correlation coefficient between 1978 and 1988 with respect to pure industrial advantages, 0.893, confirms the stability of the inter industry wage structure over time in Japan.

3.3 DISPERSIONS IN WAGE DIFFERENTIALS BY INDUSTRY

This section examines what kind of qualifications of employees and specificities of firms are crucial for controlling in the determination of pure industrial advantages. In other words, we seek the variables among many control variables which are important for control. We use weighted adjusted standard deviation (WASD) to analyze the above. The weight is the number of employees in industries. The standard deviation is an upwardly biased estimate. We follow the method used by Kruger and Summers (1988) to correct this bias.

This section uses somewhat simplified versions of wage functions

compared with those in the previous section in the sense that a somewhat fewer number of control variables are used. This is due only to
the technical reasons associated with computation. This raises weighted
adjusted standard deviations very marginally, but does not give any
significantly different result. One justification for this statement is provided by the extremely high correlation coefficient, 0.973, between
the interindustry wage differentials estimated in the previous section
and those estimated by the present method.

Table 3.3 shows 'various' weighted adjusted standard deviations
(WASD) in pure industrial advantages. This is calculated for log-wage
figures. 'Various' means that one, two, or more explanatory variables
are eliminated from the list of the control variables, and the respective
WASD is presented. The result suggests that the largest increase in
WASD is obtained when the variable of working hours is eliminated
in 1988. The next one is education. Job tenure, occupation dummy
(white-collars and blue-collars), firm size, and establishment size follow. In 1978 working hours is again the largest increase. The rank of
other variables is fairly different in 1978 compared to 1988; the next
one is sex in 1978, and education, occupation, job tenure, firm size
and establishment size follow. The fact that the contribution of both
sex and occupation had declined from 1978 to 1988 signifies that wage
differentials by sex and occupation had probably declined during the
period. It is useful to mention that equal opportunities legislation was
implemented during the period, and also that a so-called 'move toward
more white-collar jobs' than blue collar jobs in the industries went on
in Japan. These are probably responsible for the above trends.

Next, we examine the impact of adding control variables such as
human capital variables and firm size variable on WASD. Each variable is added successively, and the results are presented in Table 3.4.
We obtain the following observations. An addition of job tenure decreased WASD by 12.5 percent. Education decreased it by 13.5 percent, and a firm size by 3.6 percent in 1988. The corresponding figure
in 1978 was 15.1 percent, 13.2 percent, and 8.2 percent, respectively.
These results together with the ones in the previous section suggest
that job tenure, education, and firm size are responsible for the extremely apparent spurious wage differentials by industry. This is consistent with the paper by Tachibanaki and Taki (1990) who proposed
that the wage function which used these three variables (namely, (1)
job tenure, (2) education, and (3) firm size) is fairly successful and
sufficient in the estimation of wage determination in Japan. In other
words, these three variables determine the wage level to a greater extent.

Table 3.3   Contribution of explanatory variables to wage differentials estimated by WASD after elimination of variables

Eliminated variables	1988	1978
Working hours	0.110	0.091
Education dummies	0.099	0.088
Tenure	0.095	0.083
Blue-collar dummy	0.093	0.088
Firm-size dummies	0.089	0.083
Male dummy	0.088	0.089
Age	0.088	0.076
Regular worker dummy	0.086	0.078
No elimination	0.086	0.076
No control	0.211	0.179

Table 3.4   Contribution of explanatory variables to wage differentials estimated by WASD after addition of variables

Added variables	1988	1978
(1) No control	0.211	0.179
(2) Added except tenure, education and firm size	0.117	0.113
(3) (2) + Tenure control	0.103	0.095
(4) (3) + Education control	0.089	0.083
(5) (4) + Firm-size control	0.086	0.076

Finally, we investigate the influence of control variables in more detail, by classifying samples in 1988 further: age, tenure and firm size are subdivided. Table 3.5 shows the results, which induce the following findings. The younger age is, the smaller the WASD is. This is also true, the shorter tenure is, and equivalently the smaller firm size is. A similar finding is observed for higher education. WASD for men is smaller than for women, and is smaller for white-collars than for blue-collars. These results suggest that employees who are obliged to receive lower wage payments, say female, less educated, or blue-collar workers are likely to receive more positive (or negative) industrial advantages than those who are supposed to receive higher wage payments, say male, educated, or white-collar workers. A simple example is the following; women have greater advantage in wage payments than men in advantageous industries like finance and insurance industries, while women have greater disadvantage than men in disadvantageous industries like manufacturing. A similar argument is also possible

Table 3.5 Comparison of WASD, subdivided samples (1988)

	WASD		Correlation	
Age:				
15–29	0.064	a	a–b	0.673
30–50	0.097	b	b–c	0.771
51–	0.114	c	a–c	0.307
Tenure:				
0–4	0.069	d	d–e	0.789
5–10	0.110	e	e–f	0.879
11–	0.104	f	d–f	0.636
Size:				
10–99	0.072	g	g–h	0.804
100–999	0.073	h	h–i	0.786
1000–	0.089	i	g–i	0.488
Education:				
Secondary school	0.092		0.619	
University and				
Junior College	0.066			
Sex:				
Female	0.094		0.638	
Male	0.073			
Type of worker:				
Blue-collar	0.048		0.687	
White-collar	0.026			

for less educated versus educated, and blue-collar workers versus white-collar workers.

3.4   ECONOMIC FACTORS WHICH EXPLAIN PURE INDUSTRIAL ADVANTAGES

It is appealing to investigate why pure industrial advantages appear even after controlling for various human capital variables and firm characteristics. Since we obtained the degree of pure industrial advantages in the previous section, a natural task is to seek the cause of pure industrial advantages. There are several studies which performed a similar task. Sano (1969) and Mizuno (1973) for Japan, and Dickens and Katz (1987) for the US may be cited. It should be noted that the

Japanese studies adopted spurious industrial advantages (i.e., before-controls) which are somewhat dubious as a proper data source, for the reasons described above. Also, they did not consider a comprehensive list of causes. In sum, we would like to investigate proper causes of the appearance of pure industrial advantages, which are specific to Japanese institutional characteristics and industrial relations. The method is fairly simple. We consider a large number of economic variables, and estimate correlations between them and pure industrial advantages. Pearson correlation coefficients are estimated. It might be preferable to adopt partial correlation coefficients rather than simple correlation coefficients. Since we are going to perform another study which adopts a simultaneous equation approach in this field, partial correlations are argued elsewhere. Pearson correlation coefficients are estimated for weighted figures, with weight being the number of employees in industries. Economic interpretations are provided for these empirical results.

Data for this research are briefly explained. Two types of data on pure industrial advantages are used. The first is two-digit industrial classifications for whole industries, and two years, 1978 and 1988, are pooled. The total number of observations is 110. The second is two-digit classifications only for manufacturing industries, and again pooled. The total number of observations is 38. The former is called 'whole industry', for simplicity (Table 3.6a), and the latter is called 'manufacturing industry' (Table 3.6b). It might be interesting to look at first differences, removing the fixed effect of individual industries, since we have two years of data. That was not attempted because there were so few observations. We use a fairly large number of economic variables as candidates for explaining the causes of pure economic advantages, which are collected from various statistical sources. Therefore, industrial classifications are not perfectly identical. Although there may be some errors and biases, they are not serious because various government agencies have a policy towards the identical definition of industries. Appendix 2 shows the list of variables and their statistical sources.

It is necessary to explain the reason why variables which were used as control variables are used again as candidates for the causes of pure industrial advantages. We thought that several variables might be influential on the determination of industrial advantages. Since we use the averages or the rates of these economic variables, this is not necessarily double-counting. Let us give an example by using the age variable. Suppose that there are two industries such that the average age

Table 3.6a Correlation coefficients between pure industrial advantages and economic variables (whole industry)[a]

	WD	A	T	ED	PRO	SZ	SX	BONUS	UNION
WD	1.00								
A	-0.20*	1.00							
T	-0.12	0.25**	1.00						
ED	0.52**	-0.44***	-0.01	1.00					
PRO	-0.29***	0.30***	0.15	-0.35**	1.00				
SZ	0.35***	-0.20***	0.49***	0.17*	-0.25**	1.00			
SX	-0.22***	0.23***	0.59***	-0.03	0.09	0.09	1.00		
BONUS	0.39***	-0.41**	0.52***	0.52**	-0.26**	0.69**	0.13	1.00	
UNION	0.08	0.07	0.65***	0.03	0.01	0.70**	0.34**	0.62**	1.00
CWELF	0.36**	0.04	0.48***	0.11	-0.02	0.63**	0.30**	0.52**	0.74**
INJURY	-0.27***	0.47**	0.25***	-0.44**	0.25**	-0.06	0.35**	-0.26**	0.09
REST	-0.25***	0.35***	-0.31***	-0.30**	-0.06	-0.50**	-0.07	-0.52**	-0.48**
RED	-0.12	0.34**	-0.03	-0.16*	0.21**	-0.26**	0.17*	-0.30**	-0.08
QUIT	0.04	-0.09	-0.38***	0.12	-0.20**	-0.17**	-0.25**	-0.20**	-0.39***
HIRING	0.07	-0.18*	-0.60***	0.09	-0.33**	-0.25**	-0.48**	-0.33**	-0.59***
EMP	0.31**	-0.12	0.01	0.43***	-0.42**	0.12	-0.10	0.20**	-0.08
VACANCY	-0.36***	0.19***	-0.02	-0.25***	0.57**	-0.26**	0.14	-0.38**	-0.23***
EXPORT	-0.30***	-0.08	0.15	-0.25***	0.35**	0.11	0.28**	0.01	0.38***
CAPRET	-0.13	0.17*	0.06	-0.07	0.20**	-0.29**	0.10	-0.20**	-0.10
REGUL	0.62**	-0.26**	0.09	0.27**	-0.40**	0.60**	-0.32**	0.56**	0.36**

	CWELF	INJURY	REST	RED	QUIT	HIRING	EMP	VACANCY	EXPORT
CWELF	1.00								
INJURY	0.14	1.00							
REST	-0.54**	0.43**	1.00						
RED	0.09	0.32**	0.19**	1.00					
QUIT	-0.27**	-0.21**	0.10	0.13	1.00				
HIRING	-0.46**	-0.21**	0.36**	-0.02	0.48**	1.00			
EMP	-0.09	-0.25**	-0.04	-0.51**	0.19**	0.39**	1.00		
VACANCY	-0.32**	0.29**	0.32**	0.08	-0.05	0.13	0.03	1.00	
EXPORT	0.05	-0.01	-0.35**	-0.03	-0.20**	-0.40**	-0.26**	0.23**	1.00
CAPRET	-0.17*	-0.08	-0.01	0.06	-0.14	-0.09	0.01	0.10	0.14
REGUL	0.48**	-0.21	-0.30**	-0.35**	-0.04	-0.02	0.31**	-0.43**	-0.30**

	CAPRET	REGUL
CAPRET	1.00	
REGUL	-0.29**	1.00

Notes:
[a] Weighted by the number of workers in industries.
** : 5% significant.
* : 10% significant.
Sample size: 110.

Table 3.6b   Correlation coefficients between pure industrial advantages and economic variables (manufacturing)[a]

	WD	A	T	ED	PRO	SZ	SX	BONUS	UNION
WD	1.00								
A	0.02	1.00							
T	0.64**	0.44**	1.00						
ED	0.70**	-0.31*	0.54**	1.00					
PRO	-0.70**	0.40**	-0.43**	-0.95**	1.00				
SZ	0.28	0.35**	0.54**	0.34**	-0.18	1.00			
SX	0.81**	0.22	0.68**	0.45**	-0.43**	0.38**	1.00		
BONUS	0.77**	-0.31*	0.58**	0.79**	-0.84**	0.11	0.60**	1.00	
UNION	0.43**	-0.24	0.45**	0.42**	-0.43**	0.05	0.46**	0.72**	1.00
CWELF	0.62**	0.06	0.60**	0.38**	-0.36**	0.17	0.60**	0.64**	0.38**
INJURY	-0.15	0.69**	-0.07	-0.41**	0.36**	-0.03	-0.01	-0.44**	-0.56**
REST	-0.54**	0.45**	-0.49**	-0.64**	0.61**	-0.16	-0.46**	-0.77**	-0.75**
RED	-0.02**	-0.19	-0.13**	-0.19**	0.14**	-0.18	-0.18**	-0.06**	-0.25**
QUIT	-0.76**	-0.20	-0.65**	-0.45**	0.44**	-0.18	-0.82**	-0.59**	-0.60**
HIRING	-0.40**	0.05	-0.30**	-0.24	0.24	-0.12	-0.43**	-0.41**	-0.50**
EMP	0.14	0.02	0.26	0.39**	-0.33**	0.64**	0.05	0.09	-0.15
VACANCY	-0.58**	-0.08	-0.49	-0.36**	0.36**	0.03	-0.45**	-0.56**	-0.47**
EXPORT	0.06	-0.60**	-0.05	0.16	-0.21	-0.11	0.17	0.37**	0.56**
CAPRET	0.19	0.29*	0.48**	0.14	0.01	0.53**	0.34**	0.02	0.14
CAPITAL	0.53**	0.17	0.58**	0.29*	-0.22	0.14	0.50**	0.52**	0.66**
HI	0.45**	-0.11	0.21	0.20	-0.28*	0.07	0.39**	0.47**	0.49**
RD	0.17	-0.61**	0.02	0.38**	-0.49**	-0.04	0.12	0.55**	0.61**
VALUE	0.72**	-0.01	0.61**	0.62**	-0.64**	0.15	0.57**	0.80**	0.72**
PROFIT	0.47**	0.14	0.35**	0.26	-0.31*	0.10	0.31*	0.48**	0.55**

	CWELF	INJURY	REST	RED	QUIT	HIRING	EMP	VACANCY	EXPORT
CWELF	1.00								
INJURY	-0.32**	1.00							
REST	-0.62**	0.79**	1.00						
RED	0.40**	0.04	-0.10	1.00					
QUIT	-0.74**	0.16	0.48**	-0.28*	1.00				
HIRING	-0.47**	0.36**	0.54**	-0.28**	0.60**	1.00			
EMP	-0.21	-0.12	-0.14	-0.68**	0.10	0.08	1.00		
VACANCY	-0.61**	0.10	0.42**	-0.27*	0.59**	0.27	0.32*	1.00	
EXPORT	0.20	-0.63**	-0.59**	0.05	-0.16	-0.42**	-0.01	0.07	1.00
CAPRET	0.24	-0.14	-0.26	0.21	-0.24	-0.23	0.18	0.06	0.04
CAPITAL	0.90**	-0.23	-0.45**	0.38**	-0.68**	-0.37**	-0.24	-0.56**	-0.01
HI	0.50**	-0.25	-0.44**	0.04	-0.39**	-0.46**	0.14	-0.22	0.42**
RD	0.32**	-0.63**	-0.61**	0.05	-0.26	-0.55**	0.01	-0.15	0.78**
VALUE	0.83**	-0.27*	-0.55**	0.25	-0.70**	-0.40**	-0.08	-0.61**	0.06
PROFIT	0.73**	-0.10	-0.27	0.30*	-0.50**	-0.36**	-0.13	-0.44**	-0.04

	CAPRET	CAPITAL	HI	RD	VALUE	PROFIT
CAPRET	1.00					
CAPITAL	0.21	1.00				
HI	0.10	0.28*	1.00			
RD	-0.06	0.09	0.41**	1.00		
VALUE	0.07	0.79**	0.31**	0.34**	1.00	
PROFIT	0.05	0.70**	0.35**	0.26	0.79**	1.00

Notes:
[a] Weighted by the number of workers in industries.
** : 5% significant.
* : 10% significant.
Sample size: 38.

of employees is older in one industry, and is younger in another industry. If the former industry requires knowledge and skills of older employees, average productivity in this industry may be higher. It raises the industrial advantages of this industry. Average age may therefore be a candidate for the explanation of the industrial advantage.

Table 3.6 shows the estimated correlation coefficients. Since there are so many numbers in this table, we restrict our attention to the influence of economic variables on pure industrial advantages. Let us first examine the average worker characteristics of industries. Average age has a negative influence on industrial advantages (or pure wage differentials) for whole industry, while it has no influence for manufacturing industry. Average tenure is different from average age; it has no correlation with wage differentials for whole industry, while it has a strong positive correlation for manufacturing industry. Manufacturing industry evaluates firm specific human capital more highly than whole industry. The rate of university graduates to total employees, which signifies a higher education level in the industry, has a strong positive influence for both whole and manufacturing industries. The rate of blue-collar workers to total employees is influential negatively. The effect is weak for whole industry and strong for manufacturing industry. The rate of male employees has a weak positive effect for manufacturing industry.

Many of the above variables were used as control variables, as noted previously. What implications can be derived from the above observations obtained by the estimated correlation coefficients? The positive influences for manufacturing industry are observed by the rate of male employees, average job tenure, the rate of university graduates, and the rate of white-collar employees. It is possible to conclude that these characteristics raised average productivity of the industry, which is one of signs for a pure industrial advantage. Incidentally, Table 3.6b suggests that *per capita* value added (i.e., average productivity) has the strongest positive effect on pure industrial advantages. We can interpret this result in the following way. First, various variables such as average job tenure and other variables which were examined above, raise average productivity of the industry. Second, this higher productivity creates an industrial advantage. It is necessary to investigate this with a simultaneous equation model, as was proposed previously, in order to confirm whether this interpretation is correct.

The share of bonus payments over total wage payment is highly correlated with pure industrial advantages (pure wage differentials). This reflects the fact that bonuses are an indicator of firm specific human capital as proposed by Hashimoto (1979). We can conceive of another hypothesis for bonus payments. That is the profit-sharing hypothesis popularized by Weitzman (1986), and Freeman and Weitzman (1987). The present chapter does not intend to determine which hypothesis is more preferable to understand bonus payments in Japan. The rate of union participation has no impact for whole industry, while it has a strong positive effect for manufacturing industry. Combining with a strong negative effect on quits and a strong positive effect on productivity and profit, the influence of union rate may be regarded as a voice mechanism of union movements at least for manufacturing industry. This work thus supports Muramatsu (1984). However, a separate study is required to confirm the above statement (see, for example, Tachibanaki and Noda, 1992).

Next, we investigate the effect of working conditions on pure wage differentials. Non-statutory fringe benefit per employee, the rate of labour accident, and the rate of utilization of one-holiday per week are the variables which show the degree of working conditions. Non-statutory fringe benefit is positively correlated in ranks for both whole and manufacturing industries. The rate of labour accidents has a negative impact for whole industry, while it has no significance for manufacturing industry. The one-day holiday rate is negatively correlated for both whole and manufacturing industries. These observations lead us to conclude that lower wages are paid to workers in the industry with unfavourable working conditions. It is possible to affirm that it is too premature to accept the theory of compensating wage differentials. Instead, the '3K' industries argument described above for Japan is very plausible.

Variables like the rate of involuntary quit, the rate of voluntary quit, the rate of new job entry, the rate of increase in employment, and vacancy rate indicate the degree of labour mobility. Statistically significant variables are observed only by the rate of increase in employment (positively) and vacancy rate (negatively) for whole industry. Voluntary quit rate and vacancy rate are negatively related with industrial advantages for manufacturing industry. A higher industrial advantage probably lowers the rate of voluntary quit. Higher labour demand, which is indicated by the rate of increase in employment indirectly, raises wage levels. We conclude, nevertheless, that these variables related to labour mobility do not have a strong influence on industrial wage differentials on average. They are more influential on wages for newly hired employees than on those for currently employed workers.

A regulation dummy variable was introduced to examine whether government regulation on competition and business activity has an impact on industrial advantages. Table 3.6a indicates that this variable is quite influential positively for whole industry. Typical industries which receive higher benefits of regulations are finance and insurance industries, and electricity, gas, and water supply industries. See Tachibanaki (1992), who analyzed the benefit for finance and insurance industries. Besides the effect of regulations on industrial wage differentials, it is interesting to observe that a regulation dummy has higher correlations with firm size, non-statutory fringe benefit, and bonus ratio. These results suggest the necessity of investigating the effect of regulation further as well as of utilizing a more reliable measure of regulations rather than a dummy variable, since this is one of the most important variables in Japan.

The share of exports over total production has a negative effect on industrial wages for whole industry, while it is not statistically significant for manufacturing industry. The highest rate of exports is observed by several manufacturing products such as cars, electricity goods, chemical products, and machines. These manufacturing industries do not necessarily pay higher wages, but probably around average wages. A more interesting observation is given by the high positive correlation between the share of exports over total production and R&D expenditure rate, which signifies one of the causes of their success in exports.

Next, variables on market concentration rate and profit rate per employee are examined. The Herfindahl index is used to show market concentration for industries. These two variables have strong positive effects on industrial advantages. Thus, firms' ability to pay is an important source of higher wage payments. Another indicator of firms' ability such as value-added per employee (productivity) and capital–labour ratio has a strong positive effect on wages. It is noted that the variables examined above are interrelated each other to a greater extent. Finally, the rate of return to stocks, which shows one indicator of investment incentives like the Q-ratio, has no impact.

3.5   THE EFFECT OF DIFFERENT RETURNS TO LABOUR QUALITY

Section 3.3–3.4 estimated pure industrial advantages after controlling for various qualities of employees and firms, and investigated the causes of pure industrial advantages. It was assumed in these sections that differences in returns to labour forces among various industries were not observed. This assumption implies, for example, that monetary returns (i.e., wages) to university education do not differ from industry to industry. Another assumption is that the treatment of male–female wages is common for all industries. A similar argument is possible for other qualifications and characteristics such as firm size, tenure, and others. In sum, we have not considered the case in which industrial differences do not matter in the determination of returns (or wages) to various qualifications. This assumption may be somewhat unrealistic, as examined by Kawashima and Tachibanaki (1986), who investigated the difference in wage structures between competitive and non-competitive sectors. This section examines what would happen if this assumption was removed.

It is not so implausible to presume that returns to various labour qualifications are not so different by industries unless the labour markets are highly segmented. In fact, a large number of studies on wage differentials by industries, including the present one, assumed no variations by industries. It is, however, useful to investigate the case in which this assumption is removed. This section therefore starts by re-estimating the wage functions, which were estimated for whole industries in section 3.2, for each industry separately. These wage functions obviously produce different estimated coefficients of education, firm size, tenure, and other characteristics by industries. We perform this experiment only for 19 manufacturing industries (1978 and 1988). Thus, we have totally 38 different estimated returns (i.e., coefficients) to various qualifications such as education, size, sex, and others. The specification of the wage functions was simplified to reduce a heavy burden of computation. In particular, various interaction variables, which were adopted previously, were eliminated. It should be emphasized, however, that this simplification does not affect the substance of this section.

It requires a lot of space to discuss in detail the difference in the estimated returns (i.e., the coefficients) to various qualifications like education, sex, firm size, and others. The subject itself is also interesting, and thus we do not argue it here. The present section utilizes only the estimated returns, and examines the correlation between the pure industrial rents and the estimated returns.

Table 3.7 shows the correlation coefficients between the pure industrial advantages and the estimated returns to various qualifications. Several important observations derived from the correlation coefficients are described. Since the main concern is the relationship between industrial wage differentials and differences in returns to labour qualifi-

Table 3.7a Correlation coefficients between pure industrial advantages and estimated returns to various labour and firm qualifications

Return to blue-collar	0.493**
Return to male	−0.518**
Return to Senior High School	0.480**
Return to University, College	0.537**
Return to medium-scale firm	0.327
Return to large-scale firm	−0.052**
Return to tenure	
(1)0 years	0.661**
(1)5 years	0.679**
(1)10 years	0.670**
(1)15 years	0.583**
(1)20 years	0.385**
Return to outside experience	
(1)0 years	0.780**
(1)5 years	0.780**
(1)10 years	0.778**
(1)15 years	0.765**
(1)20 years	0.707**

Note:
** : 5% significant.

Table 3.7b Correlation coefficients between pure industrial advantages and estimated returns to various labour and firm qualifications

Return to blue-collar	0.493**
Return to male	−0.518**
Return to Senior High School	0.480**
Return to University, College	0.537**
Return to medium-scale firm	0.327
Return to large-scale firm	−0.052**
Return to tenure	
(1)0 years	0.661**
(1)5 years	0.679**
(1)10 years	0.670**
(1)15 years	0.583**
(1)20 years	0.385**
Return to outside experience	
(1)0 years	0.780**
(1)5 years	0.780**
(1)10 years	0.778**
(1)15 years	0.765**
(1)20 years	0.707**

Note:
** : 5% significant.

cations by industries, we concentrate on the contribution of each quality variable to the degree of wage differentials by industries.

First, the wage differentials between white-collar workers and blue-collar workers become narrower as pure industrial advantage increases. This is confirmed by the effect of a blue-collar worker dummy, indicating that occupational advantage is smaller in highly paid than low paid industries because the correlation is positive significantly.

Second, a similar story is present also for the effect of a male sex dummy. Females are treated more favourably in highly paid than low paid industries because the correlation is negative significantly. These two observations suggest that handicapped workers such as blue-collars and females should not work in low paid industries because they are treated less favourably in these industries.

Third, the different outcome appears with respect to educational attainment. The statistically significant positive correlation coefficients with both a high school graduates dummy and a university graduates dummy suggest that the return to education is more favourably assessed in highly paid than low paid industries. In other words, privileged workers in educational attainment should not work in low paid industries.

Fourth, the effect of firm size dummies is very minor because the correlation coefficient is either near zero or statistically insignificant. It is, thus, possible to conclude that the contribution of firm size to wage differentials by industry does not have any significant effect, unlike the case of occupation, sex, and education.

Fifth, the effect of job duration (i.e., job tenure) and outside experience (i.e., labour market experience prior to the current employer) is examined. The correlation coefficients between wage differentials by industry and job tenure are positive with statistical significance, and they show a minor convex nature. Thus, job tenures are evaluated more highly in highly paid than in low paid industries. However, this advantage declines as job tenure becomes longer and longer. The correlation coefficients between wage differentials by industry and outside experience are also positive, and their values are slightly higher than those for job tenure. Outside experiences in the labour market are evaluated more favourably in highly paid than in low paid industries. More importantly, the correlation coefficients do not decline as outside experiences become longer. This indicates that changing employer within highly paid industries does not affect the advantage of longer job tenure in the current employer, but keeps the advantage of outside experience. This is somewhat inconsistent with our examination of the labour market in Japan because it was believed that returns to tenure would not decline, and that returns to outside experience would not be so large. It is necessary to investigate further the relative contribution of job tenure and outside experience in relation to wage differentials by industry because the statistical tool for investigating the effect of job tenure and outside experience adopted in this chapter is not so rigorous.

3.6 WAGE DIFFERENTIALS BY SIZE OF FIRM

Wage differentials by size of firm, as we saw in the introduction, has been a popular subject in the literature at least in Japan. A so-called 'dual structure' represents the nature of the subject as emphasized by Ishikawa (1989), Odaka (1984), and others. The purpose of this section is not to examine it comprehensively, but to present only the 'pure' effect of the size of firm to wage differentials in benefiting from the fruitful data source. The method of the estimation is essentially the same as the one adopted for inter industry wage differentials. 'What kind of controls are used' is not explained seriously here to save space, but the adopted control variables are similar to the case for the inter industry wage differentials.

Table 3.8 shows the pure advantage and disadvantage by firm size. The size of firm is measured by the number of employees in a firm. Figures in Table 3.8 give advantage before and after controls. We can observe several interesting results from Table 3.8. First, both before-controls and after-controls show that there are substantial differentials between extremely large firms and extremely small firms. In other words, the degree of the advantage of working in larger firms is over 20 percent in comparison with the overall average wages, and the disadvantage is again over 20 percent. These figures are startling because economists in Japan had not thought such wide wage differentials by the size of firm existed. One reason for such wide differentials is given by the fact that this study considered extremely large firms (i.e., 5000 employees and more) and extremely small firms (i.e., 10–29 employees) separately. The usual firm size classification in many studies is only three (i.e., (1) 1000 employees and more, (2) 100–999, and (3) 10–99 employees). Wage differentials by the size of firm is much more serious than those commonly believed when we include both extremely larger and small firms.

Second, the controls for various quality variables such as education, age, sex and many others do not show any significant effect, unlike

Table 3.8 Advantages and disadvantages in wage payment by firm size (%)

Number of employees	1978		1988	
	Before[b]	After[b]	Before	After
5000–	28.61	23.11	32.10	27.16
	sample	(7448)		(8647)
1000–4999	20.49	17.03	21.86	15.96
	sample	(7356)		(7091)
500–999	9.95	5.61	9.24	2.68
	sample	(3552)		(3667)
300–499	1.01	−3.31	−1.55	−5.60
	sample	(3235)		(3038)
100–299	−7.54[a]	−12.10	−11.93	−15.37
	sample	(8215)		(7271)
30–99	−15.71	−19.90	−20.29	−23.36
	sample	(10382)		(9330)
10–29	−21.24	−25.34	−25.34	−28.78
	sample	(8355)		(7329)

Notes:
[a] Minus signs signify disadvantages.
[b] 'Before' means before controls, and 'After' means after controls by a large number of quality variables.

the case of wage differentials by industry. We observe only four to six percent points decreases due to the controls. In other words, a pure size effect is very likely as long as the inter size wage differential is considered. Larger firms are able to offer substantially higher wages than smaller firms, and their higher wages are not explained by higher qualifications of employees in these firms (see Tachibanaki 1993 for detail.

Third, another interesting result with respect to the effect of the size of firm is the dispersion of wages. Table 3.9 presents the estimated Gini coefficients for four samples, namely, male high school graduates of blue-collars who are 35 and 45 years old, and male college graduates of white-collars who are 35 and 45 years old, for various size classes of employers. It is found that wage dispersions are considerably high for smaller firms, and they decline as the size of firm becomes larger. Wage dispersions of extremely large firms are again somewhat high, but still much lower than those in smaller firms. These results show several interesting economic interpretations of the inter size wage differentials and the employer-size effect on management. A much fuller analysis is available in Tachibanaki (1993).

Table 3.9   Gini coefficients of male wage distributions for various size classes of firms

	10–29	30–99	100–299	300–499	500–999	1000–4999	5000–	Total
35 years old								
High School and blue-collar	0.162	0.137	0.117	0.114	0.111	0.092	0.093	0.128
College and white-collar		0.156	0.131	0.117	0.107	0.102	0.096	0.097	0.118
45 years old								
High school and blue-collar	0.188	0.154	0.138	0.143	0.126	0.116	0.095	0.154
College and white-collar		0.178	0.154	0.126	0.109	0.102	0.105	0.087	0.130

3.7   CONCLUDING REMARKS

This chapter investigated wage differentials by industry in Japan by using individual wage data. First, we attempted to estimate wage functions which are explained by an extremely large number of independent variables, and derived pure industrial advantages after controlling for labour qualities and firm characteristics. Second, we investigated the causes for pure industrial advantages, and tried to find what kind of economic variables are responsible for inducing them. Again, a large number of economic variables which show the condition of an industry and the labour market condition have been considered in order to estimate pure industrial advantages. Third, we considered the case in which returns to various labour qualities are different by industries in view of the fact that the previous studies assumed no differences in returns to labour qualities across industries. We investigated what happened with removal of no difference in returns. Finally, wage differentials by size of firm was touched on.

This chapter obtained the following results. First, although there appeared a considerable difference in wage payments by industries before the control, controlling for labour qualities and firm characteristics reduced the degree of spurious wage differentials by industry substantially. The important variables for the control were job tenure, education, and firm size. Incidentally, this study found that Japan had a considerably different industrial structure in wage payments from the

US at least for the one-digit industry level. Two-digit level industries within manufacturing industries are very similar between Japan and the US, while two-digit level industries in whole industries are not similar.

Second, we found that the most important economic variables which induced pure industrial advantages were 'the ability to pay' variables and variables related to productivity. The ability to pay variables and productivity variables include many variables such as profit rate, concentration rate, capital–labour ratio, and others. The variable on regulation was also important. The variables related to labour mobility turned out to be less important.

Third, data in Japan did not support the theory of compensating wage differentials. In other words, inferior working conditions in an industry have not been compensated by higher wage payments. It is anticipated that Japan will face a labour shortage economy in coming years, and thus the theory of compensating wage differentials may in future work in Japan.

Fourth, a removal of the assumption of no difference in returns to various labour qualities across industries did not alter the substance of the empirical findings obtained in the former sections. In other words, the result in section 3.6 supported the empirical analyses in former sections. It is therefore feasible to conclude that the results in this chapter are fairly robust because the two different methods produced consistent findings with respect to the relationship between pure industrial advantages and economic variables.

Finally, it was found that the inter size wage differentials were much more serious than those commonly believed, but the controls for quality variables did not matter, unlike the case of the inter industry wage differentials.

The most serious deficiency in this chapter is probably the lack of a simultaneous consideration for the causes of pure industrial advantages. It is possible to anticipate that economic variables considered in this chapter are interrelated to each other. In other words, it is possible that several variables such as tenure, firm size, and even industry may be jointly determined variables. Future work is called for which constructs a simultaneous equation model in investigating the influence of various economic variables on pure industrial advantages and size effects. It is also noted that panel data provide us with perfect information to investigate these subjects. Japan does not have any panel data, but we hope that panel data will be available in future.

Another weak point in this chapter may be less frequent references to economic theories which justify wage differentials by industry. Probably the most popular theory is the efficiency wage hypothesis which supports the existence of wage differentials by industry. A useful survey was given by Akerlof and Yellen (1986), and Katz (1986). Since this theory is currently under severe scrutiny as for example by Carmichael (1990) and Lang and Kahn (1990), we did not refer to the efficiency wage theory explicitly. In other words, since unlike in the US we have not obtained an apparent empirical support of wage differentials by industry in this chapter, it is risky to commit ourselves to the efficiency wage theory, at least for Japan. However, the important effect of profit, capital–labour ratio, and value added variables on pure industrial advantages may support the corollary of the efficiency wage theory. Further serious studies are required for Japan in order to test whether the efficiency wage theory is supported. Finally, it is expected that a revival of studies of wage differentials by the size of firm will appear in view of the fact that they appear to be more serious than those commonly believed.

Appendix 1: Notation of Variables in Table 3.1

PRO	Production worker dummy
SX	Female worker dummy
PER	Permanent worker dummy
*PRF*1	Regional dummy (1), high wage districts
*PRF*1	Regional dummy (2), low wage districts
A	Age
T	Tenure
*FSZ*1	Firm size dummy (1), 5000–
*FSZ*2	Firm size dummy (2), 1000–4999
*FSZ*3	Firm size dummy (3), 500–999
*FSZ*4	Firm size dummy (4), 300–499
*FSZ*5	Firm size dummy (5), 100–299
*FSZ*6	Firm size dummy (6), 30–99
ESZ	Establishment size
*ED*1	Senior high school dummy
*ED*2	Junior college dummy
*ED*3	University dummy
HR	Regular working hours
EHR	Excess working hours
*D*1	Industry dummy (1) construction
*D*2	Industry dummy (2) manufacturing
*D*3	Industry dummy (3) electricity, gas, heat supply and water
*D*4	Industry dummy (4) transport and communication
*D*5	Industry dummy (5) wholesale and retail trade, eating and drinking places
*D*6	Industry dummy (6) financing and insurance
*D*7	Industry dummy (7) real estate
*D*8	Industry dummy (8) services

Appendix 2: Explanation of Variables and Data Sources in Table 3.6

A	Average age
T	Average tenure
ED	Ratio of university graduates
PRO	Ratio of blue-collar employees
SZ	Ratio of employees whose number is over 1000
SX	Ratio of male employees
	Wage Structure Survey, Ministry of Labour
UNION	Union density
	Survey on Trade Unions, Ministry of Labour
CWELF	Non-legal fringe benefit per employee
REST	Ratio of employees who have only one non-working day per week
	Wage and Working Hours Survey, Ministry of Labour
INJURY	Density of Labour Injury
	Survey on Labour Injury, Ministry of Labour
RED	Separation rates initiated by employers
QUIT	Separation rates caused by personal reasons
HIRING	Entry rates
EMP	Hiring minus separation
	Employment Trend Survey, Ministry of Labour
VACANCY	Vacancy over number of workers
	Job Vacancy Survey, Ministry of Labour
EXPORT	Ratio of export over domestic output
	Input–output Table, Ministry Secretariat
CAPRET	Rate of return to stock
	Research Institute of Stocks Economy
CAPITAL	capital–labour ratio
	Industry Survey, Ministry of International Trade and Industry
HI	Hirfindahl index
	Fair Trade Commission
RD	R & D ratio over sales value
	R & D Survey, Ministry Secretariat
VALUE	Labour productivity (i.e., *per capita* value added)
	Industry Survey, Ministry of International Trade and Industry
PROFIT	Profit over employees
	Survey on Corporated Firms, Ministry of Finance
REGUL	Regulation dummy
	Regulated industries are electricity and gas, telecommunication, banking and insurance, and medical industries

Note

*The authors are very grateful to B. Holmlund, T. Ishikawa, J. Leonard, Y. Nakata, S. Nickell, M. Rebick, R. Topel and T. Toyoda for their useful comments. Any remaining deficiencies, however, are due to the authours alone.

References

Akerlof, G. and J. Yellen (1986) *Efficiency Wage Models of the Labor Market*, Cambridge, Cambridge University Press.

Brown, C. and J. Medoff (1989) 'The Employer Size-Wage Effect', *Journal of Political Economy*, vol. 97, no. 3, pp. 1027–59.

Carmichael, H.L. (1990) 'Efficiency Wage Models of Unemployment: One view', *Economic Inquiry*, vol. 28, no. 2, April, pp. 269–95.

Dickens, W.D. and L.F. Katz (1987) 'Inter-Industry Wage Differentials and Industry Characteristics', in K. Lang and J. Leonard (eds), *Unemployment and the Structure of Labor Markets*, Oxford, Basic Blackwell.

Freeman, R.F. and M.L. Weitzman (1987) 'Bonuses and Employment in Japan', *Journal of the Japanese and International Economies*, vol. 1, June, pp. 168–94.

Hashimoto, M. (1979) 'Bonus Payments, On-the-Job Training and Lifetime Employment in Japan', *Journal of Political Economy*, vol. 87, pp. 1086–1104.

Ishikawa, T. (1989) 'A Reconsideration of Dual Structure in Wages', in M. Tsuchiya and U. Miwa (eds), *Small-Size Enterprises in Japan*, Tokyo, University of Tokyo Press (in Japanese).

Katz, L.F. (1986) 'Efficiency Wage Theories: A partial evaluation', *NBER Macroeconomics Annual*, Cambridge, MA, MIT Press.

Katz, L.F. and L.H. Summers (1989) 'Industrial Rents: Evidence and Implications', *Brookings Papers on Economic Activity, Microeconomics*, pp. 209–90.

Kawashima, Y. and T. Tachibanaki (1986) 'The Effect of Discrimination and of Industry Segmentation on Japanese Wage Differentials in Relation to Education', *International Journal of Industrial Organization*, vol. 4, pp. 43–68.

Kruger, A. and L.H. Summers (1988) 'Efficiency Wages and Inter-Industry Wage Structure', *Econometrica*, vol. 56, no. 2, pp. 259–93.

Lang, K. and S. Kahn (1990) 'Efficiency Wage Models of Unemployment: A Second View', *Economic Inquiry*, vol. 27, no. 2, April, pp. 296–306.

Mincer, J. and Y. Higuchi (1988) 'Wage Structures and Labor Turnover in the United States and Japan', *Journal of the Japanese and International Economies*, vol. 2, June, pp. 97–133.

Mizuno, A. (1973) *Theory of Dynamics in Wage Structure*, Tokyo Shinhyoronsha (in Japanese).

Muramatsu, K. (1984) 'The Effect of Trade Unions on Productivity in Japanese Manufacturing Industries', in M. Aoki (ed.), *The Economic Analysis of the Japanese Firm*, Amsterdam, North-Holland.

Odaka, K. (1984)   *An Analysis of the Japanese Labor Market: Dual Structure*, Tokyo Iwanamishoten (in Japanese).

Ono, A. (1989)   *Employment Practive in Japan and Labour Market*, Tokyo Toyokeizaishimposha (in Japanese).

Sano, Y. (1969)   *An Econometric Analysis of Wage Determination*, Tokyo Toyokeizaishimposha (in Japanese).

Tachibanaki, T. (1975)   'Wage Determinations in Japanese Manufacturing Industries: Structural Change and Wage Differentials', *International Economic Review*, vol. 16, pp. 562–86.

————— (1982)   'Further Results on Japanese Wage Differentials: Nenko Wages, Hierarchical Position, Bonuses, and Working Hours', *International Economic Review*, vol. 23, no. 2, pp. 447–61.

Tachibanaki, T. and A. Taki (1990)   'Wage Determination in Japan: A Theoretical and Empirical Investigation', in H. Konig (ed.), *Economics of Wage Determination*, Berlin, Springer-Verlag.

————— (1992)   'Why are Wages in Finance and Insurance Industry in Japan so High?' in A. Horiuchi and N. Yoshino (eds), *Financial Analysis for Modern Japan*, Tokyo University of Tokyo Press (in Japanese).

————— (1993)   'The Employer Size Effect on Wage Differentials in Japan, Revived', Kyoto Institute of Economic Research, *Discussion Paper Series*, no. 377.

Tachibanaki, T. and T. Noda (1992)   'The Effect of Unions on Egalitarianism and Productivity in Japan', Kyoto Institute of Economic Research, *Discussion Paper Series*, no. 342.

Weitzman, M.L. (1986)   'Macroeconomic Implication of Profit Sharing', in S. Fischer (ed.), *NBER Macroeconomic Annual*, Cambridge, MA, MIT Press, pp. 291–335.

4 Wage Inequality and Regional Labour Market Performance in the US

USA
J31
R23

Robert H. Topel*

4.1 INTRODUCTION

In the US, fluctuations in relative wages and employment across regional markets are very large. For example, during the so-called 'Massachusetts miracle' of the 1980s, average wages of men in New England increased by 17 percent, while wages in the 'rustbelt' states of the Midwest fell by about 8 percent. At the same time, annual weeks worked increased by about 4 weeks per person in New England, but fell by about 2 weeks in the Midwest. Changes such as these are apparently demand driven in the sense that wage and employment fluctuations are positively correlated over time (Juhn, Murphy and Topel, 1991).

This chapter is an initial foray into data on regional labour market performance. My earlier work (Topel, 1986) studied the relationships among changing wage levels, demand, and migration between labour markets. Here, my main purpose is to model the determinants of changing wage *inequality* within geographic areas in the United States. It is well known that wage inequality and the returns to various measures of skill have increased since 1972.[1] It is less known that inequality has risen much more rapidly in some regions than in others. For example, changes in relative wages between the most and least skilled workers have been much larger in the West and Midwest than in the South and New England. My goal is to understand why.

The chapter begins by documenting differences in labour market performance across regions in the US. Based on this preliminary evidence, I follow with a model of (relative) wage determination within regional labour markets. The model stresses four main factors that can affect

93

wage inequality. First, changes in relative supplies of various skill groups can affect their relative wages. Second, for given supply patterns, changes in the composition of labour demand across industries can affect wages because some skill groups are disproportionately employed in certain sectors. Third, changing patterns of labour force participation by women will affect men's wages. The direction and magnitude of this effect depends on whether women and men are substitutes or complements in local production. Finally, industry specific patterns of technical change can shift the market demand for specific skill groups, raising or lowering their relative wages.

My evidence indicates that each of these factors has played a role in determining changing wage differentials in the US. Technical change favoured more skilled workers in production, thus raising their relative wages. This effect is neutral across regional labour markets, however. In contrast, shifts in net supply of different groups have a distinct geographic pattern that affects relative wages. The supply of less skilled workers declined in all areas, reflecting rising average levels of completed schooling for the American workforce. This shift in supply was largest in the Northeast and in the South, and smallest in the West. Conforming to this pattern, wages of less skilled workers declined by twice as much in the West as in the nation as a whole.

There is also evidence that increased labour force participation by women has reduced the wages of less skilled men. Specifically, the labour demand model indicates that women, who entered the labour force in unprecedented numbers over the past two decades, are better substitutes for less skilled men than for high skilled ones. In part, inequality may have risen because women have increased the 'supply' of less skilled workers. Indeed, across the nation as a whole, the estimates indicate that rising participation of women accounts for all of the decline in earning power of less skilled men. It is worth stressing that these conclusions about female participation are tentative; some caveats are discussed in the chapter.

The chapter is organized as follows. Section 4.2 describes the data, and provides preliminary evidence on the performance of regional labour markets in the US. Section 4.3 develops a labour demand model that guides the subsequent empirical work, which is reported in section 4.4. Section 4.5 concludes the chapter.

4.2   THE DATA AND EMPIRICAL SETTING: THE CPS DATA

The data for this chapter are drawn from the March Supplement of the *Current Population Surveys* (CPS) for the 23 years 1968 through 1990. The CPS is a monthly survey based on household interviews that contains demographic and economic information on members of roughly 50,000 randomly selected households in the US. These files contain the usual demographic information on individual respondents – age, education, and so on – as well as retrospective information on individuals' labour market activities during the previous calendar year, including annual earnings, weeks of employment and unemployment, and the industry and occupation of a person's main job.

Based on these data, Figures 4.1a–4.1i illustrate relative fluctuations in log wages (average hourly earnings) and employment rates (weeks worked/52) of men in the nine Census regions of the US since 1967. The base sample for these calculations is CPS men between the ages of 18 and 64. The plotted values are residuals from regressions that project wages or employment rates on region and year dummies. Thus the values shown in Figures 4.1a–4.1i measure changes in wages or employment in regional market m relative to the nation as a whole. In other words, aggregate fluctuations are removed from the data.

The data show extraordinarily large changes in wages and employment rates across regions. Especially for wages, these changes occur at 'medium frequency' in the sense that they are not simply trends or associated with brief local 'cycles'. For example, following a steady decline through 1980, average hourly wages in the Northeast rose by about 16 percentage points during the 1980s, *relative to the national average*. In contrast, wages in the Midwest fell by 8 percent between 1980 and 1985. In the far West (Pacific), average relative wages have fallen by 15 percent since 1967, with the most rapid decline in the early years.

Two additional points about Figure 4.1 are worthwhile. First, the magnitudes of changes in relative wages stand in sharp contrast to the relatively stable behaviour of aggregate wage growth during this period. This means that sluggish aggregate growth masks substantial flexibility of wages in regional markets. Second, as documented in Juhn, Murphy and Topel (1991), the within-region wage and employment changes are positively correlated. This point is fairly obvious from inspection of Figure 4.1, and it suggests that wage changes within regions are mainly demand driven.

As documented in several recent studies, wage inequality among

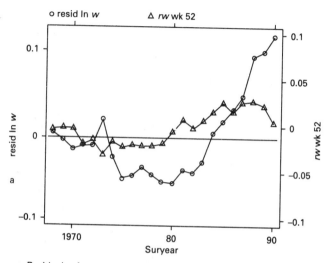

a Residuals of wage and employment, region I

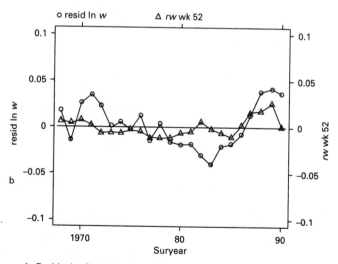

b Residuals of wage and employment, region II

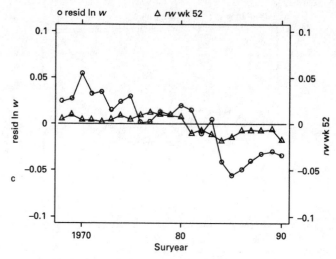

c Residuals of wage and employment, region III

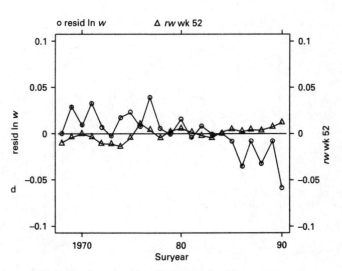

d Residuals of wage and employment, region IV

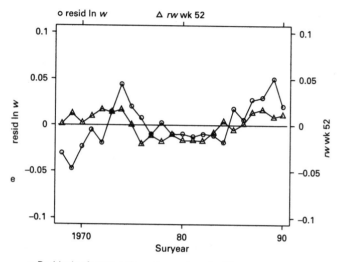

e Residuals of wage and employment, region V

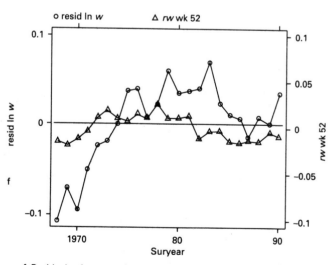

f Residuals of wage and employment, region VI

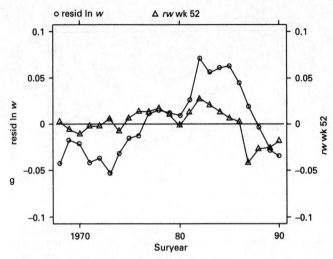

g Residuals of wage and employment, region VII

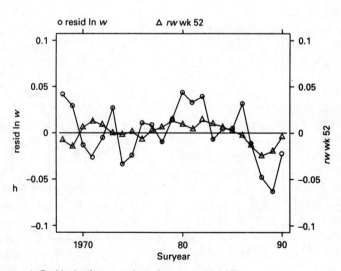

h Residuals of wage and employment, region VIII

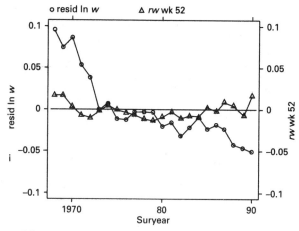

i Residuals of wage and employment, region IX

Key:
Region I	Northeast	Region IV	West North Central	Region VII	Southwest
Region II	Middle Atlantic	Region V	South Atlantic	Region VIII	Mountain
Region III	East North Central	Region VI	South Central	Region IX	Pacific

Figure 4.1   Wage and employment rates in regions of the US, 1968–90

American men has increased at a fairly steady rate since the early 1970s.[2] Figures 4.2a–4.2i illustrate changes in wage inequality within regions. In constructing these figures, I divided the distribution of male wages in each region and year into three 'skill' intervals, corresponding to the bottom, middle and top thirds of the wage distribution. The median wage for each of these categories is at the 16th, 50th, and 84th percentiles. The figures show the 84–50 wage differential and the 50–16 wage differential, indexed to 1972.

The main message of Figure 4.2 is that the wage inequality increased in all regions of the US, but that the timing and magnitude of rising inequality is not the same across regions. For example in region IX (the West) (Figure 4.2i) the wage differential between the top and bottom thirds of the wage distribution increased by 31 log points between 1972 and 1990. The corresponding increase in region I (New England) (Figure 4.2a) was only 22 points, and in region VI (South Central) (Figure 4.2f) wage inequality increased by less than 10 log points.

Table 4.1 reports results from regressions of various measures of within-region wage differentials on the overall regional wage differential, as measured in Figure 4.1. The results show that wage changes are larger among less skilled persons. On average a 10 percent increase in the relative regional wage is associated with a 13 percent

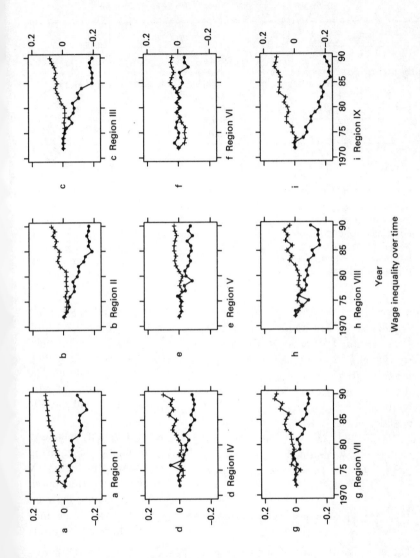

Figure 4.2 Male wage inequality by region, 1972–90

Note: The upper curve in each figure is the log wage differential between the 84th and 50th percentiles of the wage distribution. The lower curve is the differential between the 16th and the 50th percentiles. Both are indexed to 1972. See Figure 4.1 for region names.

Table 4.1   Regression coefficients relating within-region skill differentials to regional wage residuals, CPS men, 1967–89

	A Wage differential regressions					
	Percentile spread		*Age spread*		*College–High School (HS) spread*	
	90–10	80–20	HS	College	$X \leq 10$	$10 < x \leq 30$
Coefficient:	≤1.66	≤1.26	≤0.281	0.126	−0.281	0.164
t: ß = 0	(8.10)	(10.06)	(2.71)	(0.97)	(2.09)	(1.25)

	B Wage quintile regressions				
	1–20	21–40	41–60	61–80	81–100
Coefficient:	1.89	1.11	0.71	0.61	0.62
t: ß = 1	(9.47)	2.82	(4.75)	(10.83)	(8.44)

Note: Estimates in Panel *A* are OLS coefficients from a regression of the indicated within-region wage spread on the regional relative wage residual. Estimates in Panel *B* regress the wage residual for each quintile on the regional wage differential shown in Figure 4.1. The 'age spread' in panel *A* is the difference in log wages between peak earners ($x = 21-25$) and new entrants ($x = 1-5$).

narrowing of the wage gap between the first and fifth quintiles of the regional wage distribution ($\beta = -1.26$). Thus a strong local labour market – as measured by changes in average wages – reduces wage inequality. Panel B of Table 4.1 shows that most of this effect is due to extreme wage flexibility among the least skilled workers. For workers in the first quintile wages are nearly twice as flexible as the average, while high wage workers (percentiles 81–100) are more insulated from changes in local market conditions.

The reminder of the chapter tries to isolate the determinants of wage change within regional labour markets. I begin by developing a basic labour demand framework that can be applied to CPS data.

4.3   A LABOUR DEMAND FRAMEWORK

The data outlined above are suggestive of important yet poorly understood differences in local labour market performance in the US. This section develops a regional labour demand that can be implemented using microdata, and that can provide direct evidence on the determinants of local labour market performance. As in LaLonde and Topel (1989) and Katz and Murphy (1992), the end result is an inverse labour demand system in which measurable quantities affect relative wages.

The basic idea is that local labour demand is driven by patterns of regional specialization, which map aggregate product demand and technology shocks into local market effects, and by changes in relative supplies of factors of production. For example, the heavy concentration of manufacturing employment in the Midwest makes that region particularly sensitive to changes in the aggregate demand for manufactured goods. In addition, truly local shocks to labour supply or demand can also play an important role. For example, a trade pact with Canada may have disproportionate effects in areas along the US–Canadian border, while large immigration flows from Asia and Mexico may substantially increase labour supply in California.

Assume that the underlying production function in sector (industry) *j* and local market *m* is homothetic in its labour inputs (capital is ignored in what follows).[3] These inputs represent different skill categories of the labour force, which are assumed to be imperfect substitutes in local production. For example, inputs could represent demographic categories – such as schooling, experience or sex – or workers from various intervals of the skill distribution.

In the following section I will aggregate labour inputs into five categories: high, middle, and low skilled men; and high and low skilled women. I will also define industries ranging from 'low skill intensive' to 'high skill intensive' based on the average shares of these labour inputs in total employment. Leaving precise definitions of these aggregates for later, let output in industry *j* of regional market *m* be

$$Y^{jm} = \theta^j F(X_1^{jm}\tau_1^j, X_2^{jm}\tau_2^j, \ldots), \tag{1}$$

where X_i^{jm} is employment of the *i*th skill group in sector *j*, and τ_i^j indexes biased technical change that increases the 'effective' quantity of input supplied by X_i. Parameter θ^j indexes total factor productivity – factor neutral technical change in industry *j*. Notice that technical change parameters do not carry an *m* superscript; I allow technical change to be sector and factor specific, but within industries it occurs at the same pace in all regional markets. In other words, technical change has no regional component. As shown below, this assumption allows one to identify the impact of technical change from differences in regional specialization.

Given (1) and the assumption of homotheticity, the cost function in any industry is of the form $C(w, Y, \theta, \tau) = A(w/\tau)f(Y/\theta)$, which is separable in prices and the effects of scale. Applying the Envelope

Theorem (Sheppard's Lemma) and a bit of algebra, the changes in log factor demands satisfy

$$\dot{x}_i^{jm} = (E_i^j - \beta^j k^{jm})\dot{w}^m + \beta^j(\dot{p}^{jm} + \dot{\theta}^j) + \dot{\phi}_i^{jm} + \epsilon_i^{jm}, \qquad (2)$$

where E_i^j is the row vector of own and cross-price compensated demand elasticities for factor i with respect to wages, β^j is the factor-neutral elasticity of input demand with respect to changes in the price of output, p^{jm}, and k^{jm} is the vector of cost shares for each input i, satisfying $\Sigma_j k_i^{jm} = 1$. Thus the first term on the right of (2) includes both the substitution (E_i^j) and scale ($\beta^j k^{jm}$) effects of changing factor prices. The term ϕ_i^j represents biased technical change that shifts the relative demand for factor i independently of prices and total factor productivity, while the residuals ϵ_i^{jm} reflect unexplained disturbances to the demand for factor i in sector j and regional market m.

The demand system (2) is a general foundation for evaluating two important aspects of regional wage determination. First, by controlling for market-specific changes in the scale of industries, j, (2) leads to a model of *relative* wage changes for different skill groups *within* regional markets. Second, with rising supply price (finite β^j) and some additional assumptions about tradeability of goods across markets, system (2) generates a model of the determinants of changes in relative wages *across* different regional markets. The remainder of this chapter focuses on the first issue, leaving the second for subsequent research.

4.3.1 Skill Differentials within Markets

Why have skill differentials widened in the US, and why does this trend toward increased inequality vary among regions? The demand system (2) allows us to address these questions using measurable prices and quantities within regional markets.

In the system (2), the term $\beta^j(\dot{p}^{jm} + \dot{\theta}^j)$ is a fixed scale effect for each factor employed in industry j and market m. To remove these effects, let the cost share of input i be k_i^{jm} and apply the homogeneity condition that a cost-share weighted average of compensated demand elasticities must equal zero: $\Sigma_\ell k_\ell^{jm} E_{\ell i}^j = 0$. Summing over demand equations (2), this condition determines the industry scale factor $\dot{z}^{jm}$, which is a share weighted average of (log) input changes in industry j:

$$\dot{z}^{jm} = \sum k_\ell^{jm} \dot{x}_\ell^{jm}$$

$$= \beta^j k^{jm} \dot{w}^m + \beta^j (\dot{p}^{jm} + \dot{\theta}^j) + \epsilon^{jm'} \tag{3}$$

where ϵ^{jm} is a share-weighted average of the disturbances ϵ_i^{jm} to individual inputs. Notice that if factor ratios are fixed through time, then $\dot{z}$ simply measures the rate of change of industry employment.

Equation (3) subsumes the scale effects of changes in the price of output, total factor productivity, and input prices. It says that a unit increase in the price of industry j's output ($\dot{p}^{jm} = 1$) will increase input demand by β^j percent, while a unit increase in the price of input i ($\dot{w}_i^m = 1$) will reduce all input demands by β^j times the share of factor i in unit cost, k_i^{jm}. Substitution effects can be isolated by subtracting (3) from (2):

$$\dot{x}_i^{jm} - \dot{z}^{jm} = E_i^j \dot{w}^m + \dot{\phi}_i^{jm} - (\epsilon_i^{jm} - \epsilon^{jm}). \tag{4}$$

The left side of (4) measures the change in utilization of factor i relative to the change in average factor utilization, $\dot{z}^{jm}$. This change in the factor ratio depends on (1) changes in input prices, $\dot{w}^m$; (2) biased technical change that is common to all regions, ϕ_i^j; and (3) unmeasured relative demand changes that are unique to industry j and market m, $\epsilon_i^{jm} - \epsilon^{jm}$.

Equation (4) can be applied to data on wages and employment of different skill groups in different locales and industries. My main interest in this chapter is in isolating the determinants of changing relative wages of men, yet this narrowed focus does not mean that women can be excluded from the analysis. Indeed, it is plausible that one of the main factors affecting men's wages has been the sharp increase in women's labour force participation during the last two decades. As a practical matter, however, women's wages in separate markets are measured with substantial sampling error, in part because women's labour force participation is lower than for men. I therefore concentrate on the effects of changing female quantities, rather than changing prices. Specifically, I assume that skill groups for women form separate input aggregates that may substitute for men. Then rewrite (4) as a system of *conditional* demand equations in which factor ratios for women – $\dot{x}_f^{jm} - \dot{z}^{jm}$ – are treated as fixed:[4]

$$\dot{x}_i^{jm} - \dot{z}^{jm} = E_i^j \dot{w}^m + F_i^j (\dot{x}_f^{jm} - \dot{z}^{jm}) + \phi_i^j + u_i^j. \tag{5}$$

In (5), the term F_i^j is negative if women are net substitutes for men.

The parameters E_i^j must be interpreted as *conditional* demand elasticities, which hold some inputs fixed. By Le Chatlier's Principle, own price effects in (5) will be smaller than in the unconditional demand system (4).

4.3.2 Market Equilibrium

The following section estimates versions of (5) for 10 industry aggregates and 9 regional labour markets. Given these estimates, we can solve for market equilibrium changes in relative wages by aggregating over industries j. Market clearing for each input type requires that the sum of industry-specific demands equal the total market supply of the input. In log rates of changes this condition is

$$\dot{x}_i^m = \sum_j S_i^{jm} \dot{x}_i^{jm}, \tag{6}$$

where S_i^{jm} is the share of factor i employment accounted for by industry j. Now substitute the demand system (5) into the market clearing conditions (6) and solve for the vector of wage changes in market m:

$$\dot{w}^m = [E^m]^{-1} \left\{ \dot{x}_i^m - \sum_j S_i^{jm} \dot{z}^{jm} - \sum_j S_i^{jm} F_i^j (\dot{x}_f^{jm} - \dot{z}^{jm}) \right.$$
$$\left. - \sum_j S_i^{jm} \dot{\phi}_i^j - u_i \right\}, \tag{7}$$

where $E_i^m = \sum_j s_i^{jm} E_i^j$. Then $[E^m]^{-1}$ is the matrix of market-wide elasticities of complementarity (Hicks, 1932), which here relate changes in market wages to changes in observed quantities and to technical change. According to (7), within-market changes in relative wages depend on four main factors. The magnitude of each of these factors is affected by patterns of regional specialization through differences in employment shares, S_i^{jm}.

First, the term $\dot{x}_i^m - \dot{z}^m$ is the change in relative net supply (supply minus demand) of factor i in market m. Since z^m is an employment share weighted average of industry growth rates, it indexes changes in demand for factor i. If supply grows more rapidly than demand, the model indicates that wages of type i workers will fall.

The second term is a share weighted average of the effects of women's employment in each industry. If women are net substitutes for men ($F_i^j < 0$), increased employment of women will reduce men's wages. The magnitude of this effect depends on the degree of substitutability,

F_i^j, and on the change in women's factor shares over time. In effect, F_i^j transforms changes in the utilization of women $(\dot{x}_f^{jm} - \dot{z}^{jm})$ into equivalent units of type i men. So if $F_i^j < 0$, increased participation by women is equivalent to an increase in men's labour supply.

The third term reflects the impact of biased technical change. I have assumed that technical progress occurs at different rates across industries, but within an industry it occurs at the same rate across regional markets. If type i workers in region m are disproportionately concentrated in industries that have experienced i-saving technical change, this term indicates that type i relative wages will decline more rapidly in market m than elsewhere.

The last term is an aggregate of unexplained, market-specific relative demand shocks for type i workers. If these shocks play a major role in affecting relative wages, then this is evidence that truly 'local' market conditions are important.

4.3.3 Econometric Strategy

The main component of my econometric strategy is equation (7) and the elasticities of complementarity, $[E^m]^{-1}$. These can be estimated given estimates of the bracketed quantities in (7). While the first two bracketed terms can be computed directly from CPS data, terms involving women's quantities require estimates of substitution parameters F_i^j for each industry. The model also requires estimates of $\dot{\phi}_i^j$, the rate of biased technical change affecting input i in each industry, j.

Estimates of F_i^j and $\dot{\phi}_i^j$ can be derived by estimating model (5) for each industry. Given employment data by industry, region, and year, the assumption that $\dot{\phi}_i^j$ is independent of region means that $\dot{\phi}_i^j$ can be estimated from the coefficients on a vector of year dummies, D_{it}^j, that are common to input i in industry j, but that are independent of region. Intuitively, this means that technical change is identified from 'average' changes in factor ratios across regions.

Given 'first-stage' estimates of F_i^j and $\dot{\phi}_i^j$ derived from estimating industry-level models of labour demand, the second step is to estimate (7) with these estimates inserted in place of their theoretical values. So long as F_i^j and $\dot{\phi}_i^j$ are consistently estimated in the first stage, model (7) will produce consistent estimates of the elasticities of complementarity $[E^m]^{-1}$. To proceed, however, I require definitions of inputs and industry aggregates to which the model can be applied.

4.4 ESTIMATION

4.4.1 Defining Input and Industry Aggregates

The model outlined in section 4.3 can be implemented in microdata for any given definition of inputs and industries. Some 'art' is required in choosing these. My choices are guided by observed patterns of change in relative wages across markets, and prior knowledge of changes in the observable skills of American workers.

For inputs, I define five separate skill groups. High, medium and low skilled men are defined by dividing the regional wage distribution in each year into three equal parts. Then the 'wage' for each skill group is defined by the median wage in each group. Thus if group '1' indexes low skilled workers in market m, w_{1t}^m refers to the log average hourly wage of workers at the 16th percentile of the region m wage distribution in year t. By this definition, the changes in relative skill prices that are to be explained are the ones that were graphed in section 4.2. I use a similar definition of input prices for women, except there are only two skill groups: high skilled women (H) who are above the 50th percentile of the female wage distribution, and low skilled women (L) who are below it.

Given these definitions of prices, a natural choice of measured quantities might be the number of individuals in each year who fall in the indicated third (for men) of the wage distribution. An unattractive implication of this definition is that the relative supply of each skill group is fixed over time. By definition, one third of the workforce must always fall in the first third to the wage distribution. Given the rapid increase in education levels for the American workforce over this period, this would imply that increased education has had no effect on the supply of human capital. I therefore adopt an alternative strategy that allows the relative quantities of different skill groups to vary over time as education levels and other observed characteristics have changed.

The basic approach (details are available from the author) is that time-series changes in the distribution of observable characteristics in the population will change the supply of each skill type. For example, rising schooling levels should reduce the supply of less skilled workers. To account for this, I pooled the CPS over the period 1972–90 and calculated conditional wage distributions $f(P|C)$ where P denotes percentiles of the wage distribution and C is a vector of personal characteristics.[5] Then, for each region and year I predicted the share of the total workforce at each percentile P from the overall distribution $f(P|C)$

and the relative quantity of persons in market m with characteristics C, say $N_t^m (C)$. The result is a predicted relative supply of individuals, $f^m(P|t)$ at each percentile for each year t and each region, m. Secular changes in observables that are associated with higher wages – rising education levels in the labour force, for example – will shift the density $f^m(P|t)$ to the right, raising the average quality of the workforce. In terms of the model, this means declining relative supply of less skilled workers, and rising relative supply of more skilled ones. Evidence on these supply changes is presented below.

Given this definition of inputs, it remains to choose the industry aggregates where they are employed. Standard industrial classifications group detailed industries based on gross similarities of *outputs*, such as durable goods or services. Since I am interested in changes in the relative demands for skills, I chose to group detailed industries on the basis of similar labour *inputs*. I grouped 3-digit industries into 10 aggregates, ranging from low skill intensive to high skill intensive, by the following procedure.

First, for all 3-digit industries I calculated the employment shares of low, medium, and high skill workers. I then ranked industries by their skill intensities. Then industry 1 (the least skill intensive) is the set of 3-digit industries with the highest shares of low skilled workers that account for 10 percent of total employment over all regions and all years. Industry 10 (the most skill intensive) is the set of industries with the highest shares of type 3 workers who account for 10 percent of aggregate employment. Again, details of this procedure are available on request.

Given these definitions, (7) implies that there are two main reasons for differences in the evolution of wages among regional labour markets. First, holding industry composition fixed, quantities may change at different rates in different locales. For example, the labour supply of a particular skill group may change at a different rate in some regions than in others, or the demand for particular goods may increase more rapidly in some regions. Second, for given changes in quantities, varying patterns of regional specialization will generate changes in relative wages. For example, if, in some region m, employment of factor i is heavily concentrated in industries that have experienced i-saving technical change, then the wage of type i workers will fall more rapidly in m than in other regions. The remainder of this section tries to isolate the relative contributions of these factors to the evolution of wages.

4.4.2 Estimated Industry Demands for Skills

Estimates of equations (6) for the 10 industry groups defined above are shown in Tables 4.2 and 4.3. Each demand equation includes region specific relative wages for low ($w_1 - w_2$) and high ($w_3 - w_2$) skilled workers; elasticities for factor 2 ('middle' skilled workers) are implied by the homogeneity condition that the sum of own and cross-price demand elasticities for any factor is zero. Each equation also includes the estimated factor ratios for low (L) and high (H) skilled women, nine fixed region effects, and 19 unrestricted year effects. As I noted earlier, the year effects estimate the impact of (common across regions) technical change on factor ratios.

Table 4.2 reports estimated substitution effects for low skilled men. The own price effects of a change in the relative wage of less skilled men are generally negative (9 of 10 cases), and low and high skilled men are usually net substitutes. The estimates also imply that changes in the employment of low skilled women have only minor effects on the employment of low skilled men, but that high skilled women are strong substitutes for low skilled men in almost all industries. This may seem surprising, but keep in mind that the median wage for women is at about the 25th percentile of the male wage distribution. Thus entry of 'high skilled' women – with predicted wages above the female median – will mainly occur *below* the median of the male wage distribution, where strong substitution is plausible.

Even so, some of the estimated substitution effects in table 4.2 are implausibly large. For example, the estimate of -1.62 for substitution between high skilled women and low skilled men is outside the bounds indicated by theory. In theory, the parameter F_i^j is the ratio of the cross-price elasticity of demand between women and men to the own price elasticity of demand for women. This ratio should be smaller than 1.0 in absolute value, but the estimate is significantly outside of this range. There are two reasons why this may be so.

The first is measurement error. Since a cost share weighted sum of the $x_i - z$ must equal 1.0, an increase in the measured quantity of one input must lead to reduced values of $x_i - z$ for other inputs. It isn't clear why this problem should be more important for the relationship between high skilled women and less skilled men, however. In principle, one could solve the problem through choice of appropriate instrumental variables, but none are immediately apparent. The second reason, which is probably more important, is choice of industry aggregates. The skill-based definitions I have adopted may aggregate rapidly growing female inten-

Table 4.2 Estimated substitution effects for low skilled men, by industry, 1971–89

| Industry | Relative wages | | Female quantities | | R^2 |
	Low skill	High skill	Low skill	High skill	
1	−0.503	−0.004	−0.029	−1.145	0.953
	(0.143)	(0.208)	(0.096)	(0.095)	
2	−0.390	0.318	−0.090	−0.500	0.890
	(0.114)	(0.185)	(0.071)	(0.079)	
3	−0.049	0.322	−0.031	−0.018	0.913
	(0.118)	(0.184)	(0.077)	(0.079)	
4	−0.231	0.692	−0.091	−0.300	0.948
	(0.102)	(0.165)	(0.051)	(0.053)	
5	−0.185	0.346	−0.009	−0.074	0.923
	(0.100)	(0.178)	(0.027)	(0.028)	
6	−0.222	0.149	−0.040	−0.250	0.944
	(0.108)	(0.178)	(0.045)	(0.047)	
7	−0.513	−0.239	−0.092	−1.62	0.985
	(0.138)	(0.208)	(0.093)	(0.094)	
8	−0.047	0.083	−0.066	−0.343	0.944
	(0.111)	(0.179)	(0.064)	(0.069)	
9	0.109	0.498	0.042	−0.613	0.963
	(0.111)	(0.179)	(0.067)	(0.071)	
10	−0.299	0.294	0.034	−0.600	0.955
	(0.134)	(0.216)	(0.092)	(0.083)	

Note: Standard errors are in parentheses. Each model includes 9 region effects and 19 year effects, meant to measure region-neutral effects of technical change. See text for details.

Table 4.3 Estimated substitution effects for high skilled men, by industry, 1971–89

| Industry | Relative wages | | Female quantities | | R^2 |
	Low skill	High skill	Low skill	High skill	
1	0.395	−0.065	−1.00	−0.133	0.944
	(0.012)	(0.170)	(0.079)	(0.078)	
2	0.280	−0.212	−0.377	−0.311	0.965
	(0.091)	(0.146)	(0.056)	(0.062)	
3	−0.049	−0.143	−0.499	−0.330	0.936
	(0.085)	(0.133)	(0.056)	(0.057)	
4	−0.134	−0.275	−0.209	−0.228	0.837
	(0.088)	(0.143)	(0.045)	(0.046)	
5	−0.142	−0.163	−0.035	−0.026	0.909
	(0.089)	(0.145)	(0.022)	(0.023)	

Table continued on page 112

Table 4.3   continued

Industry	Relative wages		Female quantities		R^2
	Low skill	High skill	Low skill	High skill	
6	0.143	−0.000	−0.154	0.191	0.826
	(0.093)	(0.153)	(0.038)	(0.041)	
7	−0.260	0.040	−0.802	−0.568	0.979
	(0.100)	(0.152)	(0.068)	(0.068)	
8	−0.084	0.020	−0.196	−0.349	0.807
	(0.083)	(0.133)	(0.017)	(0.052)	
9	−0.090	−0.252	−0.189	−0.340	0.922
	(0.069)	(0.111)	(0.042)	(0.044)	
10	0.199	0.003	−0.286	−0.332	0.902
	(0.023)	(0.118)	(0.050)	(0.045)	

Note: See notes to Table 4.2.

sive industries with rapidly contracting industries that employ low skilled men. When combined into one 'industry' this change in relative demands between industries 'looks like' within-industry substitution of women for men. At this stage of my research, I can offer no evidence on the importance of this bias. I leave this issue for future work.

Conformable demand estimates for high skilled men (those in the upper third of the wage distribution) are shown in Table 4.3. In general, own price elasticities are smaller than in Table 4.2, and three of 10 point estimates have the wrong sign. This suggests that skilled men are more inelastically demanded. Unlike the estimates for low skilled men, *both* low and high skilled women are strong substitutes for high skilled men. This may seem implausible given the fact that the female wage distribution is shifted far to the left of the male distribution. We will find that the strong substitution effects for low skilled women are not of much consequence, however: virtually all of the increase in labour force participation of women has come at the high end of their wage distribution, among high skilled women. This means that large point estimates of substitution effects for low skilled women translate into very small effects on the employment of skilled men.

Market-wide demand elasticities for each skill group are employment share weighted averages of industry elasticities. The 2 × 2 matrix of estimated market-wide effects, E^m, is reported in Table 4.4, using weights for the West (these are typical). The diagonal terms of the market substitution matrix are negative, which is the most basic requirement of theory. Using point estimates the matrix is negative definite

Table 4.4   Estimated market-wide compensated demand elasticities for low
(1) and high (3) skilled men

	Low (1)	High (3)
Low (1)	−0.235	0.267
	(0.039)	(0.061)
High (3)	0.061	−0.105
	(0.028)	(0.043)

Note: Estimates are employment share weighted averages of own and cross-
price demand elasticities in Tables 4.2 and 4.3. Employment shares for the
West are used, but other regions produce trivially different effects. Standard
errors in parentheses.

but not symmetric, though symmetry cannot be rejected at standard
confidence levels.

4.4.3   Estimated Determinants of Relative Wages

The demand systems in Tables 4.2 and 4.3 can be used to estimate all
of the quantities on the right side of (7). Taken literally, (8) holds as
an identity, so one approach to estimating the determinants of relative
wages is simply to invert the estimated substitution matrices for each
region, one of which was illustrated in Table 4.4. These inverses provide estimates of the elasticities of complementarity that map changing quantities into changing wages in (8).

This approach proved too restrictive. As in many cases (see
Hamermesh, 1993, for example) the direct estimates of demand elasticities
shown in Tables 4.2 and 4.3 are fairly small. So if measured factor
ratios and measured wages are weakly related at the industry level, the
implied inverse demand elasticities in (7) are implausibly large.

A less restrictive approach is to use (7) as a guide for specifying a
model of wage determination in regional markets, and then to estimate
elasticities of complementarity directly. Statistically, this approach is
more consistent with the fact that I am interested in estimating $[E^m]^{-1}$,
not E^m, in the second-stage model. The first-stage models are nevertheless essential because they provide estimates of the first three quantities
in brackets of (7) – relative net supply, women's factor shares weighted
by their substitution effects, and technical change. I treat these estimated quantities as separate regressors in an unrestricted form of (7).

Before turning to the estimates, it is useful to illustrate regional patterns
of the impact of technical change on labour demands. As noted above,

my estimate of the impact of technical change is the common-across-regions component of factor ratios, after controlling for wages and female employment, in each industry. Figures 4.3 and 4.4 shows the time series of the weighted sum

$$\hat{\phi}_i^m = \sum_j S_i^{jm} \hat{\phi}_i^j, \qquad (8)$$

which enters the model of wage determination, (7), for each region, as for low- and high-skilled workers.

These estimates indicate that technical change – as I measure it from changing factor ratios – has been biased against low skilled men. Further, these effects are virtually identical across regions. This absence of regional variation means that the impact of technical change has been geographically neutral, so technical change cannot explain regional differences in the evolution of wages that were illustrated in section 4.2.[6] The only remaining candidates that can explain varying regional patterns of wage growth are differences in net supply across regions, or patterns of women's labour force participation.

Estimated determinants of relative wages are shown in Table 4.5.[7] Each measured regressor is entered with the sign it carries on the right side of (8), so theory indicates that each one should reduce relative wages. This simple prediction is confirmed. The models clearly reject the hypothesis – implicit in equilibrium condition (8) – that each regressor has the same effect on relative wages.

The effects of changes in own net supply – shown in row (1) – are strongly negative and of similar magnitude for high and low skilled men. The negative effect for low skilled men is fairly remarkable, since rising average schooling levels have caused the relative quantities of low skilled men to fall at the same time that their relative wages have declined. The resolution of this paradox is that technical change has been biased against them (see Figure 4.3), so that labour demand has fallen faster than supply. Thus the evidence in the table means that regions with less rapid reductions in net supply of less skilled workers have experienced larger declines in their relative wages.

The own quantity estimate of 0.59 for high skilled workers has a similar interpretation. On average, relative supply of high skilled men has risen more slowly than technical change has increased demand for them. So their wages have risen. Then, according to these estimates, regions with more rapid growth in the supply of high skilled workers have experienced smaller increases in high skill wages. I will present more detailed evidence on these points shortly.

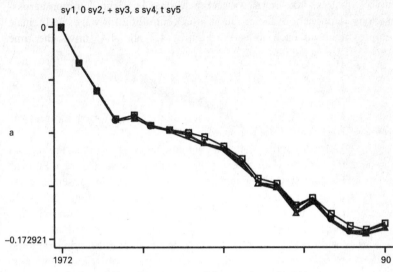

a Estimated year effects for low skill factor ratio, region I–V

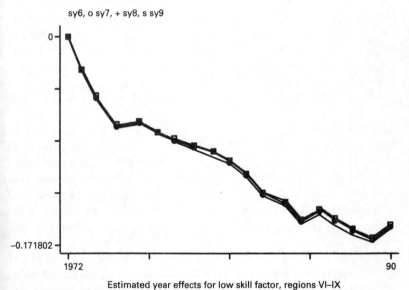

Estimated year effects for low skill factor, regions VI–IX

Figure 4.3   Estimated effects of technical change on factor ratios, low skilled men

Note: The curves show estimates of (8). Curves are not labelled because there are no important differences across regions.

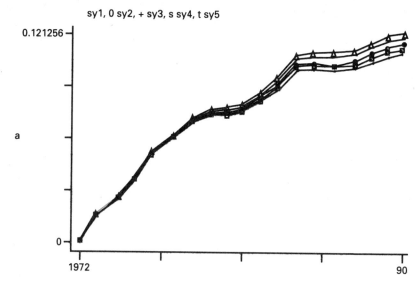

Estimated year effects for high skill factor ratio, regions I–V

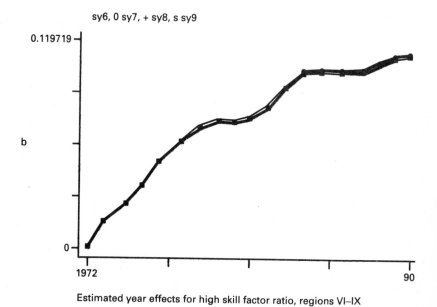

Estimated year effects for high skill factor ratio, regions VI–IX

Figure 4.4   Estimated effects of technical change on factor ratios, high skilled men

Table 4.5 Estimated determinants of relative wages of low skilled and
high skilled men, 1971–89
(Elasticities of complementarity)

Explanatory variables	Low skilled men	High skilled men
1 Net supply: $x_i^m - \sum_j S_i^{jm} z^{jm}$	−0.666 (0.105)	−0.591 (0.135)
2 Low skilled women: $-\sum_j S_i^{jm} F_{iL}^{jm}(x_L^{jm} - z^{jm})$	−1.943 (1.243)	−1.330 (0.193)
3 High skilled women: $-\sum_j S_i^{jm} F_{iH}^{jm}(x_H^{jm} - z^{jm})$	−0.962 (0.160)	−0.083 (0.199)
4 Technical change: $-\sum_j S_i^{jm} \phi_i^j$	−1.047 (0.116)	0.992 (0.152)
5 Region effects	Yes	Yes
R^2: Total	0.876	0.881
Net of region effects	0.881	0.792
Net of region effects and technical change	0.800	0.499
Observations	171	171

These effects of 'net supply' combine the impact of changing input
quantities (supply) with an employment-share weighted average of industry scales (demand). Which is more important, supply or demand?
It turns out that virtually all of the variation in net supply is due to
variation in input quantities; virtually none is due to changes in the
industry composition of demand. This is fairly surprising. I had expected that differences in regional specialization and the decline of
certain industries – durable manufacturing in the Midwest, for example – would be important determinants of changing wage inequality.
At least for the 'one-digit' skill-based industry definitions used here, I
can find no evidence for these effects.

Taken literally, the estimates also indicate that increased employment of women reduces men's wages. The pattern of the estimates is
rather odd, however. An increase in the supply of low skilled women
has a large but imprecisely estimated impact on the wages of low skilled
men, and a large (and precisely estimated) impact on the wages of
highly skilled men. In contrast, high skilled women affect only the
wages of low skilled men; their effect on high skilled men (−0.083) is
small. This pattern was unexpected, but in practice the effects of low
skilled women are unimportant. As shown below, actual changes in

the supply of low skilled women are small, so they have no appreciable effect on men's wages. Changes in the supply of high skilled women are large, however.

4.4.4 How Much Is Explained?

The estimates in Table 4.5 suggest that changes in relative net supplies and in women's labour force participation rates have played strong roles in affecting wage inequality within regions. How well does the model fit the evolution of wages across regions?

The final line of Table 4.5 records different proportions of variance in relative wages that are accounted for by the simple models. The overall R^2 of 0.88 for low skilled men includes the role of regional dummies in accounting for long-run average wage differentials across regions, so it may overstate the predictive content of the model for the time series changes in which we are interested. To account for this, the next two rows report partial R^2 statistics that net out region effects and then both region and technical change effects. For low skilled workers there is hardly any deterioration in R^2, indicating that the model does well in explaining regional differences in the evolution of wages. For high skilled men, only about half of regional differences in the evolution of wages is explained by net supply and women's employment.

Figures 4.5 and 4.6 provide graphical descriptions of the model's fit. They show the actual and predicted values of relative wages in each region for CPS survey years 1972–90. The fact that the model fits the overall trend in wages for low skilled men is not remarkable; the model attributes that component to technical change, which turns out to be a common 'trend' effect for all regions. More interesting is the fact that the model tracks well *within* regions, as was indicated by the partial-R^2 statistics in Table 4.5. For example, inspection of Figure 4.5 indicates that the largest decline in wages for low skilled men occurred in the West, and the smallest occurred in the South. The model fits these changes fairly well.

Further evidence on these points is provided in Tables 4.6 and 4.7. They record components change in relative wages, based on the regression estimates of Table 4.5 and actual changes in explanatory variables over time. For example, row 1 of Table 4.6 indicates that the relative wage of low skilled men in New England fell by 10.1 log points between 1972–3 and 1989–90.[8] The model predicts a 9.6 log point decline. This prediction is composed of four parts. First, a decline in the relative net supply of low skilled men predicts a 19.4

119

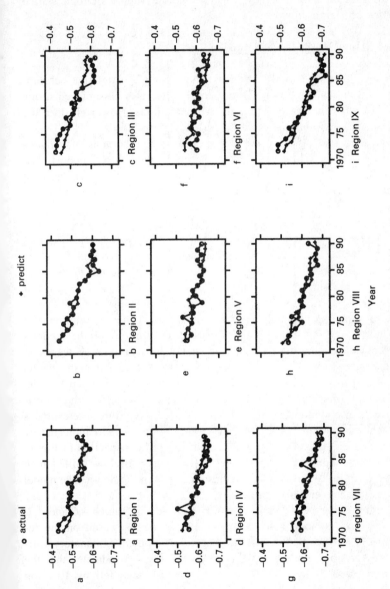

Figure 4.5 Actual and predicted relative wages of low skilled men by region, 1972–90

120

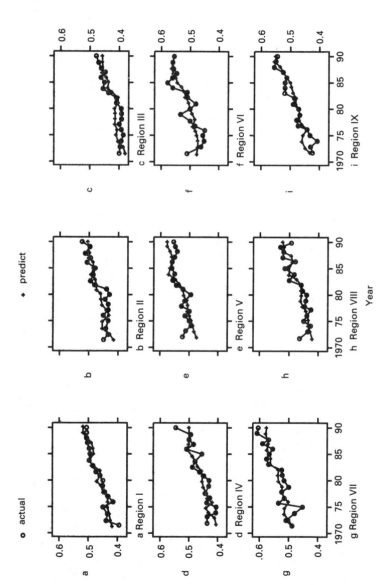

Figure 4.6 Actual and predicted relative wages of high skilled men by region, 1972–90

point *increase* in their wage. This is largely offset by a 16.4 point decline in relative wages that is caused by biased technical change. Low
skilled women had a negligible (0.002) impact on wages, but the model
indicates that increased participation by high skilled women reduced
the relative wage of low skilled men in New England by 12.8 log points.

The estimates in column (6) of Tables 4.6 and 4.7 confirm that
industry-common changes in factor ratios, which I attribute to technical change, have had region-neutral effects on wages. The model therefore attributes regional differences in relative wage changes to differences
in net supply and changes in labour force participation of skilled women.

To illustrate, wages of less skilled men fell by about 19 log points
in the West, but by only 10 points in New England. The decline in the
relative quantity of less skilled men (caused by rising schooling levels
over time) would have caused a 19.4 point *increase* in relative wages
in New England, but only a 5.1 point increase in the West. This difference is due to a much smaller increase in average schooling levels
in the West possibly because of immigration of less skilled workers
(see below). Offsetting these effects, women's participation reduced
wages by 12.6 points in New England, but by only 8.1 points in the
West. These two components predict a 9.8 log point difference in relative wage changes for the two regions, which is virtually all of the
actual difference between them. In this sense, the model indicates a
strong role for supply factors in affecting the evolution of relative wages
in regional markets. Extending this finding to aggregate wage changes,
the model indicates that the reduction in supply of less skilled workers
has been outpaced by factor-saving technical change and by growth in
supply of substitute factors. So demand for less skilled men fell, and
so did their wages.

4.4.5 Effects of Immigration on Wages

Several previous studies have used differences in immigration rates
between US cities to estimate the effects on immigration on relative
wage (LaLonde and Topel, 1992; Altonji and Card 1991; Borjas, 1987).
These studies find very small effects, even among less skilled workers,
suggesting that labour demand is very elastic and that the American
labour market can easily absorb immigrant flows. The evidence in this
chapter is different. In the far West, the large decline in relative wages
of less skilled men appears to be closely linked to an increase in labour
supply of less skilled workers, which is driven by new immigration.

The first piece of evidence on this point is shown in column (3) of

Table 4.6   Actual and predicted components of change in relative wages of low skilled men, 1972–3 to 1989–90

Region	Actual (1)	Predicted (2)	Net supply (3)	Women Low skill (4)	High skill (5)	Technical change (6)
1 New England	−0.101	−0.096	0.194	0.002	−0.128	−0.164
2 Atlantic	−0.150	−0.157	0.178	−0.006	−0.166	−0.163
3 N. Central	−0.176	−0.129	0.161	−0.005	−0.126	−0.160
4 W.N. Central	−0.094	−0.116	0.167	−0.006	−0.124	−0.158
5 S. East	−0.052	−0.089	0.174	0.001	−0.103	−0.162
6 S. Central	−0.050	−0.118	0.168	−0.005	−0.119	−0.162
7 S. West	−0.101	−0.122	0.136	−0.003	−0.096	−0.160
8 Mountain	−0.121	−0.155	0.136	−0.001	−0.130	−0.160
9 West	−0.193	−0.190	0.051	−0.008	−0.073	−0.159
Average	−0.115	−0.130	0.151	−0.003	−0.118	−0.161

Note: Predicted components are derived by multiplying the changes in explanatory variables by the regression coefficients reported in Table 4.5.

Table 4.7   Actual and predicted components of change in relative wages of high skilled men, 1972–3 to 1989–90

Region	Actual (1)	Predicted (2)	Net supply (3)	Women Low skill (4)	High skill (5)	Technical change (6)
1 New England	0.095	0.098	−0.026	0.020	−0.006	0.109
2 Atlantic	0.071	0.087	0.000	−0.012	−0.007	0.106
3 N. Central	0.075	0.071	−0.031	0.008	−0.006	0.100
4 W.N. Central	0.080	0.088	−0.014	0.004	−0.006	0.104
5 S. East	0.041	0.105	−0.039	0.039	−0.006	0.111
6 S. Central	0.072	0.082	−0.029	0.007	−0.006	0.110
7 S. West	0.115	0.088	−0.023	0.007	−0.006	0.109
8 Mountain	0.061	0.090	0.021	−0.033	−0.006	0.108
9 West	0.119	0.113	0.014	−0.004	−0.005	0.109
Average	0.081	0.091	−0.014	0.004	−0.006	0.107

Note: Predicted components are derived by multiplying the changes in explanatory variables by the regression coefficients reported in Table 4.5.

Table 4.6. Other things being equal, declining overall supply of less skilled men in the West raised their relative wage by 5.1 percent, compared to an effect of 15.1 percent in the country as a whole. Thus the decline in relative supply of less skilled men – the improvement of overall labour force quality – was only a third as large in the West as in the rest of the country. Was this because the quality of the native labour force improved more slowly in the West? Or was it because new, less skilled workers entered that labour market? Figure 4.7 provides the answer.

Figure 4.7 shows the regional evolution of the supply of less skilled (type 1) workers under two sample definitions. The line marked with an 'o' in each region uses the full sample, so these curves show the evolution of relative supply that entered into the previous estimates. On average, the labour supply of type 1 workers fell by 30 log points, but it fell by only about 10 points in the West (region 9). The CPS data do not record the immigrant status of respondents, but they do record broad ethnic categories. Since immigration flows in the 1980s came mainly from Latin America and Asia, I recalculated changes in supply on a sample that excludes Hispanics and Asians. The result is the line marked with a '+' in each figure.

There are two things to notice about the lines marked with a '+'. First, they indicate that the improvement of labour force quality among 'natives' was fairly homogenous across regions. For example, the quantity of type 1 (unskilled) native workers declined by 26 log points in the West, compared to the national average of 29 log points. Thus, in the absence of Hispanics and Asians, the model indicates that wages of less skilled workers would have fallen by similar amounts across regions. Second, with the exception of the Southwest (region 7) and West – both of which received large immigrant flows during this period – the curves coincide. This means that Hispanics and Asians increased the relative supply of less skilled workers in these regions. The effect is especially large in the West. There, the decline in unskilled supply would have been 2.6 times (0.26/0.10) greater if not for the increasing share of Hispanics and Asians in the labour force. According to the model, these 'immigrants' account for the greater increase in wage inequality in the West than in other regions.[9]

4.4.6 Women's Participation and Wage Inequality

One additional point is important. The estimates in Tables 4.5, 4.6, and 4.7 indicate that increased employment of women has reduced the

124

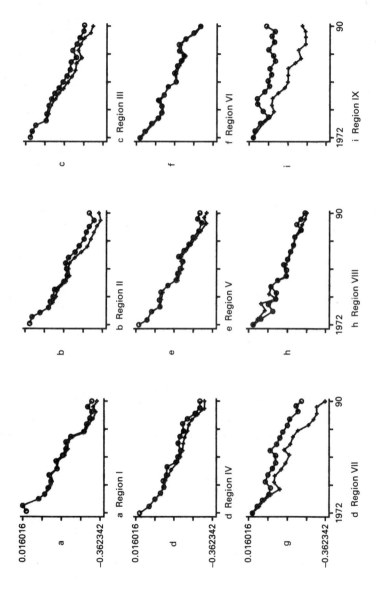

Figure 4.7 Changing relative supply of less skilled men by region and ethnicity

wages of less skilled men. The magnitude of this effect is surprising.
On average for these regions, rising participation of high skilled women
reduced the wages of less skilled men by 11.8 log points between 1972–
3 and 1989–90. This is almost of all of 13 point total change in predicted wages over this period. In other words, these estimates imply
that *if women's participation had not changed there would have been
no decline in the relative wages of less skilled men.* Thus rising labour
supply of women may have been an important contributor to the increase in US wage inequality since 1972.

I don't want to oversell this finding, however. The pattern of substitution effects that lead up to it – for example, high skilled women
substitute for less skilled men – is fairly counterintuitive. This may
indicate that the model is misspecified or that industry aggregates are
improperly defined. But the estimated effects are strong, so the possibility that women's labour force participation has adversely affected
less skilled men surely warrants further investigation.

4.5 CONCLUSIONS

This chapter invokes a fairly simple model of labour supply and demand to study the evolution of wage inequality in regional labour markets.
The results are mixed, and rather different than I had anticipated at the
outset. Aside from effects of technical change – measured by nation-
wide changes in factor ratios – I find little evidence that labour demand differences have affected relative wages. A corollary to this is
that regional differences in specialization, for example the concentration of durable manufacturing in the Midwest, do not appear to have
affected the evolution of relative wages. On the other hand, the data
indicate that regional differences in the evolution of labour supplies
have affected relative wages. Regional differences in wage inequality
seem to be driven by regional difference in supply, especially among
less skilled workers.

The model and evidence paint the following picture. Over time, technical change has favoured workers, which raises overall wage inequality.
At the same time, successive cohorts of workers have rising schooling
levels, which reduces the relative supply of less skilled workers and
reduces inequality. The former effect has dominated, on average, so
inequality has risen. Yet changes in supply vary across regional markets, so changes in relative wages do too. Regions with the greatest
increases in wage inequality are those with the smallest improvements

in labour force quality (the smallest reductions in supply of less skilled workers). Especially in the West, I provide evidence that immigration has played an important role in these supply shifts.

The chapter also provides evidence that increased labour force participation of women has reduced the wages of unskilled men, raising overall inequality. This evidence is far from definitive, but the potential importance of this effect surely warrants further research.

Notes

* Presented at the Biwako Conference, Osaka July 1992. This research was supported by the National Science Foundation. Thanks to Kevin M. Murphy and Sherwin Rosen for discussions and advice. Hsin Chang Lu provided outstanding assistance. Remaining errors are mine. I am indebted to conference participants, especially Markus Rebick, for comments.
1. See Juhn, Murphy, and Pierce (1992) for a detailed summary. Murphy and Welch (1992) analyze the determinants of the rising returns to schooling, and the role of international trade.
2. See the references in n. 1 above.
3. Results are unchanged when capital is added, so long as capital trades at a fixed price across markets and there are no substantial costs of adjustment.
4. Formally, (5) is derived by solving for women's relative wages in the female input demand equations (4), as a function of men's and women's quantities. Substituting in the male input equations yields (5).
5. The conditioning set of characteristics included seven categories for education, four for experience, and three for race.
6. There is substantial variation in estimated technical change across industries. But rough similarity of industry shares across regions implies that the impact of technical change in region-neutral.
7. Two of the regressors in these models are constructed using parameter estimates from the first-stage industry demand equations. No attempt has been made to adjust the standard errors of the second stage equation to account for the precision of these estimates. Thus standard errors in Table 4.5 are understated. See Murphy and Topel (1985) for details and methods for correcting second-stage standard errors.
8. Two-year averages are used as endpoints to reduce the effects of measurement error and other random components on actual wage changes.
9. One might object that immigration reduced the median wage of type 1 workers via sample selection rather than substitution. That is, unskilled workers may enter at the very bottom of the distribution, reducing median and average wages, but not reducing the wage of any native. To check this, I recalculated the wage distributions by region, using only 'native' workers, as defined above. Consistent with the substitution hypothesis, wages of unskilled natives declined in the West by more than in other regions. Native and full sample wage inequality measures are nearly identical.

References

Altonji, Joseph and David Card (1991) 'The Effects of Immigration on the Labor Market Outcomes of Less-Skilled Natives', in John M. Abowd and Richard B. Freedman (eds) *Immigration, Trade, and the Labor Market*, Chicago; University of Chicago Press.

Borjas, George (1987) 'Immigrants, Minorities, and Labor Market Competition', *Industrial and Labor Relations Review*, 40, April, pp. 382–92.

Hamermesh, Daniel S. (1993) *Labor Demand*, Princeton, Princeton University Press.

Hicks, John Richard (1932, 1966) *The Theory of Wages*, London, Macmillan.

Juhn, Chinhui, Kevin M. Murphy and Brooks Pierce (1992) 'Wage Inequality and the Rise in Returns to Skill', *Journal of Political Economy*, 101, June, 410–42.

Juhn, Chinhui, Kevin M. Murphy and Robert H. Topel (1991) 'Unemployment, Nonemployment, and Wages: Why Has the Natural Rate Increased with Time?', *Brookings Papers on Economic Activity*.

Katz, Lawrence F. and Kevin M. Murphy (1992) 'Changes in Relative Wages, 1963–1987: Supply and Demand Factors', *Quarterly Journal of Economics*, February, pp. 35–78.

LaLonde, Robert J. and Robert H. Topel (1989) 'Labour Market Adjustments to Increased Immigration', in R. Freeman (ed.) *Immigration, Trade, and the Labour Market*, Chicago, University of Chicago Press for NBER.

LaLonde, Robert, and Robert H. Topel (1992) 'The assimilation of immigrants in the U.S. labour market', in: R. Freeman and G. Borjas, eds., *Immigration and the workforce: economic consequences for the United States and source areas*, Chicago, University of Chicago Press.

Murphy, Kevin M. and Robert H. Topel (1985) 'Estimation and Inference in "Two-Step" Econometric Models', *Journal of Business and Economic Statistics* 3 October, pp. 370–80.

Murphy, Kevin M. and Finis Welch (1991) 'Wage Differentials in the 1980s: The Role of International Trade', in Marvin Kosters (ed.), *Workers and Their Wages: Changing Patterns in the United States*, Washington, DC, American Enterprise Institute, pp. 39–69.

Murphy, Kevin M. and Finis Welch (1992) 'The Structure of Wages', *Quarterly Journal of Economics*, February.

Topel, Robert H. (1986) 'Local Labour Markets', *Journal of Political Economy*, 94, June, pp. 111–43.

Part II

Work and Incentives

5 The Growth of the Firm and Promotions in the Japanese Seniority System

Isao Ohashi and Hisakazu Matsushige*

5.1 INTRODUCTION

Until now two reasons have been advanced to explain Japan's good economic performance – high productivity, low unemployment and steady rates of economic growth. One focuses on Japanese industrial relations which have been characterized by seniority-based wages, permanent employment and enterprise unionism, and the other attaches great importance to the labour compensation system relatively unique to Japan, that is, the bonus payment system. However, it is still a matter of some dispute quite how these features contribute to good economic performance in Japan.

In this chapter we briefly review the discussions and the explanations regarding Japan's economic performance from the point of view of the internal labor market, and attempt to present a simple model of the hierarchical firm, the main aim of which is to explain why Japanese firms are strongly motivated to expand employment. More specifically, we focus on the aspect that under the seniority wage system employment expansion works to elevate workers' incentive through increasing the probability of promotion for senior workers and to decrease the average wage through changing the age composition of employees. In later sections we test the implications of our model concerning the effects of employment expansion on the promotion probability of senior workers and on the change of the average wage, using microdata on the companies in the automobile and electric industries.

5.2   BACKGROUND

As for Japanese industrial relations, there are two interpretations – the traditional and the relative one. The former states that, immediately upon graduating from school, Japanese workers are hired by a firm and remain with the same employer until mandatory retirement about the age of 60. The employer has a policy attaching great importance to seniority in determining promotions and wages. Consequently, workers are automatically promoted to a higher position, and their wages increase with age and length of service. The traditional view insists that these employment practices are not only unique to Japan but are the core of Japanese industrial relations.

The relative interpretation of Japanese industrial practices focuses on the results of international comparisons on length of service and separation rates among Japan, US and EC countries, which have been made by Koike (1981, 1988), Hashimoto and Raisian (1985), OECD (1986), Ono (1989) and Higuchi (1991). Although some points stressed in the findings vary from researcher to researcher, they can be summarized as follows: in Japan, workers are more likely to stay in the same firm and firms attach more importance to length of service in determining wages and promotions than in other countries, hence, wage–age and wage–tenure profiles are more steeply sloped than in other countries.

As the empirical and the field studies were carried out, the relative interpretation has become prevalent among many economists. That is, people have come to understand the findings obtained by these studies as showing that the differences between Japan and other countries are one of degree. In addition, the traditional interpretation seems to be theoretically unacceptable because, in order to explain high productivity under the automatic promotion system, it depends heavily on the vague concept that Japanese workers identity themselves strongly with the group, that is, with the company at which they work. This 'groupism' argues that since the Japanese have a strongly group-oriented mentality, it is a prevalent belief among them that a company should secure a worker's job and livelihood in exchange for high worker morale. This mentality is said to have originated in the age of feudalism from the relation between master and man, or from the traditional Japanese family hierarchical system. However, in our opinion, it is unrealistic to presume that a human being works hard without any promised reward for a long working life. That is, workers work hard because remuneration for them differs depending on whether they work well or not. In reality Japanese firms widely utilize a well designed system of personnel assessment to make a decision on promotions and wage payments.

To explain why age–wage and tenure–wage profiles are steeply sloped, particularly for Japanese blue-collar workers, and why Japanese firms are productive, Koike (1977, 1988) proposed the 'Career Hypothesis', which focused on the Japanese system of skill formation characterized by extensive internal promotion, wide-ranging job rotation and egalitarian assignments of tasks among workers within a workshop. This system gives workers broad experience and intellectual skills, and makes them understand not only the structure of the machines and products but in addition the whole production process. Workers acquiring intellectual skills can deal well with unexpectedly and frequently occurring changes and something unusual, which are the most important targets for firms equipped with modern technology to cope with. They can also contribute significantly to improving efficiency through small group activities such as Quality Control (QC) circles.

Based on the findings made by Koike, Aoki (1982, 1984, 1988) developed a Japanese model of the 'hierarchical firm', which analyzes the broad aspects of Japanese firms such as the information structure, investment behavior, equilibrium growth and employment contract in the framework of the cooperative game approach, and the following section will refer in some detail to his model.

According to the human capital theory, a great amount of human investment in the earlier stages of working life makes age–wage profiles more upward sloping because it increases a worker's productivity after the investment. Based on this logic, Mincer and Higuchi (1988), and Higuchi (1991) insist that steep wage profiles in Japan are due to much investment in on-the-job training and retraining, which has been necessitated by high technological development in Japanese firms since the second World War. In addition, referring to the case studies by White and Trevor (1985), Shimada (1988), and Higuchi (1991) demonstrates that Japanese firms bear more costs to recruit workers appropriate for training. In line with these discussions, they found that the slope of tenure–wage profile is steeper and the quit rate is lower in the industries where technical progress is higher.[1]

The efficiency wage hypothesis can also provide an explanation as to why Japanese firms are productive. Lazear (1979) showed that a steep wage profile is favorable to a firm in the sense that it makes workers unlikely to shirk and cheat through increasing the loss of remuneration which separation causes. Based on this discussion, we can say that labour productivity is high in Japanese firms where steeply rising wage profiles are prevalent. Unfortunately, however, the efficiency wage hypothesis does not make clear the relation between the wage profile and the growth of the firm. Moreover, we should note that its main aim is to explain involuntary unemployment, which is quite low in Japan.

This chapter will present a simple model incorporating the mechanism proposed by the efficiency wage hypothesis into the hierarchical firm and analyze the relation between the growth of the firm and its wage structure.

Another way to explain Japan's good economic performance was proposed by Hashimoto (1979), Sachs (1979), Gordon (1982), Kahn (1984), and Freeman and Weitzman (1987). They argued that the bonus system plays a key role in explaining the combination of wage flexibility and employment stability in the Japanese labour market. In fact, according to the *Monthly Labour Survey* (Ministry of Labour, 1985), 97 percent of firms that have 30 employees or more pay bonuses twice a year and regular workers receive over 20 percent of their yearly pay in the form of semi-annual bonuses even in small-scale establishments with between 30 and 99 employees. Interpreted in the context of Weitzman's (1984) share economy model, the bonus system functions to bring about low unemployment in Japan.

However, many Japanese labour economists such as Mizuno (1985), Koshiro (1986), Brunello and Ohtake (1987), and Ohashi (1989) appear reluctant to accept the 'Bonus Hypothesis'. They tested the implications of this hypothesis for the Japanese labour market and obtained unfavorable results on the relation between bonuses and profits. In particular, Mizuno states that basic wages, to which bonuses are closely linked, are also flexible in response to economic conditions, and Ohashi stresses that, judging from the statistical significance of the effects on bonuses and from the partial correlations, labour market conditions are more influential than profits, overtime, and sales as an explanatory variable for the behaviours of bonuses and basic wages. These empirical findings require us to build an alternative model to explain Japanese economic performance.

5.3 ANALYTICAL FRAMEWORK

It has been empirically ascertained by many labour economists that long-term employment is more prevalent in Japan than in the UK, US and the EC countries, and also that age–wage and tenure–wage profiles are more steeply sloped. In this section, based on these findings, we present a simple two-period model and explore its implications for empirical analysis of the Japanese labour market.

Let us assume that the firm employs workers for two periods and workers acquire skills and knowledge from on-the-job training in the first period. The firm operating with a two-level internal organization of employees promotes some of the senior workers, who have one-period experience at the firm, to managerial positions. That is, at the beginning of the second period the firm assigns capable senior workers to positions at an upper level, such as, for example, that of foremen. The firm's decision of promotion is made on the basis of the results of personnel assessments on workers' ability and performance in the previous period. The senior workers who are not promoted are assigned the same jobs as before. This does not necessarily imply that their productivity is the same as junior workers' because they probably do their jobs better as a result of one-period work experience. Nevertheless, for simplicity of analysis, we assume both workers are the same in their ability to carry out their jobs at the lower level.[2]

It is also assumed that the ratio of foremen to all employees is in the long run fixed at x, which is determined by organizational factors such as the span of control. We will discuss this assumption more in section 5.4, because it appears controversial.

We now define the total number of employees as L, the employees in the first period as L_1, and those in the second period as L_2. Then the relation,

$$L = L_1 + L_2 \qquad (1)$$

holds. It is important to note here that in the current period L_1 is variable for the firm, but L_2 is not because it is fixed by the hiring policy in the former period.

The number of foremen is given by xL, which is assumed to satisfy the relation,[3]

$$L_2 \geq xL. \qquad (2)$$

Wages are paid to junior and senior workers by w and dw, respectively, where 'd' is larger than 1 and fixed in the long run. In addition to 'dw', the firm pays post premiums, 'a', to the senior workers who are promoted to the managerial positions. It should be mentioned here that most of the Japanese firms pay workers compensation on the basis of pay classifications rather on the skill requirements or the importance of jobs. That is, compensations are different among the workers of different personal qualifications such as age, seniority, educational background and capability even if they do the same job. Furthermore, in order for senior workers to be promoted to a managerial position, they must attain a certain level of qualification, for example, in the case of Matuda automobile company grade 3 for group leader (Hanchou), grade 4 for vice foreman, and grade 5 for foreman (Shokuchou). We should therefore interpret this as meaning that post premiums include not only post allowances but pay differentials due to different qualifications.

It is also assumed that wages and premiums are given for the individual firm because they are determined through industry-wide collective bargaining in the Spring Wage Offensive. That is, even though wage negotiation is undertaken at the level of individual company, the contracted increments or rates of change of wages are almost the same, at least among the major companies belonging to the same industry.

One may ask why senior workers not to be promoted are paid more than juniors by d, even though they do the same jobs. This is because of the seniority wage contract that wages are paid in accordance with the life-time pattern of living expenses of the worker and/or because of the implicit labour contract between the risk-neutral firm and risk-averting workers to avoid wage changes due to the uncertainty of promotion in the second period. Since these discussions are well known, we do not pursue this problem further in this chapter.

The total amount of wage payments of the firm is thus given as

$$W = wL_1 + dwL_2 + axL. \tag{3}$$

Dividing this equation by L, we have the average wage, w^*, as follows.

$$\begin{aligned} w^* &= w(L_1/L + dL_2/L) + ax \\ &= w + w(d - 1)L_2/L + ax. \end{aligned} \tag{4}$$

This shows that the average wage decreases as the level of employment increases. As discussed above, the number of seniors is given in the current period for the firm because it takes one period to train workers. This implies that the firm can change the total level of employment only through operating the number of junior workers in the current period.

Turning to the production aspect, we assume, for simplicity of analysis, the following production function

$$Y = eL, \tag{5}$$

$$e = e(xL/L_2), \qquad e' > 0. \tag{6}$$

There are two reasons why the ratio of foremen to senior workers increases productivity. One is that the seniors left out of promotion are assigned to the jobs whose duties are the same as those assigned to juniors, and hence they are greatly discouraged. In this situation the firm can not provide any effective motivation to them because the senior workers remaining at the lower rank have no possibility of promotion and do not have to worry about the result of personnel assessment.[4] The other reason is that the current ratio of foremen to senior workers gives juniors a good idea as to the probability of promotion in the next period, that is, juniors expect a higher probability of promotion as the ratio increases. This means that the expected wage profile is steeply sloped for junior workers. Thus an increase in the ratio of foremen motivates juniors through the mechanism proposed by the Efficiency Wage Hypothesis,[5] and as a result increases productivity.[6]

Assuming that the firm faces imperfect competition in the product market, we define the demand function for the firm's product as follows

$$Y = bP^{-k}, \tag{7}$$

where P is the product price, and k is the price elasticity of demand which is assumed to be constant.

Now the firm's profit can be expressed by

$$Z = PY - W = PY - (wL_1 + dwL_2 + axL). \tag{8}$$

It is assumed that the wage level is given for the firm. This assumption can be justified by the fact that the annual wage increment is determined through collective bargaining with the enterprise union in the Spring Wage Offensive and that the increment or the rate of change of the wage level is unified among the large firms in the same industry. Thus the firm maximizes its profit with respect to P, Y, and L (or L_1), subject to equations (1), (2), (5), (6) and (7).[7]

Substituting equations (1), (5), (6) and (7) into equation (8), and letting λ be the Lagrangian multiplier for the supply constraint of senior workers, we have the first-order conditions,

$$eP(1 - 1/k) + e'PxL/L_2(1 - 1/k) - (w + ax) - \lambda x \geq 0, \quad (9)$$

$$\lambda(L_2 - xL) = 0. \quad (10)$$

If the inner solutions hold, equation (9) can be expressed as

$$eP(1 - 1/k)(1 + f) = w + ax, \quad (9')$$

where f is the employment elasticity of labour efficiency, that is, $e'xL/eL_2$. This equation shows that the marginal revenue of employment expansion is equal to its marginal wage cost. The optimal solutions for output, employment, labour efficiency and the product price are given by equations (1), (5), (6), (7) and (9').

Figure 5.1, where the marginal revenue (*MR*) and the marginal cost (*MC*) are measured in terms of labour efficiency, may help in clarifying the meaning of these equations for the readers. Note here in Figure 5.1 that since f is positive, the product price is determined at a lower level than that in the case where $f = 0$, and both the levels of output and employment are higher. More importantly, by comparative static analysis we can easily know that, as product demand increases, the price of the product decreases. This is essentially because the marginal cost in terms of labour efficiency decreases as employment increases. Thus we arrive at the different result from that obtained by the traditional monopoly model.

In the case of the corner solutions, the relations,

$$eP(1 - 1/k)(1 + f) - (w + ax) > 0, \quad (9'')$$

$$L = xL, \quad (10')$$

hold. That is, the firm determines its employment at the level of L^1 in Figure 5.2, where all capable senior workers are promoted to foremen. In this situation the firm wishes to expand employment up to the level of L^2 in Figure 5.2, but it cannot, due to the shortage of capable senior workers. This case is likely to occur when the effect of employment expansion on work incentive is strong.[8]

Based on the model developed in this section, two important conclusions may be advanced. One is that the average wage decreases as

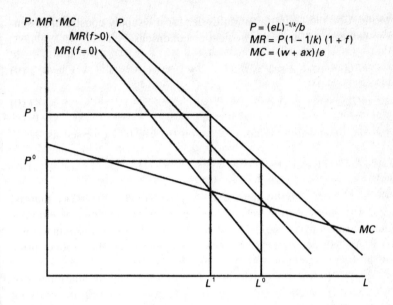

Figure 5.1   The case for the inner solutions

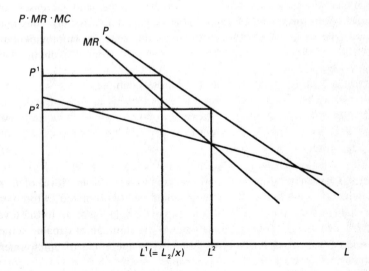

Figure 5.2   The case for the corner solutions

employment increases. From equation (4) the amount of decrease in the average wage is large when the wage profile is steeply sloped, that is, d is large. The firm is thus likely to make more profit in the seniority wage system whenever the product demand and hence employment expand. The other is that the firm has a strong incentive to promote all capable senior workers to managerial positions by expanding employment. This is because the firm can raise labour efficiency through making the expected wage profile rise steeply.

We conclude this section by comparing our model with that of Aoki (1982) and Weitzman (1983, 1984, 1985), respectively, which were developed with regard to the behaviour of Japanese firms. We first deal with Aoki's model, which aims to analyze equilibrium bargains over investment for the growth of the firm and wages paid to incumbent workers. Essentially the specification of our model is in line with Aoki's in the sense that incumbent workers benefit from employment growth in the form of probable promotion, but different in the motivation of the firm for employment growth. Aoki states that 'if the manager chooses a growth rate so as to maximize the share value after an agreement on a pay schedule with the incumbent workers, he will neglect gains from the growth of the firm accruing to employees in the form of probable promotions, and ends up with a too-low growth rate from the organizational point of view' (p. 1104). Therefore, he claims that 'the incumbent workers must exert some influence over the management so as to make their interest in the growth of the firm incorporated into the corporate policymaking'. Based on this penetrating insight, Aoki took the approach of a shareholder–employee cooperative game in order to analyze the macro phenomena in the real wage, capital accumulation and employment. In turn, our model incorporates workers' interest in employment expansion into the firm's profit in the form that the high growth rate of the firm raises the possibility of being promoted for workers and motivates them to work hard by making the expected wage profile steeply sloped.[9]

In the share economy proposed by Weitzman (1984, 1985), workers receive a proportional part of the firm's profits, which are dependent on such factors as price of output and the level of employment. It is important that under this compensation system, as long as demand and marginal revenue product curves are declining in the relevant range, revenue per worker and hence the level of wage decrease as more labour is hired. This negative relation between employment and wages gives the firm an incentive to expand employment more, as the share contract parameters are fixed and the level of employment is variable in the short run. Freeman and Weitzman (1987) attempted to test the implications of the share economy for the Japanese labour market where the bonus payment system is widely prevailing among firms.

A significant difference between Weitzman's model and that proposed here is that in the former model the employment growth of the firm is seen as detrimental to the incumbent workers in the short run because it decreases their wages. In the share economy, therefore, the possibility may arise that the incumbent workers are strongly against the firm's employment expansion even though it is beneficial to them in the long run. This is not the case in the model presented here.[10]

5.4 EMPIRICAL ANALYSIS: THE EFFECTS OF EMPLOYMENT CHANGES ON PROMOTION

Although we cannot directly test the implications and predictions of our model due to data limitation, we can empirically check the appropriateness of two basic arguments of our model. One is the assumption that the ratio of foremen to all employees is fixed in the long run, and the other is that under the seniority wage system, the average wage decreases as the level of employment increases, as shown in equation (4). In this section, we will discuss the first assumption, and consider the factors which affect the probability of a worker being promoted to a supervisory or submanagerial post such as foreman and senior foreman.

To begin with, we solve the optimal ratio of foremen to all employees in our model.[11] Maximizing the firm's profit with respect to x and L, and rearranging the first-order conditions, we have the following equation jointly with equation (9'),

$$x = fw/a, \tag{11}$$

where it is assumed that $xL < L_2$, that is, the inner solutions hold. This result is consistent with our assumption that x is fixed in the long run, as far as the wage structure, w/a, and f are stable. But we do not take this result seriously because it is an extremely simplified scenario that the span of control should be determined only from the point of view of workers' incentive.[12] It should be affected by other factors such as technology, the content of work and the hierarchical structure of the firm. Unfortunately, however, we cannot control these factors empirically.

In our context it is important to check how the span of control is affected by change in employment. More specifically, the growth rate of the company may change the composition of foreman and ordinary workers in two different ways. First, a high growth rate seems to increase the number of untrained workers relative to that of foremen. When a company expands its operation, it needs to increase the number of foremen as well as its labor force. It should be noted here that, while it may be relatively easy for a company to hire untrained workers, it may sometimes be difficult to train a sufficient number of its employees as supervisors in a short time. It is also difficult, in many cases, to find suitably qualified personnel elsewhere. However, the growth of a company may also have the opposite effect of decreasing the ratio of foremen to workers. If growth is accompanied by frequent changes of production processes, they may require additional supervisors and production managers who have leadership qualities and are able to control and coordinate their production workers.

Second, the scale of production is another factor which appears to affect the available number of foremen. It is possible to promote the division of labour by increasing the number of workers. The job of each worker is then simplified and it becomes easier for each one to understand his work: as a result, a foreman can easily supervise more workers. In addition, if the automation of the production process is introduced into the company (which tends to be a large-scale operation), it may also make it possible for a foreman to supervise more workers at any one time. For example, on an automated production line in a factory producing electronic parts, a foreman usually supervises many workers who are engaged in a similar type of job together.

It is also interesting to consider the question of whether the growth of a company equally affects the chances for promotion of different age groups. If a rapidly growing company is suffering from a shortage of supervisors, it may promote its own workers soon after it finds them to be competent enough, even at a relatively early stage in their career. This will result in a positive correlation between the growth rate of a company and the probability of its younger workers being promoted.

Based on this discussion, the equation which may be proposed to estimate this probability would be as follows:

$$ln[p/(1-p)] = a0 + a1 \times GROWTH + a2 \times D1 + a3 \times$$
$$AGE + a4 \times SCALE + a5 \times SCALE^{**}2$$
$$+ u, \text{ where}$$

p: the ratio of foremen to ordinary workers
GROWTH: the growth rate of total labour force during the past 10 years
$D1$: $D1=1$ if the company belongs to the metal machinery industry, otherwise $=0$
AGE: the average age of the labour force
SCALE: the total number of workers
u: a random term

The data on which this equation is estimated was obtained through questionnaires which were delivered by all Toyota-Roren (the Association of Unions of Toyota and related companies) to its members in 1989. The questionnaires are about the numbers of male and female blue-collar workers, foremen, and other employees in submanagerial positions such as subsection supervisors. 55 companies replied and 38 of them provided the information necessary to compile statistical tests.

Table 5.1 shows the results of OLS regressions. The first estimation shows the analysis of the ratio of foremen to the total number of blue-collar workers. There is no factor which significantly determines the ratio. Although the coefficient of *GROWTH* is positive, it is not significant. This implies that companies may increase the number of supervisors in tandem with the increase in the number of new workers so that they do not have to change the relative composition of foremen to ordinary workers.

However, when we break down and group workers according to age, in some age groups we can observe that some factors actually have an effect on the composition of foremen and ordinary workers.

The factors which alter the probability of promotion are mainly *GROWTH*, *SCALE* and *SCALE***2. The coefficients of the other variables are not statistically significant except for that of $D1$ in the case of workers between 40 and 49 years of age.

The coefficients of *GROWTH* are significantly positive in the estimated number of workers from 30 to 34 years old and the workers from 30 to 39. It would thus appear that, as noted earlier, workers in younger age groups are more likely to be promoted when a company is growing faster. A company may not further assess the ability of workers who have already been assessed and it may be said that more competent and appropriate workers are more easily found among younger workers since they are better at mastering new technology. The result of these estimations indicates that the probability of workers being promoted does not increase once they are assessed as being incompetent at some stage of their employment even if they stay longer at the same position with the company.

Table 5.1 Estimation of promotion

Age	C	Growth	D1	Age	Scale	Scale**2	R2	adjR2
TOTAL [1]	5.350 E−1 [0.772]	3.538 E−1 [0.486]	−4.053 E−2 [−1.261]	1.004 E−3 [0.518]	4.273 E−6 [1.676]		1.993 E−1	1.022 E−1
[2]	4.402 E−1 [0.668]	2.559 E−1 [0.380]			5.207 E−6 [2.146]		1.568 E−1	1.086 E−1
[30–34] [1]	8.319 E+0 [2.119]	8.350 E+0 [2.018]	2.420 E−1 [1.334]	2.271 E−3 [0.206]	−1.900 E−5 [−0.297]	1.611 E−10 [0.101]	1.634 E−1 [2.119]	3.270 E−2
[2]	8.025 E+0 [2.184]	7.807 E+0 [2.077]			−1.625 E−5 [−1.201]		1.131 E−1	6.204 E−2
[35–39] [1]	4.617 E+0 [1.623]	3.753 E+0 [1.252]	−6.352 E−2 [−0.483]	−1.351 E−2 [−1.690]	−2.592 E−5 [−0.560]	5.540 E−10 [0.479]	1.958 E−1	7.000 E−2
[2]	6.151 E+0 [2.264]	5.804 E+0 [2.089]			6.418 E−6 [−0.642]			
[30–39] [1]	3.787 E+0 [2.249]	3.287 E+0 [2.050]	6.312 E−2	−6.818 E−3	−1.589 E−5 [−0.852]	3.186 E−10 [0.357]	1.072 E−1	5.620 E−2
[2]	4.537 E+0 [2.249]	4.228 E+0 [2.050]			6.328 E−6 [−0.852]		1.072 E−1	5.620 E−2
[40–44] [1]	1.377 E+0 [0.439]	7.930 E−1 [0.241]	−7.358 E−2 [−0.506]	−9.914 E−4 [−0.113]	3.293 E−5 [2.854]		2.796 E−1	1.923 E−1
[2]	1.505 E+0 [0.515]	1.009 E+0 [0.338]			3.394 E−5 [3.158]		2.734 E−1	2.319 E−1
[45–49] [1]	−3.354 E+0 [−1.311]	−3.685 E+0 [−1.367]	−1.521 E−1 [−1.287]	1.010 E−2 [1.405]	−4.422 E−5 [−1.062]	2.053 E−9 [1.976]	4.758 E−1	3.939 E−1
[2]	−4.106 E+0 [−1.584]	−4.579 E+0 [−1.728]			4.128 E−5 [4.328]		3.486 E−1	3.114 E−1
[40–49] [1]	−2.541 E−1 [−0.155]	−7.940 E−1 [−0.461]	−2.419E−1 [−3.199]	7.358 E−5 [0.160 E−1]	−4.805 E−5 [−1.803]	2.077 E−9 [3.124]	6.865 E−1	6.375 E−1
[2]	−6.211 E−1 [0.273]	−1.071 E+0 [−0.460]			3.766 E−5 [4.499]		3.917 E−1	3.570 E−1

Note: t-statistics are in parentheses.

The coefficients of *SCALE* are estimated to be positive in the case where we regress the promotion probability of the total number of workers onto several explanatory variables. This indicates that, in general, ordinary workers in larger companies have more chances of being promoted. The increase of the scale of company gives an advantage of promotion and therefore working incentives to workers.

The examination of the relationship between *SCALE* and promotion probability in each age group shows that the relationship differs among age groups. Although the coefficients are not statistically significant, the negative coefficients in the estimations of workers 30 to 39 years old show that the probability of young workers being promoted is lower in larger companies. In contrast, the estimations of workers 40 to 49 years old show that the probability of older workers being promoted is higher in larger companies as a whole. However, it may also be important to note the fact that the coefficient of *SCALE* turns out to be negative and that of $SCALE^{**}2$ is significantly positive when we include both variables together in estimating the effect of the scale of the company on promotion. In the case of workers from 40 to 45 years old, both of the coefficients of these explanatory variables are especially significant. By calculating $-a4/(2 \times a5)$, we obtain approximately 10,000 workers. This implies that the promotion rate of older workers decreases until a company becomes very large.

We should here note that the majority of companies which were analysed in this study have less than 10,000 blue-collar workers. The positive correlation between promotion probability and the scale of companies which were observed in the estimation of whole workers may be mainly attributed to the positive correlation between those variables of older workers in sufficiently large companies.

From this, it may be implied that the growth of company has strong negative effects on the working incentive of older workers. The analysis of promotion possibility here shows that if older workers remain at the bottom rung of the hierarchical ladder, they are not benefited either by the growth of the company itself or by the result of this growth and they have less chances of promotion than younger workers until the company becomes sufficiently large.

We have, however, to consider the fact that our data may underestimate the number of supervisory workers, especially in the cases of large scale companies. The data only take into account the number of foremen and workers in submanagerial positions but not those in higher managerial positions. Considering the fact that larger companies have more layers in their job hierarchies, it is possible that workers in large companies may actually have a greater probability of being promoted when they take position of responsibility higher than those of foremen and subsection supervisors.

The discussion above may suggest a new interpretation of wage–tenure profile. Economists have observed steeper wage–tenure profiles in large and growing companies[13]. Those who support the human capital theory interpret this to mean that, in larger companies, workers undertake more human capital investment and, as a result, the workers' productivity increases at a later stage of employment in tandem with their wages. The same argument may be applied to the case of growing companies. On the other hand, those economists who emphasize imperfect information on workers' performance offer the explanation that, since it is difficult to observe each worker's performance in large companies, those companies tend to make wage–tenure profiles steeper so that workers may lose potential future wage increases if they are found to be shirking, and fired. The findings of our study, however, indicate that expanding or large companies have to increase the wages of the older workers since they need to compensate for the disadvantage which is caused by the decrease of promotion probability in so far as they wish to maintain their workers' working incentive at a high level. This also implies that companies which are highly desirous of growth need to have a wage system which increases wages automatically as workers stay longer or become older such as the Nenko wage system in Japanese companies, thus keeping work motivation high.

5.5 EMPIRICAL ANALYSIS: THE EFFECTS OF EMPLOYMENT CHANGES ON AVERAGE WAGES

This section will consider an empirical analysis of wage increments with tenure and seniority in large companies in the Japanese automobile and electric industries, both of which represent a high rate growth sector within the Japanese economy.

By differentiating equation (4) with respect to w, L and L_2,[14] we obtain

$$\Delta w^* = [1 + (d - 1)L_2/L] \, \Delta w - w(d - 1)L_2/L^2 \, \Delta L$$
$$+ \, w(d - 1)L_1/L^2 \, \Delta L_2. \tag{12}$$

The statistics of the average age of workers will be interpreted as being a representative of L_2. The average age (AGE), in the case of a two-term model, is

$$AGE = (L_1 + 2L_2)/L$$

and, using the relation that $\Delta L_1 + \Delta L_2 = \Delta L$, we have

$$\Delta AGE = (L_1/L^2) \, \Delta \, L_2.$$

By substituting this into equation (12), the following equation can be obtained for estimation purposes

$$
\begin{aligned}
\Delta w^* &= [1 + (d - 1)L_2/L] \, \Delta w - w(d - 1)L_2/L^2 \, \Delta L \\
&\quad + w(d - 1) \, \Delta AGE \\
&= [1 + (d - 1)L_2/L] \, \Delta w - w(d - 1)L_2/L \, (\Delta L/L) \\
&\quad + w(d - 1) \, AGE \, (\Delta AGE/AGE).
\end{aligned}
\tag{13}
$$

This equation means that we can predict a negative coefficient of $\Delta L/L$ and positive coefficients of $\Delta AGE/AGE$ if $d > 1$, that is, if wage increases with respect to tenure or age.

Equation (13) has been applied to the top seven companies in the automobile industry and also to the top six companies in the electronic industry. It is interesting to examine the differences among those companies since the nominated companies are producing similar goods in each industry. In addition, the annual rates of change in basic wages are coordinated among these electronic companies and although the rates of the automobile companies are determined individually, the differences are marginal.

The analysis is based on the statistical data of the annual increment in the average wages which are contracted in the Spring Wage Offensive as the representative of Δw. The wage increment is negotiated on the basis of current employment structure. After the wage change settlements, however, companies adjust their employment structure in response to various changes in economic circumstances throughout the year. As the result, the actual average wage increments Δw^* which are presented in *Report on Securities (Yuka Shoken Hokokusho)* become different from the wage increment negotiated in spring.

The data of average wages, average ages and contracted wages in the Spring Wage Offensive for individual companies are available in the *Current Report on Labor Administration* (*Rosei Jiho*) and the information regarding the number of employees is collated from the *Report on Securities*. The years from 1973 to 1989 are used for estimation purposes.

Tables 5.2 and 5.3 list the results of estimations for the automobile companies and the electronics companies, respectively. With each company, we present the results of the regression of Δw^* on $(\Delta L/L)$ and $(\Delta AGE/AGE)$.

There are several findings to be noted. Firstly, as our model describes, the negative coefficients of employment growth imply that the growth of a company decreases the average wage. In other words, the company may have an incentive to grow since growth is not accompanied by the same rate of increase in labour costs. This might be one of reasons for the fact that Japanese companies appear to be more anxious for growth than companies in other countries.

Secondly, the R^2s of the regression show the extent to which the annual increase in average wage is explained by $(\Delta L/L)$ and $(\Delta AGE/AGE)$. In the case of the automobile industry, approximately from 30 to 75 percent of an average wage increase is determined by these two variables. In the case of the electronics industry, the R^2s indicate that more than 50 percent of an average wage increase is explained by those variables in four companies.

Thirdly, our conjecture in the previous section, that wage increases with respect to tenure or age are to be found in the growing or large companies such as those being examined here, is strongly supported. In five automobile companies out of seven, the coefficients of $(\Delta L/L)$ are negative and three of them are statistically significant in one-sided test at the 5 percent criterion. The rest of the coefficients are positive but not significant. The coefficients of $(\Delta AGE/AGE)$ are positive in five companies and three of them are significant. In six electronics companies, the five coefficients of $(\Delta L/L)$ are negative. The coefficients of $(\Delta AGE/AGE)$ are positive in all electronics companies and four of them are significant. It may be thus safely concluded that 'd' in equation (12) is very likely to be greater than 1 in these industries.

A final fourth consideration is that the positive coefficients of $(\Delta AGE/AGE)$ also provide an implication for the economy where younger people are more likely to be employed than older people. The estimation shows that the employment of older workers increases labour costs. The companies therefore may be keener on reducing the number of older workers paid higher wages than young workers. This is a problem which should

Table 5.2 Wage estimations of automobile companies

	C	$\Delta L/L$	$\Delta AGE/AGE$	Adj R2	D–W
NIS (AR1)	−2106.21 [−4.5723]	2852.64 [0.2695]	91753.3 [2.7332]	0.3004	2.0038
TOY (OLS)	−1009.88 [−0.9487]	−32023.6 [−1.8496]	26187.3 [0.4294]	0.3877	1.8678
SUB (OLS)	−3316.19 [−5.0008]	−29017.2 [−1.0320]	88721.6 [1.4654]	0.3695	1.8577
HON (AR1)	−5111.2 [−3.7895]	14.4357 [0.0027]	186893 [4.2813]	0.6334	1.8100
MAZ (AR1)	−1122.55 [−0.9918]	−131978 [−2.8362]	−141823 [−1.4023]	0.3830	2.0593
SUZ (OLS)	−3485.99 [−4.6355]	−23145.8 [−1.4426]	154881 [3.0315]	0.7404	2.0428
DAH (OLS)	−1751.37 [−2.1149]	−375527.1 [−1.9801]	−167717 [−3.2318]	0.3883	1.9363

Notes: t-statistics are in parentheses.
The adjusted R^2 of AR1 are based on original data.
The Durbin–Watson statistics (D–W) are based on transformed data.

Table 5.3 Wage estimations of electronics companies

	C	$\Delta L/L$	$\Delta AGE/AGE$	Adj R^2	D–W
HIT (AR1)	−4923.77 [−4.1123]	−15032.1 [−0.5122]	224928 [2.3447]	0.5418	1.9617
TOS (AR1)	−4829.76 [−6.7344]	−17231.6 [−0.8170]	239829 [4.5491]	0.7269	2.1985
MAT (OLS)	−2598.49 [−2.3960]	−15247.2 [−1.4084]	25385.6 [0.4564]	0.1385	1.9771
MIT (OLS)	−4793.41 [−9.3813]	−24947.9 [−1.2466]	162026 [5.2157]	0.7922	2.0884
NEC (AR1)	−3786.96 [−3.8870]	1193.27 [0.0518]	135189 [2.4658]	0.3669	1.8293
FUJI (AR1)	−604.496 [−0.3554]	−31663 [−1.5496]	1826.33 [0.0876]	0.5534	1.9833

Notes: t-statistics are in parentheses.
The adjusted R^2 of AR1 are based on original data.
The Durbin–Watson statistics (D–W) are based on transformed data.

be taken into account given the increased and growing percentage of an aging labour force.

5.6 CONCLUSION

This chapter has attempted to present a model of the hierarchical firm to explain why Japanese firms are strongly motivated toward expanding employment under the seniority wage system. According to our model, since employment expansion works to elevate workers' incentive by increasing the promotion probability for senior workers and to decrease the average wage through changing the age composition of employees, the firm's incentive to grow is higher than the traditional theory of the firm implies. Interestingly, facing an increase in the product demand, the firm decreases its product price, because the marginal cost in terms of labour efficiency decreases as production and hence employment expand.

To support our model empirically, we regressed the ratio of foremen to ordinary workers on the growth rate, the average age of the labour force and the total number of workers of a company. When we estimate the equation for all age groups together, we found that promotion possibility increases when a company is expanding its number of employees. It is also interesting to note that workers in younger age groups are more likely to be promoted to a higher rank when a company is growing faster. This is probably because a company may not further assess the ability of workers who have already been assessed as being incompetent at some stage of their employment, and because more competent workers are more easily found among younger workers since they are better at mastering new technology.

We also analyzed empirically the effects of employment changes on the average wages by regressing the actual average wage increments on the contracted ones, the rates of change of employment and the changes of the average age of employees. The results are favourable to our model. In particular, the negative effect of employment changes on the average wages is statistically significant. It may thus be proposed that expansion is beneficial even for a firm.

Notes

* The authors would like to thank Naoki Mitani, Atsushi Yashiro, Hiroyuki Chuma, Charles Brown, Stephen Nickell and other participants at the Biwaxo conference, Osaka (July 1992) for their helpful suggestions. We also wish to thank Yoko Sano and Takao Kato, seminar participants at Osaka City University for very helpful comments. Financial support from the Kikawada Foundation is gratefully acknowledged.

1. Supporting the traditional view, Ono (1989) claims that as a determinant of wage profiles, ages are more important than tenure, external experience and education in Japan. Here 'more important' means that age is statistically significant as an explanatory variable even if the other determinants are controlled, and the variability of wages explained by age is large. Ono's findings imply that the 'Career' hypothesis and the human capital theory are not powerful in explaining the Japanese wages.

2. According to the case studies made by Meddoff and Abraham (1980), senior workers are not necessarily more productive in the jobs of the same grades.

3. Some senior workers are probably not appropriate for managerial position in ability or in character. In this case the potential source of foremen is less than L_2. But this does not significantly change our analysis.

4. This is one of the serious problems of aging workers which Japanese firms face today.

5. See Yellen (1984) for a survey on this hypothesis.

6. Along the line of Carmichael(1983) we can interpret xL/L_2 as representing the duration of assuming a foreman for an individual senior. That is, if the ratio increases, he can be promoted earlier in the second period and become more motivated. In this case, the firm is assumed to hire workers at every point of time and a senior is promoted when a vacancy due to retirement appears in a senior position.

7. As pointed out by Professor H. Chuma at the 30th Memorial Conference in Osaka, we can analyze our model in terms of the growth rate of the firm instead of the level of activity. In this case we must particularly assume, for simplicity of analysis, that the firm is in a steady state where the inflow of its labor force is equal to the outflow. In turn, the model developed in this chapter implicitly assumes that the firm does not maximize its profit for the multiple periods, but only for the current period.

8. One can argue that this automatic promotion does not necessarily motivate workers to work hard, yet we assume that when workers cheat or shirk, they are assessed badly by the firm or dismissed. When dismissed, they cannot obtain a higher wage in the next period, and when assessed badly, they will be looked upon as being inappropriate for a higher position. This possibility for junior workers not to be promoted can be easily introduced to the present model.

9. Ariga, Brunello, Ohkusa and Nishiyama (1992) also analyzed the effects of the firm's growth on the promotion possibility of incumbent workers, their optimal skill level, the span of control and the wage–tenure profile, focusing on the tradeoff between production efficiency and the minimization of the agency costs. It is important to note that in their model the rate of growth is given for the firm. Our model, however, assumes that the wage–tenure profile is given in the short term.

10. After having written this chapter, we read Brunello's interesting paper(1992), which shows that 'with internal promotion the bargained profit sharing parameter can be positive even if insiders face no unemployment risk' (Brunello, 1992, p. 571).
11. Professors Nickell and Segawa kindly recommended us to do this.
12. This does not deny that workers' incentive is an important factor in determining the span of control. In reality many Japanese firms provide special staff posts, which are seemingly managerial under titles such as assistant section chief and directive aide, to those who are left off the lines. But this is only for white-collar workers, and does not seem to motivate them fully.
13. See Higuchi(1991), for example.
14. We assumed in the theoretical model that L_2 is fixed because the firm can not control L_2, but here in this empirical analysis we differentiate equation (4) with L_2 since L_2 changes as time passes.

References

Ariga, K., G. Brunello, Y. Ohkusa and Y. Nishiyama (1992) 'Corporate Hierarchy, Promotion and firm Growth: Japanese Internal Labor Market in Transition', *Journal of the Japanese and International Economies*.
Aoki, M. (1982) 'Equilibrium Growth of the Hierarchical Firm: Shareholder–Employee Cooperative Game Approach', *American Economic Review*, December pp. 1097–1110.
——— (1987) *The Cooperative Game Theory of the Firm* (Oxford, Clarendon Press.
——— (1988) *Information, Incentives, and Bargaining in the Japanese Economy* New York/Cambridge University Press.
Brunello, J. (1992) 'Profit Sharing in the Internal Labour Market', The *Economic Journal*, vol. 102, May, pp. 570–77.
Brunello, J. and F. Ohtake (1987) 'Bonusu Chingin No Ketutei Mekanizumu to Koyou: Kigyo Betu Deita Niyoru Saikou' (The Determination of Bonuses and Wages, and Employment: A Reconsideration by Firm Microdata), Osaka University Economics, vol. 37.
Carmichael, L. (1983) 'Firm-Specific Human Capital and Promotion Ladders', *Bell Journal of Economics*, vol. 14, Spring, pp. 251–58.
Freeman, R. and M.L. Weitzman (1987) 'Bonuses and Employment in Japan', *Journal of the Japanese and the International Economies*, vol. 1, June, pp. 168–94.
Gordon, R.J. (1982) 'Why U.S. Wage and Employment Behavior Differs from that in Britain and Japan', Economic Journal, vol. 92, March, pp. 13–44.
Hashimoto, M. (1979) 'Bonus Payments, On-the-job Training, and Lifetime Employment in Japan', *Journal of Political Economy*, vol. 87, October, pp. 1084–104.
Hashimoto, M. and J. Rasian (1985) 'Employment, Tenure, and Earnings Profiles in Japan and the United States', *American Economic Review*, vol. 75, September, pp. 721–35.
Higuchi, Y. (1991) *Nihon Keizai to Syugyoo Koudou* (Japanese Economy

154   *The Growth of the Firm and Promotions in Japan*

and Employment Structure) Tokyo, Toyokeizai Sinposya.

Kahn, G.A. (1984) 'International Differences in Wage Behaviour: Real, Nominal or Exaggerated?' *American Economic Review*, vol. 74, May, pp. 155–59.

Koike, K. (1977) *Shokuba no Rodo Kumiai to Sanka – Roshi Kankei no Nichibei Hikaku* (A Comparative Study of Industrial Relations on The Shopfloor in the United States and Japan), Tokyo, Toyokeizai.

Koike, K. (1981) *Nihon no Jukuren* (Skill Formation Systems in Japan), Tokyo, Yuhikaku.

Koike, K. (1988) *Understanding Industrial Relations in Modern Japan*, London; Macmillan.

Koshiro, K. (1986) 'Gainsharing, Wage Flexibility and Macro-Economic Performance in Japan', *Discussion Paper Series*, Faculty of Economics, Yokohama National University.

Lazear, E.P. (1979) 'Why Is There Mandatory Retirement?', *Journal of Political Economy*, vol. 87, December, pp. 1261–84.

Medoff, James L. and G.A. Katharine (1980) 'Experience, Performance, and Earnings', *Quarterly Journal of Economics*, vol. 95, December, pp. 703–36.

Mincer, J. and Y. Higuchi (1988) 'Wage Structures and Labor Turnover, in the United States and Japan', *Journal of the Japanese and International Economies*, vol. 2, June, pp. 97–133.

Mizuno, A. (1985) 'An Economic Analysis of Wage Flexibility and Employment Fluctuation in Japan', *Pacific Economic Papers*, no. 124, Canberra, Australia–Japan Research Center.

Ohashi, I, (1989) 'On the Determinants of Bonuses and Basic Wages in Large Japanese Firms', *Journal of the Japanese and International Economies*, vol. 3, December, pp. 451–79.

Ono, A. (1989) *Nihonteki Koyo Kankou to Rodo Shijo* (The Japanese Employment Practices and the Labor Market), Tokyo, Toyo Keizai Shinposha.

Organization for Economic Cooperation and Development (OECD) (1977) *Flexibility in the Labour Market*, (Paris, OECD, 1986).

Sachs, J. (1979) 'Wages, Profits, and Macroeconomic Adjustment: A Comparative Study', *Brookings Pap. Econ. Act.* vol. 2, pp. 269–319.

Shimada, H. (1988) *Hyuman Wea no Keizaigaku* (The Economy of Human Ware), Tokyo, Iwanami Shoten.

Weitzman, M.L. (1987) 'Some Macroeconomic Implications of Alternative Compensation Systems, *Economic Journal,* vol. 93, December, pp. 763–83.

Weitzman, M.L. (1984) *The Share Economy*, Cambridge, MA/ Harvard University Press.

——— 'The Simple Macroeconomics of Profit Sharing', *American Economic Review*, vol. 75, December, pp. 937–53.

White, M. and M. Trevor (1985) *Under Japanese Management*, London, Heineman Educational.

Yellen, J. (1984) 'Efficiency Wage Models of Unemployment', *American Economic Review*, vol. 74, May, pp. 200–5.

6 Effects of Job Training and Productivity Growth on Retention of Male and Female Workers in Japan

Yoshio Higuchi*

6.1 INTRODUCTION

The relationship between the low job turnover rate and the seniority wage system in the Japanese labour market has drawn the attention of specialists both at home and abroad and has been invoked by many researchers. The relationship of the job separation rate and the wage structure has been analyzed from several economic perspectives such as human capital theory (Hashimoto and Raisian, 1985; Mincer and Higuchi, 1988), information sharing among employees (Aoki, 1988), stimulation of work motivation (Shapiro and Stiglitz, 1984; Spark, 1986) and the avoidance of cheating (Lazear, 1979). It has also been approached from a cultural perspective (the Japanese cultural background of upbringing and historical tradition). However, this relationship has mostly been discussed in connection with male employees. In fact, there have been few studies of the Japanese female retention rate.

In present day Japan, females account for 40 percent of the total labour force. As a result, it is possible that by limiting our analyses to male employees, we may be losing sight of the overall characteristics of the Japanese labour market. Many Japanese companies point out that the biggest problem in employing female workers as core members of the companies is their high job separation rate. It is said that Japanese companies put emphasis on internal job experience to provide job training through on-the-job training (OJT) and by sharing information. For these companies, the low separation rate of workers is essential in order to develop human resources.

Table 6.1   Job separation rates of male and female employees in the US and Japan (annual rates, %)

	US (1977)		Japan (1977)		Japan (1987)	
	Male	Female	Male	Female	Male	Female
Total	17.3	19.7	4.6	13.3	7.0	15.5
Age 18–24	36.4	33.8	8.8	17.8	19.5	23.4
25–34	18.6	20.2	4.3	18.8	7.1	20.8
35–44	12.2	15.0	2.5	8.5	4.2	11.6
45–54	8.2	11.8	1.9	6.8	4.0	9.0
55–59	8.9	9.7	4.4	10.3	9.5	12.9

Note: Total separation rates are calculated from the data between age 18 and 59 in the US, between age 15 and 64 in 1977, and between age 15 and 59 in 1987 in Japan. Also, Japanese separation rates in the row of age 18–24 are those between age 15 and 24, and those in the row of age 55–59 in 1977 are between age 55 and 64. In the US data, those who were temporarily laid off and recalled in a year are not included as separators.

Sources: US, *Current Population Survey* (S. E. Haber, E. J. Camar and G. Green, A New Method for Estimating Job Separation by Sex and Race, *Monthly Labor Review*, June 1983).
Japan, *Employment Structure Survey*.

On the other hand, economic theory shows that companies with high quasi-fixed labour costs including human capital tend to require their workers to have long working hours (Rosen, 1969; Ohashi, 1990). Long and rigid working hours assigned by Japanese firms might prevent female workers from staying in companies for many years.

By making cross-comparisons of industries and schools within Japan, this chapter will attempt to examine the impact of increased job training and productivity on the wage structure and the firm retention rates of not only male but also female workers. By examining the working environment in this manner, the chapter will consider the strengths and weaknesses of the Japanese labour market.

Table 6.1 shows the job separation rate by age and sex in Japan and in the US. Although the job separation rate has risen in recent years in Japan, in the case of male workers, the rate remains substantially lower than in the US. Of interest is that there is very little disparity in separation rates between American males and females while in Japan, the separation rate for females is dramatically higher than for males.[1] The reasons for this discrepancy between Japan and the US lie in the different roles attached to males and females in the household and the Japanese male's role as the breadwinner. At the same time, this role difference may be interrelated with the greater level of anticipation placed on male workers within the firm. However, it might be true that these roles of male and female in households and in firms are influenced not only by cultural elements but also by economic reasons such as a change in labour shortage conditions. To examine the impact that job training has on work force retention rates, we shall refer to a survival analysis based on data for the younger segment of the Japanese workforce. This examination will also enable us to consider the situation by relating background factors such as supply and demand behaviour.

Section 6.2 will explain the theoretical framework and the data used in this chapter. Section 6.3 will disclose the estimated wage equations for males and females and the survival analysis findings. By examining these equations, we will attempt to study the impact of job training on both male and female wage structures as well as on retention rates. Job training will be divided into several categories by content. In section 6.4, the data and references used for section 6.3 will be analyzed in greater detail according to levels of schooling. Findings have shown that, particularly in the case of females, the effects of job training and productivity on retention rates are different by educational level. In the case of female high school graduates, job training has proved to be effective in increasing the firm retention rate; however, in the case of female university graduates, findings based on human capital theory are not conclusive. Furthermore, examples of decisive factors for a high firm retention rate among female university graduates are flexibility of the companies in accommodating working hours to employees' needs and the existence of a childcare leave programme. Section 6.5 will present provisional concluding remarks.

6.2 THE SURVIVAL MODEL AND PRELIMINARIES

Theories of human capital investment in worker skills have been used to explain tenure and experience wage profiles and to link them to turnover patterns across workers. The greater emphasis on training and retraining, much of it specific to the firm, is supposed to result in steeper wage trajectories and in low job separation rates.

In this chapter, we apply this human capital hypothesis to the Japanese labour market, and study whether the above relationship is apparent in both male and female workers by making cross-comparison of various industrial sectors in Japan.

It is quite difficult to approach job training quantitatively as a statistic. Data pertaining to this issue has not been used extensively except for some specialized research (Lillard and Tan, 1986; Mincer, 1984). However, in this chapter, the human capital hypothesis will be examined, and our remarks will be based on the *Survey on Labor Management of Female Workers* carried out by the Ministry of Labor in 1984.[2] This survey considered labour policies in firms and the rate of training, among other items. As shown in Table 6.2, the survey probed 11 items for both male and female workers. Since the survey was carried out through a reply questionnaire, the accuracy of the training execution cannot be fully guaranteed. Furthermore, there is also the problem that the available data merely represent statistical rates for firms that have conducted 11 job training courses and whose results have been totalled by industry and by firm size. However, at the moment, this is the only available reference survey on training for males and females. Therefore, by relying on these data, we shall examine the human capital hypothesis.

To begin with, let us study the relationship of the rate of firms conducting training and the labour productivity growth rate for each industrial sector. We can interpret this relationship in two ways. First, in industrial sectors enjoying buoyant productivity growth and fast technological advancement, we can hypothesize that training is imperative for building new skills or improving already existing skills (Mincer and Higuchi, 1988). The other interpretation is that job training is very effective in raising labour productivity.

Table 6.3 shows the correlation coefficients of the variables. According to Table 6.3, the correlation coefficient is low for basic training that is conducted when an employee joins the company. Statistically, this value is not significant. On the other hand, job training that is conducted at a later date to gain further knowledge or skill, and knowledge and skills training that is deemed necessary for job transfer or promotions is assumed to yield high correlation coefficients. This kind of training is conducted more actively in industrial sectors where productivity growth rates are higher. Furthermore, cross-comparisons of males and females show that, for introductory training, the correlation coefficient is higher for females; however, when it comes to more advanced training for building skills, it is higher for males.

Table 6.2 The proportion of firms giving job training by content (%)

Content of job training	Proportion of firms giving that kind of job training	The same content for male and female workers	Different content for male and female workers	Training only for male workers	Training only for female workers	Proportion of firms not giving that kind of job training
1. Attending to customers	54.6	75.8	6.4	3.9	13.9	45.4
2. General and basic knowledge and skill such as orientation	58.1	83.3	6.5	8.5	1.7	42.0
3. Basic knowledge and skill at each division and occupation	67.7	72.1	12.3	14.2	1.4	32.3
4. Improvement in knowledge and skill at current job	66.1	57.7	9.6	32.1	0.6	33.9
5. Required knowledge and skill in the reassigned but same-level position	32.9	49.3	10.4	39.9	0.4	67.1
6. Required knowledge and skill in the higher-level position before reassignment	34.3	40.9	13.3	45.6	0.2	65.7
7. Required knowledge and skill in the higher-level position after reassignment	36.1	40.1	10.4	49.5	0.0	63.9
8. Required knowledge of supervisor	29.8	36.2	6.1	57.8	0.0	70.2
9. Required knowledge of supervisor after promotion	33.6	35.7	5.9	58.4	0.0	66.4
10. Required knowledge for promotion to the managerial position	28.5	24.6	3.0	72.4	0.0	71.5
11. Required knowledge for promotion to the managerial position after promotion	35.5	25.4	3.2	71.4	0.0	64.5

Source: Survey on Labour Management of Female Workers, Ministry of Labour, 1984.

Table 6.3   Correlation coefficients between the execution rate of job training in firms and the growth rate of labour productivity by industry

Content of job training	Male	Female
1. Attending to customers	0.1128	0.0530
2. General and basic knowledge and skill such as orientation	0.1919	0.2765*
3. Basic knowledge and skill at each division and occupation	0.3555*	0.4942*
4. Improvement in knowledge and skill at current job	0.4613**	0.5769**
5. Required knowledge and skill in the reassigned but same-level position	0.5387**	0.5676**
6. Required knowledge and skill in the higher-level position before reassignment	0.5502**	0.5032**
7. Required knowledge and skill in the higher-level position after reassignment	0.5664**	0.4964**
8. Required knowledge of supervisor	0.5226**	0.4139**
9. Required knowledge of supervisor after promotion	0.5306**	0.4516**
10. Required knowledge for promotion to the managerial position	0.5335**	0.3221*
11. Required knowledge for promotion to the managerial position after promotion	0.5278**	0.3424*

Note: The productivity is the average annual growth rate of real labour productivity between 1982 and 1987 (at market prices calendar year, 1980, *Annual Report on National Accounts*). The number of industries is 20, shown in footnote 5.
**: 1% significant.
*: 5% significant.

Source: *Survey on Labour Management of Female Workers*, 1984.

To examine the impact each type of job training has on retention rates, we shall apply survival analysis here. The *Employment Structure Survey* that was executed in 1987 surveyed the record of job changes, employment history, the number of years of tenure, the industrial sector and the firm size at the previous job and the current job. To carry out the survival analysis, a non-censored sample (leavers) was established consisting of employees with a job separation record, regardless of whether they are presently employed or out of the labour market. A censored sample (stayers) consisted of employees who did not have a job separation record and who were still currently employed by the same company that they had joined upon graduation. The effects of each factor are analyzed based on the maximum likelihood estimation method (Miller, 1981; Kiefer, 1988; Tachibanaki and Taki, 1990).

T represents the period from joining a firm until separation, and X represents the explanatory variables for job duration, including job training variables. We hypothetically express the duration of employment by a stochastic variable: $T = \exp(X'\beta)T_0$. T_0 represents the period from joining a firm until the person at the $X = 0$ baseline leaves the job and forms the hypothetical distribution. Establishing y and y_0 as the logarithm for T and T_0 respectively brings us to (1)

$$y = X'\beta + y_0. \tag{1}$$

Under these circumstances, the survival probability (continued employment rate) in t years after joining the firms becomes

$$\text{prob}(T > t\,/X) = \text{prob}(T_0 > \exp(-X'\beta)t). \tag{2}$$

Usually, for this type of model, μ is designated as the constant term for demonstrating the difference in the duration length from joining a firm until the job separation activities for the individual to the baseline. σ is then introduced as the scale parameter.

Let us now consider the likelihood of the occurrence of a job separation for each of the two kinds of samples. Since the non-censored sample consists of those who already have separated from their jobs, job tenure from the time of hire until job separation (period T) from the previous job is conclusive and observable. Assuming that the probability function of job separation for the period T is $g(T)$, the likelihood of a sample of this nature will be $g(T)$. On the other hand, for those who are still employed by the company that they first joined, t will represent the period from joining up until the time that this survey was conducted. The overall employment duration including the period up until the time when a job change occurs in the future is then established as T. Taking into consideration that this employee has never resigned from a job, we can conclude that the likelihood of this sample is the probability that the employee will remain for the period t : prob $(T \geq t) = G(t)$. Assuming then that the flag, δ_i, for those who have separated from firms is 1 and that for those who stay on is 0 and establishing the probability function and the probability of remaining as $f(W)$ and $F(W)$ instead of $g(T)$ and $G(T)$ respectively after converting the variables so that $W_i = (y_i - X_i'\beta)/\sigma$, the likelihood for the overall sample will be represented by equation (3)

$$\log L = \Sigma_i \{(\delta_i \log (f(W_i)/\sigma) + (1 - \delta_i) \log (F(W_i))\}. \qquad (3)$$

The parameter which maximizes the above equation will be none other than the maximum likelihood of this model.

Assuming that the time from joining a firm until separation is in accordance with the Weibull distribution, we shall make an estimate for each parameter. We also estimated the survival model assuming the log normal distribution and the log logistic distribution, but our conclusions remained unchanged.[3]

At the same time, let us use the rates of firms in the industrial sectors relevant to the samples and which have carried out job training as the explanatory variable X for (1) to examine the effects of job training on retention rates. Furthermore, we add the educational level dummy variable for each sample (dummy variables for high school, junior college and university graduates, respectively, with junior high school graduates as the comparison base) while $K1$ and $K2$ are established as firm size dummy variables (dummy variables for a firm with 100–999 employees, with 1000 employees or more, and with less than 100 workers as a comparison base) as explanatory variables. Finally, dummy variables will also be provided to show whether each sample lives in one of the 11 major cities or not. Since the item on wage rates was not included in the survey, it must be estimated from another data source. We use the wage rate level and wage–tenure slope by sex in the corresponding industry of the sample that are estimated in the following way from the 1987 *Basic Wage Structure Survey*

$$\log w = c_0 + c_1 S + c_2 S^2 + c_3 K1 + c_4 K2 + c_5 A + c_6 A^2$$
$$+ c_7 T + \Sigma_j \gamma_j \text{IND}_j + \Sigma_j \Theta_j \text{IND}_j \times T. \qquad (4)$$

In this equation, S represents the educational level, A represents the age, T represents the number of years of job tenure. As a wage rate, the hourly wage rate including the annual bonuses of regular employees was used. Instead of the age variable, we might have to put the external job experience as an independent variable, in accordance with human capital theory. But our data source does not include the item of job history, and the variable, external job experience, defined by age−years of schooling−6, cannot be measured, in particular for female workers because they have been out of the labour market. The industrial IND_j is a dummy variable of medium industrial classification (20 industries) with the food manufacturing industry used as the comparison base.[4] The estimated coefficients, γ_j and Θ_j, represent the relative levels of the wage standard and the effects of the job tenure on wages in the respective industries when compared to the base industry. The γ_j and the Θ_j are used as the independent variable X for equation (3) in the survival analysis. By doing so, we are supposed to be able to quantitatively grasp how wage levels and the number of years of continuous employment affect the job duration in the respective industries.

6.3   ESTIMATED EFFECTS OF JOB TRAINING ON THE WAGE STRUCTURE AND RETENTION RATE

First, for each firm, let us study the impact of firm job training on the wage structure. We shall use the 1987 *Basic Wage Structure Survey* referred to earlier. Table 6.4 shows the estimated wage rate equations for males and females as shown in equation (5). H represents the execution rates (percent) of job-training in companies corresponding to the sample respondents.

$$\log w = c_0 + c_1 S + c_2 S^2 + c_3 A + c_4 A^2 + c_5 K1 \qquad (5)$$
$$+ c_6 K2 + c_7 T + c_8 T^2 + c_9 H + c_{10} H \times T$$

The estimated coefficients, shown in Table 6.4, of the educational level, the age and the number of years of job tenure show the theoretically expected positive effects on the wage rate. Male–female cross-comparisons reveal that the impact difference by the scale of the firm was greater among females.

Let us now study the estimated findings of c_9. For both 'Job Training for Basic Knowledge and Skill at each Division and Occupation' as well as 'Job Training for Improvement in Knowledge and Skill at

Table 6.4 The estimated results of wage equations on job training

	Job training for basic knowledge and skill at each division and occupation		Job training for improvement in knowledge and skill at current job		Labour productivity growth rate	
	Male	Female	Male	Female	Male	Female
Constant	0.16315 (2.024)	0.22056 (1.556)	0.38456 (5.071)	0.25658 (1.806)	0.37562 (4.949)	0.21273 (1.490)
School year	0.02131 (2.054)	0.08984 (4.185)	0.01793 (1.703)	0.09941 (4.580)	0.02374 (2.221)	0.11302 (5.169)
(School year)^2	$0.1843E - 2$ (4.560)	$0.8828E - 4$ (0.101)	$0.2075E - 2$ (5.065)	$-0.1952E - 3$ (−0.221)	$0.2007E - 2$ (4.826)	$-0.6948E - 3$ (−0.782)
Age	0.06614 (41.939)	0.02797 (12.265)	0.06497 (40.643)	0.02769 (12.003)	0.06440 (39.741)	0.02696 (11.581)
Age^2	$-0.6855E - 3$ (−36.538)	$-0.3563E - 3$ (−12.320)	$-0.6691E - 3$ (−35.202)	$-0.3491E - 3$ (−11.933)	$-0.6626E - 3$ (−34.357)	$-0.3374E - 3$ (−11.431)
Medium firm	0.11715 (19.204)	0.20304 (19.609)	0.11730 (18.953)	0.20765 (19.819)	0.11787 (18.741)	0.21419 (20.259)
Large firm	0.26309 (42.782)	0.35349 (31.601)	0.26632 (42.696)	0.36973 (32.551)	0.26709 (41.951)	0.39199 (34.392)
Tenure	0.01485 (8.198)	0.03312 (11.145)	0.02971 (28.321)	0.04596 (21.816)	0.03453 (36.055)	0.05090 (27.082)
Tenure^2	$-0.3770E - 3$ (−15.186)	$-0.7193E - 3$ (−12.167)	$-0.3633E - 2$ (−14.418)	$-0.7392E - 3$ (−12.378)	$-0.353 E - 3$ (−13.811)	$-0.7564E - 3$ (−12.553)
Job training (productivity growth)	$0.3793E - 2$ (9.058)	$0.3444E - 4$ (6.471)	$0.1762E - 2$ (6.193)	$0.1931 E - 4$ (3.637)	$0.5564E - 2$ (4.321)	$-0.2197E - 3$ (−0.131)
Job training $\times$ Tenure	$0.3102E - 3$ (13.132)	$0.4597E - 5$ (8.910)	$0.1582E - 3$ (9.907)	$0.3732E - 5$ (7.263)	$0.2690E - 3$ (3.324)	$0.8991E - 3$ (5.353)
R^2	0.6648	0.5083	0.6552	0.4973	0.6444	0.4886

Current Job' indicated on Table 6.4, c_9 generally indicates a statistically significant positive figure. This shows the high wage rates in industries which have high job training execution rates. The estimated value of c_{10} is also a significant positive figure, reflecting the high wage–tenure slope in industries where job training is regularly carried out. On the other hand, coefficients for males and females show that the figure is by no means smaller for females. Even for females, there is a visible impact of job training on the growth of wage rates, or the tenure–wage slope. Similar findings were obtained for other types of training although these will not be discussed here.[5]

Next, we examine the impact of job training on the retention rate. Table 6.5 shows the statistics of the sample means and standard deviations which were used. The target sample was limited to relatively young males and females who were recruited as regular full-time employees between 1978 and 1987 and had been out of school for 15 years or less. We used this data to conduct the survival analysis and the results are shown in Table 6.6. Column (1) shows the estimated findings which were sought without wage variables, while Column (2) shows the estimated findings including wage variables.

Let us first look at the results for males (Table 6.6a). Such results indicate that the higher the educational level and the greater the scale of the firm, the higher the retention rate. Next, let us study the results from the perspective of the effect of job training. Column (1) shows that the effect of general, basic knowledge and skills training was not great in males and females. On the other hand, job training for gaining further knowledge and perfecting skills, as well as for job transfer proved to be statistically highly effective in elevating the retention rate. Column (2), in which wages were added as an explanatory variable verified that both the wage rate level and the wage slope were highly effective in elevating the retention rate. However, here, job training took a negative coefficient. In other words, if wage levels or slopes are the same, the retention rate in the firms carrying out job training frequently is low. This proves that even when job training is conducted frequently, as long as it is not connected with higher wages, it simply increases efforts and expenses of employees, while resulting in a lower retention rate.

Next, let us look at the results for females (Table 6.6b). In terms of the scale of the firm the results were the same as for males. However, in terms of the educational level, there was very little difference between university and junior college graduates. This factor will be taken up in depth in section 6.4. In terms of the effect of job training, there

Table 6.5 Sample means and standard deviations

Variable	Definition	Male		Female	
		Mean	Std. Dev.	Mean	Std. Dev.
Total sample					
Number of observations		25,173		37,764	
Dummy variable for					
High School	1 if High School graduate	0.4930	0.5000	0.5829	0.4931
Junior College	1 if Junior College Graduate	0.0798	0.2709	0.2819	0.4499
College	1 if College graduate	0.3993	0.4898	0.0974	0.2966
Medium-size firm	1 if employed at a firm with 100–999 workers	0.3906	0.4879	0.2762	0.4471
Large-size firm	1 if employed at a firm with more than 1000 workers	0.3944	0.4887	0.2815	0.4498
Large city	1 if living in the 11 largest cities	0.1873	0.3902	0.1719	0.3773
Wage rate[a]		−0.0020	0.0601	0.0723	0.0776
Wage slope[b]		0.0037	0.0057	0.0041	0.0065
Age		25.6781	3.7642	25.0064	3.5967
Job tenure	Years of job tenure	4.1771	2.1647	3.4545	1.9113
Sample of leavers					
Number of observations		5,223		15,914	
Dummy variable for					
High School		0.5635	0.4960	0.6097	0.4878
Junior College		0.0814	0.2734	0.2598	0.4386
College		0.3035	0.4598	0.0832	0.2762
Medium-size firm		0.4430	0.4968	0.2681	0.4430
Large-size firm		0.2150	0.4109	0.1989	0.3992

167

Large city	0.1689	0.3747	0.1808	0.3849
Wage rate	−0.0135	0.0463	0.0632	0.0761
Wage slope	0.0034	0.0052	0.0035	0.0063
Age	26.9891	3.7456	26.6683	3.2156
Job tenure	2.5240	1.4631	2.6821	1.4874
Sample of stayers				
Number of observations	19,950		21,850	
Dummy variable for				
High School	0.4746	0.4994	0.5634	0.4960
Junior College	0.0793	0.2703	0.2979	0.4573
College	0.4244	0.4943	0.1078	0.3102
Medium-size firm	0.3769	0.4846	0.2822	0.4501
Large-size firm	0.4414	0.4966	0.3417	0.4743
Large city	0.1922	0.3940	0.1654	0.3716
Wage rate	0.0010	0.0629	0.0790	0.0781
Wage slope	0.0038	0.0058	0.0045	0.0066
Age	25.3348	3.6930	23.7960	3.3691
Job tenure	4.6099	2.1095	4.0170	1.9878

Notes:

[a] The difference in the estimated coefficient of industry dummy variable from that of the base industry (= food prod. industry) in the semi-logarithmic equation of hourly wage rate shown in section 6.2.

[b] The difference in the estimated coefficient of the product of industry dummy variable and job tenure from that of the base industry (= food prod. industry) in the semi-logarithmic equation of hourly wage rate.

Table 6.6a The estimated results of survival analysis on job training (Male)

	Job training for general and basic knowledge and basic skill such as orientation		Job training for basic knowledge and skill at each division and occupation		Job training for improvement in knowledge and skill at the current job		Job training for required knowledge and skill in the reassigned higher position	
	(1)	(2)	(3)	(4)	(5)	(6)	(7)	(8)
Constant	1.61966*	2.36098*	1.70749*	2.47004*	1.02462*	2.36004*	1.69500*	2.12379*
	(430.595)	(451.759)	(255.850)	(335.156)	(77.265)	(132.088)	(645.962)	(738.14)
Job training	0.00328*	−0.00905*	0.00150	−0.00914*	0.01181*	−0.00788*	0.00327*	−0.00807*
	(10.615)	(29.358)	(1.253)	(26.503)	(55.669)	(7.084)	(7.532)	(25.172)
Wage rate		3.74791*		3.42268		3.72687*		3.65669*
		(163.651)		(159.265)		(93.497)		(155.727)
Wage slope		27.12600*		21.0095*		19.9825*		20.13170*
		(57.978)		(54.440)		(30.485)		(52.301)
High school	0.37726*	0.38776*	0.38563*	0.38614*	0.37556*	0.37920*	0.38247*	0.38571*
	(50.727)	(53.519)	(53.034)	(53.159)	(50.448)	(51.247)	(52.217)	(53.075)
(Junior College	0.49352*	0.50157*	0.51139*	0.49902*	0.48207*	0.49589*	0.50699*	0.49749*
	(57.555)	(58.481)	(62.112)	(57.979)	(55.321)	(57.145)	(61.230)	(57.662)
University	0.65622*	0.65907*	0.67937*	0.65272*	0.64027*	0.64504*	0.67143*	0.65125*
	(135.888)	(134.941)	(147.298)	(132.756)	(131.571)	(129.492)	(144.619)	(132.251)
Medium firm	0.30088*	0.28954*	0.30001*	0.29490*	0.29265*	0.29024*	0.29608*	0.29675*
	(130.082)	(119.818)	(128.932)	(123.978)	(122.939)	(120.134)	(125.239)	(125.272)
Large firm	0.98623*	0.90745*	0.98403*	0.91849*	0.96025*	0.92791*	0.97882*	0.92272*
	(859.026)	(712.245)	(854.219)	(734.911)	(814.064)	(750.239)	(843.624)	(742.550)
Large city	0.03525	0.04989	0.03600	0.04634	0.04235	0.04579	0.03829	0.04397
	(1.324)	(2.651)	(1.381)	(2.291)	(1.910)	(2.235)	(1.560)	(2.062)
Scale para.	0.82330	0.82261	0.82370	0.82204	0.82323*	0.82232*	0.82375*	0.82183
	[0.0099]	[0.0099]	[0.0099]	[0.0099]	[0.0099]	[0.0099]	[0.0099]	[0.0099]
Log likelihood	−16109.7	−16023.3	−16114.4	−16024.5	−16086.7	−16034.5	−16111.3	−16025.3

Notes: Figures in parentheses are χ^2 statistics

Figures in brackets are standard deviations.

*: Significant at the 1% level.

Table 6.6b The estimated results of survival analysis on job training (Female)

	Job training for general and basic knowledge and skill such as orientation		Job training for basic knowledge and skill at each division and occupation		Job training for improvement in knowledge and skill at the current job		Job training for required knowledge and skill in the reassigned higher position	
	(1)	(2)	(3)	(4)	(5)	(6)	(7)	(8)
Constant	1.52884* (1791.83)	1.72892* (1370.81)	1.52346* (1271.86)	1.27682* (523.526)	1.04219* (778.254)	0.98334* (530.926)	1.44845* (2664.93)	1.36178* (1885.68)
Job training	-0.00032 (0.401)	-0.00525* (51.132)	-0.00022 (0.107)	0.00302* (11.146)	0.01121* (270.198)	0.01103* (169.90)	0.00369* (20.742)	0.00450* (17.441)
Wage rate		1.59703* (243.017)		2.01731* (301.708)		1.91689* (382.519)		1.96817* (356.582)
Wage slope		3.15360 (3.862)		-8.1827* (26.288)		-14.678* (104.697)		-8.62266* (32.295)
High School	0.14603* (33.409)	0.11902* (22.522)	0.14521* (33.156)	0.11667* (21.613)	0.13747* (29.952)	0.13216* (27.758)	0.14196* (37.719)	0.11923* (22.529)
Junior College	0.25739* (94.551)	0.15505* (33.966)	0.25632* (94.0282)	0.16379* (37.727)	0.23860* (81.910)	0.18108* (46.251)	0.25564* (93.590)	0.16606* (38.764)
University	0.23139* (56.471)	0.11602* (14.132)	0.23044* (55.782)	0.13265* (18.302)	0.23272** (57.444)	0.16061* (26.900)	0.23652* (58.916)	0.13546* (19.080)
Medium firm	0.24052* (367.060)	0.27284* (474.033)	0.24085* (361.445)	0.26640* (444.288)	0.22140* (312.483)	0.24718* (383.311)	0.23458* (364.844)	0.26625* (445.919)
Large firm	0.56343* (1510.72)	0.56678* (1557.56)	0.56322* (1450.14)	0.55413* (1439.69)	0.50179* (1185.98)	0.51986* (1265.72)	0.54649* (1388.36)	0.55342* (1450.94)
Large city	-0.12336* (80.485)	-0.12058* (78.001)	-0.12366* (80.972)	-0.12255* (80.451)	-0.11458* (69.867)	-0.11106* (65.501)	-0.12307* (80.226)	-0.12178* (79.442)
Scale para.	0.66263* [0.0043]	0.65699* [0.0042]	0.66261* [0.0043]	0.65763* [0.0042]	0.66056* [0.0043]	0.65663* [0.0042]	0.66252* [0.0043]	0.65750 [0.0042]
Log likelihood	-33766.1	-33488.8	-33766.3	-33509.1	-33623.6	-33427.4	-33755.8	-33506.0

Notes: Figures in parentheses are χ^2 statistics.
Figures in brackets are standard deviations.
*: Significant at the 1% level.

was no pronounced effect resulting from general or introductory training. However, job training to gain further knowledge and skills or to get a promotion proved overall to be significantly effective in raising the retention rate. The effect-value remained significant in comparison with males even after the wage rate variable was included. On the other hand, the wage rate levels have large and positive coefficients but the wage–tenure slopes have negative coefficients in the case of females.

Table 6.7 shows the simulation results of several cases based on these estimated coefficients.

6.4   DIFFERENCES IN MALE AND FEMALE RETENTION RATES AMONG EDUCATIONAL LEVELS

How different are the respective retention rates among males and females classified according to educational level, scale of the firm and place of residence? Table 6.8 shows the findings of the survival analysis based on pooled data comprised of male and female samples. F represents the female dummy variable, so the estimated coefficient which was obtained by multiplying the variables of the educational level, scale of the firm and large city dummy should designate the disparity between males and females for each factor. Estimated findings showed negative values for all factors. Compared with the comparison base (a junior high school graduate employed in a small company and who lives outside a large city), there was a bigger disparity in retention rates among males and females who had a higher level of education, who worked for larger companies and who resided in larger cities. Particularly in terms of educational levels, the disparity between males and females was wider for university graduates than for junior high school, high school and junior college graduates. According to the 1990 *White Paper on Industrial Relations* (Japan Productivity Center), 81 percent of Japanese large companies in a questionnaire selected the high separation rate of female university graduates as a reason impeding them from developing human resources so that females become core workers. This relatively low retention rate of female university graduates will be studied in the following parts of this section.

To examine these factors, we conducted a survival analysis by using samples classified by sex and by educational level, and adding industrial dummy variables (20 industries), scale of the firm dummy variables and urban area dummy variables.[6] If we compare the coefficients between males and females by their educational levels in the 20

Table 6.7 The simulation results of firm retention rates (%)

	5th Year	*10th Year*
Male Workers		
Base case	86.26	70.96
(large firm, High School graduate, large city, the average percentage of job training)		
Large firm, Junior College graduate	87.82	73.98
Large firm, University graduate	89.84	77.98
Medium firm, High School graduate	71.71	46.22
Medium firm, Junior College graduate	74.66	50.76
Medium firm, University graduate	78.58	57.15
Non-large city	85.59	69.69
Industry with the highest percentage of firms giving job training	89.71	77.73
(electricity, gas, heat supply, and water = 91.2%)		
Industry with the lowest percentage of firms giving job training	82.79	64.51
(textiles = 52.6%)		
Female Workers		
Base case	57.22	20.30
(large firm, High School graduate, large city)		
Large firm, Junior College graduate	61.94	25.46
Large firm, University graduate	61.67	25.15
Medium firm, High School graduate	42.59	8.74
Medium firm, Junior College graduate	48.08	12.35
Medium firm, University graduate	47.76	12.12
Non-large city	62.54	26.17
Industry with the highest percentage of firms giving job training		
(finance and insurance = 67.5%)	75.20	44..31
Industry with the lowest percentage of firms giving job training (lumber and wood products = 27.3%)	56.88	19.96

Notes: Job training is for improvement in knowledge and skill at the current job. The simulation is based on the estimated results shown in Column (5) in Table 6.6.

Table 6.8   The estimated results of survival analysis by pooled data of
male and female workers

	Estimated coefficient	x^2 value
Constant	1.74967*	1616.41
High School	0.35297*	61.848
Junior College	0.46311*	71.230
University	0.61575*	171.519
Medium firm	0.26253*	138.502
Large firm	0.85569*	963.963
Large city	0.02917	1.256
F	−0.23066*	20.839
High School × F	−0.20236*	15.044
Junior College × F	−0.19589*	10.136
University × F	−0.37560*	43.231
Medium firm × F	−0.01248	0.233
Large firm × F	−0.27133*	76.173
Large city × F	−0.15683*	27.682
Scale parameter	0.69990*	[0.0040]
Log likelihood	−50014.9	

Notes: F is the dummy variable for female workers. The number in brackets
is the standard deviation.
*: 1% significant.

industrial sectors, we can tell if the workforce retention rate is high
for female university graduates in the industry that has a high retention rate for male high school graduates. Table 6.9 shows the resulting correlation coefficients. Table 6.9 reveals that between male and
female high school graduates, between female junior college and female university graduates, and between male junior college and university graduates, there exists a significant positive correlation. However,
between male and female university graduates, we observed a statistically significant negative relationship. In other words, for university
graduate workers, in industries with a high retention rate among males,
the retention rate among females was low. What is the reason behind
this?

Table 6.10 shows the relationship of job training and retention rate
according to sex and educational level. For males, job training proved
effective for elevating the retention rate in all educational categories.
In fact, the higher the educational level, the greater the impact. We
used this finding to simulate the retention rate of medium-size firm
employees who had been with the same company for 10 years. In the
public utility industry which posted the highest job training execution

Table 6.9 Correlation coefficients matrix between retention rates of male and female workers by educational level

	Female Junior College	Female University	Male High School	Male Junior College	Male University
Female High School graduates	0.4200*	−0.2218	0.5211*	0.2902	0.6506**
Female Junior College graduates		0.4886**	0.1464	0.3211	0.0965
Female University graduates			−0.2880	−0.0554	−0.5220**
Male High School graduate				0.8060**	0.7712**
Male Junior College graduates					0.5484**

Notes: *: 10% significant.
**: 5% significant.
Correlation coefficients are calculated based on the estimated coefficients of industry dummy variables in survival analysis. Firm size dummy variables are included in the equations.

Table 6.10 The estimated results of survival analysis on job training by educational level

	Job training for improvement in knowledge and skill at the current Job					
	Male			Female		
	High School	Junior College	University	High School	Junior College	University
Constant	1.83783*	1.02213*	0.89217*	1.09678*	1.34978*	2.00306*
	(163.400)	(5.559)	(18.726)	(964.058)	(467.42)	(231.189)
Job training	0.00527*	0.01902*	0.02249*	0.01272*	0.01009*	−0.00639
	(6.365)	(9.487)	(59.098)	(241.973)	(52.543)	(4.696)
Medium firm	0.31364*	0.30198*	0.32474*	0.29506*	0.10138*	0.02739
	(84.619)	(11.013)	(37.783)	(346.977)	(18.401)	(0.337)
Large firm	0.98273*	0.61599*	1.04913*	0.46303*	0.43795*	0.80780*
	(490.281)	(28.874)	(282.555)	(586.048)	(300.127)	(287.934)
Large city	−0.01246	0.13687*	0.09906*	−0.08876*	−0.10677*	−0.13795*
	(0.083)	(1.796)	(3.721)	(22.214)	(20.415)	(10.855)
Scale para.	0.82067*	0.80967*	0.84583*	0.66282*	0.62513*	0.68608*
	[0.01307]	[0.03414]	[0.01880]	[0.00548]	[0.00793]	[0.01553]
Log likelihood	−8736.6	−1321.3	−5357.3	−20113.1	−8854.0	−3024.6

Notes: Figures in parentheses are χ^2 statistics.
Figures in brackets are standard deviations.
*: Significant at the 1% level.

rate, the retention rate of high school graduates is 50.7 percent, while in the textile industry where the job training execution rate was lowest, the retention rate was 9.0 percent lower at 41.7 percent. Among junior college graduates, the retention rates in the two industries were 71.8 percent and 44.0 percent, respectively, showing a difference of 27.8 percent. Among university graduates in the two industries, the difference was a wide 30 percent, with rates of 75.3 percent and 45.3 percent, respectively.

On the other hand, among females, significant increases in effectiveness were marked for high school and junior college graduates, but not for university graduates. Similar estimations were conducted on types of job training other than training for improvement in knowledge and skills at the current job shown in Table 6.10. Among female high school graduates, increases in retention rates were also marked for most other types of job training, but for female university graduates, several types of job training resulted in negative coefficients.

Another finding worth noting for females was the difference in retention rates between the size of the firm according to educational level. Among high school and junior college graduates, both the large firm dummy and the medium firm dummy resulted in significant, positive coefficients. Among university graduates, the large firm dummy took a very high coefficient compared with high school and junior college graduates; however, when it came to the medium firm dummy, this coefficient was not significant. In other words, among university graduates, there was a pronounced difference in retention rates between large firms and other firms. On the other hand, the rate difference between small and medium firms remained marginal. This marginality in the difference can be attributed to the small number of university graduates employed by small firms.

Estimated findings in Table 6.6 show minor differences in retention rates between female junior college and university graduates. The reason for this is believed to be the impact of the specification of the equation which was based on the hypothesis that the scale of the firm has the same effect in each educational level. Table 6.10, in which the estimation was conducted by educational level, shows that particularly in the case of large firms, the retention rate was clearly higher for university graduates than for junior college graduates. Similar estimated findings were confirmed when all female samples in Table 6.6 were used to make estimations without adding the firm size dummy variable to the explanatory variable.

Table 6.11 shows the impact of labour productivity growth on the

Table 6.11 The estimated results of survival analysis on the growth rate of labour productivity

	Male				Female			
	Total	High School	Junior College	University	Total	High School	Junior College	University
Constant	1.91753* (1277.97)	2.51127* (7800.06)	2.72687* (1356.64)	3.05559* (4737.18)	1.56447* (3928.37)	1.74318* (31656.4)	1.97022* (19322.9)	2.24793* (5750.03)
Productivity	0.02010* (30.954)	0.03220* (42.693)	-0.01836 (2.417)	0.00879 (1.902)	0.01878* (126.524)	0.03589* (297.17)	-0.00305 (0.894)	-0.06570* (107.25)
Growth rate	0.06790 (4.708)	0.04970 (1.237)	0.13687 (1.756)	0.07670 (1.998)	-0.09877* (49.704)	-0.05510* (8.231)	-0.08680* (13.024)	-0.19378* (20.092)
Large city								
High School	0.63118* (137.521)				0.23624* (84.339)			
Junior College	0.74693* (127.800)				0.38878* (208.465)			
University	1.07502* (362.426)				0.49390* (253.008)			
Scale para.	0.84238* [0.0102]	0.84551* [0.0136]	0.81930* [0.0347]	0.86051* [0.0193]	0.67717* [0.0044]	0.67875* [0.0057]	0.63772* [0.0082]	0.70523* [0.0163]
Log likelihood	-16626.5	-9023.2	-1341.5	-5604.2	-34580.3	-20614.3	-9093.7	-3180.9

Notes: Figures in parentheses are χ^2 statistics.

Figures in brackets are standard deviations.

*: Significant at the 1% level.

retention rate in the corresponding industrial sector. In the case of female high school graduates, productivity growth had a pronounced impact on the retention rate, but for female university graduates, the reverse was markedly evident, posting a negative effect.

The above findings imply that factors other than job training and wages also strongly affect the job separation behavior of female university graduates. Let us study this from the post-resignation perspective. 47.6 percent of female high school graduates who separated from their jobs went on to work for other firms, while only 35.9 percent of university graduates did so. The remaining 64.1 percent left the job market. It is believed that when a worker leaves one firm to work for another, the structuring of job training, wage levels and the wage slope are key criteria for selecting a firm. Moreover, when one is induced to consider leaving or staying with a firm because of marriage or child-birth, the most relevant factor might be the length of the assigned working hours by the firm. According to our estimated survival model, the retention rate of female workers is clearly low in the firms with long working hours (Higuchi and Abe, 1992). Simulation results based on the estimated parameters show the female retention rate in the long working-hour firms such as 203 hours a month is 10.2 percent in 10 years, in comparison with 25.0 percent in short working-hour firms such as 162 hours.

Also, whether the company is equipped with a programme that can accommodate the worker's circumstances might be a key variable influencing the female retention rate. For example, if working hours could be flexibly adjusted to the needs of the worker, this flexibility could increase the retention rate. One example of this programme is the childcare leave programme. Let us look at the effects of leave programmes on the retention rate. The findings are as shown in Table 6.12. To obtain these findings, the rates of companies with childcare leave programmes in the industrial sectors corresponding to the samples were added as explanatory variables (from the 1985 *Survey on Labor Management of Female Workers*). Even when the scale of the firm and places of residence were controlled, retention rates of female workers remained high for firms with childcare leave programmes. This effect was particularly pronounced for females with a higher educational background.[7] Let us use these estimated findings to simulate the retention rate of female workers who reside in a large city and who have been working for the same large firm for 10 years. For this estimation, we conducted a cross-comparison between the service industry which had the highest rate of companies with a childcare leave

Table 6.12 The estimated results of survival analysis on childcare leave programmes (female sample)

	All sample		High School grad.		Junior College grad.		University grad.	
Constant	1.24811* (2171.49)	1.29271* (2274.71)	1.49536* (7143.44)	1.51059* (6936.29)	1.36468* (2532.18)	1.35623* (2438.50)	1.21979* (523.266)	1.21602* (508.547)
Childcare leave prog.	0.02594* (469.882)	0.01752* (152.895)	0.01434* (81.569)	0.00647* (12.194)	0.03562* (296.943)	0.02426* (88.227)	0.04567* (121.705)	0.04667* (78.096)
Wage rate		1.05400* (90.395)		0.97709* (50.523)		1.30658 (36.600)		-0.18018 (0.155)
Wage slope		0.17574 (0.02237)		0.07454 (0.00258)		2.42991 (1.20423)		1.98291 (0.175)
High School	0.16648* (44.250)	0.13604* (29.4411)						
Junior College	0.20757* (62.297)	0.15576* (34.476)						
University	0.15396* (25.227)	0.10821* (12.368)						
Medium firm	0.29422* (534.778)	0.29403* (539.05)	0.35584* (478.998)	0.35350* (477.279)	0.18221* (58.834)	0.18078* (58.369)	0.05487 (1.409)	0.05656 (1.481)
Large firm	0.62337* (1848.43)	0.59590* (1666.41)	0.59574* (932.945)	0.56662* (831.289)	0.56900* (502.24)	0.52493* (419.185)	0.70555* (231.979)	0.70618* (227.474)
Large city	-0.10996* (64.848)	-0.11543* (71.646)	-0.09954* (27.846)	-0.10784* (32.807)	-0.08691* (13.938)	-0.08301* (12.772)	-0.08270* (4.020)	-0.08246* (3.994)
Scale para.	0.65713* [0.00424]	0.65559* [0.00423]	0.66400* [0.00549]	0.66217* [0.00548]	0.61500* [0.00778]	0.61359* [0.00775]	0.67361* [0.01519]	0.67365* [0.01519]
Log likelihood	-33530.6	-33440.3	-20200.8	-20149.4	-8736.24	-8692.41	-2967.81	-2967.70

Notes: Figures in parentheses are χ^2 statistics.
Figures in brackets are standard deviations.
*: Significant at the 1% level.

programme and the steel industry which had the lowest rate.[8] The difference in the retention rates between the two industries was 10.8 percent for high school graduates, 28.2 percent for junior college students and 33.9 percent for university students.

This difference in the effects of childcare leave programmes on retention rates by educational level might be observed because of selecting our sample from those with the same duration, 15 years, regardless of education level. Namely, while the upper age limit of high school graduates is 33 years old, that of university graduates is 37 years old. If the average marriage ages or childbirth ages are the same among differently educated women, more university graduates with childbirth might be included in our sample, because of a different upper age limit. In order to avoid this kind of sample selection bias, we estimated the survival model by using another dataset with the same upper age limit, 35 years old. But our conclusion, that for more educated women, there is a larger positive effect of childcare leave programmes on retention rates, remained unchanged. The estimated coefficient of high school graduates is 0.0168, that of junior college graduates is 0.0498, and that of university graduates is 0.0740 (scale parameters are 0.663, 0.665 and 0.720, respectively).

The correlation coefficients of the percentages of companies implementing childcare leave programmes according to the industrial sector and the productivity growth rates shows a negative value of −0.3931 (significant at the 10 percent level). The findings in Table 6.11 reveal that for female university graduates, the productivity growth rate had a negative effect on the workforce retention rate. It is possible that this negative effect was further fuelled by inflexible working hours. It is not known how many workers actually took childcare leave, but if this index is proof that this system backs the retention of female workers, it could result in changing the retention rate of female workers.[9]

6.5   CONCLUDING REMARKS

The findings of the human capital empirical research show that for males, human capital theory plays a key role in Japan. Firms that reinforce job training have a higher tenure–wage profile curve. On the other hand, while introductory job training for developing general knowledge and skills conducted shortly after recruitment did not have a clear impact on the retention rate, job training improving knowledge and skills definitely elevated the retention rate. Moreover, a similar relationship was observed among female high school graduates. However, this was not so for female university graduates. Among female university graduates, additional influential factors include the length of the assigned working hours and the availability of programmes which benefit female workers, such as the childcare leave programme.

To date, the survey target of analyses on the retention rate in Japan has been focused on males. The necessary level of "time" did not change greatly according to various stages in life for male workers relative to female workers. However, to analyze the retention rate of female workers, it is also necessary to take into account the shift in the role-allocation of family members in present day Japan. Furthermore, it is very likely that this shift will also serve as a key issue for future studies conducted on males.

The cost of living varies according to the age group. But personal income can be adjusted at any moment through savings and loans. On the other hand, time is only available in the present, that is, one can't borrow time from the future for present use. It is not easily adjustable in the way that income is.

A questionnaire was prepared to probe problems related to human resource development of female workers. More than half of the companies mentioned separation after a short period (the 1985 *Survey on Labor Management of Female Workers*). This comparative rate rose further in the case of females in a major career path, where it accounted for more than 80 percent (the 1990 *White Paper on Industrial Relations*). Even if a firm spends a great deal of time and money on job training, many female workers will leave the company before they are able to make full use of their newly gained knowledge and skills. However, as shown by the analytical findings in this chapter, in companies that provide a working environment that caters to females, a high retention rate can be observed. Therefore, companies keen on elevating the retention rate of female workers must consider not only wages but also other factors such as flexible working hours and the overall improvement of the working environment.[10]

It is expected that Japan will continue to see a decrease in the number of younger workers, as well as the continued aging of the overall population. The absolute number of overall labour force is predicted to decrease after the year 2000. Under these circumstances, greater reliance will have to be placed on female workers. When this happens, how are companies going to cope with the harmony of labour management and a working environment that can cater to the needs of females? The labour policies of Japanese companies must change, and such changes must include making revisions to items related to the wage and the working hours system.

Notes

*   I gratefully acknowledge helpful and constructive comments on an earlier version of this chapter by Corinne Boyles and Toshikazu Mattushige and other participants at the Biwawo conference, Osaka (July, 1992). I am also grateful to Masahiro Abe for his excellent research assistance. Needless to say, I am solely responsible for any remaining errors.

1. In comparison to other advanced countries, there is a wide wage gap between male and females workers in Japan. For Sweden, the ratio of male–female average wages was 100:90 in 1980. Given an average male wage of 100, in the UK, the female wage was 79, in West Germany, 72, and in the US, 66, while in Japan female wages were substantially lower at 54 (Mincer, 1985). In Japan, this wide disparity between the average wages of males and females is mainly caused by the differences in the attributes of male and female workers such as educational level, the number of job tenure years, and age. If male and female workers have the same school years, job tenure years and age, the wage gap on average would shrink to a ratio of about 100:80 (Higuchi, 1991). In the Japanese wage structure, however, job tenure and age play major roles in determining wages. It is the difference in the average number of continuous years of employment between males and females which widens the wage gap. In this sense, it can be considered that an analysis of the difference in the work force retention rate between males and females is important for examining characteristics particular to the Japanese labour market.

2. In Japan, a law calling for equal opportunity in the employment of males and females was implemented in April 1986. This law prohibits unfair treatment of females in terms of recruitment, training and promotion. This survey was executed in 1984 before the implementation of this law and thus surveys the situation of labour policies for both males and females at that time.

3. In the case of female workers, if the marriage age is limited, the distribution of job separation by age might be bimodal in the periods shortly after joining companies and marriage. But the observed ages of job separation of the female workers do not show the bimodal distribution. When this tendency is strong, the assumption of unimodal distribution concerning separation age is not suitable.

4. The 20 industries are as follows: (1) Foods; (2) Textiles; (3) Lumber and wood products; (4) Chemical and allied products; (5) Petroleum and coal products; (6) Rubber products; (7) Ceramic, stone, and clay products; (8) Iron, steel, and non-ferrous metal products; (9) Fabricated metal prod-

ucts; (10) General machinery; (11) Electrical machinery; (12) Transportation equipment; (13) Precision instruments and machinery; (14) Miscellaneous manufacturing industries; (15) Electricity, gas, heat supply, and water; (16) Wholesale and retail trade, eating, and drinking places; (17) Finance and insurance; (18) Real estate; (19) Transport and communication; and (20) Services.

5. Let us then compare the impact of the number of years of job tenure on wage rates for males and females respectively. Roughly speaking, the impact appears greater for females. It looks as though these estimated findings are affected by a selectivity bias since the retention rate is higher for high income earners and low for low income earners. To diminish the effect of this selectivity bias, it would be necessary to implement a simultaneous estimation of wages and job separation behaviour. Unfortunately, we were unable to implement such an estimation since an appropriate estimation method has not been developed.

6. Estimation according to educational level was not implemented for junior high school graduates due to the small size of the sample.

7. Childcare leave was implemented in April 1992 in Japan. The law requires that a company grant childcare leave to an employee who requests it. Such leave is available to either the mother or the father. Such childcare leave continues until a child's first birthday. Moreover, for an employee with a pre-elementary school aged child, the company is required to create a working environment that will promote working conditions that leave time for childcare by curtailing working hours and implementing other accommodating policies.

8. School teachers are excluded in calculating the rate of the firms with childcare leave programmes. Most schools have childcare leave programmes and the retention rates of teachers are low. If we include school teachers in our sample, the effects of childcare leave programmes become larger than those in the text.

9. Meitzen (1986) and Light and Ureta (1992) are good sources as these reports survey differences between the male and female job separation behaviour in the US. Moreover, Altonji and Paxon (1988) analyze the effects of working hours on job separation behaviour.

10. It was pointed out in Oi (1962) and Rosen (1969), as well as in Ohashi (1990) that when fixed costs are high, including the costs of job training, firms decrease the number of workers and increase the number of working hours. Moreover, Hashimoto and Yu (1980) noted that as to workers with larger firm specific human capital, the downturn in a business cycle was dealt with by adjusting the number of working hours and wages, rather than by adjusting the number of workers. However, there are few studies analyzing the relationship of fixed costs and the retention rate on the nature of the working-hours system in present-day Japan, although revisions to the working-hours system have now become imperative.

References

Altonji, A.G. and C.H. Paxon (1988)   'Labor Supply Preference, Hours Constraints, and Hours-Wage Trade-offs', *Journal of Labor Economics*, vol. 6, no. 2.

Aoki, M. (1988)   *Information, Incentives, and Bargaining in the Japanese Economy*, Cambridge, Cambridge University Press.

Hashimoto, M. and B.T. Yu (1980)   'Specific Capital, Employment Contracts, and Wage Rigidity,' *Bell Journal of Economics*, vol. 11, no. 2.

Hashimoto, M. and J. Raisian (1985)   'Employment, Tenure, and Earning Profiles in Japan and the United States', *American Economic Review*, vol. 75, September, pp. 721–35.

Higuchi, Y. (1991)   *Nihon Keizai to Syugyou Koudou* (Japanese Economy and Employment Structure), Tokyo, Toyo Keizai Sinposya.

Higuchi, Y. and M. Abe (1992)   'Roudou Jikan Seido to Jyuugyouin no Kigyou Teichakuritu' ('Working Hour System and Retention Rates of Workers'), *Economic Journal*, vol. 43, no. 3.

Kiefer, N.M. (1988)   'Economic Duration Data and Hazard Functions', *Journal of Economic Literature*, vol. 26, no. 2.

Lazear, E.P. (1979)   'Why Is There Mandatory Retirement?' *Journal of Political Economy*, vol. 87, December, pp. 1261–84.

Light, A. and M. Ureta (1992)   'Panel Estimates of Male and Female Job Turnover Behavior: Can Female Nonquitters Be Identified?', *Journal of Labor Economics*, vol. 10, no. 2.

Lillard, L.A. and H.W. Tan. (1986)   'Private Sector Training: Who Gets it and What are its Effects?', Rand Corporation.

Meitzen, M.E. (1986)   'Differences, in Male and Female Job-quitting Behavior', *Journal of Labor Economics*, vol. 4, no. 2.

Miller, Jr. R.G. (1981)   *Survival Analysis*, New York, John Wiley.

Mincer, J. (1984)   'Labor Mobility, Wages, and Job Training', *DOL Report*.

———— (1985)   'Intercountry Comparison of Labor Force Trends and of Related Developments', *Journal of Labor Economics*, vol. 3, no. 1, Part 2.

Mincer, J. and Y. Higuchi (1988)   'Wage Structures and Labor Turnover in the United States and Japan', *Journal of the Japanese and International Economies*, vol. 2, June, pp. 97–133.

Ohashi, I. (1990)   *Rodo Shijo no Riron*, (The Theory of the Labor Market), Tokyo, Toyo Keizai Sinposya.

Oi, W. (1962)   'Labor as a Quasi-Fixed Factor', *Journal of Political Economy*, vol. 70, no. 6, pp. 538–55.

Rosen, S. (1969)   'On the Interindustry Wage and Hours Structure', *Journal of Political Economy*, vol. 77, no. 2.

Shapiro, C. and J.E. Stiglitz (1984)   'Equilibrium Unemployment as a Worker-Discipline Device', *American Economic Review*, vol. 74, no. 3, pp. 433–44.

Spark, R. (1986)   'A Model of Involuntary Unemployment and Wage Rigidity: Worker Incentive and the Threat of Dismissal', *Journal of Labor Economics*, vol. 4, no. 4.

Tachibanaki, T. and A. Taki (1990)   'The Effects of Individual Characteristics and of Parametrics and Non-parametric Approach on Job Duration in Japan', Kyoto Institute of Economic Research, Discussion Paper, no. 293.

7 Interindustry and Firm Size Differences in Job Satisfaction Among Japanese Workers

Tsuneo Ishikawa*

7.1 INTRODUCTION

It is often pointed out that despite the recent rise in the levels of income and wealth the greater part of Japanese households do not feel much comfort and richness in actual living. No doubt long working hours, long commuting time, heavy congestion, and exorbitant rise of land prices in the major metropolitan area go a long way in explaining such impoverishment.

Another important determinant of the richness of living, however, is the richness of the quality of work life. This is because work is not only a means to acquire goods and services necessary for living but is also a field of activity in which people exhibit their ability and responsibility, thereby contributing to society and in which they simultaneously further their ability itself. Are Japanese employers responding positively to such expectations on the part of workers? Does the degree of fulfilment of such expectations differ greatly among individuals depending on which employer worked for and which type of job held?

This chapter looks on such a feature as a problem of distribution of job satisfaction among individuals, and investigates the factors that determine the current state of distribution using a micro survey data on individual attitudes and consciousness.[1] The dataset for the present study is the workers' responses to the *Survey on the Accumulation of Assets and on Worker Life in Major Metropolitan Areas* conducted by the Ministry of Labour in November, 1990.[2] The purpose of this survey is to investigate the effect on workers' asset formation and work attitudes of the widened gap in wealth distribution that arose on account of the acute rise in land and stock prices after 1985. It asks the level, purpose as well as the (historical) source of workers' wealth holding and at the same time raises various questions on worker attitude towards work as well as on the concept of fairness with respect to income and wealth distribution. Among the responses to these questionnaires this chapter focuses on those concerning individual workers' evaluation of job satisfaction.

Related to the present study is a long-standing empirical investigation on the relationship between organizational setups and incentive mechanisms of firms and the extent of worker commitment towards jobs. Such investigations have traditionally belonged to the fields of industrial sociology and psychology, on the one hand, and of labour management and control, on the other.[3] These studies have usually been carried out in the context of within or across specific organizations. Since the advent of concern on work motivation as an important determinant of labour productivity and macroeconomic unemployment, however, there is a growing trend for such studies to be intermeshed with mainstream economic analysis.

Among the existing literature the most recent and perhaps methodologically the most relevant study to the present one is that of Lincoln and Kalleberg (1990).[4] They have chosen the city of Atsugi (on the outskirts of Tokyo) as the study site and conducted a sample survey on manufacturing establishments and the workers therein. From the establishments are collected the information on detailed organizational characteristics and from workers are collected the information on individual attributes, occupational and job characteristics, hierarchical positions, the nature of social bonds with fellow workers, and both pecuniary and non-pecuniary job rewards, and the responses to the queries on the extent of work commitment and job satisfaction. The authors then related these responses to the foregoing explanatory variables.

Lincoln and Kalleberg's main conclusion is that the high work commitment of the workers observed (which confirms earlier investigations carried out in Japan) is a contrived one in the sense that it is derived from the operation of a wide-ranging inducement apparatus set up inside Japanese firms (which is against the 'culturalist' view). While the high commitment of workers is certainly a major success for Japanese employers it simultaneously entails a large gap between the expectations and the reality on the part of workers, which is why they have been observed to express relatively low job satisfaction.[5]

The present study partly complements Lincoln and Kalleberg's detailed work in that it has a much larger sample frame, covering the entire (non-agricultural) industrial as well as occupational spectrum and covering the three major metropolitan areas of Japan. It is thus particularly suitable to obtaining a birds-eye view of the distribution of job satisfaction among Japanese workers and of factors that tend to associate with job satisfaction.

The organization of this chapter is as follows. Section 7.2 summarizes the general nature of the data. Section 7.3 spells out the observed characteristics of job satisfaction on various dimensions and discusses the basic conceptual framework within which different job satisfaction scores may appear. Section 7.4 presents a model and the estimation result of the ordered Probit analysis as applied to workers' evaluation of whether or not due reward is paid for their effort. Section 7.5 discusses the result of a similar ordered Probit analysis as applied to the workers' evaluation of the extent of challenging and stimulating experience on the job. Section 7.6 concludes by summarizing the main findings, discussing the general implications and noting the qualifications of the present analysis.

7.2 CHARACTERISTICS OF THE DATA

The data comes from the population of regularly employed married household head who is employed in a privately owned establishment with 30 or more regular employees in three major metropolitan areas (Tokyo, Nagoya and Osaka). The survey chose persons randomly: 10 persons each from 1200 establishments that were in themselves selected randomly on the basis of the 1986 *Establishment Census*. The questionnaire form was delivered to each sampled individual via establishment, and the response was mailed back directly to the sender from the individual. 5600 responses were thus collected from individuals, the response rate being 46.3 percent. Because of the condition that a worker must be a married household head to be included in the sample, responses by female persons were limited to only 1.4 percent of the total samples. Hence, this chapter restricts the analysis to responses by male individuals only, and furthermore, to those made by individuals aged 25 and above. It appears that the second condition enables the analysis to focus on people who have largely completed the search and the job-matching processes.

Table 7.1 shows the mean attributes of the respondents as classified by each age group. It also shows the distribution of annual labour earnings as well as that of net worth which (which includes the mar-

Table 7.1   Mean attributes of the sample[a]

Age group	25–34	35–44	45–54	55–	Total
Schooling (years)	14.9	14.2	13.1	12.6	13.9
Duration of service (years)	7.8	15.9	23.3	20.5	16.8
Occupation					
• Profess./technical	25.8	22.2	17.9	19.3	21.4
• Managerial	8.4	25.5	36.1	37.8	26.0
• Skilled/production operatives	3.0	3.9	5.8	4.9	4.4
• Clerical, sales and others	62.8	48.4	40.2	38.0	48.2
Firm size (%)					
• large (1000 and more employees)	55.9	55.0	52.1	32.2	52.0
• medium (100–999 employees)	33.8	35.0	35.5	48.3	36.3
• small (less than 100 employees)	10.3	10.0	12.4	19.5	11.7
Industry (%)					
• Construction	9.6	11.4	9.2	10.7	10.3
• Manufacturing (incl. mining)	23.7	24.0	30.4	23.6	25.8
• Utility	2.9	2.4	2.8	2.3	2.6
• Transportation and communication	7.5	10.3	16.0	12.7	11.7
• Wholesale and retail	23.4	25.2	21.0	15.0	22.5
• Finance and insurance	8.5	8.4	5.7	3.4	7.1
• Real estate	2.2	1.2	0.9	3.2	1.5
• Service	22.1	17.0	14.0	29.0	18.5
Employed earnings[b] (10,000 yen/year)					
• Bottom quartile	355	451	507	329	418
• Median	460	625	730	600	600
• Top quartile	705	964	1,083	1,076	983
Net worth (10,000 yen)					
• Bottom quartile	–31	413	1,099	1,514	265
• Median	500	2,900	4,600	5,900	3,000
• Top quartile	5,247	8,565	12,854	15,280	10,488
Sample size	1,203	2,096	1,641	559	5,549

Notes:
[a] Mean figures are calculated by excluding missing values.
[b] The composition of the *Census of Wages* (Ministry of Labour, surveyed in June, 1990) samples for the corresponding population of workers, i.e., male regular workers aged 25 and above who are employed in a privately owned

establishment with 30 or more regular employees in three major metropolitan areas (Tokyo, Nagoya and Osaka) is as follows:
Schooling = 13.1 years, Duration of service = 13.8 years,
Production workers' ratio (= Production workers in mining, construction and manufacturing industries workers in all industries) = 20.0%
Firm size: Large firms = 43.8%, Medium firms = 19.1%
           Small firms = 38.1%
Industry: Construction = 5.6%,
           Manufacturing (incl. mining) = 40.1%,
           Utility = 1.0%,
           Transportation and communication = 13.6%,
           Wholesale and retail = 18.1%,
           Finance and insurance = 4.8%,
           Real estate = 1.3%, Service = 15.7%.

ket value of the golf club membership). Reflecting the recent acute rise in the land price in these metropolitan areas there indeed is an immense difference between the dispersion of earnings and that of net worth as measured by the ratio of respective mean values of the top and the bottom quartiles of the distribution (2.4 for the former and 39.6 for the latter for the age groups combined).[6]

As the accompanying note to Table 7.1 shows, however, there exist certain sampling biases in this survey. The manufacturing industry is underrepresented as compared with non-manufacturing industries, and even within the manufacturing industry blue-collar workers seem to be rather heavily underrepresented as compared with white-collar workers. Similarly small-sized firms are underrepresented *vis-à-vis* medium- and large-sized firms. Subsequent analysis shows that such sampling biases indeed call for cautious qualifications when overall evaluation of the distribution of job satisfaction is made.

7.3 WORKER CONSCIOUSNESS OF JOB WORTH AND INDICES OF JOB SATISFACTION

The study begins by looking at the workers' views on the meaning they attach to the job (hereafter termed *job worth*). The survey asks the respondent which of the following three alternative views is the closest to his own:

(a) Job worth derives from intrinsic interest in the job, so that the levels of earnings and assets are irrelevant;

(b) Job worth does not derive solely from earnings and assets, yet in

Table 7.2   Workers' views on job worth

Content of job worth	Age 25–34	Age 35–44	Age 45–54	Age 55–
	%	%	%	%
Intrinsic interest in the Job	8.7	8.4	9.8	15.7
Moderate amount of earnings and assets	80.6	81.0	79.7	70.8
Earnings and assets alone	10.7	10.6	10.4	13.5
Total	100.0	100.0	100.0	100.0

Note: Percentage ratios are calculated by excluding missing values.

order for meaningfulness to be felt the job must assure earnings and assets that would at least enable the job holder to own a house;
(c) Job worth depends squarely on the levels of earnings and assets that can be acquired from the job.

It is to be stressed that this is not a question about the respondent's current state of affairs but about his idea in general. Table 7.2 summarizes the responses for each age group.

As seen from Table 7.2, the view that some moderate amounts of earnings and assets are to be secured by the job is supported by the greater part of the population. Yet at the same time, each of the polar views that either intrinsic interest or pecuniary reward alone is important is taken by about 10 percent and that adherence to intrinsic interest in the job shows a notable increase among older people (i.e., aged 55 and over). Between the young (aged 25–34) and the medium age (aged 35–44 and 45–54) groups there seems to be little difference in the concept about job worth.

The increased evaluation of intrinsic job interest among the older people may be explained, first, by a life-cycle effect of decreased monetary needs as they complete the process of child rearing and of paying back housing mortgages, and second, by a particular cohort effect that they passed through a period of dire economic severity during and immediately after the Second World War. It is difficult, however, to distinguish these two effects in the data.

On the other hand, it is worth noting that the young generation, reared in the age of material affluence and often suspected of having discontinuity in ideas and values (as the popular word 'new human beings' connotes), is not different from the age groups 35–44 and 45–54 in terms of what they look for in the job.[7]

About the respondent's current state of job satisfaction the survey asks whether or not

A. due reward for effort is attained in terms of pay and promotion,
B. the job allows one to exhibit one's own ability fully,
C. the job involves new challenges and is stimulating,
D. the job involves broad realm of responsibility.

For each item the respondent chooses one of the five categories: 'satisfied', 'somewhat satisfied', 'neither satisfied nor dissatisfied', 'somewhat dissatisfied', and 'dissatisfied'. Note that A not only refers to current pay but also refers to past history and future prospects on promotion within the firm. In effect, it asks whether the respondent's past and current effort has been fairly rewarded. Its content may largely be construed as pecuniary. B, C, and D, on the other hand, clearly refer to non-pecuniary attributes of the job.

Figure 7.1 shows for each questionnaire item the proportions of those workers in the sample as grouped by age whose response was either 'satisfied' or 'somewhat satisfied', and Figure 7.2 shows the same proportions for those whose response was either 'dissatisfied' or 'somewhat dissatisfied'. (Hereafter, the categories 'satisfied' and 'somewhat satisfied' are frequently aggregated and are simply termed *satisfied*, and similarly for the categories 'dissatisfied' and 'somewhat dissatisfied', termed *dissatisfied*.

Figures 7.1 and 7.2 may give the overall impression that the job satisfaction level of Japanese workers is on the whole high, especially with regard to non-pecuniary dimensions. However, the previously noted sampling bias in the distribution of respondents and the analysis below (sections 7.4 and 7.5) jointly show that the bars of Figure 7.1 are overstated while those of Figure 7.2 are understated. Hence it would be quite misleading to accept these absolute numbers at their face value.[8]

Comparison of Figures 7.1 and 7.2 shows that, for each age group, the item for which the frequency of satisfaction exhibits the highest score is D (broadness of responsibility) while that exhibiting the lowest score is A (due reward for effort). B (exhibit ability fully) and C (stimulating) hold intermediate positions, and yet for each age group B gets a slightly higher frequency score than C. The frequency of workers expressing dissatisfaction on each of the four items also gradually declines with age, but for age 55 and over the tendency reverses itself, if not sharply. In particular, a significant rise occurs in the proportion of people who express dissatisfaction over D (broadness of responsi-

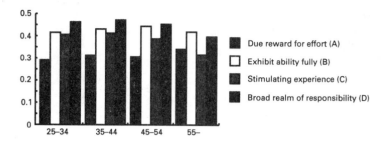

Figure 7.1   Satisfaction about job

Note: The height of each bar represents the proportion of individuals who responded with the answer of either being 'satisfied' or 'somewhat satisfied'.

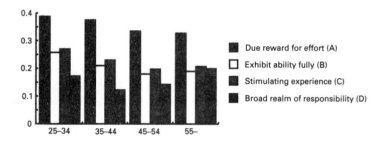

Figure 7.2   Dissatisfaction about job

Note: The height of each bar represents the proportion of individuals who responded with the answer of either being 'dissatisfied' or 'somewhat dissatisfied'.

bility). It is not difficult to imagine that mandatory retirement and other personnel practices that move the older people's work-place rather drastically are the cause of such a reversal.

What, then, determines the workers' responses to these questions? What sort of correlations are present among the responses to four questions within each individual? In particular, does dissatisfaction on pecuniary rewards (A) tend to be compensated for by satisfaction on non-pecuniary rewards B, C, D (thus facilitating the 'equalizing difference' argument) or do both tend to be assortative?

The first question will for now (pending the discussion in the concluding section) be answered as follows. Items A, B, C, and D all contain elements that depend individuals' inherent framework of values

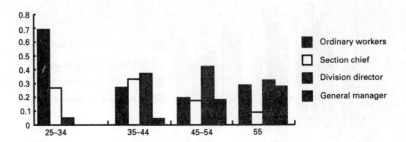

Figure 7.3 Distribution of hierarchical ranks among respondents

and subjective valuation. Evaluation of 'due reward for effort' obviously depends on what one regards as the proper concept of 'effort' and then on what one considers as a 'fair reward'. The judgement also seems likely to depend on one's observation of the 'effort' expended by other workers in the local reference group.[9] Evaluation of whether or not the job allows one to 'exhibit ability fully' depends much on how exactly one understands one's own ability, including one's potential. Evaluation of whether the job is 'stimulating' or not is naturally influenced by one's perception of the gap between one's already achieved ability and one's potential ability. It is a well established proposition in psychology that tasks that are far apart from an individual's potential ability are more painful than pleasant stimulation, while tasks which contribute little to developing one's potential ability are hopelessly boring.[10] Finally, evaluation of the 'broadness of responsibility' depends much on how one sets out the appropriate context of responsibility for oneself.

The proposition that individuals' responses to items A, B, C, and D are intermediated by their respective framework of evaluation seems to be attested by the fact that despite the existence of large differences in the shape of the distribution of hierarchical ranks (note that rank is clearly an important objective element influencing the amount of pecuniary as well as non-pecuniary rewards) between age groups (as seen in Figure 7.3) the frequencies of satisfaction and dissatisfaction on all items as shown in Figures 7.1 and 7.2 do not differ much between age groups.

On the other hand, even if each individual has his/her own framework of reference it does not necessarily mean that it is distributed completely randomly over individuals. It is perhaps appropriate to construe as follows. Based on the levels of past learning and experience individuals form certain expectations as to what constitutes a fair achievement level on each of the four items A, B, C, and D. 'Effort' is then

192   *Job Satisfaction: Interindustry and Firm Size Differences*

Table 7.3   Correlation among various job satisfaction indices[a]

	A	B	C	D
A	1.0	0.392	0.333	0.335[b]
B	(0.542)	1.0	0.536	0.472
C	(0.484)	(0.702)	1.0	0.487
D	(0.470)[b]	(0.627)	(0.635)	1.0

Notes:
[a] The definition of job satisfaction indices are as follows:
  A = Due reward for effort.
  B = Exhibit ability fully.
  C = Involves new challenge and stimulation.
  D = Involves broad realm of responsibility.
[b] The measure of association in the upper-right box is the square root of Cramer's Mean Squared Quotient. The figures in parentheses in the lower-left box are the ordinary correlation coefficients by regarding the satisfaction indices as continuous variables.

interpreted in a widest sense including not only highly motivated and attentive direct productive effort but also conscious deferral of leisure and accumulation of knowledge as well as affective capacity either in school or on the job. The fair achievement level thus commonly depends on an individual's level of schooling and occupational history, and one may safely suppose the existence of a relatively stable structure of evaluation among individuals.

Simultaneous to conceiving the fair achievement levels individuals evaluate the achievement levels realized by their current job. And depending on the magnitude of the gap between the fair and realized levels they form a judgement in terms of five category levels, 'satisfied' through 'dissatisfied'. In sum, when the gap becomes sufficiently large, they express 'dissatisfaction'.

Turning to the second question, the categorical responses to each job satisfaction item have been assigned numerical values of 5 for 'satisfied,' 4 for 'somewhat satisfied,' 3 for 'neither satisfied nor dissatisfied,' 2 for 'some what dissatisfied,' and 1 for 'dissatisfied.' The extent of correlation among different items is then calculated using these numerical values. The figures in the upper-right corner of Table 7.3 give the square root of Cramer's mean squared quotient (i.e., a measure of association for discrete variables) while the figures in parentheses in the lower-left corner give the usual correlation coefficient (taking the numerical indices to be continuous variables). In terms of the squared root of mean square quotient, the correlations between A index and B, C, and D indices are around 0.3–0.4, while those among B, C, and D indices are around 0.5.[11]

The relatively high correlations among B, C, and D indices are naturally expected, for the amount and quality of information handled and the extent and realm of decision making normally go together in shaping up the objective job environment that commonly underlies the psychological mappings of B, C, and D indices. The positive correlations between A and B, C, D indices, on the other hand, provide *prima facie* evidence that pecuniary and non-pecuniary job rewards do not stand in a compensatory relationship. That is, those who are satisfied (dissatisfied) with the quality of the job are more likely to be simultaneously satisfied (dissatisfied) with pecuniary rewards than the reverse.

7.4 DETERMINANTS OF SATISFACTION WITH RESPECT TO DUE REWARDS FOR EFFORT

Suppose that a fair level of reward as conceived by individuals in the light of their past and current experience can, for each age group, be expressed by a common linear function of education, duration of service (tenure in the firm), occupation and commuting time. As the level of past effort is not directly measurable, education and duration of service are taken to be its proxy variables. They measure the cumulated time devoted to acquiring the general background knowledge and affective capacities and those that are specific to the firm. Furthermore, for some occupational types past efforts to acquire abilities specific to the job are taken into consideration. Professional and technical jobs, management jobs, and skilled worker and production operative jobs are considered to belong to such categories. The length of commuting time is also regarded as one, if not major, dimension of effort. A statistical error term is further introduced to take account of any other influence that may not be directly measured by the above variables. Differences in the individuals' framework of values clearly constitute one of such influences.

On the other hand, the realized level of reward as perceived by a worker depends on education, duration of service, and occupational type. It is further influenced by the size of firm and industrial difference. The possibility that asset holding affects the worker's perception is also considered. Another possibility to examine is the influence of hierarchical ranks acting independently of the preceding variables. Other non-measured influences are stacked in a separate statistical error term.

By following the framework of analysis discussed in the previous section, an individual's job satisfaction is supposed to depend on the magnitude of the gap between the realized level of reward and what is conceived as a fair level of reward. This gap, to be called the *satisfaction score* and denoted by y, is then expressed for individual i in each age group by

$$y_i = b_0 + b_1 \text{ educ}_i + b_2 \text{ tenure}_i + b_3 \text{ sptech}_i + b_4 \text{ manage}_i$$
$$+ b_5 \text{ prod}_i + b_6 \text{ commtime}_i + b_7 \text{ net worth}_i + b_8$$
$$\text{large}_i + b_9 \text{ small} + b_{10} \text{ manuf} + b_{11} \text{ util}_i + b_{12}$$
$$\text{transcom}_i + b_{13} \text{ wholret}_i + b_{14} \text{ finins}_i + b_{15} \text{ realest}_i$$
$$+ b_{16} \text{ service}_i + u_i \qquad (1)$$

In some parts of estimation an additional term, b_{17} rank$_i$, is included. The explanatory variables are defined as follows:

educ	= years of schooling, tenure = duration of service
sptech	= dummy for professional and technical jobs
manage	= dummy for managerial jobs
prod	= dummy for skilled worker or production operative jobs
commtime	= commuting time (1 for less than 30 minutes, . . ., 5 for more than 2 hours)
net worth	= real and net financial wealth held in 10 million yen (the market value of golf club membership included)
large	= dummy for large firms with 1000 or more employees
small	= dummy for small firms with less than 100 employees
manuf	= dummy for manufacturing (including mining) industry
util	= dummy for utility industry
transcom	= dummy for transportation and communication industry
wholret	= dummy for wholesale and retail industry
finins	= dummy for financial and insurance industry
realest	= dummy for real estate industry
service	= dummy for service industry
rank	= hierarchical rank in the employed firm (1 for an ordinary worker, 2 for a section chief (*Kakari-cho*) and equivalent, 3 for a director (*Kacho*) and equivalent, and 4 for a general manager (*Bucho*) and equivalent)

dummy variables take the value 1 if the respondent belongs to the category in question, and take the value 0 otherwise.

The statistical error term u$_i$ is defined as the difference between the two error terms defined earlier. The normalization assumption is that u_i takes 0 as its mean, and 1 for its variance. (This gives the scaling factor for the measurement of the *satisfaction score* discussed above.) It is further supposed that u_i is distributed normally.

Given the foregoing assumptions, the degree of satisfaction on each item can be analyzed in terms of an ordered Probit model. Suppose that within each age group there are four threshold values 0, a_1, a_2, a_3 ($0 < a_1 < a_2 < a_3$) with respect to the *satisfaction score* y_i such that

<domain of y>	<the response>
$y_i < 0$	→ 'dissatisfied'
$0 \leqq_i < a_1$	→ 'somewhat dissatisfied'
$a_1 \leqq y_i < a_2$	→ 'neither satisfied nor dissatisfied'
$a_2 \leqq y_i \, a_3$	→ 'somewhat satisfied'
$a_3 \leqq y_i$	→ 'satisfied'

The coefficients $b_0, \ldots, b_{16}$ (and b_{17}) and the unknown threshold values a_1, a_2, a_3 are then simultaneously estimated by the maximum likelihood method.[12] The coefficients b_j ($j = 1, 2, \ldots, 16, 17$) express the size of the contribution of each factor on the *satisfaction score*. Among these coefficients b_1 through b_5 indicate the net contribution to satisfaction which is defined as each factor's contribution to the realized level of reward net of its contribution to the fair level of reward.

When (1) is estimated for each age group and the results are contrasted with the result of a pooled estimation (whereby all age groups are pooled together), it is shown that the null hypothesis that the vector of coefficients ($b_0, \ldots, b_{16}, a_1, a_2, a_3$) is the same for all age groups is not rejected (in terms of the likelihood ratio test).[13] Therefore, only the result of the pooled estimation will be discussed in the sequel. The estimation result is shown in Table 7.4.

It is perhaps easier to understand the implications of this result by looking at Figures 7.4 and 7.5. Figure 7.4 presents two curves. First, the upward sloping curve shows the relationship between the estimated deterministic part of the *satisfaction score*, hereafter to be called *xb-score*, and the predicted probability value that an individual's response is either 'somewhat satisfied' or 'satisfied', i.e.,

$$Pr\{y_i \geqq \hat{a}_2\} = Pr\{u_i \geqq \hat{a}_2 - x_i\hat{b}\}$$
$$= 1 - F(\hat{a}_2 - x_i\hat{b})$$

Table 7.4.   Ordered Probit regression results on pooled data

| | All ages (25–) | |
	(1)	(2)
const.	1.100	1.013
	(0.150)	(0.151)
educ	−0.00151	−0.00169
	(0.00820)	(0.00838)
tenure	−0.00367	−0.0128
	(0.00224)	(0.00244)
sptech	−0.107	−0.130
	(0.0473)	(0.0474)
manage	0.364	0.199
	(0.0444)	(0.0478)
prod	−0.175	−0.0804
	(0.108)	(0.109)
commtime	−0.0332	−0.0358
	(0.0214)	(0.0214)
net worth	0.0222	0.0165
	(0.00399)	(0.00404)
large	0.357	0.438
	(0.0420)	(0.0429)
small	−0.203	−0.254
	(0.0647)	(0.0650)
manuf	−0.0915	−0.0442
	(0.0649)	(0.0652)
util	0.332	0.448
	(0.120)	(0.121)
transcom	−0.0107	0.0542
	(0.0795)	(0.0799)
wholret	−0.0925	−0.0824
	(0.0663)	(0.0664)
finins	0.389	0.403
	(0.0832)	(0.0834)
realest	−0.105	−0.139
	(0.155)	(0.155)
service	0.0502	0.0656
	(0.0702)	(0.0704)
rank	−	0.214
	−	(0.0229)
A1	0.885	0.895
	(0.0268)	(0.0271)
A2	1.738	1.760
	(0.0322)	(0.0326)
A3	3.133	3.177
	(0.0481)	(0.0488)
Diff. FS	0.560	0.692
	(0.0643)	(0.0660)
Diff. MF	0.481	0.447
	(0.0724)	(0.0726)
Num. of obs.	3,595	3,595
Log Likelihood	−4,994.8	−4,950.7

Note: Dependent variable = satisfaction index A on due reward for effort.

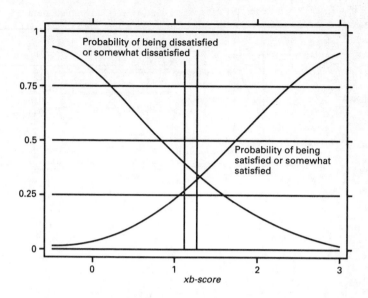

Figure 7.4   The relationship between *xb-score* and the probability of
satisfaction with respect to due rewards for effort

where ^ indicates the estimated value, $x_i\hat{b}$ is a vector notation for the
deterministic part of the RHS of (1), and $F(\ )$ is the cumulative density function of a standard normal variable. Second, the downward
sloping curve shows the relationship between the *xb-score* defined
previously and the predicted probability value that the individual's response is either 'somewhat dissatisfied' or 'dissatisfied,' i.e.,

$$Pr\{y_i < \hat{a}_1\} = Pr\{u_i < \hat{a}_1 - x_i\hat{b}\}$$
$$= F(\hat{a}_1 - x_i\hat{b}).$$

Quite obviously from the specification (1), the higher is the *xb-score*
on the horizontal axis, the higher is the probability of being satisfied
and the lower is the probability of being dissatisfied. The predicted
probability value along each curve can be reinterpreted, via the law of
large numbers, as the proportion of workers having the same *xb-score*
who responds as such. Among the two vertical lines, the right hand
one expresses the mean value of *xb-score* in the sample. The probability levels implied by the intersection points of this line with the
two curves conceptually correspond to the bar graphs of Figures 7.1
and 7.2 (except that the former represents the mean values over four

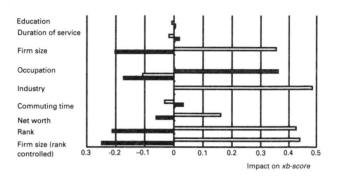

Figure 7.5   Determinants of job satisfaction with respect to due rewards
for effort

Notes:
The standard of comparison and the unit change of each factor chosen to
evaluate the impact on *xb-score* are as follows:

Factor	Upper Bar (Black)	Standard of Comparison	Lower Bar (White)
(1) Education	Junior High School graduate	High School graduate	College graduate
(2) Duration of service	5 years	10 years	15 years
(3) Firm size	Small (−99 employees)	Medium (100–999 employees)	Large (1000–employees)
(4) Occupation	Skilled worker/ produc. operat. (blue-collar)	White-collar (clerical, sales and others)	Prof./technic. (white) managerial (grey)
(5) Industry	Manufacturing	Wholesale and retail	Finance and insurance
(6) Commuting time	−0.5 hour	0.5–1 hour	1–1.5 hours
(7) Net worth	Mean of bottom quartile (2.65 million yen)	Median (30 million yen)	Mean of top quartile (104.88 million yen)
(8) Rank	Ordinary worker	Section chief	General manager
(9) Firm size, rank controlled	Smal	Medium	Large

The bars for (1)–(7) are drawn on the basis of estimated coefficients for
equation (1) while the bars (8)–(9) are drawn on the basis of those for equation (1) with the addition of the rank variable.

Table 7.5. The relationship between the deviation in *xb-score* from its
sample mean and the changes in the probabilities of satisfaction and
dissatisfaction (%)

Δxb–Score	−0.8	−0.6	−0.4	−0.2	+0.2	+0.4	+0.6	+0.8
Δ Probability of satisfaction	−21.7	−17.6	−12.8	−6.7	+7.8	+15.6	+23.3	+31.1
Δ Probability of dissatisfaction	+31.1	+23.3	+15.6	+7.8	−6.7	−12.8	−17.6	−21.7

Source: Figure 7.4.

age groups[14]). The vertical line on the left hand side will be explained
later.

The horizontal bar chart of Figure 7.5, on the other hand, shows the
estimated impact of a unit change in some selected variables on the
xb-score. The horizontal axis represents a change in the *xb-score*. By
looking at these bars simultaneously with Figure 7.4 prediction can be
made as to how large a change in the probability of being satisfied or
that of being dissatisfied the specified change in the explanatory variables would generate. Because of the non-linearity involved the magnitude of the probability changes, in general, depends on where on the
horizontal axis one measures from. Table 7.5 illustrates the numerical
impact in question as measured from the calculated mean *xb-score* of
the sample.

From Figure 7.5 the following characteristics are observed. First,
the effects of schooling and duration of service are negligibly small.
This holds in spite of their importance as determinants of earnings and
hierarchical ranks.[15] The most plausible interpretation of this result seems
to be that an increase in schooling or duration of service not only
raises the actual rewards but also raises the conceptual level of fair
rewards. It is therefore consistent with the assumption that schooling
and duration of service are proxies for individuals' past effort.

Second, the effects of commuting time and net worth are in the expected direction. Their quantitative significance, however, is relatively
small. The coefficient of commuting time is not even statistically
significant. The coefficient of net worth is statistically strongly significant
(at the 1 percent level), yet the difference in *xb-score* generated by the
top and bottom quartiles of the distribution of net worth (which may
be identified as the *haves* and *have-nots*, respectively) is 0.23, amounting
to relatively little in its effect on satisfaction (see Table 7.5). One caveat
is that the non-response rate on the net worth figure amounts to about

a third of the total sample, which calls for a further examination to ascertain if such a magnitude of missing values might not generate a downward bias in the estimation of the net worth effect.

The estimated net worth coefficient provides an answer, if not a conclusive one, to the suspicion raised frequently recently that the widened gap in the distribution of wealth might be badly affecting the work motivation of Japanese workers. The answer from this study does not buttress this suspicion, at least as long as the wealth gap stands at the current level. Yet it does impart a warning that a further worsening in the distribution of wealth would possibly incur deterioration of job satisfaction which, in view of the notion of job worth held by the great majority of workers, would lead to a decline in work motivation.

Third, among occupational types there are rather sizeable differences in the degree of job satisfaction concerning rewards for effort between managerial and blue-collar (skilled worker and production operatives) jobs and between managerial and professional or technical jobs. In terms of *xb-score* the former amounts to 0.54 while the latter amounts to 0.47. The blue-collar and professional/technical workers indeed have relatively strong dissatisfaction about rewards for effort when compared with white-collar workers in general.[16]

Fourth, among the industrial categories there exists little difference between the manufacturing and the wholesale/retail sectors, yet there is a sizeable difference between these two industries and the finance/insurance sector. In terms of *xb-score*, the latter amounts to 0.48. (The estimated difference in the two coefficients $b_{14} - b_{10}$ together with its standard error is shown as 'Diff. MF' near the bottom of Table 7.4.) Between the manufacturing and finance/insurance sectors there exists around 24–36 percent difference in annual wage earnings throughout age groups after controlling for schooling, duration of service, occupational types and firm size, and such an earnings differential clearly lies in the background for such a big differential in satisfaction. (Further discussion is made in the concluding part of the chapter.)

Fifth, concerning hierarchical ranks, there exists a large difference between a general manager and an ordinary worker. The *xb-score* differs by as much as 0.64. The fact that satisfaction is high among high ranking workers and is low among low ranking workers is not necessarily obvious, however. For, if each rank is paid what workers in that rank regard as fair and if promotion occurs in ways workers regard as fair, then a significant part of the difference in question must disappear. What would still remain is the dissatisfaction with respect to the scarcity of the opportunity for promotion and/or the hierarchical structure itself. It seems, therefore, that differences in satisfaction among different ranks reflect complaints that exist around the operation of personnel management inside firms.

Sixth, and finally, there appears to be a large difference among firms of different sizes in their capacity to generate job satisfaction.[17] Between large firms (with 1000 or more employees) and small firms (with less than 100 employees) the *xb-score* differs by 0.56 (i.e., see 'Diff. FS' (= $b_8 - b_9$) recorded near the bottom of Table 7.4). In Figure 7.5, there is another bar placed at the bottom which represents the effect of firm size, this time controlling for the rank of individual (thus corresponding to the estimates of Column (2) of Table 7.4). This implies that, comparing among workers with the same rank, there is 0.64 difference in terms of *xb-score* between large and small firms. The gap of 0.08 that occurs depending on whether or not the rank is controlled arises mainly from the fact that the probability of assuming a higher position is larger in small firms than in large firms.[18]

Viewed from the opposite angle, even if small firms are more likely to promote individuals the effect in reducing the job satisfaction differential between large and small firms is at most 13 percent (=0.08/ 0.64). Naturally the existence of large wage-*cum*-non-wage benefit differentials between large and small firms lie at the heart of the matter.

It has been remarked earlier that there exists a significant underrepresentation of the manufacturing industry, blue-collar workers and small firms in the current sample. Although by no means a fully justifiable procedure, a rough adjustment of the mean *xb-score* was made on the basis of column (1) estimates, using the mean schooling and duration of service figures and the industrial, firm size, and white-collar/blue-collar composition figures of the 1990 *Census of Wages* data. The result is shown as the left hand side vertical line in Figure 7.4. Adjusted figures show that individuals who are not satisfied with respect to the fairness of reward are indeed much larger in proportion than those who are satisfied.

7.5 DETERMINANTS OF JOB SATISFACTION WITH RESPECT TO NON-PECUNIARY QUALITIES

What about the satisfaction indices B(exhibit ability fully), C(stimulating), and D(broadness of responsibility)? As shown in section 7.3 there exist relatively high correlations among these indices. In fact, the ordered Probit analyses for the respective indices (conducted separately for each age group) have arrived at qualitatively very similar results. This implies that the explanatory variables at hand have quite analogous effects on each of the three non-pecuniary dimensions of job satisfaction.[19] In the following, the non-pecuniary attributes of the job will be represented by index C, namely whether or not the job provides challenge and stimulating experiences.

Basically the same model as in the case of satisfaction on due rewards for effort is employed. The only modification is that of excluding the variables 'commtime' and 'net worth' as they seem irrelevant to the question of challenge and stimulating experience on the job. The results of estimation are given in Table 7.6.

Figures 7.6 and 7.7 are depicted for each age group on the basis of estimated coefficients in Table 7.6. Considering the two vertical lines in Figure 7.6, the right hand one shows the unadjusted mean of the *xb-score*, while the left hand one shows its adjusted mean explained previously. The size of adjustment is largest among the age group 25–34.

The impact of each factor on the *xb-score* is summarized by Figure 7.7 (prepared analogously to Figure 7.5), this time drawn for each age group. It is apparent that certain features differ significantly among age groups.[20]

First, while the net impact of schooling and duration of service on satisfaction is negligible (just as in the case of satisfaction on due rewards) there is a single exception to the rule, i.e., the effect of schooling for age group 25–34, which is positive and statistically significant. Between high school and college graduates the *xb-score* differs as much as 0.27. Note also that the rank variable is not statistically significant for this age group. These results imply that, in the life stage during which promotion is not yet a major concern, schooling differentials play a leading role in allocating individuals to jobs with rich learning opportunities which, in turn, facilitate the major source of challenge and stimulation.

Second, observing among different industries the advantage of the finance/insurance industry over manufacturing industry noted previously in the case of satisfaction on due rewards still holds for the young age group (aged 25–34) as the *xb-score* differential reaches 0.6 (see 'Diff. MF' coefficient at the bottom of Table 7.6). The advantage of the finance/insurance industry, however, declines monotonically with age. For the age group 45–54, it effectively disappears, and for the age group 55 and above the tendency is the reverse: it is now the manufacturing industry which has the advantage (0.34 in *xb-score*, although not statistically significant).[21] It is to be remarked that these features

Table 7.6. Ordered probit regression results on data for each age group

	Age 25–34		Age 35–44		Age 45–54		Age 55 –	
	(1)	(2)	(1)	(2)	(1)	(2)	(1)	(2)
const.	-0.165	-0.178	1.256	1.185	1.149	1.0182	1.126	1.0606
	(0.354)	(0.354)	(0.214)	(0.214)	(0.205)	(0.206)	(0.279)	(0.282)
educ	0.0681	0.0659	0.00141	-0.0183	0.0116	-0.0157	0.00939	-0.000098
	(0.0197)	(0.0198)	(0.0112)	(0.0116)	(0.0111)	(0.0118)	(0.0176)	(0.0185)
tenure	-0.000477	-0.00299	-0.00338	-0.0107	-0.00403	-0.00968	-0.00349	-0.00440
	(0.00957)	(0.00998)	(0.00453)	(0.00466)	(0.00364)	(0.00374)	(0.00391)	(0.00395)
sptech	0.215	0.213	0.166	0.157	0.214	0.202	0.575	0.533
	(0.0784)	(0.0784)	(0.0622)	(0.0623)	(0.0781)	(0.0783)	(0.138)	(0.140)
manage	0.236	0.212	0.309	0.176	0.272	0.102	0.292	0.196
	(0.115)	(0.119)	(0.0587)	(0.0619)	(0.0634)	(0.0681)	(0.110)	(0.125)
prod	-0.196	-0.198	-0.188	-0.107	-0.148	-0.0106	-0.0980	-0.0709
	(0.202)	(0.202)	(0.131)	(0.132)	(0.127)	(0.129)	(0.257)	(0.258)
large	0.294	0.302	0.230	0.285	0.353	0.425	0.162	0.179
	(0.0754)	(0.0759)	(0.0552)	(0.0558)	(0.0639)	(0.0649)	(0.119)	(0.120)
small	-0.104	-0.109	-0.151	-0.177	-0.0543	-0.129	-0.0144	-0.0127
	(0.113)	(0.113)	(0.0844)	(0.0846)	(0.0909)	(0.0918)	(0.130)	(0.130)
manuf	0.200	0.203	0.176	0.207	0.214	0.290	0.172	0.209
	(0.119)	(0.119)	(0.0853)	(0.0856)	(0.102)	(0.103)	(0.182)	(0.183)
util	0.256	0.267	0.208	0.311	0.183	0.321	0.138	0.207
	(0.206)	(0.207)	(0.167)	(0.168)	(0.184)	(0.185)	(0.343)	(0.346)
transcom	0.111	0.117	-0.172	-0.111	-0.0790	0.0443	-0.121	-0.0864
	(0.155)	(0.155)	(0.103)	(0.103)	(0.113)	(0.115)	(0.200)	(0.201)

Table continued on page 204

204

Table 7.6. continued

	Age 25–34		Age 35–44		Age 45–54		Age 55 –	
	(1)	(2)	(1)	(2)	(1)	(2)	(1)	(2)
wholret	0.423	0.417	0.101	0.0901	0.318	0.354	0.232	0.253
	(0.122)	(0.122)	(0.0851)	(0.0852)	(0.106)	(0.106)	(0.189)	(0.189)
finins	0.801	0.790	0.400	0.376	0.253	0.327	−0.171	−0.130
	(0.150)	(0.150)	(0.109)	(0.109)	(0.144)	(0.145)	(0.297)	(0.298)
realest	0.374	0.346	−0.216	−0.249	0.643	0.763	0.065	0.0739
	(0.230)	(0.233)	(0.223)	(0.224)	(0.301)	(0.302)	(0.293)	(0.293)
service	0.105	0.0998	0.0321	0.0121	0.349	0.409	−0.00248	0.0244
	(0.124)	(0.124)	(0.0912)	(0.0914)	(0.115)	(0.116)	(0.172)	(0.173)
rank	—	0.0496	—	0.218	—	0.235	—	0.0832
		(0.0560)		(0.0314)		(0.0342)		(0.0508)
A1	0.682	0.683	0.790	0.802	0.835	0.851	0.690	0.692
	(0.0445)	(0.0445)	(0.0389)	(0.0395)	(0.0502)	(0.0511)	(0.0738)	(0.0740)
A2	1.552	1.553	1.734	1.758	1.992	2.027	1.981	1.986
	(0.0550)	(0.0550)	(0.0459)	(0.0466)	(0.0587)	(0.0599)	(0.0936)	(0.0939)
A3	2.900	2.902	3.124	3.165	3.386	3.444	3.178	3.187
	(0.0751)	(0.0751)	(0.0605)	(0.0614)	(0.0751)	(0.0767)	(0.123)	(0.123)
Diff. FS	0.398	0.411	0.381	0.462	0.407	0.554	0.177	0.192
	(0.116)	(0.116)	(0.0847)	(0.0856)	(0.0939)	(0.0965)	(0.145)	(0.145)
Diff. MF	0.601	0.586	0.224	0.170	0.0387	0.0374	−0.343	−0.339
	(0.128)	(0.129)	(0.0969)	(0.0974)	(0.125)	(0.125)	(0.278)	(0.278)
Num. of obs.	1181	1181	2067	2067	1593	1593	522	522
Log Likelihood	−1653.1	−1652.7	−2813.6	−2789.4	−2052.7	−2029.1	−680.6	−679.3

Note: Dependent variable = satisfaction index C on stimulating experience.

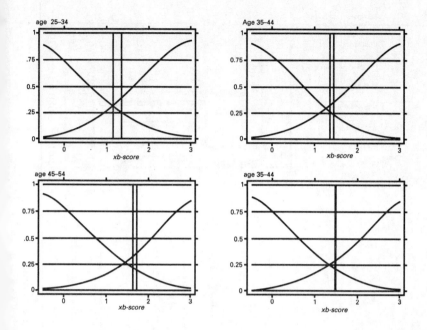

Figure 7.6 The relationship between *xb-score* and the probability of satisfaction with respect to the existence of stimulating experience on the job

Note: In each figure, the upward sloping curve represents the probability of being satisfied or somewhat satisfied, while the downward sloping curve represents the probability of being dissatisfied or somewhat dissatisfied.
Source: Table 7.6.

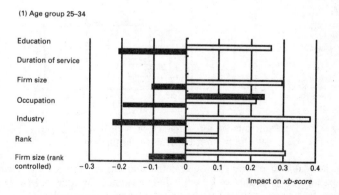

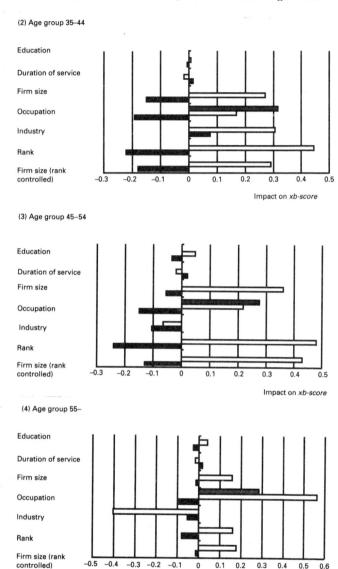

Figure 7.7   Determinants of job satisfaction with respect to the existence
of stimulating experience on the job

Note: The standard of comparison and the unit change in each explanatory
factor is identical with that of Figure 7.5. The commuting time and net worth
variables have been excluded from the set of explanatory variables.

also hold for B and D indices. This result indicates that the finance/insurance industry, while maintaining comparative advantage in terms of rewards for effort, does not succeed in maintaining comparative advantage in the long run over the intrinsic quality of the job. Alternatively speaking, some form of a compensating relationship in the life-time between pecuniary and non-pecuniary rewards is operating among a certain subset of industries.

The foregoing discussion has dealt with characteristics that are specific to age. Another point that is characteristic of non-pecuniary qualities of the job (*vis-à-vis* pecuniary rewards) is the place occupied by professional/technical workers. It has already been noted that these jobs are positioned close to blue-collar workers in terms of satisfaction on pecuniary rewards, yet with respect to the existence of challenging and stimulating experience they are positioned close to managerial jobs. The advantage of professional/technical jobs over blue-collar jobs in terms of *xb-score* amounts to 0.35–0.4 for the age groups up to 45–54, and then jumps to 0.68 for the age group 55 and above, far surpassing that of managerial jobs. Therefore, more than any other type of job, workers with this type of job continue to receive stimulating experience even when they become older.

Concerning the impact of firm size, a similar feature to the case of pecuniary rewards is observed, except that its effect diminishes for the age group 55 and above. There is a sizeable difference (0.3–0.4 in terms of *xb-score*) between large and small firms in their capacity to generate satisfaction about stimulating experience among workers and, moreover, such a difference does not diminish much even if the relative ease of getting promotion in small firms is taken into account.

7.6 CONCLUDING REMARKS

This chapter has analyzed the determinants of job satisfaction among Japanese workers by using micro survey data on worker attitudes collected in three major metropolitan areas of Japan. More specifically, the chapter has examined how workers' job satisfaction relates to such factors as education, job tenure in the firm, industry, occupation, firm size, and wealth holding.

Job satisfaction has been considered in two dimensions; first, how worker's effort is rewarded in terms of pay and promotion, and second, how stimulating an experience the job provides. The former may be regarded as largely, though not exclusively, pecuniary, while the latter concerns an intrinsic or a non-pecuniary quality of the job. In fact, the latter is taken to represent two other non-pecuniary qualities of the job explored in the survey, whether or not the job allows the worker fully to exhibit his/her ability and whether or not the job allows the holder to exercise a broad realm of responsibility. The major findings of the chapter are as follows.

First, on both pecuniary and non-pecuniary dimensions the difference in firm size has notable impact on the degree of satisfaction. The advantage of large firms does not diminish even if the tendency (confirmed within the data) for workers in small firms to be promoted more easily than their counterparts in large firms is taken into consideration.

Second, as compared with ordinary white-collar (clerical, sales, and service) jobs, blue-collar jobs are clearly at a disadvantage on both dimensions of job satisfaction. Against the same standard, professional/ technical jobs have an advantage with respect to non-pecuniary qualities (whose extent increases as workers become older) but are at a disadvantage with respect to (satisfaction about) pecuniary rewards. This appears to be one of the very few cases in the data for which something close to the principle of equalizing difference is operating.

Third, industry-wise, there exists a significant difference in the degree of satisfaction concerning pecuniary rewards between the manufacturing and wholesale/retail industries, on the one hand, and the finance/ insurance industry, on the other. Yet, with respect to the capacity of providing stimulating experience (and other non-pecuniary qualities) the relative advantage of finance/insurance industry declines quickly with age, and it may even turn into a disadvantage for workers in the old age group.

Fourth, even though the levels of education and firm job-tenure certainly enhance wage earnings and the chances of getting to a higher rank, they have virtually no effect at all on workers' job satisfaction in both dimensions. (The single exception is the effect of education on young workers' feeling of stimulating experience on the job.) Such discrepancy in the results may be explained by the simultaneous rise in the levels of rewards (in both dimensions) that workers consider as fair and those that they actually receive.

Fifth, there exists a statistically significant wealth effect on the degree of satisfaction concerning pecuniary rewards, yet quantitatively its effect is a relatively mild one. Therefore, the acute rise in the skewness of wealth distribution that Japan experienced recently has yet to affect seriously the work motivation of individuals, in particular, the young workers who do not own land in the urban area. The present result does facilitate a conclusion, however, to the effect that a further worsening in the dispersion of wealth distribution might possibly adversely affect the motivation of workers as a whole by increasing the number of workers who feel that they are not paid a fair reward.

So much for the findings. Overall one may be inclined to point out a paradox. The paradox is that workers in the manufacturing sector (blue-collar workers, in particular, but not limited to them) which boasts of internationally renowned productivity and quality of product exhibit relatively low scores in terms of job satisfaction, or to be more precise, high incidence of worker dissatisfaction about the job on both pecuniary and non-pecuniary grounds. The manufacturing sector in Japan is also associated with an intricate network of small subsidiary firms, and the smallness of firm size is shown to be an additional factor contributing to the incidence of worker dissatisfaction.

It is perhaps not far-fetched to relate such high incidence of dissatisfaction to the existence of dualistic division in the labour market that is most heavily enmeshed in the manufacturing industry.

A parallel study by the author based on the micro dataset of the *Census of Wages* and employing the methodology of switching regressions (as applied by Dickens and Lang, 1985) has delineated the existence of a clear dualistic wage structure in the overall Japanese labour market. One component, the primary sector, is represented by an earnings equation with high rates of return to both education and experience (both internal and external) and is generally associated with high wages, while the other component, the secondary sector, is represented by an earnings equation with almost no returns to education and external experience but with a moderate rate of return to internal experience and yet is generally characterized by low wages and relatively long working hours. The moderate rate of return on internal experience is not much of a blessing for secondary sector workers, for either voluntarily or involuntarily they tend to move among firms frequently, thereby losing the opportunity to reap any benefit. Incidence of the secondary sector turned out to be particularly high in the manufacturing industry, and especially among the blue-collar jobs. As the secondary sector job is associated with little learning opportunities such workers may also naturally feel discontent with respect to the non-pecuniary qualities of the job.[22]

One general implication of this study concerning worker welfare, and more specifically for enriching the life-long quality of work life for Japanese workers, might be to raise the specialty content of the job.[23] It would be particularly helpful to older workers. In terms of practice, however, it may not be so simple, for it would certainly require a major reappraisal and restructuring of the personnel management system. More specifically, examination of possible tradeoffs that such a modification in job content would entail, e.g., deteriorating breadth of knowledge held by workers, must be made. In any case, in an increasingly aging society like Japan such a reappraisal would certainly be a welcome move on the part of workers, and it might even facilitate a profitable source of organizational innovation for employers.

This study concludes by pointing out two qualifications of the present analysis. The first concerns the limitation of the data. Because of the sampling design, attitudes of workers employed in very small firms (with less than 30 employees) are not considered, and because of the smallness of the samples female workers have been excluded from the analysis. Yet as far as the excluded female samples are concerned they tend to exhibit a higher incidence of job dissatisfaction than male counterparts, which accords well with the popular expectation. It is also unfortunate that the survey lacks the data on working hours. One of the main dependent variables, rewards for effort, could have been analyzed much further had there been information on working hours.

The second qualification pertains to the basic methodology adopted in the analysis. The point is that there may be an alternative interpretation to the respondents' answer of 'neither satisfied nor dissatisfied' concerning job satisfaction indices. A fairly large proportion of workers actually chose that answer. The interpretation adopted in this study has been that the size of the gap between the fair and the realized levels of reward for an individual with that particular answer lies in between the range generating satisfaction and the range registering complaint. It is based on the presumption that all individuals have a considered opinion and evaluation of their jobs when they are given a questionnaire. Without such preparation, however, individuals may simply refuse or avoid answering the question that delves deeply into their identity by taking the choice 'neither satisfied nor dissatisfied'. Although the estimation results (Tables 7.4 and 7.6) indicate consistency of the data with the present interpretation (cf. the meaningfulness of the boundary coefficients), it does not necessarily mean that the alternative interpretation is foreclosed by the data.

The distinction of well-considered responses from those that are not certainly requires a more refined design of the questionnaire form. A more refined survey should also contain questions on the possible concrete sources of job satisfaction (like the ones collected by Lincoln and Kalleberg) the lack of which has led the present study to rest at a rather superficial level of relating job satisfaction to the observable environment of employment.

Notes

* I would like to thank Kuramitsu Muramatsu, Motohiro Morishima, and Mari Sako as well as other participants of the conference for helpful discussions and Paul Ryan, Atsushi Seike and Hiroshi Yoshikawa for valuable comments and criticisms on earlier versions of the chapter. I would also like to thank Yoshie Ohta and her staff at the Ministry of Labour for not only permitting me to use the data but also conducting a special inquiry to improve a portion of it. Finally, I would like to acknowledge the financial support provided by the Tokyo Center for Economic Research under its project entitled *The Problem of Human Resources and Their Future Perspectives in Japan*.
1. Discussion of the distribution of such subjective scores as whether or not 'expectation' is 'fulfilled' obviously faces, in principle, the difficulty known as interpersonal utility comparisons. Yet as long as individual differences in preferences are random and are statistically independent of the observable individual attributes and characteristics of the workplace that are chosen as the explanatory variables of the present analysis it can be examined whether or not there exists stable dependence of 'satisfaction' on the variables just listed. This constitutes the major presumption of the analysis below.
2. For an overall discussion of the findings from the survey see Ministry of Labour (1991a).
3. The classic works in the fields of industrial sociology, industrial psychology, and labour management and control include Blauner (1964), Whyte (1955) and Edwards (1979), respectively.
4. Lincoln and Kalleberg (1990). This includes a useful survey of the existing literature on work commitment and job satisfaction in Japan (see pp. 53–62). I am indebted to Mari Sako for informing me of the existence of this work at the conference.
5. Another major purpose of Lincoln and Kalleberg's study not mentioned in text is comparison of work attitudes between Japanese workers and American workers, for which they have conducted a similar survey in the city of Indianapolis. Interested readers are also referred to this portion of their study.
6. Respondents were frequently found to err about knowledge of the size of the firm they worked in. (This became apparent when several individuals who belonged to the same establishment answered differently about firm size.) After weeding out all the questionable responses the author requested the Ministry of Labour to investigate the correct size of the firm; they then kindly tracked down all the names of the establishments to which questionable samples belonged and obtained the correct figures of firm size by using their own records of establishments. Corrected firm

size figures are employed throughout the analysis reported in this chapter.

Another difficulty with the data was that missing values appeared frequently concerning the value of real wealth holding. In cases where information on the date and method of acquisition (either through new purchase or through inheritance) is obtained the missing values are estimated by assigning the mean value of the real assets having similar physical attributes in the respective area (Tokyo, Nagoya or Osaka).

Finally, non-responses with respect to the ownership of the golf club membership were identified as zero holding.

7. This aspect on job worth seems quite independent of the frequently discussed changes in the importance that workers attach to family or individual leisure life as compared with life at work or life in an organization. Across age cohorts young workers are observed to show relatively more concern on the former. This aspect of changes in worker consciousness is surveyed and discussed in Ieuji (1986 pp. 6–14) and Ministry of Labour (1991b). Also Muramatsu (1992), in a survey on white-collar workers in the automobile and automobile parts industries in the Nagoya area, notes the simultaneous existence of the tendency for the value orientation towards family life to increase among the young workers and the tendency for the feeling of the necessity of job worth (i.e., meaningfulness of the job) to remain constant across the age groups, which seems to support the hypothesis that the two facets of valuation are independent (see Muramatsu, pp. 60–1).

9. The author is indebted to a criticism of Paul Ryan with regard to the ambiguity of the meaning of 'effort' used in an earlier version of the chapter.

10. See Scitovsky (1992, pp. 34–5), in particular the discussion on the Wundt curve.

11. The Mantel–Haenszel chi-square statistics obtained indicate that the null hypothesis that there exists a linear relationship between any two of B, C, and D indices is rejected by a wide margin. Hence, there is no reason to suppose that these indices are substantively identical. On the other hand, it will later be stated (see n. 19 below) that the model in this chapter is not powerful enough to be able to delineate the causes of different responses to each of these indices.

12. For a more detailed explanation about the estimation method, see Maddala (1983, pp. 46–9).

13. In fact, in terms of the likelihood ratio test the null hypothesis that all the coefficients are identical among four different age groups was not rejected, with the chi-square test statistic equalling 42.22 with 60 degrees of freedom.

14. When compared with Figures 7.1 and 7.2, the calculated value of the satisfaction probability tends to be underestimated. This discrepancy results from the exclusion of those samples with missing values on net worth in the regression procedure. The excluded samples amounted to 1831 in the total sample size of 5519.

15. For annual wage earnings the rates of return on schooling and job tenure in the firm are estimated as follows. The explanatory variables in the log-earnings equations are identical with those in equation (1), with controls on firm size, occupation and industry:

Age group	25–34	35–44	45–54	55–
Schooling (%)	4.6	2.9	3.2	3.7
Job tenure (%)	3.4	0.9	0.8	1.6

All of these coefficients are statistically significant at the 1 percent level.

The next figures represent the estimated coefficients on the same set of variables when an ordered Probit model is applied to the individual's position in the hierarchy (with the numerical assignment of 4 for a general manager, 3 for a division director, 2 for a section chief, and 1 for an ordinary worker) whereby firm size dummies are included as the other explanatory variables:

Age group	25–34	35–44	45–54	55–
Schooling	0.152	0.177	0.208	0.181
Job tenure	0.131	0.0476	0.0335	0.0112

These figures express the impact of each variable on the *xb-score*, just as in the main text. The effect of job tenure is thus found monotonically to decline with age, while that of schooling is found to stand still. All the coefficients are statistically significant at the 1 percent level.

16. The estimated coefficients of occupational dummies in the log earnings functions reported in n. 15 above are as follows:

Age group	25–35	35–44	45–54	55–
Professional/Technical	−0.0220	0.0265	0.000505	0.165
	(0.0207)	(0.0162)	(0.0231)	(0.0624)
Managerial	0.0358	0.140	0.133	0.262
	(0.0308)	(0.0150)	(0.0186)	(0.0523)
Skilled/Production	0.0249	−0.112	−0.112	0.0582
	(0.0786)	(0.037)	(0.0424)	(0.132)

The figures in parentheses are standard errors. The base of the occupational dummies is taken to be the white-collar occupation other than three categories listed above.

17. A statistically significant positive effect of plant size on worker job satisfaction (as well as on workers' feeling of commitment towards work) has also been found (see Lincoln and Kalleberg, 1990, p. 228, Table 8.1).

18. In fact, the coefficients of firm size dummies in the ordered Probit equations described in n. 15 above are:

Age group	25–34	35–44	45–54	55–
Large firms	−0.394	−0.342	−0.336	−0.273
Small firms	0.182	0.118	0.422	−0.0106

where the base of firm size is taken to be the medium-sized firm with 100–999 regular employees. The coefficients for large firms are all statistically significant at the 1 percent level, whereas for small firms only the estimate for the age group 45–54 is statistically significant at the 1 percent level.

19. This also highlights the limitation of the present data. Had it contained information on objective job characteristics such as those collected by Lincoln and Kalleberg, differences in the responses to the three items of non-pecuniary attributes could have been analyzed further.

20. In fact, the likelihood ratio test similar to the one described in n. 13 above conducted on B, C, and D indices, respectively, has shown that, in each case, the null hypothesis of identical coefficients among different age groups is rejected at the 1 percent significance level.

21. One possible explanation for the reversal of the coefficient in the finance industry may be that workers there tend to move to subsidiary or related firms from their late 40s so that few workers in high ranking positions remain in the sample for the age group 55 and above. As a matter of fact, the sample counts of this particular group of workers turned out to be only 19, which no doubt explains the statistical weakness of the estimate. Yet the composition of these 19 samples in terms of the hierarchical position occupied turned out to be 7 general managers, 1 division director, 1 section chief and 9 ordinary workers, and 1 unknown. Therefore, the above conjecture does not seem to hold.

22. The switching regression results referred to in the text is reported in Ishikawa and Dejima (1993). For the pioneering contribution applying this methodology in the context of a US study, see Dickens and Lang (1985, pp. 792–805).

23. See the proposal made in Seike (1992).

References

Blauner, R. (1964) *Alienation and Freedom: The Factory Worker and His Industry*, Chicago, University of Chicago Press.

Dickens, W. and K. Lang (1985) 'A Test of Dual Labor Market Theory', *American Economic Review*, vol. 75, September.

Edwards, R. (1979) *Contested Terrain: The Transformation of the Workplace in the Twentieth Century*, New York, Basic Books.

Ieuji, Y. (1986) 'Jyakunenso no Kinro Ishiki no Henka to Kigyo Keiei' (Changes in the Work Consciousness of the Young and Firm Management), *Rodo Tokei Chosa Geppo*, vol. 38, June, pp. 6–14.

Ishikawa, T. and T. Dejima (1993) 'Measuring the Extent and Nature of Duality in Japanese Labour Market', a paper presented at the International Workshop, 'Europe, Japan and the United States: Technological Progress and Financial Structure', (Turin, 1–3 April). The Japanese version appeared in T. Ishikawa (ed.), *Nihon no Shotoku to Tomi no Bunpai* (Distribution of Income and Wealth in Japan), Tokyo, University of Tokyo Press, 1994.

Lincoln, J.R. and A.L. Kalleberg (1990) *Culture, Control and Commitment: A Study of Work Organization and Work Attitudes in the United States and Japan*, Cambridge, Cambridge University Press.

Maddala, G.S. (1983) *Limited-Dependent and Qualitative Variables in Econometrics*, Cambridge, Cambridge University Press.

Ministry of Labour (1991a) *Shisan Kakusa to Kinrosha Seikatsu ni kansuru*

Kenkyukai Hokokusho (The Report of the Research Group on Wealth Dispersion and Worker Life), August.

Ministry of Labour (1991b) *Gendai Wakamono no Shokugyo Ishiki: Shokugyo Ishiki no Henka ni Taiou suru tameni* (Occupational Consciousness of the Contemporary Young), September.

Muramatsu, K. (1992) 'Howaito Karar no Hatarakigai to Noryoku Shugi' (The Job Meaningfulness for White Collar Workers and Meritocracy), *Nanzan Keizai Kenkyu*, vol. 7, October, pp. 60–1.

Scitovsky, J. (1992) *The Joyless Economy: The Psychology of Human Satisfaction*, 2nd edn, New York, Oxford University Press.

Seike, A. (1992) *Koreisha no Rodo Keizaigaku* (The Labour Economics of the Elderly), Tokyo, Toyo Keizai.

Whyte, W.F. (1955) *Money and Motivation: An Analysis of Incentives in Industry*, New York, Harper & Row.

8 Pay and Performance

Charles Brown*

USA
J31
J33
J41

A critical link between the labour market and the performance of the firm is the ability of the firm to attract, retain, and motivate workers. This personnel function is largely absent from the simplest textbook models of the firm's demand for labour, either because workers are assumed to be identical and effort is ignored, or because firms are assumed to determine and pay each worker the value of his/her marginal product if these marginal products differ. If all workers are paid exactly the value of what they produce, the labour cost per unit of output is the same whether one hires able, hard-working employees or less able, lazy ones.

While such a simplification is defensible for studying many problems, it is more realistic to view personnel policies as firms do, as a key component of their ability to remain profitable and even to survive. Indeed, concerns about competitiveness have refocused firms' attention on strengthening the link between pay and performance (Greeley and Oschner, 1986; Mitchell, Lewin and Lawler, 1990).

Once one allows that individual workers' wages differ from their marginal products, attention is necessarily focused on the reasons for such disparities, and the wage-setting institutions and other consequences that result. That, broadly, is the subject of this chapter.

In section 8.1, I present a number of different models of wage determination, focusing on individual workers who differ in their ability or levels of effort rather than on labour as a homogeneous factor of production. Section 8.2 offers a broad empirical overview of the quite limited evidence on the rules and institutions of wage-setting in the U.S. In section 8.3, I contrast piece rates and time rates as methods of determining individual workers' pay. In section 8.4, I consider evidence that the wage distribution is compressed, in that workers who produce more do not earn proportionately more than less productive co-workers, and then in section 8.5 explore the relationship between worker performance and turnover. In section 8.6, I present survey evidence on workers' perceptions of the pay–performance link at their workplace, and of their employer's willingness to match outside offers

216

for superior workers. In section 8.7, I offer some concluding observations.

Wherever possible, I focus on differences in pay and performance for workers doing similar work, ideally for the same employer. Perhaps the major omission that results is neglect of profit-sharing and related mechanisms which tie part of all workers' pay to the profits (or other outcome measures) of the organization as a whole.[1] Another implication of this focus is that attention is directed toward occupations where firms have several workers doing similar work, and therefore away from executive compensation issues.[2]

8.1 THEORIES OF INDIVIDUALS' WAGE DETERMINATION

Simple textbook models in which each worker receives a wage equal to his or her marginal product ignore two reasons why this equality might not be realized in practice: (1) a worker's output is not easily observed, and often the cost of measuring that output precisely is too high; (2) workers who are uncertain about what their marginal products will be may prefer a more egalitarian wage distribution as insurance.

The economic interactions that are generated by these two features of the labour market are both interesting and complex. Lacking perfect information about each worker's contribution, employers search for wage-setting rules that are attractive to productive workers and encourage them to work hard. Workers, concerned that they may turn out to be less able or just unlucky may have an interest in a more equal wage distribution, but employers who offer such insurance must concentrate on retaining those who learn that they are highly productive.

A substantial body of research has explored these and related themes. This section is therefore deliberately selective, focusing on models that are most closely related to the available data.

8.1.1 Paying the Conditional Expectation of Marginal Product

A useful starting point is Aigner and Cain's (1977) model of competitive employers, who have imperfect information about workers' productivity. To emphasize the role of wage determination in indirectly selecting the quality of a firm's workforce, effort levels supplied by workers are implicitly assumed constant. Competition leads the firm to set each worker's wage equal to the expected value of his/her marginal product conditional on available information. Let the worker's true marginal product be q, and let y be an imperfectly measured version of q, with the measurement error $e = y - q$ uncorrelated with q. One can think of y as a 'test score' prior to hiring or a 'performance evaluation' on the job; given that the model does not have an inter-temporal dimension either interpretation is appropriate. The key assumption is that e is uncorrelated with q, rather than with y: we have an errors in the variables model, not an omitted variables model. Less critically, e has mean zero; q, y and e are assumed to be normally distributed.

The firm sets the wage w equal to the conditional expectation of q given y:

$$w(y) = E(q|y) = \alpha y + (1 - \alpha)E(q)$$

where $\alpha = \text{var}(q)/\text{var}(y)$. Thus, the employer averages the imperfect indicator of productivity and the unconditional mean, with the weight on the latter larger the less accurate is y. This in turn means that the wage varies α-for-one rather than one-for-one with differences in *true* performance q:

$$E(w|q) = \alpha E(y|q) + (1 - \alpha)E(q) = \alpha q + (1 - \alpha)E(q)$$

Now suppose there are two groups with possibly different distributions of q and y, but with group membership unerringly measured. In Aigner and Cain's original paper, differences by race or sex were stressed, but the same analysis applies to schooling or age. Competitive employers would apply the above wage-setting rules to each group separately. With group membership well measured, differentials between groups would accurately reflect differences in productivity between groups; imperfect measurement of performance leads to within-group redistribution compared to the perfect measurement, $\alpha = 1$ 'textbook' outcome.

It is easy to show that if all employers make the same error in measuring a particular worker's performance, competition would force firms to offer wages according to the above rules. If other firms offered workers their expected marginal product, the alternative wage of workers any one firm might hire would equal this expected marginal product. Consequently, the firm cannot attract any worker to whom it offers less, and cannot afford to offer more.

But it is unlikely that the errors that firms make in either predicting or in measuring performance are identical at different firms. If these errors differ across firms, a worker's expected marginal product at one firm may be higher or lower than his/her wage elsewhere, and so the right wage-setting rule is not obvious. Hashimoto and Yu (1980) considered a related problem, and their results suggest that the same qualitative results would continue to hold in this more realistic setting.

8.1.2 Piece Rates and Time Rates

Rather than taking the accuracy with which employers measure output to be given, Lazear (1986) allowed the firm to choose between measuring output precisely at a cost per worker of θ and not monitoring output at all (except perhaps that some minimum level is attained). If output is measured precisely, the worker receives $q - \theta$; if output is not measured, the worker receives a fixed wage or 'salary' s. For any given value of s, workers with $q - \theta > s$ will opt for piece rates and those with $q - \theta < s$ will choose time rates. In equilibrium, the value of s must adjust so that it is equal to the mean value of q among those who opt for time rates.

Two predictions emerge from this model: first, if the cost of a piece rate system is higher, fewer workers will find it worth 'paying' θ to have their output measured precisely, and the fraction of workers who receive piece rates will fall. Second, because each of the piece rate workers earns more than s, the average wage of piece rate workers exceeds the average wage of salaried workers. And, to relate this model to that discussed in section 8.1.1, notice that the pay–performance relationship is attenuated (in the strong version of the model, absent) for time rated workers but not for the piece rate workers.

A similar analysis applies if we think of method of pay as motivating a worker with a fixed level of ability rather than guiding the matching of firms and workers. Those working under piece rates have a substantial marginal incentive to work harder, which those working under time rates do not have. Consequently, those working under piece rates exert a higher level of effort, and earn more; those working under time rates exert the minimum level of effort that the firm can detect cheaply and which it requires as a condition for employment.[3]

Treating 'selection' and 'motivation' separately has a cost, missing the fact that 'ability' and 'effort' are often substitutes. One notion of ability is that more able individuals produce a given output with less effort, so that 'ability' and 'energy level' are hard to distinguish. In Brown (1990a) I outlined a model in which utility equals the wage minus the psychic cost of effort on the job, and the latter cost increases with output but is inversely proportional to ability. Piece rates encourage workers to work harder and earn more, but only the more able find this package more attractive than lower wages and lower effort under time rates.

I also discussed a model with three methods of pay, piece rates, merit pay, and standard rates. Under piece rates output is monitored precisely and wages are tied to output. Under standard rates, little is spent monitoring output and wages depend only slightly on output. Merit pay serves as an intermediate category, with less precise measurement and a weaker link to wages than under piece rates, but more than under standard rates. Not surprisingly, the model predicts that wages of those working under merit pay will lie between the wages of piece rate and standard rate workers doing similar work.

8.1.3 Principal–agent Models

In the 'classic' principal–agent model, the principal (firm) observes the output of the agent (worker) precisely, but cannot tell to what extent that output reflects effort (which reduces worker utility) and random factors (which do not directly affect the worker's utility). For example, the agent may be growing crops on land owned by the principal, who can measure the amount harvested but cannot determine whether good (bad) harvests reflect high (low) levels of diligence by the agent or simply (un)favourable growing conditions. If the random factors change the level of output but not the marginal product of effort, with risk-neutral landowners and workers the optimal contract would in effect be a piece rate contract: the worker would rent the land for a fixed fee and then keep all of the output.

More commonly, it is assumed that the landowner is risk-neutral but the worker is risk-averse. In this case 'share-cropping' arrangements emerge: the worker's earnings are equal to an intercept plus a share of the output.[4]

Both tenant farmers and CEOs are faced with major fluctuations due to factors that cannot be precisely measured in the profitability of their efforts. This is less obviously true in many other applications. For blue-collar workers, major random factors (machine breakdown) can be observed and minor week-to-week fluctuations in output can be smoothed by tying pay to a moving average of output. In the case of higher-level white-collar workers, an important source of uncertainty is just how productive the worker will turn out to be; but once that is known, those with productive draws have an incentive to court outside offers, undermining the ability of the firm to provide insurance to those with less favourable draws.[5] One solution to this problem is to under-pay new workers and overpay old ones (Milgrom and Roberts, 1992, p. 336).

Another source of uncertainty for the worker is the errors made by supervisors in assessing performance, in situations where precise measurement is too costly. Here again an important implication of the theory is that the relationship between wages and either true or measured performance is reduced the less reliable is the performance assessment (Milgrom and Roberts, 1992, pp. 221–3).

Baker (1992) assumes that both the firm and the worker are risk-neutral, but that the worker's output cannot be measured with enough precision to be the basis of a legal contract. Instead, a performance measure is available which imperfectly reflects the value of the worker's output but is clear enough to both sides that pay can be tied to it. Random factors influence the effect of effort on both the value of the worker's output and on the performance measure (as well as perhaps influencing the level of these variables). Baker shows that the response of pay to the performance measure is again higher the better is the performance measure. But in this context it is the extent to which the marginal impact of effort on the performance measure mirrors the marginal impact of effort on the value to the firm of the worker's output, rather than the correlation between the performance measure and the value of output, that determines how 'good' the performance measure is.

Just as models with ability differences among workers often neglect worker effort, the principal–agent models tend to underplay the importance of worker ability and outside opportunities. That the firm must meet the level of utility available elsewhere is formally included as a constraint. But it is assumed that that outside level is known to both the firm and the worker, and that in effect the firm can tailor its contract with the worker to this knowledge. As a result, one misses the role of the worker's output or performance level as an indicator of the likely outside options of the worker.

8.1.4 Relative Performance Evaluation

Risk-averse agents would prefer to be compensated for effort, which they control, rather than output or performance evaluations that are subject to random shocks or measurement errors. In many cases these sources of uncertainty can be reduced by using relative comparisons in setting compensation, so long as the ability of agents in the comparison group to effect each others' performance is not a problem.[6]

The idea that contracts can be improved by taking such information into account is an important one, but it does not change the general conclusions of the models discussed so far. Basically, the group mean can be used to filter out some of the random shock in output or the measurement error in the performance evaluation, and the transformed output or performance measure is used in setting pay.

8.1.5   Rank order Contests

In each of the models discussed so far, except for some contracts that emerge in the principal–agent literature, pay is a continuous function of output or performance. An alternative compensation structure combines relative comparison and payment based on rank order. Sports competitions are the clearest and perhaps most visible use of this idea. But it has also been used to understand the incentives provided by promotions, where typically one worker is given a rise which is far too large to be explained by the firm having revised its estimate of his/her productivity to such a large extent (Lazear and Rosen, 1981).

When agents are risk-neutral and identical, an appropriately chosen compensation rule based only on rank order can attain the same first-best level of effort as a piece rate system. A rank order contest compresses the wage distribution to the extent that extreme values of output do not generate extreme values of pay. But it increases pay inequality when outputs of the competitors are nearly equal. Indeed, Nalebuff and Stiglitz (1983) observed that a typical rank order contest with equally able agents can often be improved upon by adding a third outcome ('tie') in which both contestants receive an intermediate prize if the difference between them is below some level chosen before the contest begins. The absence of 'ties' in labour market promotion contests is therefore somewhat puzzling.

The attractiveness of contests to risk-averse agents is, however, overstated by the stylized contests which are typically analyzed. In particular, promotion contests have the undesirable feature of introducing uncertainty about whether and when a promotion will become available – when one's superior will retire or resign or him/herself be promoted, and whether the number of positions to which one might be promoted will grow or shrink in response to the general fortunes of the firm. In this important sense, golf tournaments are different, because barring rain the first-place check is sure to be handed out at the end of play on Sunday.

8.1.6 Workers' Concern for Relative Position

Introspection suggests that workers often evaluate their compensation relative to that received by their coworkers. This observation leads to two quite different lines of thought. First, as suggested by Frank (1984), if workers care about their pay relative to that of their coworkers, being more satisfied when they are paid comparatively higher wages (as well as, in traditional models, absolutely higher wages), then the distribution of compensation is more unequal than the distribution of wages: high paid workers get the psychic bonus of being *relatively* well paid, while low paid workers bear the extra burden of being paid less than others. Frank argues that this tends to compress the wage distribution.

Second, such comparisons may engender sufficient unhappiness that supervisors are discouraged from creating serious performance-related wage differentials, and morale may suffer badly if they do. Compensation specialists are fond of noting that an overwhelming majority of workers feel they are above average. Serious merit pay schemes necessarily challenge this perception for a significant fraction of the firm's workers. Milgrom and Roberts (1992, p. 370) note that managers often avoid making sharp distinctions in merit increases as a way of reducing the inherent unpleasantness of the task: apparently those who are dissatisfied outweigh the appreciation of those who would gain from more differentiation.

8.1.7 Career Concerns

Implicit in the earlier models in which firms pay workers the expected value of their marginal products conditional on the information available about them is the corollary that pay should evolve over time in response to what can be observed about the workers' performance. In models in which both effort and ability affect output, the market's learning about ability has interesting implications for the incentives to work hard at different points in one's career (Gibbons and Murphy, 1992).

Early in one's career, a worker has two reasons to work hard: because hard work will increase one's pay in the short run, and because as the market observes one's performance one's pay will respond in the long run. When wages are linked to current performance, the intercept in this wage function incorporates all the available information about how productive the worker (probably) is; being more productive in this period will increase that intercept in the future.[7]

Thus, early in the career the relationship between performance and wages may be relatively weak, because of the additional incentive provided by this future payoff – the career concern. In addition, workers may initially be uncertain about their own ability, and prefer some insurance in the form of a compressed pay structure. As careers advance, the relationship between pay and performance should grow stronger: the future payoff to good performance today is reduced, and as both workers and firms learn about workers' abilities, low ability workers can no longer find high ability workers willing to join in ability 'insurance'.

8.1.8 Discharges

Employers have two carrots to reward better workers, higher pay in their current job and the promise of future promotions; they also have two sticks to punish bad performance, lower pay and the threat of discharge. So far we have said relatively little about discharges. The models discussed so far have little explanation for why workers whose performance is poor are discharged rather than just being paid a low wage that reflects the firm's estimate of their performance.[8]

One explanation – which may well have considerable validity – is that if the wage a firm offers falls below a particular level, it is an almost certain indication that the worker will look for work elsewhere, contributing little effort and perhaps considerable disruption on the current job. This is basically an *ad hoc* amendment to the previous models, which did not consider the possibility of discharge and its implications for optimal choice of other aspects of the firm's compensation policy.

Efficiency wage models, on the other hand, have discharges as the centrepiece of the analysis. Here workers are paid more than they can expect elsewhere, and the threat of losing this difference (added to the cost of finding a new job) provides an incentive to work hard and not be discharged for shirking. Unfortunately, in emphasizing the incentive to avoid discharge, effort levels are typically stripped down to a choice between working as expected or shirking, and ability differences among workers are ignored. While the models have strong implications about wage differentials between firms that do and do not use efficiency-wage approaches – the efficiency-wage firms pay higher wages to make a discharge really sting – they do not address the distribution of wages within a firm among workers doing similar work.

Lazear (1979) argued that firms should back-load compensation, again to make discharge sting and hence encourage workers to work hard even if they are not closely watched. This approach suggests that wages will vary with seniority holding performance constant, as workers earn less than their marginal product when young and more when old, but again has no obvious implications for how more and less productive workers at a given age and seniority level will be compensated.

8.2 EVIDENCE ON WAGE-SETTING

Given the importance of firms' wage-setting behavior for understanding labour markets, the topic has stunningly little hard evidence of the sort one is accustomed to in other areas in labour economics. For example, recent increases in wage inequality in the US and most other high GDP countries have been studied extensively. During the period, both pay for performance and high commitment workplaces have received increased attention, at least in the US. Yet despite the potential of pay for performance to increase within-firm wage differentials and high commitment workplaces to increase between-firm differentials, there is no empirical basis for assessing their contribution to recent wage inequality. The fragmentary and sometimes dated evidence we have is, however, often interesting. That evidence is considered in this section.

Cox (1971) reported that in 1968–70, 14 percent of the plant workers in metropolitan areas and virtually none of the office workers received incentive pay (Table 8.1). Because the sample excluded establishments with less than 50 workers, and incentive pay is less common in smaller establishments (Brown, 1990a), the 14 percent figure probably overstates what one might expect in a full national sample. 'Plant workers' include workers in wholesale and retail trade who are on commission, though they account for a minority of those receiving incentive pay.

At least in establishments of this size, formal wage-setting systems which define a pay range for each job were much more common than wage-setting in the absence of such a system: only 13 percent of the plant workers and 28 percent of the office workers were in this latter 'no formal rate policy' group. Opportunities to earn more in a particular job by superior performance were much more limited for the plant workers. 36 percent of them were in 'single rate' plans that provide 'the same rate to all experienced workers in the same job classification', and another 16 percent progressed through the range of rates for their job based on seniority. So, for just over half of the plant workers,

Table 8.1 Distribution of workers by method of wage payment

Method of payment	Metropolitan Areas, 1970[a]		All Areas, 1984[b]	
	Plant workers (%)	Office workers (%)	Professional/ administrative workers (%)	Technical/ clerical workers (%)
Paid time rates	86	99	100	100
Formal rate policy	73	72	81	79
Single rates	36	3	–	2
Range of rates	37	69	81	77
Length of service	16	11	1	11
Merit review	9	36	68	53
Combination	12	22	11	14
Individual determination	13	28	18	20
Incentive pay	14	–	–	–
Piece rates, etc.[c]	12	–	–	–
Commissions	2	–	–	–

Notes:
[a] Source: Cox (1971, Table 1). Establishments with less than 50 workers (less than 100 in manufacturing, public utilities, and retail trade in 12 largest cities) excluded.
[b] Source: Personick (1984, Table 1). Establishments with less than 50, 100, or 250 workers (depending on industry) excluded.
[c] For the sample of plant workers, this included individual piece rates, 5%; group piece rates, 1%; individual production bonuses (for production in excess of quota), 3%; and group production bonuses, 3%.
– : less than 0.5%.

the only way to earn more by working harder would be to qualify for a promotion. For office workers, in contrast, single rate and seniority driven progression were less common (3 and 11 percent of workers, respectively), with merit reviews correspondingly more important.

Personick (1984) confirmed these general patterns with more recent data (but based on a somewhat different sampling frame) for office workers. Among both professional and administrative workers and among technical and clerical workers, four-fifths were paid under formal systems with a range of wages attached to each job.[9] Progression through the range is based on merit, or a combination of merit and seniority. Moreover, the ranges are broad enough that at least in principle they provide a good deal of room for within-grade merit increases: the maximum wage in a given pay grade is typically about 50 percent higher than the minimum.

Based on these two studies, one might expect that in a typical establishment the within-job wage variation would be higher for white-collar workers. That is indeed the case. Buckley (1985) found that in establishments with more than one worker in a job classification, the median while-collar occupation had a 22 percent within-grade differential, but for the median blue-collar occupation it was only 7 percent.

Curiously, though, the formal pay systems often start all workers in a given job at the same wage. This is clearest in 'single rate' systems, but often occurs in the range of rate systems used by white-collar workers. Personick (1984, p. 27) reported that a quarter of the professional and administrative employees, and 42 percent of the technical and clerical employees, worked under systems where new hires are typically paid the minimum of the rate range. The models in section 8.1 have employers using all available information in setting wages. Employers devote significant resources to screening workers – i.e., making forecasts of their likely productivity – but then frequently do *not* use this information in setting starting wages.

Paying workers an hourly wage that depends on previous merit reviews is similar to incentive pay in that it should be more attractive than a single rate or seniority driven system to the more able or hard-working employees. But the relationship of pay and performance over time is quite different. Under piece rates, one's pay depends on one's output over some recent accounting period. Under conventional merit pay plans, however, a merit rating is translated into a wage *increase* that becomes part of the 'base'. Thus, for a young worker planning to remain with the firm to retirement, a favourable merit rating in one period translates into a higher wage in many succeeding periods.

The relationship between the merit review and the resulting wage increase has another interesting feature, at least in the strong majority of firms that are included in compensation surveys: the higher one is in the pay grade, the smaller the proportional increase associated with a given merit rating. Thus, for example, being rated 'outstanding' might raise wages of those at the bottom of the range by 9 percent, but raise wages of those near the top by only 5 percent (National Research Council, 1991, p. 116).

The fact that merit pay increments typically become part of the base means that one's wage at any one time depends on the sequence of previous performance ratings. This corresponds, at least qualitatively,[10] to the outcome predicted by learning models, in which evidence of past productivity is used to estimate the worker's true ability. Limiting raises for those higher in the pay range for the job is, however, likely to affect more senior workers. Thus, a better rating is worth less to them not only because the increased base will apply to fewer remaining years with the firm, but also because it translates into a smaller increment per year. This is at least superficially contrary to the implications of the career concerns model, and to the evidence for CEOs reported by Gibbons and Murphy (1992).

It is important to recognize that wage increases reported attributable to 'merit' may in fact be more accurately understood as seniority driven if the merit ratings are all more or less the same. Perhaps the classic example of this mislabelling is the federal civil service, where annual rises were given to workers with satisfactory performance with amazing regularity. The President's Panel on Federal Compensation (1976, p. 50) found that less than 2 percent of federal General Schedule (non-executive white-collar) workers had their regular within-grade step increases delayed or withheld, and only 2 percent received the extra step increase for which extraordinary performers were eligible: 'The regular within-grade increase has effectively become an automatic length-of-service increase.' Such uniformity in turn created pressure for 'real' merit increases in the most recent round of civil service reform. One federal manager, however, explained to me how one evades pressure to differentiate merit increases: one simply gives the top increases to different workers each year!

While private employers' 'merit' rises have not become divorced from their intended purpose to this extent, it remains a problem. (Greeley and Ochsner, 1986; Milgrom and Roberts, 1992, pp. 402–6).

Within-grade wage increases are of course not the only reward for superior performance: better workers can look forward to being pro-

Table 8.2 Importance of seniority in production decisions

Promotion practice	Employee group			
	Union hourly %	Non-union hourly %	Non-exempt salaried %	Exempt salaried %
Junior employer never promoted ahead of senior employee	33	15	15	0
Junior employee promoted only if *significantly* better	43	41	45	48
Junior employee promoted if better than senior employee	24	44	41	52

Source: Abraham and Medoff (1985, Table 3).

moted. While promotions undoubtedly serve this purpose, they are limited in two important ways. First, performance is not the only factor in making promotion decisions: seniority is explicitly mentioned as a factor in typical promotion rules for unionized workers, and preference for the senior worker unless the less senior worker is *significantly* better is common even among non-union workers. Based on a survey of medium and large firms (50 or more workers, and $1 million or more in sales), Abraham and Medoff (1985) conclude that 'perhaps 60 percent of U.S. employees work in settings in which seniority leads to a substantial preference in promotion decisions'. While the preference for more senior workers is less common for professional and managerial ('exempt' workers) than for others, it is non-negligible even for this group (see Table 8.2).

Second, promotions may be less common and less valuable than one might have guessed. McCue (1992) found that about 5 percent of workers reported a within-firm promotion in the previous year. She estimated that over a 40-year work career these promotions account for about a 0.12 increase in ln-wage, compared to a 0.60 increase in ln-wage from all sources (normal wage growth, within-firm promotions, and changes of firm). Only a quarter of the promotions and of the associated wage increases are estimated to occur after the first 20 years of working.

McCue's definition of 'promotion' is a relatively strict one, however. Respondents (from the Panel Study of Income Dynamics) were asked how long they had been in their current position and, if in that position for less than one year, were asked about the change of position, with 'promotion' a candidate explanation. Those who receive promotions that change one's title but not one's duties – or that recognize, after the fact, that a worker has been doing higher-level work than called for in his/her job description – may well report themselves in the same 'position' and therefore be counted as not having had a promotion.

In contrast, Bishop (1990) found that in a sample of workers who had been working for their current employer for about a year, one-third had been 'promoted' according to their employer's report. It is hard to judge how much of the difference between the two promotion rates is due to different definitions and how much to real differences in promotion rates in the first year and later years on the job.

8.3   PIECE RATES AND TIME RATES

Of the models summarized in section 8.1, the one which has received the most empirical attention contrasts the precise measurement and output-linked pay under piece rates to time rates, where workers are paid by the hour with little direct relationship to how much they produce. Two implications of that model are that piece rate workers should receive higher pay than those paid time rates, at least within a given occupation–industry market, and that factors which make costly the precise measurement of the value of what is produced will discourage the use of piece rates. In the empirical literature, those paid group incentives or those paid bonuses for production over a quota are often grouped with those paid piece rates.

The hypothesis that those paid piece rates earn more than those paid time rates has been verified in a number of studies. King (1975) found that incentive rated workers in auto dealer repair shops earned 20–50 percent more per hour than time rated workers in the same occupation and metropolitan area, and that this differential had remained stable for at least a decade. Pencavel (1977) reported that among punch-press operators in Chicago, those who worked under incentive pay earned 7 percent more than those paid under time rates. Seiler (1984) found that incentive paid workers earned 14 percent more than those paid time rates among those making footwear and men's and boys' suits and coats.

The Bureau of Labour Statistics *Industry Wage Survey* (IWS) reports often tabulate earnings of those paid under incentive pay and those paid time rates by occupation. A sampling of these results is presented in Table 8.3. In most IWS reports, the differentials are gross differentials that do not hold constant factors correlated with both wages

Table 8.3 Wages under incentive pay and time rates

Industry (and years)	Occupation	Mid-1970s			Most recent	
		% receiving incentive pay	% wage differential[a]		% receiving incentive pay	% wage differential unadjusted
			Adjusted	Unadjusted		
Men's and boys' shirts (1974, 1987)	Cutters, machine	35	16	9	26	13
	Spreaders	34	24	31	36	36
	Sewing machine operators	96	12	5	98	5
Men's and boys' suits and coats (1976, 1989)	Cutters, cloth		11		61	7
	Finish pressers, machine		31		90	2
	Sewing mach. operators (coats)		18		92	9
	Sewing mach. operators (trousers)		16		95	11
Wood household furniture (1974, 1987)	Assemblers, furniture, exc. chairs	23	16	14	13	19
	Offbearers, machine	16	15	22	12	36
	Ripsaw operators	17	16	12	12	26
	Sanders, furniture, machine	19	16	19	11	22
	Tenoner operators	22	8	2	14	14
Iron and steel foundries (1973, 1986)	Chippers and grinders	31	18	20	29	18
	Moulders, machine	64	2	14	59	18
Structural clay products (1975, 1986)	Kiln setters and drawers	46	17	25	39	31
	Offbearers, machine	35	18	33	20	36
	Pugmill operators	26	20	25	18	24

Note:
[a] Wage differential = Wage difference (incentive − time) divided by average wage.

and method of pay, such as union status, establishment size, region or detailed type of product. In a few of the reports, however, 'net' differentials that held these factors constant were calculated. Table 8.3 focuses on these industries and occupations,[11] when a recent report was also available.

Calculation of net differentials was begun in the 1970s, but not continued. Hence, where available data permit, Table 8.3 presents the net differentials from the mid-1970s, plus the gross differential from the same report and the gross differentials for the same industries and occupations from a recent report.

These differentials are often sizeable; more often than not they exceed 15 percent. Unlike most other wage differentials, controlling for available 'other' factors does not reduce the gross differential in any predictable way: the net differentials are about as large as the gross differentials. And while incentive pay has become less common, *even within detailed occupation and industry*,[12] the premium for incentive pay has not declined.

The finding that those paid under incentive pay earn more than those who are not is strongly confirmed by the data, but dividing those paid time rates according to the degree of incentive they face yields a surprising result. As noted earlier, some time rate workers' pay is linked to performance (though more weakly than for those paid piece rates) because merit increases depend on performance; we expect such workers to earn more than those paid based only on their job classification and perhaps their seniority. However, this prediction appears to be inconsistent with the data.

In Brown (1992) I used establishment-level data from the IWS to investigate this relationship. The data were drawn from 10 industries and over 3000 establishments. The empirical strategy was to regress the mean ln-wage of blue-collar workers on the fraction of workers in the establishment working under different methods of pay, along with controls for the occupational distribution of the establishment and establishment characteristics like unionization, number of employees, and location. Workers were grouped according to method of pay into three categories: those working under incentive pay, those working under merit pay (where time rates are adjusted to some evaluation of the workers' output), and those paid standard rates (where pay depends only on one's job classification or that classification plus seniority). Holding constant the establishment characteristics, including the occupational distribution, larger proportions working under incentive pay meant higher wages (as expected) but larger proportions working under merit pay meant *lower* wages, even compared to standard rates.

These differences were statistically significant (*t*-ratios of about 8) and held within individual industries and when only non-union workers were considered. The finding that merit pay is associated with lower wages than standard rates seems to be robust statistically but is puzzling theoretically.

One possibility is that standard rate firms substitute pre-employment screening and more aggressive discharge policies for differentiated pay to produce skilled and hard-working employees. Working backwards, it does make sense that *if* a firm was committed to relatively undifferentiated pay it would have an extra incentive to screen workers carefully before hiring – the less pay varies with output, the greater the gain to the firm from finding a worker who produces more. But it's difficult to see, within the terms of a standard competitive model, why a firm that had invested a lot in choosing the best worker would not tie pay to just how good it thought that best worker was – and yet that is, roughly, what standard rate firms appear to do. Greater reliance on firing seems a more promising explanation – standard rate firms have an unusually strong incentive to discharge inadequate performers (since if they don't have to pay them as much as good workers), and the monitoring level needed to identify (and defend discharging) the worst workers may well be less costly than that required by annual merit reviews.

Another possible explanation begins with the observation that unionized workers receive higher wages *and* most often have standard rate systems. Casual empiricism suggests that workers often dislike merit pay reviews and the pay differentiation they produce. It is at least possible that among non-union workers, some are better 'organized' than others, and are better able to obtain both higher wages *and* the preferred independence from supervisors' whims. Given that both industry and employer size were held constant in the empirical work, the differences in ability to extract good 'deals' must be across same-sized establishments in a particular industry if they are to account for the empirical finding.

Note, however, that the prediction that those working under incentive pay earn the highest wages was confirmed in my data, as in a number of earlier studies. So any explanation of why merit pay workers do not earn more than standard rate workers must also account for the fact that the standard model works so well for those receiving incentive pay.

The hypothesis that choice of method of pay is sensitive to the costs of precise measurement that piece rates require has been less studied, but is confirmed by the data. For example, one would expect piece rates would be easier to administer when workers have a narrow set of routine duties rather than a variety of duties. Moreover, since piece rates create an incentive to produce many low quality pieces unless quality can be adequately monitored, jobs requiring attainment of precise standards may be candidates for piece rates but those that require workers to generalize, evaluate, and decide would not be. Matching data on method of pay of individual workers to independent evaluations of the content of their (narrowly defined) jobs (Brown, 1990a) confirmed both of these expectations. Piece rates were also more common in larger organizations, presumably because the fixed cost of setting up and fine-tuning the piece rate system can be spread over more workers. However, a measure of occupational concentration, designed to identify where (given establishment size) fewer different jobs are present and so again the cost per worker of a piece rate system would be reduced, was only weakly related to use of piece rates.

On balance, then, both the wage differences associated with piece rates and the relative extent of utilizing piece rates behave as predicted by the standard model. But 'merit pay' does *not* seem to be an intermediate category between piece rates and standard rates, at least in terms of wage rates.

8.4 COMPRESSION OF WITHIN-FIRM WAGE DISTRIBUTIONS

A theme which emerged at several points in the discussion of the theories in section 8.1 is that pay is likely to be 'compressed' – i.e., among workers in a firm doing similar work, wages will vary less than proportionately with output. These models also make clear why this prediction will be difficult to test empirically: they often assume (realistically) that employers do not have perfect measures of each worker's productivity. If the employer can't measure productivity accurately, how can the econometrician?

Bishop's (1987) solution to this problem was to focus instead on the relationship between wages and *reported* productivity. He obtained data from a sample of firms contacted in late spring 1982, which asked about the last worker hired prior to August 1981 (i.e., at least eight months earlier), and another worker hired in the preceding two years for a similar job. For each worker in the pair, both starting and most recent wage are available. The distinctive feature of the data, however, is that the workers' supervisor was asked to evaluate the productivity of both workers at various points (second week, third through twelfth week, and time of survey (or as of separation)), on a numerical scale that ran from zero for 'absolutely no productivity' to 100 for the maximum productivity any employee in the position can obtain. To minimize the effects of differences across firms in the subjective scaling of the responses, Bishop focused on *differences* in wages and performance (and other characteristics like schooling) between the two workers at each firm.

Bishop found that the elasticity of wages with respect to reported productivity is 0.08 for starting wages and 0.22 for most recent wage (the latter being after about a year on the job). When one controls for a set of education and experience variables, these elasticities fall to 0.03 and 0.19, respectively. I interpret the 0.03 as saying that either employers do not have much indication of future productivity from variables not included in Bishop's regressions (such as references from previous employers or interview impressions) or they do not use them in setting initial wages.

Bishop also considered whether unionization and employer size alter the estimated performance–pay relationship. In union establishments the elasticity of pay with respect to performance was half or less of its value in non-union establishments, though the union–non-union difference was not statistically significant. The elasticity was also smaller in larger establishments, falling to zero when establishment size reaches 400 workers. This latter finding means that if we weighted establishments by their level of employment the average elasticity would be considerably smaller than the 0.2 average value in the sample.

These results are clearly inconsistent with the hypothesis that wages vary proportionately with reported productivity scores. They are probably also inconsistent with the hypothesis that wages vary proportionately with true productivities, but the latter are reported with error in Bishop's data. For this latter hypothesis to be true, roughly 80 percent of the variance in the reported productivity score must be error. That seems unlikely given that the productivity scores come from supervisors presumably well placed to report them. But several factors could contribute to serious measurement errors in the reported productivity variable: the regressions use *differences* in reported scores between workers,[13] and the productivity reports for workers who have left the firm may be subject to recall error that is not the same for all workers. I think it is plausible that such errors exaggerate the true of extent of compression but it is implausible that this fully accounts for increments to performance receiving less than proportionate increments in wages.

In section 8.2 it was noted that under conventional merit pay, improved productivity in one period raises the wage in all subsequent periods, so the increment to the present value of compensation is larger than the increment to current wages. Given the short tenure of Bishop's sample this possibility cannot be tested directly. But Bishop does find that controlling for current performance, earlier performance has no effect on wages, which points against the idea that the present value of the wage responds more fully than the current wage.

The remaining literature I have been able to locate on whether those employees are more productive receive comparably higher wages is limited to case studies. Their common finding is that in a number of settings where the employer can measure performance well, wages vary less than proportionately with output, and in some cases not at all.

Weiss (1980) studied output of workers paid group incentives. Among workers in the same group (who receive the same wage, apart from a small seniority premium) with the same supervisor doing the same job (typically $N < 20$), 'the output of the most productive worker was often more than three times as great as the least productive worker' (p. 528).

Akerlof (1982) used data initially collected by Homans (1954) to motivate his 'gift exchange' model of the labour market. The data refer to cash posters, whose job it was (long before computers) to record customers' utility payments. Those who handled less than 300 such transactions received a 'mild rebuke' from their supervisor; those who handled more than 300 received neither higher wages not significant opportunities for promotion. Despite this almost totally compressed wage structure, the average cash poster exceeded the 300 per hour standard by 17 percent, and the two best (of 10) handled 40 percent more transactions – and with a lower error rate – than the worst two.

Frank (1984) reported on several markets in which wages *do* vary with output, but apparently much less than proportionately. In a sample of 13 auto dealerships, a salesperson selling an extra car receives only about a fourth of the gross margin (sales price less wholesale price). Similarly, in a sample of real estate brokers, an agent selling an extra house keeps just over half of her firm's commission on the sale. Increasing either of these shares to (or close to) one would mean that the auto dealership or realty company would be unable to cover fixed costs. But since these fixed costs are largely fixed – i.e., do not increase if a salesperson or agent makes another sale – the puzzle is why dealerships and realtors don't 'sell' jobs and then pay something close to the full commission.[14]

Each of these studies, by itself, is easily dismissed as an outlier; together they somewhat reinforce Bishop's conclusion. Recall, also, from section 8.2 that the typical range between the best and worst paid workers in a typical blue-collar job at a given workplace is 7 percent. Except in situations where workers work to a standard set below the capability of the typical worker, it is hard for me to imagine that the best worker produces only 7 percent more than the worst.

8.5 TURNOVER

The relationship between turnover and performance – whether those who leave a firm are the most or least productive workers – is complicated by a number of factors. Turnover can be initiated by both firms and workers. Presumably, firms encourage or dictate the departures of their least productive workers, though why they discharge workers rather than simply offering an appropriately lower wage is not clear. Worker-initiated turnover, on the other hand, is more complicated. Among workers with similar alternatives, those paid least by their current employer should be most likely to leave, and these will be the least productive if there is even a weak pay–performance correlation. However, one might expect that on average those who are most productive will have the best outside alternatives, and so compressed wage structures risk losing these most productive workers (Fama, 1980, p. 292). It is the relationship between turnover and worker productivity that is therefore of interest here.

Bishop (1990) studied this relationship in the same sample of firms he used in his earlier study of wages and performance. Given that average firm in his sample is small, and that within firms jobs with higher turnover rates are more likely to be selected, one expects high turnover rates and this expectation is confirmed: in the (approximately) one year since they were hired 17 percent of the workers quit and layoffs and discharges each felled an additional 6 percent of the workers. Since each firm in his sample had hired *two* workers for (roughly) the same job, he was able to relate differences in their probability of involuntary separations and quits to differences in rated performance in the first three months[15] on the job.

Not surprisingly, he finds that better performing workers are less likely to be involuntarily separated (laid off or discharged): a one standard deviation improvement in performance reduces this rate by 11 percentage points. A smaller (7 percentage point) reduction is also found for quits.

Dividing the sample by union status and establishment size produces perhaps the most interesting findings. Union workplaces have essentially no relationship between involuntary turnover and performance: while discharges are triggered by poor performance, they are very infrequent, and poorer performers are not overrepresented among layoffs. Union workplaces also have little relationship between quits and performance. As establishment size increases, the tendency for poorer performers to be subject to involuntary separations becomes stronger, because discharges are more important relative to layoffs (and, of course, discharges are related to performance). But the tendency for poorer performers to quit vanishes in larger establishments (about 200 workers). This lines up well with Bishop's earlier results on wage compression being more pronounced in larger and unionized workplaces.

In interpreting these results, a simple model is helpful. Suppose that q_i is worker i's true marginal product with this firm, y_i is the firm's estimate of q_i and $w_i = b_0 + b_1 y_i$ is the firm's wage offer. Let a_i be the worker's (best) *alternative* wage offer, which is based on z_i, the alternative firm's estimate of the worker's value there: $a_i = c_0 + c_1 z_i$. The worker quits if $a_i > w_i$. Finally, assume q, y, and z are normally distributed.

These are two different questions we might ask about voluntary turnover in this model: Do those who remain with the firm have higher estimated productivity than those who leave? Do those who remain with the firm have higher true productivity than those who leave. Algebraically, the answers to these questions correspond to

$$\text{sign } E(y|\, w > a) - E(y) = \text{sign cov}[y, b_1 y - c_1 z]$$

and

$$\text{sign } E(q|\, w > a) - E(q) = \text{sign cov}[q, b_1 y - c_1 z]$$

respectively.

As a benchmark, consider what happens if the alternative offer is from a firm just like the current firm except that it has a different (but equally accurate) estimate of q. Then we might expect $b_1 = c_1$ and of course $\text{var}(y) > \text{cov}(y, z)$. The issue is not whether the firm's wage structure is compressed (b_1 is 'small') but how it compares to other

Table 8.4 Performance and turnover: electronics manufacturer

Performance quintile	Turnover rate in	
	First 6 months (%)	*Next 12 months* (%)
Lowest	9.0	6.0
Second	8.0	8.0
Third	6.0	7.0
Fourth	7.5	10.5
Highest	10.5	11.5

Source: Weiss (1987, Figures 7.4a–b).

firms'. But in this benchmark case the second expression is zero: $b_1 = c_1$ and $cov(q, y) = cov(q, z)$.

Departures from this benchmark case could go in either direction. Since y is based on actual observation of workers on the job but z is not (y is presumably not eagerly shared with rival firms), one might expect $cov(q, y) > cov(q, z)$. This would make the *true* productivity of those who remain higher. Alternatively, given the particular sample it is likely that sampled jobs are 'entry'-level jobs which individuals leave when they have established a 'track record'. If so, one might presume that on average the alternative jobs are higher skill, and so place a higher value on differences in worker quality. In this situation, the first expression need no longer be positive.

Note also that the first covariance is necessarily larger than the second, since they differ by $b_1 cov(y - q, y)$ which is positive. Thus, the finding that voluntary turnover is unrelated to *measured* performance for moderately-large firms means that the effect of such turnover on true performance is likely to be negative.

Most other studies of consequences of compressed wage structures on turnover have been case studies. Weiss (1987) studied a large electronics manufacturer with an unusual but interesting pay system. New workers were paid piece rates but after achieving a specified level of performance they were transferred to group incentive pay, and the size of the group leaves almost no relationship between individual output and pay.[16] Weiss found that output became much less dispersed once this transition is made, so initial (piece rate) output provides a better indication of the worker's ability and potential effort level. Turnover by performance quintile is given in Table 8.4. In the first six months, turnover was highest among the extremes of the distribution. Weiss attributed the high turnover rates among poor performers to supervisors' pressure to improve or leave, and the turnover rates among the best workers to their desire to find alternative employment where their superior performance is rewarded. In the next 12 months turnover is unambiguously higher among the better performers.

The federal government has received relatively more attention than private firms, in part because the compression of its wage structure is well known but also because it does not regard the relevant data as highly sensitive. Perhaps surprisingly, the military has been a cooperative source of data, and unsurprisingly that data offers large samples and high quality information. While the compensation structure of the US military has become a great deal more market-oriented (with enlistment and re-enlistment bonuses targeted to hard-to-fill occupational specialties), pay remains only loosely linked to performance. In particular, within pay grade there is *no* merit pay component, and the link between performance and promotion is also attenuated by institutional considerations.

Ward and Tan (1985) studied the impact of ability and job performance on re-enlistment decisions in eight military occupations in all four branches of the armed forces. Level of schooling and scores on the ability test given to individuals entering the military indicate general ability is positively related to earnings in civilian jobs. Ward and Tan also inferred performance in the military from the speed at which the individual attained two key early promotions. They found that those with higher scores on their index of military performance were more likely to re-enlist, while those with higher general ability scores (and, less consistently, those with more schooling) were less likely to do so.

In a more recent study (Brown, 1990b), data were available for Army enlistees completing their first term of enlistment (roughly, three years of service) deciding whether to re-enlist. For each soldier in three occupational fields (infantry, mechanical maintenance, and administration) the data included the general ability test given at entry,[17] a test score that reflects mastery of his military occupation (and is treated by the Army as a performance indicator), a cruder version of Ward and Tan's speed of promotion variable, and whether the individual was ineligible to re-enlist (roughly 15 percent of the sample was ineligible).

If we interpret the general-ability test as an indicator of performance and opportunities in civilian jobs and the military test as an indication of performance in the Army, the results again have a strong comparative-advantage flavour. Despite the fact that the two indicators are positively related, those with higher general-ability scores are *less* likely to re-enlist and those with higher military scores (or faster promotion) are *more* likely to re-enlist. This general pattern remains in a multi-variate framework when the effects of ineligibility are removed from the data.

The relatively favorable experience of the armed forces in retaining its top rated enlistees is surprising, given the quite small pay increments associated with superior performance.[18] While fringe benefits are an important part of the pay structure, they are either provided equally to all (medical care) or depend on salary (pensions) and so are not differentially attractive to the most competent. The most plausible explanation is that non-financial 'compensation' is positively related to performance: either favorable treatment is accorded top performers by their peers and supervisors, or (reversing the line of causation) those who find military life most attractive turn out to be the most effective performers. The extent to which non-financial compensation can be manipulated by civilian organizations to retain top performers is unclear.

A study of federal civilian white-collar employment (US Merit Systems Protection Board, 1989) also found turnover rates[19] lower among higher rated employees. Of the top five merit rating categories, the bottom two account for less than 1 percent of all workers, and 11 percent of the workers in these categories resigned. In the top three categories, accounting for 21, 37, and 41 percent of the workers, resignation rates were 3.1, 2.5, and 4.3 percent respectively.

An important limitation of these federal studies is that the data give no indication as to how different the turnover–performance relationship might be if the pay–performance relationship were amplified. Some clues are contained in a merit pay experiment at some US Navy laboratories, for non-clerical white-collar workers (Miller, 1988). Available turnover data (for the first and third year of the experiment) show overall turnover rates for the white-collar workers were similar in the experimental and control labs (slightly lower in the former), but were 40 percent lower among those with superior performance ratings.

On balance, my reading of the evidence is that turnover rates for higher rated employees tend to be somewhat lower than for lower rated employees, though apart from the small non-union firms in Bishop's sample the difference is not very large. And as noted above one expects the relationship between turnover and 'true' performance to be even less negative; in Weiss' data, where performance is well measured and performance incentives absent, it is positive. When one realizes that some 'voluntary' turnover may be immediately motivated by the prospect of involuntary turnover, it seems quite possible that genu-inely voluntary turnover is more common among better performers. Of course involuntary separations are much more (negatively) related to rated performance; even though they are less common than worker-initiated separations, they account for the majority of the negative re-lationship between overall turnover and performance, at least among low-tenure workers.

8.6 WORKERS' VIEW OF THE PAY–PERFORMANCE LINK AND OFFER-MATCHING

Since salary compression would seem to invite raiding a firm's best employees by other firms, it is natural to ask whether firms typically match outside offers for good employees or permit such workers to leave in order to maintain the salary structure – and whether offer matching is more or less common in firms that try hard to align pay with performance in the first place. In principle, this latter relation-ship could go either way: firms that adopt 'egalitarian' salary struc-tures may suffer more losses of valued employees if they do not match, but such matching presumably violates the principles that led to an egalitarian structure in the first place.

A recent survey of a nationally representative sample of workers by the Survey Research Center at the University of Michigan provides evidence on workers' perception of the pay–performance link and on the elusive subject of offer-matching. From September 1992 through March 1993, respondents to the Monthly Survey of Consumers who were currently employed as private wage and salary workers were asked about the importance of performance (compared to seniority) in deter-mining layoffs, wages, and promotions. The exact questions posed were:

If your employer had to reduce its workforce permanently, which do you think would be more important in deciding who is let go – length of service with the company or job performance?

In determining *wages* or salaries where you work, which is more important – length of service with the company or job performance?

In determining who gets promoted at the place where you work, which is more important – length of service with the company or job performance?

A final question dealt with offer-matching:

If someone who was a *good* worker was offered 10 percent more pay by another employer, do you think your employer would be likely to match the higher pay or would they lose the worker to the higher-paying employer?

Summary statistics for these questions are presented in Table 8.5. Given the earlier evidence that the pay–performance link is not terribly strong, the substantial majorities who find job performance more important than seniority in determining wages is surprising, as is the perceived importance of merit in layoffs. Given this perceived importance of merit, the reported unwillingness of employers to match even a modest (10 percent) wage hike offered by another employer is striking.

Correlations among the four employer strategies suggest that workers whose pay depends on performance are likely to respond that layoffs and promotions are also performance-related, though the correlations among these three performance versus seniority questions are modest (0.3 to 0.4). The most interesting correlations, however, are between these three answers and that regarding offer-matching. Basically, offer-matching is unrelated to the importance of performance in allocating rewards: workers whose pay is performance-related are slightly more likely to report that their employer would match an outside offer than are those whose pay is seniority driven.

Given Bishop's findings that the pay–performance link is strongest in small, non-union workplaces, it is natural to ask how these responses relate to the size and union status of the workplace. The second panel of Table 8.5 shows that performance counts for less in union-sector decisions, but the relationship between these outcomes and employer size is quite weak. Offer-matching is less common in union workplaces – not surprising given contract restrictions on wages – and it is also less common in larger firms.

That offer-matching is less common in larger firms is consistent with an emphasis on the importance of relative comparisons by workers. The cost of matching an outside offer for one employee is not only the dollar cost of the rise, but also the possibility that others rated equally or higher will regard themselves as unfairly paid. Whether this dissatisfaction is born in the form of lower morale or offset with higher wages, it is likely to be larger the more employees in the comparison group.

Table 8.5 Pay, performance, and offer-matching

	Layoffs 1 = Performance 0 = Seniority	Wages 1 = Performance 0 = Seniority	Promotions 1 = Performance 0 = Seniority	Offer-matching 1 = Match offer 0 = Lose worker
Sample means	0.80	0.80	0.85	0.33
Correlation matrix				
Layoffs	1.00			
Wages	0.38	1.00		
Promotions	0.30	0.41	1.00	
Offer-matching	0.11	0.12	0.08	1.00
Union and employer size effects[a]				
Union contract	−0.287	−0.295	−0.109	−0.128
	(0.043)	(0.043)	(0.038)	(0.051)
Ln (Establishment	−0.007	0.003	−0.004	−0.007
employment)	(0.008)	(0.008)	(0.007)	(0.009)
Ln (firm	−0.003	−0.008	0.007	−0.028
employment)	(0.005)	(0.005)	(0.005)	(0.006)

Notes:
[a] Dummy variables for 12 broad industry categories are also included in these regressions.
$N = 1109$.

Source: University of Michigan Survey of Consumers, September 1992–March 1993.

8.7 CONCLUDING OBSERVATIONS

The evidence in the preceding sections has the feel of a collage, not a tightly woven tapestry. At least in the US, we have not achieved the level of cooperation by business firms that has been achieved with households in participating in large scientifically chosen samples. Since data on performance is perhaps inevitably better collected from firms than households, assembling relevant evidence has lagged behind innovative theoretical work on this topic more decisively than is true in most other topics studied by labour economists.

My reading of the evidence is that there is considerable compression of the wage distribution within firms: improved performance does not increase wages in the same proportion. While difficulty in measuring individual workers' contributions with confidence is no doubt part of the problem, the within-firm compression appears to exceed what could be explained on that account. This does not lead to a wholesale exodus of the best performers. Firms weed out the least successful workers and accept *roughly* proportionate turnover by the more successful; whether this is because other firms offer equally modest rewards to excellent performance or because superior workers collect enough non-financial compensation to discourage leaving is unclear. Moreover, at least judging from workers' perceptions, matching outside offers of good workers does not appear to be widespread enough to counteract the likelihood of better workers generating such offers. It thus appears that the firms are passing up the opportunity to manage their turnover more aggressively by widening the spread of rewards they offer.

That managers are reluctant to engage in sharp differentiation has been widely noted. There are two interpretations of this observation. One is that this, too, reflects a principal–agent problem – it would be 'good' for the firm to be more meritocratic, if only the owners of the firm could get the lower-level managers to be so. The other is that workers prefer relatively equal wage distributions and compensation policies that violate this preference either reduce morale and productivity or require substantial investments in a personnel system that can 'sell' itself to the workers. I believe there is a germ of truth in both.

Information technology has begun to expand the range of feasible monitoring activities and output-linked compensation schemes for many workers, and this trend seems likely to continue. To date popular press reports have emphasized workers' beliefs that they are being expected to work much harder for little or no additional compensation. The rewards from a systematic analysis of this (un)natural experiment are high indeed.

If improvements in the technology of monitoring or upper management prevailing upon lower-level managers leads to a stronger link between pay and performance, the consequences would be potentially important both for firms so affected and for the economy more generally. Performance-based pay has some of the characteristics of supply-side economics. In particular, the reward to greater diligence on the job is increased, so we would expect more effort from affected workers. And, at least in principle, a tighter pay–performance link would raise the wages of the most productive while reducing the wages of those who are less productive, so that the overall income effect on effort should be less an issue than it is when taxes are reduced. Finally, while reductions in marginal tax rates tend to exaggerate inequality between high and low paid occupations, and between workers and owners of capital, reallocating pay within each occupation in favour of the more productive has (at least in the short run) only within-occupation effects. It is worth stressing, however, that if *some* firms adopt a more performance driven pay structure, part (and perhaps much) of the improvement in productivity that might result comes at the expense of other firms, whose best workers are drawn away.

Notes

* Prepared for the Biwako conference, Osaka (July 1992). The chapter has been revised in response to very helpful comments from Masahiro Okuno, Mari Sako, and Toshiaki Tachibanaki, and the general discussion at the conference.
1. Blinder (1990) offers some quite interesting evidence on this subject.
2. On executive compensation, see Ehrenberg and Milkovich (1987) and Rosen (1990).
3. What is being finessed here is the question of why those paid time rates exert any effort at all. Lazear assumed there was a level of effort that firms could observe costlessly, and that is likely to be relatively low level – showing up for work and at least going through the motions. Another possibility is that if one has to be on the job and at least appear to be working, there is a level of effort below which utility actually falls. A final possibility is to imagine that pay does increase with performance under time rates (through some merit review) though this relationship is much weaker than under piece rates.
4. In simple one-period principal–agent problems a less continuous payoff often proves optimal. For a critique of these solutions and a justification of simple linear rules, see Holmstrom and Milgrom (1987).
5. Even if the fact that the worker is able is known only to the firm and

the worker and not to other firms, the worker who learns that he/she is successful can move to firms that offer less compressed pay structures, since such a worker's interest in insurance is reduced.

6. In some cases, an agent could adversely influence the performance of a competitor, or fail to provide assistance that would otherwise be desirable. Another concern is that the agents could collude, each reducing effort without lowering the relative performance (and hence pay) of any group member.

7. Of course the market realizes that people are working harder for that reason. But an individual worker still has the incentive to work hard: if one doesn't, the market can't tell that the worker individually has chosen not to 'play the game' this period, and so makes negative inferences about the worker's ability from the low level of output.

8. In some principal–agent models with discontinuous payoffs, a low payoff to unsatisfactory workers is sometimes thought of as similar to discharge. But in the real world unsatisfactory workers are paid for the work they perform up to their discharge (which may be adjusted down to reflect their bad performance, but often is not) and *then told they cannot continue for this employer*. So a static principal–agent model really cannot capture the economics of discharges, which require an intertemporal model.

9. Personick's sample used different establishment-size cutoffs in different industries but in general this cutoff was higher than in Cox's. This difference, rather than any true change over the 15 years between the studies, may account for the larger share of workers under formal plans in Personick's data.

10. Learning models typically posit additive errors, in which the wage would be based on a sum of changes due to measures of performance, whereas the typical merit system uses proportional changes that cumulate multiplicatively.

11. The only pattern I can detect to the industries chosen is that they tend to have significant use of incentive pay. Occupations studied tend to be ones with significant numbers of workers in them. Thus, the industry–occupation combinations are *not* chosen by any formal random sampling of industries or occupations, but I believe they are broadly representative of occupations in which incentive pay is common.

12. This decline is part of a longer-term and more general decline in the use of incentive pay. For a detailed study of this decline in the machinery industry, see Keefe (1991).

13. Differencing does remove differences between workplaces in the scaling of these reports. But if there is a component of reporting error that is uncorrelated across the two reports in a single workplace, differencing will intensify the importance of this error relative to the true variance of performance.

14. One *possible* explanation is that 'full' commissions would lead to overly aggressive selling, to the detriment of the employer. Some anecdotal 'evidence': a local appliance store in Ann Arbor advertises that its sales people are *not* on commission and so have no incentive to try to sell pricier models. I am told that Saturn, a US car venture spun from General Motors that continually stresses its unconventionalness, pays its auto

salespersons straight salaries, again to enhance their credibility with potential customers.
15. More precisely, productivity in the third through twelfth week on the job is the main performance indicator.
16. He also indicated that promotion opportunities are nil.
17. Education data were also available, but for the cohort studied 90 percent of the sample had graduated from high school.
18. Indeed, Smith, Sylwester, and Villa (1991, p. 85) compared those who left the service to those who remained and found that having an above-average early promotion record in the Army increased civilian earnings (of those who left) more than it increased military compensation (for those who remained).
19. Those moving from one federal agency to another were not counted as having separated.

References

Abraham, Katharine G. and James L. Medoff (1985) 'Length of Service and Promotions in Union and Nonunion Work Groups', *Industrial and Labor Relations Review*, vol. 38, no. 3, April, pp. 408–20.

Aigner, Dennis and Glen Cain (1977) 'Statistical Theories of Discrimination in Labor Markets', *Industrial and Labor Relations Review*, vol. 30, pp. 175–87.

Akerlof, George A. (1982) 'Labor Contracts as a Partial Gift Exchange', *Quarterly Journal of Economics*, vol. 97, no. 4, November, pp. 543–69.

Baker, George P. (1992) 'Incentive Contracts and Performance Measurement', *Journal of Political Economy*, vol. 100, no. 3, June, pp. 598–614.

Bishop, John H. (1987) 'The Recognition and Reward of Employee Performance', *Journal of Labor Economics*, vol. 5, no. 4, part 2, April, pp. 36–56.

———— (1990) 'Job Performance, Turnover, and Wage Growth', *Journal of Labor Economics*, vol. 8, no. 3, July, pp. 363–86.

Blinder, Alan S. (ed.) (1990) *Paying for Productivity*, Washington, DC, Brookings Institution.

Brown, Charles (1990a) 'Firms' Choice of Method of Pay', *Industrial and Labor Relations Review*, vol. 43, no. 3 (supplement), February, pp. 165–82.

———— (1990b) 'The Quality Dimension in Army Retention', *Carnegie-Rochester Conference Series on Public Policy*, vol. 33, pp. 221–56.

———— (1992) 'Wage Levels and Method of Pay', *Rand Journal of Economics*, vol. 23, no. 3, Autumn, pp. 366–75.

Buckley, John E. (1985) 'Wage Differences Among Workers in the Same Job and Establishment', *Monthly Labor Review*, vol. 105, no. 3, March, pp. 11–16.

Cox, John Howell (1971) 'Time and Incentive Pay Practices in Urban Areas', *Monthly Labor Review*, vol. 91, no. 12, December, pp. 53–6.

Ehrenberg, Ronald G. and George T. Milkovich (1987) 'Compensation and Firm Performance', in Morris Kleiner *et al.* (eds), *Human Resources and the Performance of the Firm*, Madison, WI, Industrial Relations Research Association.

Fama, Eugene (1980) 'Agency Problems and the Theory of the Firm', *Journal of Political Economy*, vol. 80, no. 2, pp. 288–307.

Frank, Robert (1984) 'Are Workers Paid Their Marginal Product?', *American Economic Review*, vol. 74, no. 4, September, pp. 549–71.

Gibbons, Robert and Kevin J. Murphy (1992) 'Optimal Incentive Contracts in the Presence of Career Concerns: Theory and Evidence', *Journal of Political Economy*, vol. 100, no. 3, June, pp. 468–505.

Greeley, Thomas P. and Robert C. Ochsner (1986) 'Putting Merit Back into Salary Administration', *Topics in Total Compensation*, vol. 1, no. 1, Fall, pp. 15–22.

Hashimoto, Masanori and Ben T. Yu (1980 'Specific Capital, Employment Contracts, and Wage Rigidity', *Bell Journal of Economics*, Autumn, pp. 536–49.

Holmstrom, Bengt and Paul Milgrom (1987) 'Aggregation and Linearity in the Provision of Intertemporal Incentives', *Econometrica*, vol. 55, March, pp. 231–59.

Homans, George C. (1954) 'The Cash Posters', *American Sociological Review*, vol. 19, December, pp. 724–33.

Keefe, Jeffrey (1991) 'Why Are Wage Incentives Obsolete?', unpublished paper, October.

King, Sandra (1975) 'Incentive Pay in Auto Repair Shops', *Monthly Labor Review*, vol. 98, no. 9, September, pp. 45–8.

Lazear, Edward P. (1979) 'Why Is There Mandatory Retirement?', *Journal of Political Economy*, vol. 87, December, pp. 1261–84.

———— (1986) 'Salaries and Piece Rates', *Journal of Business*, vol. 53, no. 3, pp. 405–31.

Lazear, Edward P. and Sherwin Rosen (1981) 'Rank Order Tournaments as Optimum Labor Contracts', *Journal of Political Economy*, vol. 89, pp. 841–64.

McCue, Kristin (1992) 'Promotions and Wage Growth', unpublished paper, March.

Milgrom, Paul and John Roberts (1992) *Economics, Organization, and Management*, Englewood Cliffs, NJ, Prentice-Hall.

Miller, Demaris (1988) 'Turnover in Navy Demonstration Laboratories, 1980–1985', Washington, DC, Office of Personnel Management, December.

Mitchell, Daniel J.B., David Lewin, and Edward W. Lawler III (1990) 'Alternative Pay Systems, Firm Performance, and Productivity', in Alan Blinder (ed.), *Paying for Productivity*, Washington, DC, Brookings Institution, pp. 15–87.

Nalebuff, Barry J. and Joseph E. Stiglitz (1983) 'Prizes and Incentives: Towards a General Theory of Compensation and Competition', *Bell Journal of Economics*, vol. 14, no. 1, Spring, pp. 21–43.

National Research Council, Committee on Performance Appraisal for Merit Pay (1991) *Pay for Performance: Evaluation Performance Appraisal and Merit Pay*, Washington, DC, National Academy Press.

Personick, Martin E. (1984) 'White-collar Pay Determination under Range-of-rate Systems', *Monthly Labor Review*, vol. 104, no. 12, December, pp. 25–30.

Pencavel, John (1977) 'Work Effort, On the Job Screening, and Alternative Methods of Remuneration', in Ronald Ehrenberg (ed.), *Research in Labor Economics*, vol. 1, Greenwich, CT, JAI Press, pp. 225–58.

President's Panel on Federal Compensation (1976) *Staff Report*, Washington, DC, Government Printing Office.

Rosen, Sherwin (1990) 'Contracts and the Market for Executives', NBER, *Working Paper*, no. 3542, December.

Seiler, Eric (1984) 'Piece Rate vs. Time Rate: The Effect of Incentives on Earnings', *Review of Economies and Structure*, vol. 66, no. 3, August, pp. 363–76.

Smith, D. Alton, Stephen D. Sylwester and Christine M. Villa (1991) 'Army Re-enlistment Models,' in Curtis Gilroy, David Horne and D. Alton Smith (eds), *Military Compensation and Personnel Retention: Models and Evidence*, Alxandria, VA, US Army Research Institute.

US Merit Systems Protection Board (1989) *Who is Leaving the Federal Government?: An Analysis of Employee Turnover*, Washington, DC, US Government Printing Office.

Ward, Michael P. and Hong W. Tan (1985) 'The Retention of High-Quality Personnel in the US Armed Forces', *RAND Report*, R-3117-MIL, February.

Weiss, Andrew (1980) 'Job Queues and Layoffs in Markets with Flexible Wages', *Journal of Political Economy*, vol. 88, no. 3.

———— (1987) 'Incentives and Worker Behavior: Some Evidence', in Haig R. Nalbantian (ed.), *Incentives, Cooperation, and Risk Sharing*, Totowa, NJ, Rowman & Littlefield, pp. 137–50.

Part III

Employment and Unemployment

9 Unemployment in the OECD Countries

Richard Layard and Stephen Nickell* OECD
E24
J64

9.1 INTRODUCTION

Unemployment varies a great deal, both across countries and over time (see Table 9.1.) In particular, since the early 1960s, unemployment has risen in every OECD country but whereas some of the increases have been relatively slight, as in the US, in other countries, such as Spain, the rises have been truly staggering. It is our purpose to try and explain both the trends in unemployment in each country, and the differences in the levels of unemployment across the countries.

To help us on our way, a number of facts are worth noting. First, few unemployed individuals have deliberately chosen to become unemployed. Furthermore, in Europe, the proportion of workers who enter unemployment is much lower than in the US and has risen little over the last twenty years. Second, in many countries, unemployment has risen sharply at given levels of vacancies. Third, the rise in European unemployment has been associated with a massive increase in long-term unemployment. Thus nearly half of Europe's unemployed have now been out of work for over a year. Fourth, there is no systematic correlation between levels of unemployment and the wage gap[1] (see Gordon, 1988, for example). Unemployment is not high simply because real wages are 'too high'.

In order successfully to analyze unemployment patterns, we require a theoretical framework which is flexible enough to encompass the institutional structures (with regard to wage-setting, for example) which occur in the different OECD countries, and is consistent with the above facts. This will be the topic of the first two sections of the chapter. We should then be in a position to explain the unemployment experiences of the different countries, and this will be the subject of our third section. Finally we provide a summary and some general conclusions.

Table 9.1   Unemployment in OECD countries, 1960–90 (%)

	1960–8	1969–73	1974–9	1980–5	1986–90
Belgium	2.3	2.4	6.3	11.3	9.5
Denmark	2.0	1.4	5.5	9.3	8.6
France	1.7	2.6	4.5	8.3	9.8
W. Germany	0.7	0.8	3.2	6.0	5.9
Ireland	5.0	5.6	7.6	12.6	16.2
Italy	3.8	4.2	4.6	6.4	7.7
Netherlands	1.2	2.0	5.1	10.1	8.8
Spain	2.4	2.7	5.3	16.6	18.7
UK	2.6	3.4	5.1	10.5	8.7
Australia	2.2	2.0	5.0	8.6	7.2
New Zealand	0.2	0.3	0.8	3.9	5.6
Canada	4.7	5.6	7.2	9.9	8.3
US	4.7	4.9	6.7	8.0	5.8
Japan	1.4	1.2	1.9	2.4	2.5
Austria	1.6	1.1	1.5	3.0	3.4
Finland	1.8	2.3	4.4	5.1	4.3
Norway	2.0	1.7	1.8	2.6	3.5
Sweden	1.3	1.8	1.5	2.4	1.7
Switzerland	0.1	0.0	1.0	1.7	1.9

Note: OECD standardized rates except for Denmark, Ireland, New Zealand, Austria, Sweden for which unstandardized rates are used and Italy and Switzerland for which some adjustments are made (see Appendix 2).

9.2   A BASIC THEORETICAL FRAMEWORK

The model we develop builds on an analysis of pricing, employment and wage determination at the level of the firm. An assumption of identical firms then enables us to generate the simple aggregate model set out at the beginning of section 9.3. The idea of the present section is to demonstrate how the macro model we use rests on straightforward micro foundations. However, once we have obtained our aggregate model, we shall indicate how it may be extended to reflect a more complex underlying structure.

9.2.1   Pricing and Employment Decisions

The identical firms in the economy are labelled $i = 1 \ldots F$. Each has a constant returns technology of the form

$$y_i - k_i = \alpha(n_i - k_i) + \epsilon_i, \tag{1}$$

where y_i = value added output, k_i = capital stock (predetermined), n_i = employment (all in logs) and ϵ_i = productivity shock (serially uncorrelated).[2] Firms are price-setters and thus face downward sloping demand curves. In order to specify the demand side, we first note that the aggregate technology has the form

$$y - k = \alpha(n - k) + \epsilon, \tag{2}$$

which follows from the identical firms' assumption. Based on this, we next define $\bar{y}$ as the level of output corresponding to full utilization of resources. That is,

$$\bar{y} - k = \alpha(l - k) \tag{3}$$

where l = labour force, assumed fixed for simplicity. The technology shock is set to its mean level.

Real demand in the economy, y_d, we suppose takes the quantity theory form

$$y_d = m - p \tag{4}$$

where m = money stock, p = value added price (GDP deflator). Demand is allocated equally across firms, so if f is the log of the number of firms, the share of demand for each is $y_d - f$. We then specify the demand curve facing the firm as

$$y_{di} = -\eta[p_i - p] + y_d - f, \tag{5}$$

p_i = the firm's value added price, η = the demand elasticity.

Firms' decisions are taken as follows. When prices are set, wages and demand levels are known but aggregate prices are not. Output is then determined by firms supplying whatever is demanded at the predetermined price.[3] Employment is set to produce the output. This ordering of events is arbitrary but is of no great significance in the present context of explaining unemployment. Furthermore, we do not incorporate adjustment costs at this stage, merely indicating the consequence when we reach the final aggregate model.

Pricing is based on (expected) marginal cost, mc^e, which is given by

$$mc_i^e = w_i + \frac{(1 - \alpha)}{\alpha} (y_{di}^e - k_i) - \frac{\epsilon_i}{\alpha} - \log \alpha \qquad (6)$$

Short-run profit maximization then yields

$$p_i = -\log \kappa + mc_i^e, \quad (\kappa = 1 - 1/\eta) \qquad (7)$$

where κ is an index of product market competitiveness. If we now combine (5), (6), and (7), we have a price equation of the form

$$p_i - w_i = -\log \alpha\kappa + \frac{(1 - \alpha)}{\alpha} (y_d - k) -$$

$$\frac{\eta(1 - \alpha)}{\alpha} (p_i - p^e) - \frac{\epsilon_i}{\alpha} \qquad (8)$$

Prices are influenced by wage costs (w_i) and expected competitors' prices (p^e) as well as by demand, because marginal costs are increasing. In order to aggregate, we may simply note that $p_i = p$, $w_i = w$, $\epsilon_i = \epsilon$ because firms are identical. Hence (8) becomes

$$p - w = -\log \alpha\kappa + \frac{(1 - \alpha)}{\alpha} (y_d - k) -$$

$$\frac{\eta(1 - \alpha)}{\alpha} (p - p^e) - \epsilon/\alpha.$$

It is convenient to separate cyclical demand effects from long-run productivity effects, and this we do by noting that $y_d - k = (y_d - \bar{y}) - \alpha(k - l)$, from (3). So the price equation becomes

$$p - w = -\log \alpha\kappa + \frac{(1 - \alpha)}{\alpha}(y_d - \bar{y}) - (1 - \alpha)(k - l) -$$

$$\frac{\eta(1 - \alpha)}{\alpha} (p - p^e) - \epsilon/\alpha. \qquad (9)$$

Finally we allow the mark-up of prices on marginal cost to be sensitive to the cycle, so we specify

$$-\log \alpha\kappa = \beta_0 - b_1(y_d - \bar{y}) \qquad (10)$$

where here we have the mark-up falling in booms. We shall have more
to say on this issue below. Combining (9) and (10) yields a final aggregate price equation of the form

$$p - w = \beta_0 + \left(\frac{(1 - \alpha)}{\alpha} - b_1\right)(y_d - \bar{y}) - (1 - \alpha)(k - 1)$$

$$- \frac{\eta(1 - \alpha)}{\alpha}(p - p^e) - \epsilon/\alpha. \tag{11}$$

For the purposes of our macro model, we require this price equation,
the demand equation (4) and an Okun's law-type equation connecting
demand and (un)employment. Since firms supply whatever is demanded
at the predetermined price, aggregate output, y, must equal aggregate
demand,[4] y_d. So (2) implies

$$y_d = \alpha(n - k) + \epsilon$$

and subtracting (3) yields

$$(y_d - y) = -\alpha u + \epsilon \tag{12}$$

where u = the aggregate unemployment rate (= $l - n$).

9.2.2 Aggregate Demand and Price Behaviour

In order to specify a general macroeconomic framework, it is necessary to generalize our price equation (11). We shall, however, retain
the very simple demand and technology captured by (4) and (12), because additional complexity here adds little in the way of further insight into unemployment patterns. A slightly more general version of
the price equation may be written as

$$p - w = \beta_0 + \frac{\beta_1}{\alpha}(y_d - \bar{y}) + \frac{\beta_{11}}{\alpha}\Delta(y_d - \bar{y}) -$$

$$\beta_2(p - p^e) - (1 - \alpha)(k - 1) - \epsilon/\alpha \tag{13}$$

The only additional term is that reflecting changes in demand, $\Delta(y_d - \bar{y})$. Such a term will enter if there are costs of adjusting factors of
production.[5] The argument rests on the fact that, in the presence of
quasi-fixed factors, marginal costs are steeper in the short run than in

the long run. Hence, when demand and output increase, the short-run upward pressure on prices is greater than the long-run upward pressure.

In subsequent analyses, it will become clear that the parameters of the price equation are crucial determinants of the behaviour of the economy in both the short and the long run. The three key parameters are β_1, β_{11}, and β_2. Starting with the first, β_1 is the long-run or level demand effect on prices. As we can see from our illustrative model (11), this depends on the impact of both marginal cost $[(1 - \alpha)/\alpha]$ and the mark-up on marginal cost $[-b_1]$. What do we know about β_1? First, it is generally agreed that it is small. The lack of responsiveness of prices to demand fluctuations is a well known feature of pricing behaviour (see Coutts *et al.*, 1978; Encaoua and Geroski, 1986; Brack, 1987 for evidence from a number of countries). Second, there is fairly general agreement that β_1 is smaller if firms operate in a less competitive environment (see, again, Encaoua and Geroski, 1986; Brack, 1987).

Aside from this, not much else seems to be known. For example, there is little consistent evidence on the slope of short-run marginal cost curves and on the cyclical behaviour of the price mark-up on marginal cost. Thus marginal costs slope up in US industries according to Bils (1987), slope down in most of German manufacturing according to Flaig and Steiner (1990), slope down in the 'big three' US car companies according to Berndt *et al.* (1990) and are U shaped in US car plants according to Aizcorbe (1990). In fact the last seems the most plausible since it is very hard to believe that marginal costs are not increasing in the vicinity of full capacity, otherwise why would delivery lags rise so strongly in booms? (Carlton, 1989). If marginal costs slope down, what is the point of keeping customers waiting when supplying them immediately is cheaper?

Concerning the price mark-up on marginal cost, there are few studies, with many more being devoted to the behaviour of mark-ups on average cost. Again the evidence is mixed. Bils (1987) find mark-ups to be countercyclical, Flaig and Steiner (1990) find them to be procyclical. Berndt *et al.* (1990) find a procyclical mark-up at GM and Ford, and a countercyclical mark-up at Chrysler.

Turning to the second key parameter, β_{11}, this depends on the costs associated with adjusting factors of production. The more sluggish is the response of capital and labour to exogenous shifts, the more we would expect costs, and hence prices, to respond to fluctuations in demand in the short run.

The last important parameter, β_2, is associated with the price surprise and reflects the extent of nominal inertia. There is, of course, an extensive literature on nominal inertia in price setting, much of it usefully summarized in Blanchard and Fischer (1989, Chapter 8). In our simple model, nominal inertia arises because firms are unaware of aggregate prices when setting their own price. However, we can allow β_2 to reflect nominal inertia from any source, and the key question is, what can we expect it to depend upon? The model set out by Ball *et al.* (1988) looks at the equilibrium frequency of price changes in the context of a menu cost model, and concludes that this is increasing in the overall level of inflation, the variance of both aggregate and firm specific shocks, and the second derivative of the profit function with respect to price. This last is a measure of the cost to the firm of deviating from its static profit-maximizing price. Generally speaking, this cost is increasing in the demand elasticity, so price changes are less frequent when the demand elasticity is low and the product market environment is less competitive. This last is consistent with the evidence presented in Carlton (1986, p. 655).

To summarize, therefore, the key parameters of price-setting behaviour are those associated with the level (β_1) and change (β_{11}) of demand, and with nominal inertia (β_2). Theory and evidence suggest that β_1 is lower and β_2 is higher, when the product market is less competitive. Furthermore, we would expect the change effect, β_{11}, to be larger, the greater the costs associated with adjusting labour and capital.

9.2.3 Wage Determination

We now turn to the important question of wage determination. As a foundation for our macro model, we consider decentralized wage-setting, leaving any discussion of centralized or coordinated wage bargaining until later. In the context of our simple micro foundations, we shall suppose that wages are set prior to prices, but conditions in the external labour market are known.

The following three factors are common to most models of wage determination. First, firms and workers are concerned with outside opportunities, A. Firms are concerned because both recruitment and retention as well as perhaps motivation, all depend on A. Workers are concerned because A reflects what is available if they leave their current employment. Second, workers are concerned with job security, that is, with employment prospects inside their firm. Third, firms are concerned with profit prospects.

In order to specify outside opportunities, A, we argue that these depend on alternative wages, W, unemployment benefits, B, and the chances of being in work. To be more precise about this latter point, what matters are the chances of obtaining a job from unemployment when searching with given 'effectiveness', c. Search effectiveness here means anything which influences the speed with which an individual achieves a suitable job match at given levels of unemployment and vacancies. Thus it not only includes the intensity with which the individual looks for work but also the intensity of employer search, the acceptability of the individual to prospective employers, and so on. So suppose H is the number of hires per period from unemployment. Then the chances of getting a job, for an unemployed person of unit effectiveness, are given by H/cU, where U is the number of unemployed and c is the average search effectiveness of the unemployed. On average (in steady state), the number of hires from unemployment is equal to the number of exits from employment into unemployment, sN, where s is the exit rate. So we now have,

$$\text{chances of getting a job} = H/cU = sN/cU$$
$$= \frac{s(1 - u)}{cu}$$
$$\simeq s/cu$$

where u is the unemployment rate. In the light of this, we may define outside opportunities, A, as

$$A = W(1 - \phi(cu/s)) + B\phi(cu/s) \tag{14}$$

where ϕ represents the proportion of the relevant period for which a worker of unit search effectiveness can expect to be unemployed were he to lose his job. This is clearly increasing in cu/s, which is the average length of time an unemployed individual can expect to remain unemployed before obtaining a suitable job.[6] Thus $\phi' > 0$.

Turning to the second important factor, namely employment prospects within the firm, here we shall suppose that workers are concerned with longer-term prospects in the sense that prospects are evaluated at the average level of the price mark-up on marginal cost, $-\log \bar{\kappa}$ (see equation (7)). Combining this with (6) and noting that $y^e_{di} - k_i = y^e_i - k_i = \alpha(n^e_i - k_i)$, then employment prospects must satisfy

$$p^e_i - w_i = -\log \alpha\bar{\kappa} + (1 - \alpha)(n^e_i - k_i) \tag{15}$$

where we suppose that the productivity shock, ϵ_i, is not known when wages are set. Rewriting (15) in unlogged form yields

$$N_i^e = K_i(W_i/\alpha\bar{\kappa}\,P_i^e)^{-1/(1-\alpha)} \tag{16}$$

which reveals how employment prospects are influenced by wages. Finally, on the firm's side, the prospects for operating profit are the key factor and these may be written as

$$\Pi_i^e = \frac{(1-\alpha\bar{\kappa})}{\alpha\bar{\kappa}}\,W_iN_i^e. \tag{17}$$

Within this overall framework, we shall now present two examples of models of wage determination, the first involving unions, the second not.

9.2.4 A Union Model of Wage Determination

Here we use the Nash bargaining framework, assuming that wages only are bargained over. As we have already indicated prices, and hence employment, are set unilaterally by the firm.[7] In the Nash bargain we suppose that the workers' objective less the fall-back is given by

$$(W_i - A)S(W_i)$$

where S is the probability that the representative employee will remain employed or the 'survival' probability. In Appendix 1, we demonstrate that S depends on the number of employees who are party to the wage bargain, N_{ti} (the number of 'insiders') relative to expected employment, N_i^e. That is

$$S = S(N_{ti}/N_i^e(W_i)) \quad (S' < 0). \tag{18}$$

With the firm's contribution to the Nash bargain being expected operating profit, Π_i^e, wages emerge as the solution to

$$\max_{W_i}[(W_i - A)S(W_i)]^\beta\Pi_i^e(W_i) \tag{19}$$

where β serves as an indicator of union power in the bargain. In Appendix 1, we show that wages satisfy

$$\frac{W_i - A}{W_i} = \frac{1 - \alpha\bar{\kappa}}{\epsilon_{SN}(W_i) + \alpha\bar{\kappa}/\beta} \tag{20}$$

where $\epsilon_{SN} = \partial \log S(N_{ii}/N_i^e)/\partial \log N_i^e > 0$. From (20) we see that the wage mark-up on outside opportunities is decreasing in the elasticity of survival with respect to expected employment, ϵ_{SN}, and in the average level of product market competition, $\bar{\kappa}$, and it is increasing in union power, β.

In order to generate a wage equation on the basis of (20), we take (log) differentials using the definitions of A, N_i^e, S. This yields

$$dw_i = \lambda_i[dp_i^e + (1 - \alpha)(dk_i - dn_{ii})] +$$
$$(1 - \lambda_i)[dw - c_1 d(cu/s) + c_2 db] + c_3 d\beta \tag{21}$$

where $b = B/W$, the benefit replacement ratio, and

$$\lambda_i = \frac{(1 - \alpha\bar{\kappa})N_i\epsilon'_{SN}}{(\epsilon_{SN} + \alpha\bar{\kappa}/\beta)^2(1 - \alpha)N^e}$$

$$\left[(1 - \phi(1 - b)) + \frac{(1 - \alpha\bar{\kappa})N_i\epsilon'_{SN}}{(\epsilon_{SN} + \alpha\bar{\kappa}/\beta)^2(1 - \alpha)N^e}\right]^{-1}$$

$$c_1 = \frac{\phi'(1 - b)}{1 - \phi(1 - b)}, \ c_2 = \frac{\phi}{1 - \phi(1 - b)}, \ c_3 = \frac{\alpha\bar{\kappa}(1 - \alpha\bar{\kappa})}{\lambda_d(\beta\epsilon_{SN} + \alpha\bar{\kappa})^2},$$

λ_d = denominator of λ_i, $\epsilon'_{SN} > 0$ (see Appendix 1). Note that $0 \le \lambda_i < 1$.

This equation serves as the foundation for our model of wage determination. Wages are a weighted sum of the 'inside' firm specific factors (notably expected prices, p_i^e, and a productivity measure, $k_i - n_{ii}$) and the 'outside' factors (w, c, u, b), with union power, β, generating an extra term. The parameter λ_i may thus be termed the insider weight. This equation is, however, based on a union bargaining model and so we must also consider a non-union alternative.

9.2.5 A Non-union Model of Wage Determination

Here we consider a model which takes explicit account of job vacancies. Wages are set by the firm to influence accessions in order to ensure that the firm operates as near to full capacity as possible. To keep things simple, suppose we have fixed coefficients, *ex post*. So if the firm has capital stock, K_i, then the number of available job slots, N_i^*, is given by

$$N_i^* = K_i v, \tag{22}$$

where v is constant in the short run. We next assume a production function of the form

$$Y_i = N_i(K_i/N_i^*)^{1-\alpha} \quad (N_i \leq N_i^*). \tag{23}$$

We can thus define the number of vacancies as $(N_i^* - N_i)$, each vacancy reflecting an unfilled job slot. Suppose we have an accessions function a (W_i/A), $a' > 0$, which captures the flow of accessions per vacancy. Then employment must satisfy

$$N_{it} - N_{it-1} = a(W_{it}/A)(N_i^* - N_{it}) - sN_{it}$$

where s is the (fixed) separation rate. Note that A is again given by (14).

Within this framework, we show in Appendix 1 that if the firm sets wages and employment, then wages will satisfy

$$dw_i = \lambda_i[dp_i^e + (1 - \alpha)(dk_i - dn_i^*)] +$$
$$(1 - \lambda_i)[dw - c_1d(cu/s) + c_2db] \tag{24}$$

where, in this case, the weight, λ_i, is given by

$$\lambda_i = \left[1 + \frac{a\eta_a}{s(1 + \eta_a) + r + a} \right]^{-1} \quad (0 < \lambda_i < 1).$$

The parameter r is the discount rate and $\eta_a = a'W_i/aA$, the accessions elasticity.

The form of equation (24) is almost identical to the union equation (21). There are only two notable differences. In the union model, the capital stock is normalized on the number of 'insiders', N_{Ii}, whereas here it is normalized on the predetermined number of job slots, N_i^*. Second, there is no union power term.

9.2.6 The Aggregate Wage Equation

Returning to the union model, the linearized wage equation based on
(21) has the form

$$w_i = c_0 + \lambda_i[p_i^e + (1 - \alpha)(k_i - n_{li})] +$$
$$(1 - \lambda_i)(w - c_1(cu/s) + c_2b) + c_3\beta \qquad (25)$$

Using our identical firms assumption, we may aggregate to obtain,
after some rearrangement,

$$w - p = c_0/\lambda - \frac{(1 - \lambda)}{\lambda} c_1(cu/s) - (p - p^e) +$$
$$(1 - \alpha)(k - n_l) + \frac{(1 - \lambda)}{\lambda}c_2b + \frac{c_3}{\lambda}\beta \qquad (26)$$

In order to develop a more general model, we require a number of
additions and extensions. Consider first the number of insiders, n_l. The
simplest assumption here is to suppose that the number of employees
who are party to the wage bargain is equal to last period's employment less the proportion δ who quit voluntarily. Thus, so long as δ is
small, we have

$$n_l = n_{-1} - \delta.$$

From this we find that the term $(k - n_l)$ can be written

$$(k - n_l) = k - n_{-1} + \delta$$
$$= (k - l) + u_{-1} + \delta \qquad (27)$$

So this 'insider' term generates a positive lagged unemployment effect
on wages. It is this effect which is the foundation of so-called insider
hysteresis.

The next term we must look at more closely is cu/s, where c/s is the
ratio of the search effectiveness of the unemployed to the entry rate
into unemployment. As we have already noted, the effectiveness of the
unemployed depends on the intensity of both unemployed and employer
search, and on the acceptability or suitability of unemployed individuals to prospective employers. These depend on a number of exogenous

factors which we shall label z_1, and discuss later, but also on an endogenous factor, namely the proportion of long-term unemployed, LTU. This latter influences effectiveness because the evidence suggests that the long-term unemployed both search less intensively (because of demoralization, for example) and are less acceptable to employers (see, for example, Daniel, 1990 for the first, and Meager and Metcalf, 1987 or Winter-Ebmer, 1991, for the second). This suggests that we may write c/s as

$$c/s = \alpha_{10}(z_1) - \alpha_{11}LTU. \tag{28}$$

The proportion of long-term unemployed is endogenous because it is, itself, influenced by unemployment. Typically it increases in the long run when unemployment goes up but, in the short run, things are rather different. When unemployment is actually increasing, there is generally a rise in the inflow and this naturally tends to *reduce* the long-term proportion because of the increased number of recent entrants. Overall, therefore, we tend to have a relationship of the form

$$LTU = \alpha_{20}(z_2) + \alpha_{21}(z_2)u - \alpha_{22}(z_2)\Delta u/u, \tag{29}$$

where z_2 are the exogenous variables influencing LTU, to be discussed later.

Using (28) and (29) and omitting reference to z_1, z_2 for convenience, we find that the term cu/s becomes

$$cu/s = (\alpha_{10} - \alpha_{11}\alpha_{20})u - \alpha_{11}\alpha_{21}u^2 + \alpha_{22}\Delta u \tag{30}$$

Thus the dynamics of long-term unemployment introduces an element of 'outsider' hysteresis. If we now include the insider effect (27) and the long-term unemployed effect (30) in our basic wage equation (26), we obtain

$$w - p = c_0/\lambda + (1 - \alpha)\delta - $$
$$\left[c_1(\alpha_{10} - \alpha_{11}\alpha_{20})\frac{(1 - \lambda)}{\lambda} - (1 - \alpha)\alpha'\right]u$$
$$- \left[\frac{(1 - \lambda)}{\lambda}c_1\alpha_{22} + (1 - \alpha)\alpha'\right]\Delta u - (p - p^e)$$
$$+ (1 - \alpha)(k - l) + \frac{(1 - \lambda)}{\lambda}c_2b + \frac{c_3}{\lambda}\beta. \tag{31}$$

We have made two adjustments to obtain this. First we have omitted the term in u^2 arising from (30). Here, we shall simply note that this is one of several possible reasons why the unemployment effect might be concave (see Nickell, 1987, for example). Second, we have weighted the lagged unemployment effect arising from insider hysteresis by a parameter, $\alpha'(< 1)$. We do this because this insider effect only appears in the union model. Since economies are never completely unionized, its impact in the aggregate equation will be somewhat attenuated.

Before finishing with wage determination models, one final element must be introduced, namely, real wage resistance. Real wage resistance occurs if workers resist falls in their living standards consequent on tax increases or adverse terms-of-trade shocks by pressing for higher wages. In our union model, such effects do not arise, because any shifts which change the wedge between consumer and product prices influence W_i and A in exactly the same fashion, so entering multiplicatively in the Nash objective and leaving the wage outcome unchanged. In reality, of course, we know that real wage resistance arises because individual wellbeing depends not only on the absolute level of real income but on its level relative to that ruling in the past. Once we allow for this possibility in our model, then (product) wages will rise in response to adverse *changes* in labour taxes or shifts in the terms of trade. We shall not present this result formally here but simply add in the appropriate term to our wage equation.

As a consequence of this analysis, we end up with a wage equation of the general form

$$w - p = \gamma_0 - \gamma_1 u - \gamma_{11}\Delta u - \gamma_2(p - p^e) +$$
$$(1 - \alpha)(k - l) + z_w \tag{32}$$

where z_w includes the union effect, β, the benefit replacement ratio, b, and the real wage resistance effects discussed above.

9.2.7 The Parameters of the Wage Equation

Along with the parameters of the price equation, the parameters of the wage equation are of critical importance in determining the behaviour of the aggregate economy. The key parameters are γ_1, γ_{11} and γ_2. Starting with the first of these, γ_1, this measures the impact of unemployment on wage-setting. In order to analyze this parameter we must trace back its determinants from equation (31). Here we see that γ_1 is given by

$$\gamma_1 = c_1(\alpha_{10} - \alpha_{11}\alpha_{20})(1 - \lambda)/\lambda - (1 - \alpha)\ \alpha'. \tag{33}$$

The parameter α_{10} depends on those factors which influence the search effectiveness of the unemployed relative to the entry rate into unemployment (c/s). Search effectiveness is clearly diminishing in the generosity of the benefit system as measured by the replacement ratio, b, and the duration of benefit entitlement, BD. It will also be diminishing in the degree of mismatch between the skill or regional distribution of the unemployed relative to the available job vacancies, mm. Finally, we shall argue that search effectiveness will be enhanced by so-called labour market spending, LMS. This measures state expenditure on labour market programmes to assist the unemployed in finding work (e.g. expenditure on training, mobility and the like, see OECD, 1988, for a complete discussion). One other factor worth mentioning here is the degree of 'employment protection'. This reflects the extent to which governments impose costs on firms who wish to reduce their labour force. This has two effects. An increase in employment protection tends to reduce the flow from employment to unemployment(s) *and* search effectiveness(c), by making firms more reluctant both to fire and hire. The net effect on c/s is indeterminate which is consistent with the conflicting evidence (see Lazear, 1990; Bentolila and Bertola, 1990, for examples of this conflict).

The parameter α_{20}, which enters with a negative sign (see equation (33)), reflects the exogenous factors which influence the extent of long-term unemployment. The important ones are benefit duration, BD, and labour market spending, LMS, which influence α_{20} positively and negatively respectively. Their impact on γ_1 is therefore negative and positive as before. Finally, it is worth noting that α' tends to be increasing in unionization which will thus have a negative effect on γ_1 (see equation (33)).

This whole discussion has been based on decentralized models of wage determination. What if wage bargaining tends to be more coordinated? The standard argument here is that the higher the degree of coordination, the more responsive are wage outcomes to the state of the labour market. The idea is that, as bargaining becomes more coordinated, the greater will be the apparent impact of the wage bargain on unemployment and the smaller will be its apparent impact on real wages (because the impact of the wage bargain on aggregate prices will become greater). As a consequence, the parties to the wage bargain will take more account of the unemployment position when setting the wage (see Layard *et al.*, 1991, chapter 2, for a full discussion).

Turning to the parameter associated with the change in unemployment or hysteresis parameter, γ_{11}, we see from (31) that this is increasing in α_{22} and α'. The first of these, α_{22}, is increasing in the importance of long-term unemployment in the economy and so, from arguments already rehearsed, γ_{11} is increasing in benefit duration, *BD*, but diminishing in labour market spending, *LMS*. It may also be increasing in unionization via α'. The next question is how the hysteresis parameter is influenced by the extent of coordination in wage bargaining. Since it depends partly on the power of insiders in the wage bargain, we might suspect that there is a difference here between who is more coordinated, unions or employers. If unions are more coordinated, this will surely raise the power of insiders, whereas if employers are more coordinated this will reduce their power. Overall, therefore, we hypothesize that γ_{11} is increasing in union coordination and decreasing in employer coordination.

Finally, we come to the nominal inertia parameter, γ_2. Standard arguments lead one to associate γ_2 with the structure of labour contracts. If these are longer, this will tend to raise nominal inertia but the extent of indexation and synchronization will clearly tend to reduce it.

9.2.8 The Wage Equation and the *u/v* Curve

In the Introduction, we noted as one of our important facts, the sharp rise in unemployment at given levels of vacancies in many countries. In order to incorporate this into our general framework, we investigate the relationship between vacancies and unemployment. The key relationship here is the so-called matching function which relates the number of job hires from unemployment to the number of effective unemployed searchers, *cU*, and the number of available vacancies, *V*. Suppose that the number of hires, *H*, satisfies

$$H = M(cU, V) \qquad (M_1, M_2 > 0)$$

where *M* reflects the matching technology (see, for example, Hall, 1977; Jackman *et al.*, 1989). Both considerations of theory and the empirical evidence suggest that *M* has the constant returns property.[8] In steady state, the number of hires from unemployment equals the flow into unemployment, *sN*, thus yielding

$$sN = M(cU, V)$$

or

$$\frac{sN}{cU} = M\left(1, \frac{V}{cU}\right) \qquad \text{by constant returns}$$

or

$$\frac{s(1 - u)}{cu} = M\left[1, \frac{v(1 - u)}{cu}\right] \tag{34}$$

where v is the vacancy rate, V/N. This is the steady state u/v curve or Beveridge curve.[9] It is easy to show that it slopes down, and shifts outwards with a rise in search effectiveness, c. Consequently any adverse shifts in those factors which influence search effectiveness will raise wages at given unemployment and cause the u/v curve to move outwards. This provides the connection between the increase in long-term unemployment and the rise in unemployment at given vacancies noted in the Introduction. This completes our discussion of the foundations of the aggregate model, and in the next section we consider its operation.

9.3   THE MACROECONOMICS OF UNEMPLOYMENT

We now analyze the structure of our macro model and its response to shocks of various kinds. In particular we highlight the role played by the key parameters of the price and wage equations discussed in section 9.2. These are particularly important for our purpose, because it is cross-country differences in these parameters which go a long way towards explaining the different unemployment patterns.

Gathering together the equations of the model, we have

Okun's law $(y_d - \bar{y}) = -\alpha u + \epsilon$ (35)
(equation (12))

Demand $y_d = m - p$ (36)
(equation (4))

Prices
(equation (13)) $p - w = \beta_0 + \dfrac{\beta_1}{\alpha}(y_d - \bar{y}) + \dfrac{\beta_{11}}{\alpha}\Delta(y_d - \bar{y})$

$$- \beta_2(p - p^e) - (1 - \alpha)(k - l)$$
$$- \epsilon/\alpha \tag{37}$$

Wages
(equation (32))

$$w - p = \gamma_0 - \gamma_1 u - \gamma_{11}\Delta u - \gamma_2(p - p^e)$$
$$+ (1 - \alpha)(k - l) + z_w \tag{38}$$

It is convenient to write the price equation with unemployment as the demand variable, so using (35) and (37) gives

$$p - w = \beta_0 - \beta_1 u - \beta_{11}\Delta u - \beta_2(p - p^e) -$$
$$(1 - \alpha)(k - 1) - \frac{\beta_3}{\alpha}\epsilon \tag{39}$$

where $\beta_3 = 1 - \beta_1 - \beta_{11} > 0$ so long as a favourable productivity shock reduces marginal cost at constant employment.[10]

Before going on to analyze this model, it is worth noting that many economists, particularly in the US, tend to view the price equation (39) as a labour demand equation and the wage equation (38) as a labour supply equation with z_w reflecting labour supply shocks. While the model is certainly open to this interpretation, it is somewhat restrictive. Since price-setting firms probably produce the majority of OECD output, a price equation interpretation of (39) is to be preferred. However, this is a minor issue. Much more important is the labour supply interpretation of the wage equation. To us, this seems wholly misplaced. Non-competitive forms of wage determination predominate in the OECD and while changes in the benefit replacement ratio can be viewed as shifting the labour supply curve, it requires a real intellectual contortion to look at changes in union power or real wage resistance in this fashion. As a consequence we shall persist with our current interpretation of this model, while emphasizing that the labour demand–labour supply interpretation is perfectly consistent with the model in a formal analytical sense.

Bearing this in mind, we shall now discuss the equilibrium, the unemployment–inflation tradeoff, and the response of the economy to demand and supply shocks.

9.3.1 Equilibrium

The equilibrium rate of unemployment in this model, u^*, is the stationary value ($\Delta u = 0$) corresponding to a zero productivity shock

($\epsilon = 0$) and price expectations fulfilled [$p = p^e$]. Solving the model yields

$$u^* = \frac{\beta_0 + \gamma_0 + z_w}{\beta_1 + \gamma_1} \tag{40}$$

Thus equilibrium unemployment depends essentially on the autonomous elements of wage pressure, z_w, in particular, union effects, benefit effects and real wage resistance (see the discussion around equation (32)). So shifts over time in equilibrium unemployment will flow from changes in these variables but will also depend crucially on the scaling factor, $(\beta_1 + \gamma_1)^{-1}$. This term is often known as the Real Wage Rigidity (RWR) parameter (see Grubb *et al.*, 1983, for example). The larger the extent of real wage rigidity, the bigger will be the equilibrium shifts in unemployment corresponding to any given change in wage pressure. So, as we shall see, this parameter plays an important role in explaining the different patterns of unemployment in the various countries.

9.3.2 The Unemployment–inflation Tradeoff

If we eliminate the real wage from the wage and price equations (38, 39), we obtain the unemployment–inflation tradeoff,

$$u + \frac{(\beta_{11} + \eta_{11})}{(\beta_1 + \gamma_1)}\Delta u + \frac{(\beta_2 + \gamma_2)}{(\beta_1 + \gamma_1)}(p - p^e) =$$
$$\frac{\gamma_0 + \beta_0 + z_w - \beta_3 \epsilon}{\beta_1 + \gamma_1} \tag{41}$$

or

$$u - u^* + \frac{(\beta_{11} + \gamma_{11})}{(\beta_1 + \gamma_1)}\Delta u + \frac{(\beta_2 + \gamma_2)}{(\beta_1 + \gamma_1)}(p - p^e) = -\frac{\beta_3 \epsilon}{\beta_1 + \gamma_1} \tag{42}$$

This reveals those factors which must be associated with a deviation of unemployment from equilibrium. In particular, there must be a price surprise unless unemployment is rising or falling, or there is a productivity shock. Another way of writing this equation is

$$\Delta p = \Delta p^e + \frac{\gamma_0 + \beta_0}{\gamma_2 + \beta_2} - \frac{(\beta_1 + \gamma_1)}{(\beta_2 + \gamma_2)} u - \frac{(\beta_{11} + \gamma_{11})}{(\beta_2 + \gamma_2)} \Delta u +$$

$$\frac{z_w - \beta_3 \epsilon}{(\beta_2 + \gamma_2)}. \tag{43}$$

This is often known as a Phillips Curve (see, for example, the discussion in Gordon, 1990) despite the fact that it is not a wage equation. Equations of this type, along with the definition of u^* given in (40), are particularly useful for analyzing unemployment patterns because they represent a fundamental supply-side constraint. This is particularly clear if we suppose that price expectations satisfy

$$\Delta p^e = \Delta p_{-1}. \tag{44}$$

This assumption is apposite for the last two decades within the OECD because, during this period, the inflation process appears to have a unit root. That is, the assumed expectations formation mechanism is consistent with the stochastic process driving inflation.[11] Given this assumption, the supply-side constraint becomes a genuine unemployment–inflation tradeoff of the form

$$(u - u^*) + \frac{(\beta_2 + \gamma_2)}{(\beta_1 + \gamma_1)} \Delta^2 p = - \frac{(\beta_{11} + \gamma_{11})}{(\beta_1 + \gamma_1)} \Delta u - \frac{\beta_3 \epsilon}{(\beta_1 + \gamma_1)}. \tag{45}$$

Thus we have a tradeoff between deviations of unemployment from u^* and changes in inflation. This tradeoff may be temporarily shifted in a favourable direction if unemployment is rising or there is a favourable productivity shock. The former arises because of the short-run reduction in inflationary pressure via hysteresis effects, when the level of economic activity is actually falling. Overall, however, (45) acts as a constraint in the sense that demand fluctuations can move the economy around on it but cannot shift it in the long term.

The parameter which actually represents the tradeoff is $(\beta_2 + \gamma_2)/(\beta_1 + \gamma_1)$, which is sometimes known as the degree of Nominal Wage Rigidity (NWR). It also represents the unemployment cost (in percentage point years) of bringing inflation down by 1 percent, so it is also a measure of the so-called Sacrifice Ratio. However, this simple tradeoff is, strictly speaking, a closed economy concept. In an open economy things can be a little more complicated. One of the autonomous wage pressure factors in z_w is real wage resistance and this may arise from adverse movements in the terms of trade. In terms of understanding or explaining unemployment patterns, it is quite possible to condition on such terms-of-trade shifts, particularly when major components of the shifts are exogenous, as with the oil shocks. However if one explicitly recognizes that terms-of-trade movements are not strictly exogenous, then the supply-side tradeoff may be developed further. The first step is to define equilibrium unemployment to be the level consistent with stable inflation *and* balanced trade. Then to utilize a trade balance equation to eliminate the endogenous elements of the terms-of-trade, thereby obtaining a three way tradeoff between unemployment, changes in inflation and the trade balance. We shall not pursue this here (see Layard *et al.*, 1991 or Nickell, 1990) but merely note that in making cross-country comparisons of unemployment, it may be necessary to control for the trade balance as well as the rate of change of inflation.

9.3.3 The Response of the Model to Shocks

The next stage is to investigate how the key variables respond to various kinds of shock. The three types of shock we specify are,

productivity	ϵ
money supply	$\Delta m = \Delta m_{-1} + \epsilon_m$
wage	$z_w = \overline{z}_w + \epsilon_w$

where ϵ, ϵ_m, ϵ_w are all white noise. We now suppose that both ϵ and ϵ_w are zero when unemployment is at its equilibrium value and hence $\overline{z}_w$ replaces z_w in the definition of u^* given in equation (40). Taking the model as given by (35)–(38) and assuming model consistent (rational) expectations,[12] we find that unemployment satisfies

$$(u - u^*) = \frac{\beta_{11} + \gamma_{11}}{(\beta_1 + \gamma_1 + \beta_{11} + \gamma_{11})} \ (u - u^*)_{-1} - \frac{(\beta_2 + \gamma_2)}{\Omega} \ \epsilon_m$$

$$+ \frac{(\beta_2 + \gamma_2 - \beta_3)}{\Omega} \ \epsilon + \frac{\epsilon_w}{\Omega} , \qquad (46)$$

where

$$\Omega = \alpha \ (\beta_2 + \gamma_2) + (\beta_1 + \gamma_1 + \beta_{11} + \gamma_{11}).$$

The following points are worth noting. First, the degree of persistence in the economy depends on the hysteresis parameters $(\beta_{11} + \gamma_{11})$. To be more precise, it depends on the ratio of the change effects of economic activity (unemployment) on wages and prices to the level effects, that is $(\beta_{11} + \gamma_{11})/(\beta_1 + \gamma_1)$. Indeed if the level effects are zero, unemployment deviations follow a random walk and we have a pure hysteresis model of the type discussed in Blanchard and Summers (1986). Second, the impact of the money shock depends on the extent of nominal inertia in wage- and price-setting, $(\beta_2 + \gamma_2)$. This is, of course, a standard result in one-good models.[13] Third, nominal inertia reduces the favourable effects of positive productivity shocks whose impact on unemployment is indeterminate, although it is easy to show that the impact on output is always positive. Fourth, nominal inertia reduces the unfavourable effects of adverse wage shocks. Finally, the higher are the effects of economic activity on wages and prices, $(\beta_1 + \gamma_1)$ (i.e., the lower is real wage rigidity, RWR), the greater is the stability of the economy in response to any kind of shock. This is probably the most important point to bear in mind.

It is worth briefly commenting on the impact of the shocks on real wages because their cyclical behaviour has been the subject of so much debate over the last 50 years. Recall that here we are talking about wages relative to the GDP deflator. A favourable productivity shock will raise real wages, as will a positive wage shock. However the impact of a positive demand shock can go either way. In fact real wages will rise if and only if

$$(\gamma_1 + \gamma_{11})\beta_2 > (\beta_1 + \beta_{11})\gamma_2. \qquad (47)$$

So in order to obtain procyclical real wages *in response to demand shocks*, we need a tendency for nominal prices to be stickier than nominal wages $(\beta_2 > \gamma_2)$ and for economic activity to have a bigger impact on wage-setting than on price-setting $(\gamma_1 + \gamma_{11} > \beta_1 + \beta_{11})$. So if cycles are predominantly generated by demand shocks allied to nominal inertia, real wages can either be procyclical or countercyclical depending on the parameter configurations. Two particular cases are worth noting. If product markets are competitive and there is, therefore, no nominal inertia in price-setting, then $\beta_2 = 0$ and real wages are countercyclical. On the other hand, if there is pure mark-up pricing (i.e., no demand effect), then $\beta_1 + \beta_{11} = 0$ and real wages are procyclical.

To summarize, therefore, if cycles are generated by demand shocks, the real wage can be either procyclical or countercyclical. If cycles are generated by productivity shocks, it will be procyclical and if cycles are generated by wage shocks, it will be countercyclical. Since, in reality, all types of shock occur, it is hardly surprising that real wages exhibit no clear-cut cyclical tendencies and that there is no correlation between unemployment and the wage gap as noted in the Introduction.

This completes our analysis of the model and in section 3.4 we shall see what light it sheds on the unemployment experiences of the OECD countries.

9.4 UNEMPLOYMENT PATTERNS IN THE OECD

As we have already seen in Table 9.1, there are very large variations in unemployment across countries, particularly in the 1980s. Our purpose here is to use the framework we have set up in the previous sections to shed some light on both cross-country and intra-country variations in unemployment. We begin with an investigation of the levels of unemployment in the 1980s.

9.4.1 Explaining Cross-country Variations in Unemployment

Our aim is to explain the average level of unemployment in the 1980s across 20 OECD countries. We select the period 1983–8 because unemployment was relatively stable over these years so that dynamic effects are minimized. We begin with our expression for equilibrium unemployment, which we repeat here for convenience.

$$u^* = \frac{\beta_0 + \gamma_0 + z_w}{\beta_1 + \gamma_1} \tag{40}$$

When discussing wage models we concluded that the main elements of z_w, the factors generating wage pressure, were union power, the benefit replacement ratio and real wage resistance. Since we are concerned with longer-run averages and the real wage resistance effects are essentially temporary rather than permanent, we ignore them in this analysis which leaves us with union power, which we measure by the coverage of collective bargaining, $UCOV$, and the benefit replacement ratio, RR. In addition to variations in z_w across countries, we must also take account of variations in the parameters β_1 and γ_1. Recall that these reflect the impact of the level of economic activity on price and wage setting respectively.

In our discussion of price equations in section 9.2, we noted that there is some evidence to suggest that β_1 is increasing in the level of product market competition. Unfortunately, we are unable to locate any consistent measures of product market competition across our various countries, so this variable must be ignored. With regard to the wage parameter, γ_1, we are more fortunate. The analysis of wage determination in section 9.2 indicates that the unemployment effect on wages, γ_{11}, is negatively related to the unemployment benefit replacement ratio, *RR*, and the duration of unemployment benefit entitlement, *BD*, and positively related to the extent of labour market spending, *LMS*, and the degree to which wage bargaining is coordinated across unions, *UNCD*, and across employers, *EMCD*. This suggests that we may write u^* as

$$u^* = \frac{\overset{+}{\beta_0} + \overset{+}{\gamma_0} + z_w \, (UCOV, RR)}{\underset{-\quad - \quad + \quad + \quad +}{\beta_1 + \gamma_1 \, (RR, BD, LMS, UNCD, EMCD)}} \qquad (48)$$

In order to analyze actual levels of unemployment, the discussion in section 9.3 indicates that we must correct for differences across countries in changes in the rate of inflation, $\Delta^2 p$, and the trade balance (normalized on GDP), TB. Thus, incorporating (48), we have a linear relationship of the form

$$u = \alpha_{10} + \alpha_{11}UCOV + \alpha_{12}RR + \alpha_{13}BD - \alpha_{14}LMS - \alpha_{15}UNCD$$
$$- \alpha_{16}EMCD - \alpha_{21}\Delta^2 p + \alpha_{22}TB \qquad (49)$$

which we use to explain average unemployment levels in the 1980s across 20 OECD countries. The data are reported in Table 9.2 and the resulting regression has the form

$$u = 2.03 + 0.15 \, RR + 0.93 \, BD - 0.13 \, LMS + 1.88 \, UCOV$$
$$\quad\;\; (7.2) \qquad (3.1) \qquad\;\; (2.6) \qquad\;\;\; (1.9)$$

$$- 1.13 \, UNCD - 4.36 \, EMCD - 0.46 \, \Delta^2 p + 0.29 \, TB,$$
$$\quad (1.7) \qquad\qquad (7.7) \qquad\qquad (3.7) \qquad\;\; (2.2)$$

$N = 20$, $\bar{R}^2 = 0.92$, se = 1.3, t ratios in brackets.

As can be seen, this equation is highly successful in explaining the cross-section variation in unemployment in our 20 countries, with the six institutional variables plus corrections for inflation and trade position explaining over 90 percent of the variation. Key factors are the

Table 9.2 Explaining unemployment across the OECD, 1983–8

	u	BD	RR	LMS	UCOV	UNCD	EMCD	$\Delta^2 p$	TB
Belgium	11.3	4	60	7.4	3	2	2	−3.6	2.30
Denmark	9.0	2.5	90	7.9	3	3	3	−3.0	1.33
France	9.9	3.75	57	3.9	3	2	2	−6.5	0.42
Germany	6.7	4	63	10.4	3	2	3	−1.7	3.87
Ireland	16.4	4	50	5.0	3	1	1	−7.6	2.89
Italy	7.0	0.5	2	0.8	3	2	1	−8.9	0.42
Netherlands	10.6	4	70	2.7	3	2	2	−0.1	4.25
Portugal	7.7	0.5	60	7.4	3	2	2	−12.7	−7.59
Spain	19.8	3.5	80	2.1	3	2	1	−5.8	0.86
UK	10.7	4	36	4.6	3	1	1	1.4	−0.54
Australia	8.4	4	39	2.8	3	2	1	1.1	−2.01
New Zealand	4.6	4	38	13.1	2	2	1	1.4	−1.57
Canada	9.9	0.5	60	4.3	2	1	1	−1.8	1.96
US	7.1	0.5	50	2.4	1	1	1	−0.5	−2.65
Japan	2.7	0.5	60	5.6	2	2	2	−0.3	2.91
Austria	3.6	4	60	5.6	3	3	3	−1.9	0.42
Finland	5.1	4	75	12.9	3	3	3	−1.6	1.00
Norway	2.7	1.5	65	9.8	3	3	3	−3.5	3.16
Sweden	2.2	1.2	80	34.6	3	3	3	−3.8	2.35
Switzerland	2.4	1.0	70	3.7	2	1	3	−0.3	0.39

Notes:
Variables: u = percentage unemployment rate, 1983–8. BD = duration of benefit entitlement in years (1985). Indefinite is set at 4 years. RR = percentage benefit replacement ratio (1985). LMS = expenditure on 'active' labour market programmes per unemployed person as a percentage of output per person (1987). $UCOV$ = percentage of workers covered by union collective agreements (3 = over 75, 2 = 25–75, 1 = under 25). $UNCD$ = union coordination in wage bargaining (3 = high, 2 = middle, 1 = low). $EMCD$ = employer coordination in wage bargaining (3 = high, 2 = middle, 1 = low) $\Delta^2 p$ = change in inflation 1983–8 in percentage points. TB = 100 x current balance ÷ GDP, 1983–8 average. For sources and detailed definitions, see Appendix 2.

unemployment benefit system and the method of wage determination, where note that employer coordination is of vital importance in allowing labour market slack to suppress inflationary pressure and hence reduce unemployment. We also tried including a proxy for employment protection (the proportion of manufacturing employees with less than two years' job tenure, an inverse measure), but its impact was negligible (t = 0.4).

However, this is obviously a rather crude exercise. The next step is to see to what extent we are able to explain the time series variation in unemployment within each country.

9.4.2 Explaining Time-series Variations in Unemployment

To analyze the fluctuations in unemployment in the OECD countries, we use equation (46) as the foundation. If we drop the productivity shock, ϵ, substitute out u^* and assume that $\alpha(\beta_2 + \gamma_2)/(\beta_1 + \gamma_1 + \beta_{11} + \gamma_{11})$ is small, then (46) can be rewritten as

$$u = \frac{(\beta_{11} + \gamma_{11})}{(\beta_1 + \gamma_1 + \beta_{11} + \gamma_{11})} \, u_{-1} + \left[1 - \frac{(\beta_{11} + \gamma_{11})}{(\beta_1 + \gamma_1 + \beta_{11} + \gamma_{11})}\right]$$

$$\frac{1}{(\beta_1 + \gamma_1)} \left[(\beta_0 + \gamma_0) - (\beta_2 + \gamma_2)\Delta^2 m + \bar{z}_w \right.$$

$$\left. + \frac{(\beta_1 + \gamma_1 + \beta_{11} + \gamma_{11})}{\alpha(\beta_2 + \gamma_2) + (\beta_1 + \gamma_1 + \beta_{11} + \gamma_{11})} \, \epsilon_w\right] \qquad (50)$$

We drop the productivity shock because we have no consistent measure and our assumption that $\alpha(\beta_2 + \gamma_2)/(\beta_1 + \gamma_1 + \beta_{11} + \gamma_{11})$ is small[14] may be justified by the fact that $\alpha < 1$ and the average estimated value of the other term reported in Layard *et al.* (1991, chapter 9) is 0.16. However, despite this assumption, we do not set the coefficient on ϵ_w to unity because we feel it is worth investigating whether or not the response of unemployment to wage shocks is reduced by nominal inertia.

Our aim is to estimate equation (50) for 19 OECD countries simultaneously, allowing the parameters to depend on institutional factors, guided by our analysis in section 9.2. Taking each of the parameters in turn, we start with the lagged dependent variable. The price hysteresis parameter, β_{11}, depends on the extent of labour adjustment costs. Our (inverse) proxy for this is the proportion of manufacturing employees who have been in their current job for less than two years, *PL2*. In our discussion of the wage hysteresis parameter, γ_{11}, in section 9.2, we conclude that it is increasing in benefit duration, *BD*, union coverage, *UCOV*, and union coordination, *UNCD*, whereas it is decreasing in labour market spending, *LMS*, and employer coordination, *EMCD*. We have already analysed β_1 and γ_1, and so we shall model the lagged dependent variable coefficient as

$$\frac{\beta_{11} \overset{-}{(PL2)} + \gamma_{11} \overset{+}{(BD,} \overset{-}{LMS,} \overset{+}{UCOV,} \overset{+}{UNCD,} \overset{-}{EMCD)}}{\beta_1 + \gamma_1 \underset{-}{(RR,} \underset{-}{BD,} \underset{+}{LMS,} \underset{+}{UNCD,} \underset{+}{EMCD)}}$$

$$= a_{10} - a_{11}PL2 + a_{12}BD + a_{13}RR - a_{14}LMS + a_{15}UCOV$$
$$+ a_{16}UNCD - a_{17}EMCD. \tag{51}$$

The only variable with an ambiguous sign is union coordination whose effect will probably be positive because its impact via γ_1 appears to be weak in the cross-section regression reported above.

The next parameter to look at in equation (50) is $1/(\beta_1 + \gamma_1)$ and this we have already considered. In the light of this previous discussion we propose to specify it as

$$1/(\beta_1 + \gamma_1) = a_{20} + a_{21}BD + a_{22}RR - a_{23}LMS - a_{24}UNCD -$$
$$a_{25}EMCD. \tag{52}$$

The 'constant terms' in equation (50), namely $(\beta_0 + \gamma_0)$, we simply capture by including country dummies. So the next substantive parameters are those relating to nominal inertia, namely $(\beta_2 + \gamma_2)$. In section 9.2, we noted that price stickiness, β_2, is negatively related to the overall level of inflation, $\overline{\Delta p}$, and the variance of aggregate nominal shocks which we measured by the variance of changes in nominal income, VNI.[15] The degree of wage stickiness, γ_2, is inversely related to the flexibility of wage contracts, FWC, which we capture using indices of their duration, indexation and synchronization. Thus we have

$$\beta_2\underset{-}{(VNI,} \overset{}{\underset{-}{\overline{\Delta p}})} + \gamma_2\underset{-}{(FWC)} = a_{30} - a_{31}VNI - a_{32}\overline{\Delta p} - a_{33}FWC. \tag{53}$$

Finally, we must specify our measures of wage pressure $\overline{z}_w$, ϵ_w. The key factors here which we are able to measure are the replacement ratio, union effects and real wage resistance effects. Note that here we must have time series for each country. This is not difficult for the replacement ratio, RR but, with regard to union effects, things are more tricky. Following Newell and Symons (1985, 1987), we use a simple 'wage explosion' dummy, XP, which takes the value unity after 1970 in all countries. This captures the impact of the sudden and well documented surge of union wage pressure which occurred in most OECD countries in the late 1960s (see, for example, Newell and Symons,

1989). Concerning real wage resistance, by far the most important overall factors in the OECD were the terms-of-trade shocks, and these we measure by taking the change in the real price of imports weighted by the import share, $s_m \Delta (p_m - p)$. In the light of this discussion it seems sensible to suppose that the replacement ratio and the union effects represent long-run sources of wage pressure, $\bar{z}_w$, whereas the change in the real price of imports is a temporary shock, ϵ_w. So in equation (50), we specify wage pressure as

$$\bar{z}_w + \frac{(\beta_1 + \gamma_1 + \beta_{11} + \gamma_{11})}{\alpha(\beta_2 + \gamma_2) + (\beta_1 + \gamma_1 + \beta_{11} + \gamma_{11})} \epsilon_w = a_{41}XP + a_{42}RR$$

$$+ (1 + a_{51}VNI + a_{52}\overline{\Delta p} + a_{53}FWC)s_m\Delta(p_m - p) \qquad (54)$$

where we simply allow the coefficient on ϵ_w to be influenced by the nominal inertia effects $(\beta_2 + \gamma_2)$ and not by the other parameters $(\beta_1 + \gamma_1 + \beta_{11} + \gamma_{11})$. This we do because, given our assumptions, the impact of the second group of parameters on the coefficient is an order of magnitude smaller.[16]

We are now in a position to write down our unified employment equation for the OECD economies. Based on (50)–(54), we have

$$u_{it} = a_i + (a_{10} - a_{11}PL2_i + a_{12}BD_i + a_{13}RR_i - a_{14} LMS_i$$

$$+ a_{15}UCOV_i + a_{16}UNCD_i - a_{17}EMCD_i)u_{it-1} +$$

$$[1 - (a_{10} - a_{11}PL2_i + a_{12}BD_i + a_{13}RR_i - a_{14}LMS_i$$

$$+ a_{15}UCOV_i + a_{16} UNCD_i - a_{17}EMCD_i)][a_{20} + a_{21}BD_i$$

$$+ a_{22}RR_i - a_{23}LMS_i - a_{24}UNCD_i - a_{25}EMCD_i]$$

$$[-(a_{30} - a_{31}VNI_i - a_{32}\overline{\Delta p_i} - a_{33}FWC_i)\Delta^2 m_{it} + a_{41}XP_{it}$$

$$+ a_{42}RR_{it} + (1 + a_{51}VNI_i + a_{52}\Delta p_i + a_{53}FWC_i)s_m\Delta$$

$$(p_m - p)_{it}] \qquad (55)$$

For reference purposes, in Table 9.3, we present those country-specific variables which are not in Table 9.2. Then, in Table 9.4, we present an estimated version of equation (55) for 19 OECD countries over the period 1956–88. Some variables are omitted because they proved to be both numerically and statistically insignificant. Overall, however, the equation looks highly satisfactory with the relevant variables all being correctly signed. That is all very well but, before discussing

Table 9.3 Variables used in Equation (55)

	PL2	Δp	VNI	FWC
Belgium	18	4.5	0.11	4
Denmark	27	6.6	0.05	6
France	18	6.8	0.05	3
Germany	19	3.8	0.08	4
Ireland	22	6.3	0.29	2
Italy	13	8.5	0.23	4
Netherlands	28	4.8	0.12	5
Spain	13	9.6	0.17	5
UK	28	7.0	0.21	2
Australia	39	6.2	0.14	6
New Zealand	39	7.3	0.22	6
Canada	33	5.1	0.11	2
US	39	4.1	0.06	1
Japan	21	4.8	0.25	4
Austria	28	4.4	0.06	4
Finland	28	7.3	0.13	3
Norway	28	3.7	0.08	4
Sweden	28	5.4	0.05	4
Switzerland	28	4.1	0.12	0

Notes:
*Variables: PL*2 = percentage of manufacturing employees with tenure less than two years. The numbers for Spain, New Zealand, UK, Austria, Norway, Sweden, Switzerland were not available in the original source and are simply based on the data for related countries. $\overline{\Delta p}$ = average inflation rate (GDP deflator). *VNI* = variance of changes in log nominal GDP. *FWC* = *LWC+IWC+SWC; LWC* = 2 if contracts 1 year or less, = 1 if contracts between 1 and 3 years, = 0 if contracts 3 years or more; *IWC* = 2 if indexation is widespread, = 1 if some indexation, = 0 if no indexation; *SWC* = 2 if wage contract renewals are more or less completely synchronized, = 1 if there is some synchronization, = 0 if there is no synchronization. For sources, see Appendix 2.

the equation in detail, we must find out how well it explains the data.

In Table 9.4, we present the R^2 for each country. Then, in Table 9.5, we present the regression standard errors of this model and for comparison, the same statistic for individual country autoregressions containing a constant, two lags on unemployment and a time trend. The results indicate first, that the structural model explains over 90 percent of the variation in unemployment in 11 countries and under 80 percent in only 3 (Norway, Sweden and the US). Relative to the country

Table 9.4   OECD unemployment equation (19 countries, 1956–88)

$$u_{it} = \text{Country dummy} + \underset{(39.7)}{(0.83} - \underset{(3.4)}{0.11PL2_i} + \underset{(7.3)}{0.041BD_i} + \underset{(7.1)}{0.095UNCD_i}$$

$$- \underset{(7.9)}{0.69EMCD_i)}u_{it-1} - \left[1 - (0.83 - 0.11PL2_i + 0.041BD_i \right.$$

$$\left. + 0.095UNCD_i - 0.069EMCD_i) \right]\left[\underset{(4.3)}{1.47} + \underset{(4.0)}{0.34BD_i} - \underset{(4.0)}{0.25EMCD_i} \right]$$

$$\left[- \left[\underset{(4.8)}{0.57} - \underset{(3.9)}{3.87VNI_i} - \underset{(2.2)}{0.10FWC_i} \right] \Delta^2 m_{it} + \underset{(2.7)}{0.028XP_{it}} \right.$$

$$\left. + \underset{(4.4)}{0.20RR_{it}} + \left[1 + \underset{(4.0)}{0.58FWC_i} \right]s_m \Delta\left[p_m - p \right]_{it-1} \right]$$

Notes:
t-ratios in parentheses.
Equations estimated by non-linear 3SLS(SUR) in TSP 4.2A.
Variables: i = country, t = time, u = unemployment rate, $PL2$ = *proportion* of employees in manufacturing with job tenure less than 2 years, BD = benefit duration, $UNCD$ = union coordination in wage bargaining, $EMCD$ = employer coordination in wage bargaining, s_m = share of imports, $p_m - p$ = real price of imports, XP = dummy taking value unity after 1970, RR = benefit replacement ratio, m = money stock (M1), FWC = flexibility of wage contracts, VNI = variance of changes in log GDP. All time-invariant variables have means set to zero. Data sources given in Appendix 2. Fuller definitions appear in notes to Tables 9.2 and 9.3.
R^2 for each country are as follows: Belgium, 0.96; Denmark, 0.95; France, 0.99; Germany, 0.93; Ireland, 0.95; Italy, 0.86; Netherlands, 0.97; Spain, 0.98; UK, 0.94; Australia, 0.90; NZ, 0.90; Canada, 0.88; US, 0.72; Japan, 0.91; Austria, 0.87, Finland, 0.82; Norway, 0.42; Sweden, 0.58; Switzerland, 0.85.

Table 9.5   Regression standard errors (%) for model of Table 9.4 with comparison

	Table 9.4	Comparison model $u_{it} = \omega_{0i} + \omega_{1i}u_{it-1} + \omega_{2i}u_{it-2} + \omega_{3i}t$
Belgium	0.724	0.714
Denmark	0.666	0.827
France	0.346	0.397
Germany	0.621	0.677
Ireland	0.924	0.895
Italy	0.584	0.578
Netherlands	0.675	0.708
Spain	1.005	0.677

Table 9.5 continued

	Table 9.4	*Comparison model* $u_{it} = \omega_{0i} + \omega_{1i}u_{it-1} + \omega_{2i}u_{it-2} + \omega_{3i}t$
UK	0.872	0.855
Australia	0.833	0.854
New Zealand	0.574	0.562
Canada	0.787	0.971
US	0.829	1.001
Japan	0.177	0.178
Austria	0.327	0.328
Finland	0.775	0.625
Norway	0.438	0.451
Sweden	0.379	0.358
Switzerland	0.447	0.409

specific autoregressions plus trend, the structural model has a regression standard error which is lower in 10 out of 19 cases and much higher in only 2 cases (Spain, Finland). Overall, therefore, the structural model, which has a mere 14 parameters plus 19 country dummies, is as good in explaining the dramatic fluctuations in unemployment in 19 countries over 33 years as a set of individual country autoregressions, including trends, which have a total of 76 parameters. The explanatory power of our model is thus not inconsiderable.

The parameters indicate the crucial importance of the benefit and wage bargaining structures in determining patterns of unemployment. Benefit duration has a significant role in increasing both persistence and the impact of wage pressure and demand shocks, whereas employer coordination in wage bargaining has an equally important role in reducing both these factors. Union coordination, on the other hand, tends to increase persistence as predicted but appears to have no effect in reducing the impact of shocks[17] (the omitted coefficient in Table 9.4 is 0.0073(0.5)). The replacement ratio appears to play no role in generating persistence (its coefficient is negligible and is omitted), but it does appear as a significant wage pressure variable influencing the equilibrium rate.

The only other significant factor affecting persistence is our proxy for employment flexibility (the negative of employment adjustment costs), namely *PL2*, which has a powerful negative effect. The important nominal inertia variables are the variance of nominal shocks, *VNI*, and wage contract flexibility, *FWC*. These are negatively related to nominal stickiness and both of them tend to reduce the impact of nominal shocks ($\Delta^2 m$), whereas only the latter increases the impact of import price shocks [$s_m \Delta(p_m - p)$]. The average inflation rate ($\overline{\Delta p}$) seems to have no effect on either of these and is omitted.

To give some idea of the orders of magnitude involved, if we start with the real wage rigidity factor, ($\beta_1 + \gamma_1)^{-1}$, which translates wage pressure shocks into unemployment, we find that the typical 'successful' countries have values of this parameter from one-third to one-half as great as the typical 'unsuccessful' countries. Representative numbers include Switzerland (0.63), Sweden (0.70), Japan (0.71), Norway (0.80), US (0.96) among the more successful countries and UK (2.15), Ireland (2.15), Belgium (1.90), Netherlands (1.90) among the least successful countries.

The degree of persistence provides similar wide divergencies. Taking the mean lag in years as a suitable measure,[18] we find Switzerland (2.5), Japan (3.8), US (3.2), Sweden (4.8) whereas the UK, Ireland, Belgium and the Netherlands all have a value between 7.1 and 9.1 – two or three times more persistence. Of course all these numbers are the consequence of a very crude exercise and the actual values should be treated with scepticism. However, they are indicative of the potential importance of some of these characteristics in explaining the very different patterns of unemployment experience across the OECD.

9.5   COMPARISONS WITH OTHER WORK AND CONCLUSIONS

Our broad empirical conclusions indicate, first, that levels of unemployment and the size of the unemployment response to shocks depends on the structure of the unemployment benefit system and the mechanism of wage determination. Second, the persistence of unemployment depends again on the benefit and wage determination systems, and also on the degree of employment flexibility. Third, the impact of nominal shocks is negatively influenced by the degree of nominal flexibility in wage bargaining and the average variance of nominal shocks over the sample period.

With regard to the benefit structure, while the evidence suggests that the level of the replacement ratio is of some importance in explaining unemployment patterns, a key feature of the system appears to be the duration of benefit eligibility. Restricting benefit duration to between 6 and 18 months serves to prevent the build-up of long-term unemployment. This reduces both the impact of adverse shocks and the duration of their effects. Limiting benefit duration does not necessarily mean that the system has to be very harsh. When benefits run out, the system can be constructed to ensure that an alternative is made available in the form of either training or employment, as in Sweden, for example. While some work has been done on the relationship between the level of benefits and unemployment with mixed results (see Minford, 1983, or Burtless, 1987, for example), there has been little analysis of the impact of other aspects of the benefit structure, although Emerson (1988) has quite a lot to say about the broader implications for the labour market.

This absence of alternative evidence does not apply to the structure of wage bargaining where, following the seminal work of McCallum (1983), and Bruno and Sachs (1985), there has been a great deal of work. McCallum (1983) found that the level of strike incidence during the 1960s was inversely related to economic performance after the first oil shock whereas Bruno and Sachs (1985) discovered a positive relationship between performance and the degree of centralization of wage bargaining or 'corporatism'. Results along similar lines are presented in Newell and Symons (1987), Bean *et al.* (1986) and Alogoskoufis and Manning (1988). Both Freeman (1988) and Calmfors and Driffil (1988) were critical of this work, because they thought that a high level of decentralization should also work well and, in the former case, because the construction of corporatism indices is such a subjective business. In the context of our results, it seems likely that a low level of unionization (i.e., a decentralized economy) is helpful but that if unions are an important factor, then coordination in wage bargaining among employers is particularly helpful, something not emphasized in previous work, although Soskice (1990) presents compelling reasons why it is likely to be important.

Notable work on unemployment persistence includes Alogoskoufis and Manning (1988), and Barro (1988). The latter finds that unions tend to raise persistence except in the presence of centralized bargaining. Again he makes no distinction between employee and employer coordination, which in the case of persistence, appear to have opposite effects. Alogoskoufis and Manning (1988), on the other hand, emphasize the role of sluggish employment adjustment, something that also appears in our results as well as in those of Newell and Symons (1985). We were, however, unable to find any relationship between unemployment *levels* and employment adjustment costs, which is inconsistent with the results of Lazear (1990) although not with those Bentolila and Bertola (1990).

Turning to the role of nominal inertia; we were able to find a role for both the variance of nominal shocks and the flexibility of wage contracts in reducing the impact of money supply shocks. In the former case, this is consistent with the standard work on cross-country comparisons of the output–inflation tradeoff which is, in our context, the same as nominal wage rigidity (see Lucas, 1973; Alberro, 1981). The fact that wage contract flexibility also serves to enhance the impact of terms-of-trade shocks confirms the result of Bruno and Sachs (1985) who note that wage contract flexibility (which they refer to as nominal wage responsiveness) was bad for economic performance following the first oil shock.

Overall, therefore, our results encompass most of the previous work on cross-country comparisons of economic performance and extend them, notably by emphasizing the importance of benefit duration and employer coordination in wage bargaining.

Appendix 1: Wage Model

Union Wage Model

From equation (19), the wage solves

$$\max_{W_i} \; [(W_i - A)S(W_i)]^\beta \Pi_i^e(W_i).$$

The first-order condition may be written as

$$\frac{\beta}{W_i - A} - \frac{\beta}{S}\frac{\partial S}{\partial W_i} - \frac{N_i^e}{\Pi_i^e} = 0$$

which implies that

$$\frac{W_i - A}{W_i} = \left[-\frac{W_i}{S}\frac{\partial S}{\partial W_i} + \frac{W_i N_i^e}{\beta \Pi_i^e} \right]^{-1}. \tag{A1}$$

From equations (1) and (2), we may eliminate P_i from (16) to find that the elasticity of employment wages is given by

$$\frac{\partial \log N_i}{\partial \log W_i} = -1/(1 - \alpha\bar{\kappa}). \tag{A2}$$

Furthermore, the wage share, from (17) is

$$\frac{W_i N_i^e}{\Pi_i^e} = \frac{\alpha\bar{\kappa}}{1 - \alpha\bar{\kappa}} \tag{A3}$$

So

$$-\frac{W_i}{S}\frac{\partial S}{\partial W_i} = -\frac{\partial \log S}{\partial \log W_i}$$

$$= -\frac{\partial \log S}{\partial \log N_i} \cdot \frac{\partial \log N_i}{\partial \log W_i}$$

$$= \frac{\epsilon_{SN}\,\bar{\kappa}}{1 - \alpha\bar{\kappa}}. \quad \text{from (A2).}$$

Using this fact and (A3) enables us to rewrite (A1) as

$$\frac{W_i - A}{W_i} = \frac{1 - \alpha\bar{\kappa}}{\epsilon_{SN}(W_i) + \alpha\bar{\kappa}/\beta}$$

which confirms equation (20).

Turning to the survival probability S, let us suppose that employment, N_i, can be written as

$$N_i = \tilde{\phi}N_i^e.$$

where $\tilde{\phi}$ is a unit mean random variable. Then if N_{li} is the number of employees who are party to the wage bargain, their probability of survival is

$$S_i = \text{prob}\ (N_i > N_{li}) + \frac{E(N_i \mid N_i \leq N_{li})}{N_{li}}\ \text{prob}\ (N_i \leq N_{li})$$

$$= P\ (\tilde{\phi} > N_{li}/N_i^e) + \frac{N_i^e}{N_{li}}\ E\left[\tilde{\phi} \mid \tilde{\phi} \leq \frac{N_{li}}{N_i^e}\right] P\left[\tilde{\phi} \leq \frac{N_{li}}{N_i^e}\right]$$

$$= S\ [N_{li}/N_i^e(W_i)].$$

This confirms equation (18). For the properties of S, let $N_{li}/N_i^e = x$. Then we have

$$S(x) = P(\tilde{\phi} > x) + x^{-1}F(\tilde{\phi} \mid \tilde{\phi} \leq x)P(\tilde{\phi} \leq x).$$

Let $\tilde{\phi}$ have a density h, CDF, H and recall $\tilde{\phi} \geq 0$ with a unit mean. So S can be written

$$S(x) = 1 - H(x) + x^{-1}\int_0^x \tilde{\phi}h(\tilde{\phi})d\tilde{\phi} > 0 \tag{A4}$$

$$S'(x) = -x^{-2}\int_0^x \tilde{\phi}h(\tilde{\phi})d\tilde{\phi} < 0 \tag{A5}$$

$$S''(x) = 2x^{-3}\int_0^x \tilde{\phi}h(\tilde{\phi})d\tilde{\phi} - x^{-1}h(x) \tag{A6}$$

Then

$$\epsilon_{SN} = -xS'(x)/S(x) > 0 \text{ from (A4), (A5)}$$

$$\epsilon'_{SN} = x\left[\frac{S'(x)}{S(x)}\right]^2 - \frac{1}{S(x)}\ (S'(x) + xS''(x))$$

$$= \frac{1}{S(x)}\ [S'(x) + h(x) - \epsilon_{SN}S'(x)] \text{ from (A4), (A5).}$$

If we evaluate this in stationary equilibrium, then $x \leq 1$ and it is easy to show that for all symmetric, single-peaked distributions, $S'(x) + h(x) > 0$ and hence $\epsilon'_{SN} > 0$.

Non-union Wage Model

Assuming price taking behaviour, the firm chooses the wage path which solves

$$\max \Sigma \frac{1}{(1 + r)^t} [P_{it}N_{it} v^{-(1-\alpha)} - W_{it}N_{it}]$$

subject to $N_{it} - N_{it-1} - a (W_{it}/A_t)(N_i^* - N_{it}) + sN_{it} = 0 \qquad (A7)$

$N_{it} \leq N_i^*.$

Recall that the technology is given by (22), (23) and $a (W_{it}/A_t)$ is the accessions function. Furthermore $N_i^* - N_{it}$ is the number of vacancies. The first-order conditions for an interior solution are

$$\frac{1}{(1 + r)^t} [P_{it}v^{-(1-\alpha)} - W_{it}] - \mu_{it}(1 + a + s) + \mu_{it+1} = 0 \qquad (A8)$$

$$- \frac{N_{it}}{(1 + r)^t} + \frac{\mu_{it}a'}{A_t} (N_i^* - N_{it}) = 0 \qquad (A9)$$

where μ_{it} is the multiplier associated with the constraint (A7). Defining $\eta_a = a'W_{it}/aA_t$, in stationary equilibrium, wages satisfy,

$$W_i = \frac{P_i (K_i/N_i^*)^{1-\alpha}\eta_a s}{s(1 + \eta_a) + a (W_i/A) + r} \qquad (A10)$$

Noting that A is given by equation (14), then taking log differentials of (A10) yields equation (24) in the main text.

Appendix 2: Data Appendix

Unemployment

OECD standardized rates except for Denmark, Ireland, New Zealand, Austria, Sweden where unstandardized rates are used and Italy and Switzerland which are described below. Except for Italy, the published OECD standardized rates are similar to the 'unemployment rate on US concepts', calculated by the US Bureau of Labor Statistics (BLS), *Comparative Labor Force Statistics for 10 Countries 1959–88* (mimeo). For Italy we use the BLS numbers 'on US concepts', which exclude those who, while registered as unemployed, have performed no active job search in the last 4 weeks. For 1985 and earlier we multiply the BLS numbers by 7.5/6.3 to allow for a break. For Switzerland we use registered unemployment times three, this being the factor for 1980 shown in the Census of that year.
Source: OECD Employment Outlook, June 1990, Tables R.18, R.19, 37, 38 except for Italy and Switzerland.

Benefit Duration

Duration of eligibility to some form of benefit paying over $120 per month in 1985.
Source: Mainly US Dept. of Health and Social Services, *Social Security Programs Throughout the World 1985 (Reserve Report No. 60)* and Eurostat, *Definition of Registered Unemployed*, 1987, Theme 3, Series E.

Replacement Ratio

Gross benefits for a single person under 50 as a percent of the most relevant wage (normally gross except in Germany) in 1985.
Source: As with benefit duration.
For the time series, we use a similar definition.
Source: Emerson (1988).

Labour Market Spending

Expenditure on 'active' labour market programmes per unemployed person as a percentage of output per person in 1987.
Source: OECD, *Employment Outlook*, September 1988, Table 3.1.

Union Coverage, Union Coordination, Employer Coordination

These are defined in Table 9.2 and described in Layard *et al.* (1991, Annex 1.4).

PL2

The percentage of manufacturing employees with tenure less than two years. *Source:* Metcalf (1986).

Flexibility of Wage Contracts

This index is described in Table 9.3.
Source: Bruno and Sachs (1985, Table 11.7 with minor adjustment).

The other variables include money stock (M1), import prices, GDP deflator, nominal GDP, trade balance. These are all taken from the LSE Centre for Economic performance, OECD dataset. This is described by David Grubb in LSE Centre for Labour Economics, *Working Paper*, no. 615, with updates by Andrew Newell and Mark Walsh.

Notes

* We are most grateful to Assar Lindbeck and John Martin for useful comments on an earlier draft of this chapter. This research was funded by the Economic and Social Research Council.
1. The wage gap refers to the difference between the current real wage and that which would generate a demand for labour corresponding to full employment. In most OECD countries, this gap tended to rise in the late 1970s and fall in the 1980s. However, unemployment rose throughout. The basic reason for the absence of any correlation is that when firms set prices, there is no systematic relationship between product wages and employment, particularly in the presence of nominal inertia. This contrasts with the situation where firms are price-takers and the employment/real wage relationship is then constrained by the standard neoclassical labour demand curve. Only in this case is the wage gap a useful concept.
2. If the overall productivity shock were serially correlated, then we could incorporate the predetermined part into the capital stock and include the innovation as the shock.
3. This is obviously a simplifying assumption which avoids complexities due to rationing, shifts in inventories, and so on. Such complexities typically make the dynamics of the model more complicated without influencing its basic structure.
4. Note that the output of the i_{th} firm is equal to y_{di} and when we aggregate (5), we see that total output must equal y_d.
5. See Layard *et al.* (1991, Chapter 7), for a formal demonstration.
6. Note that an increase in the average search effectiveness of the unemployed, at given unemployment, *raises* the average length of time any particular individual can expect to remain unemployed, because there is more competition for the available vacancies.
7. We make this assumption because it corresponds to the facts as set out in Oswald and Turnbull (1985).

8. Consider the following example given in Hall (1977). Suppose U unemployed job-seekers are searching randomly over V vacancies. If each seeker makes one application per period, the probability that a seeker applies for a particular vacancy is 1/V. The probability that no seeker applies for a particular vacancy is thus

$$\left[1 - \frac{1}{V}\right]^{U} \simeq e^{-U/V}$$

So, if firms are prepared to hire any applicant, the probability that a vacancy is filled per period, H/V, is given by

$$H/V = 1 - e^{-U/V}.$$

So

$$H = V\,(1 - e^{-U/V})$$

which exhibits constant returns. For evidence in favour of this assumption, see Layard *et al.* (1991, chapter 5).

9. This derivation makes a number of assumptions. However, the model can easily be extended without changing the overall structure. For example s can be endogenized or we can incorporate on-the-job searchers without difficulty (see Layard *et al.*, 1991, chapter 5).

10. Note there is also a term in ϵ_{-1} arising from the appearance of $\Delta(y_d - y)$ in (37). We simply ignore this because it has no important implications and clutters up the algebra.

11. Of course, such an assumption about expectations is not model consistent and will, therefore, not be robust to significant changes in the overall policy regime. However it is quite satisfactory for explaining the events of the last 25 years.

12. Here we suppose expectations to be model consistent in order to isolate those factors in the economy which will generate persistence once we rule out the consequences of model inconsistent expectations.

13. Once we have more than one good, it is very easy to construct models without nominal inertia in which government expenditure policy has real consequences, usually via supply-side substitution mechanisms. See Grandmont (1989) for a general discussion and references.

14. This assumption enables us to write the actual coefficient on $\Delta^2 m$, that is $(\beta_2 + \gamma_2)(\beta_1 + \gamma_1 + \beta_{11} + \gamma_{11})/[(\beta_2 + \gamma_2)\,\alpha + (\beta_1 + \gamma_1 + \beta_{11} + \gamma_{11})]$, as $(\beta_2 + \gamma_2)$.

15. Other possible factors include the variance of firm specific shocks and the degree of product-market competition, neither of which are measurable across all the countries.

16. The coefficient on ϵ_w is $(\beta_1 + \gamma_1 + \beta_{11} + \gamma_{11})/[(\beta_2 + \gamma_2)\alpha + (\beta_1 + \gamma_1 + \beta_{11} + \gamma_{11})]$. From this, we see that

$$|\partial \text{ coefficient}/\partial\beta_1|/|\partial \text{ coefficient}/\partial\beta_2| = (\beta_2 + \gamma_2)/(\beta_1 + \gamma_1 + \beta_{11} + \gamma_{11})$$

which we have assumed to be small. So the impact of the parameters β_1, γ_1, β_{11}, γ_{11} is small relative to the impact of β_2, γ_2.
17. This is hardly surprising given the weakness of this factor in the cross-section regression.
18. Note that the mean lag in years is [1 - lagged dependent variable coefficient]$^{-1}$.

References

Aizcorbe, A.M. (1990) 'Procyclical Labor Productivity, Increasing Returns to Labor, and Labor Hoarding in US Auto Assembly Plant Employment', US Bureau of Labor Statistics, mimeo.
Alberro, J. (1981) 'The Lucas Hypothesis on the Phillips Curve: Further International Evidence', *Journal of Monetary Economics*, vol. 7, no. 2, pp. 239–50.
Alogoskoufis, G.S. and A. Manning (1988) 'On the Persistence of Unemployment', *Economic Policy*, 7, pp. 427–69.
Ashenfelter, O.C. and R. Layard (1983) 'Incomes Policy and Wage Differences', *Economica*, vol. 50, no. 198, pp. 127–43.
Ball, L., N.G. Mankiw and D. Romer (1988) 'The New Keynesian Economics and the Output–Inflation Trade-Off', *Brookings Papers on Economic Activity*, 1, pp. 1–65.
Barro, R. (1988) 'The Persistence of Unemployment', *American Economic Review*, vol. 78, no. 2, pp. 32–7.
Bean, C.R., R. Layard and S.J. Nickell (1986) 'The Rise in Unemployment: A Multi-Country Study', *Economica*, vol. 53, no. 210(s), pp. S1–S22.
Berndt, E.R., A.F. Friedlander and J. S.-E.W. Chiang (1990) 'Interdependent Pricing and Mark-up Behaviour: An Empirical Analysis of GM, Ford and Chrysler', NBER, *Working Paper*, no. 3396, Cambridge MA, NBER.
Bentolila, S. and G. Bertola (1990) 'Firing Costs and Labour Demand: How Bad is Eurosclerosis?', *Review of Economic Studies*, vol. 57(3), no. 191, pp. 381–402.
Bils, M. (1987) 'The Cyclical Behaviour of Marginal Cost and Price', *American Economic Review*, vol. 77. no. 5, pp. 838–55.
Blanchard, O.J. and L.H. Summers (1986) 'Hysteresis and the European Unemployment Problem', *NBER Macroeconomics Annual 1986*, Cambridge, MA, MIT Press.
Blanchard, O.J. and S. Fischer (1989) *Lectures in Macroeconomics,* Cambridge, MA, MIT Press.
Blum, A.A. (1981) (ed.) *International Handbook of Industrial Relations*, London, Aldwych Press.
Brack, J. (1987) 'Price Adjustment within a Framework of Symmetric Oligopoly: An Analysis of Pricing in 380 U.S. Manufacturing Industries, 1958–71', *International Journal of Industrial Organization*, vol. 5, no. 3, pp. 289–302.
Bruno, M. and J.D. Sachs (1985) *Economics of World Wide Stagflation*, Oxford, Basil Blakwell.

Burtless, G. (1987) 'Jobless Pay and High European Unemployment', in R.Z. Lawrence and C.L. Schultze (eds), *Barriers to European Growth*, Washington, DC, The Brookings Institution.

Calmfors, L. (ed.) (1990) *Wage Formation and Macroeconomic Policy in the Nordic Countries*, Oxford: SNS and Oxford University Press.

Calmfors, L. and J. Driffill, (1988) 'Centralisation of Wage Bargaining and Macroeconomic Performance', *Economic Policy*, 6, pp. 13–61.

Carlton, D.W. (1986) 'The Rigidity of Prices', *American Economic Review*, vol. 76, no. 4, pp. 637–58.

————— (1989) 'The Theory and the Facts of How Markets Clear: Is Industrial Organization Valuable for Understanding Macroeconomics?', in R. Schmalensee and R.D. Willig (eds), *Handbook of Industrial Organization*, vol. 1, Amsterdam, North-Holland.

Coutts, K., W. Godley, and W. Nordhaus, (1978) *Industrial Pricing in the United Kingdom*, Cambridge: Cambridge University Press.

Daniel, W.W. (1990) *The Unemployed Flow*, London, Policy Studies Institute.

Dore, R., J. Bounine-Cabalé, and K. Tapiola (1989) *Japan at Work: Markets, Management and Flexibility*, Paris, OECD.

Emerson, M. (1988) *What Model of Europe?*, Cambridge, MA, MIT Press.

Encaoua, D. And P. Geroski (1986) 'Price Dynamics and Competition in Five OECD Countries', *OECD Economics Studies*, vol. 6, Spring, pp. 47–74.

Flanagan, R.J., D.W. Soskice, D.W. and L. Ulman (1983) *Unionism, Economic Stabilization, and Incomes Policy: European Experience*, Washington, DC, Brookings Institution.

Flaig, G. and V. Steiner (1990) 'Markup Differentials, Cost Flexibility, and Capacity Utilization in West-German Manufacturing', Augsburg University, *Volkswilschaftliche Diskussionreiche*, no. 40.

Freeman, R.B. (1988) 'Labour Market Institutions and Economic Performance', *Economic Policy*, 6, pp. 64–78.

Gordon, R.J. (1988) 'Wage Gaps vs. Output Gaps: Is There a Common Story for All of Europe?', in Giersh, H. (ed.), *Macro and Micro Policies for More Growth and Employment: Keil Symposium*, Tübigen, J.C.B. Mohr, pp. 97–151.

————— (1990) 'What is New-Keynesian Economics', *Journal of Economic Literature*, vol. 28, no. 3, pp. 1115–71.

Grandmont, J.M. (1989) 'Keynesian Issues and Economic Theory', CEPREMAP, *Discussion Paper*, no. 8907, Paris, CEPREMAP.

Grubb, D., R. Jackman, and R. Layard, (1983) 'Wage Rigidity and Unemployment in OECD Countries', *European Economic Review*, vol. 21, no. 1/2, pp. 11–39.

Hall, R.E. (1977) 'An Aspect of the Economic Role of Unemployment', in G.C. Harcourt (ed.), *The Microeconomic Foundations of Macroeconomics*, London, Macmillan.

Jackman, R., R. Layard and C.A. Pissarides (1989) 'On Vacancies', *Oxford Bulletin of Economics and Statistics*, vol. 51, no 4, pp. 377–94.

Layard, R., S. Nickell, and R. Jackman, (1991) *Unemployment: Macroeconomic Performance and the Labour Market*, Oxford, Oxford University Press.

Lazear, E.P. (1990) 'Job Security Provisions and Employment', *Quarterly Journal of Economics*, vol. 105, no. 3, pp. 699–726.

Lucas, R.E., Jr (1973) 'Some International Evidence on Output–Inflation Tradeoffs', *American Economic Review*, vol. 63, no. 3, pp. 326–34.

McCallum, J. (1983) 'Inflation and Social Consensus in the Seventies', *Economic Journal*, vol. 93, no. 372, pp. 784-805.

Meager, N. and H. Metcalf (1987) 'Recruitment of the Long Term Unemployed', Institute of Manpower Studies, *IMS Report*, no. 138.

Metcalf, D. (1986) 'Labour Market Flexibility and Jobs: A Survey of Evidence from OECD Countries with Special Reference to Great Britain and Europe', London School of Economics, Centre for Labour Economics, *Working Paper*, no. 870.

Minford, P. (1983) 'Labour Market Equilibrium in an Open Economy', *Oxford Economic Papers*, vol. 35, Supplement, pp. 207–44.

Newell, A. And J.S.V. Symons (1985) 'Wages and Unemployment in OECD Countries', London School of Economics, Centre for Labour Economics, *Discussion Paper*, no. 219.

——— (1987) 'Corporatism, Laissez-Faire and the Rise in Unemployment', *European Economic Review*, vol. 31, no 3, pp. 567-601.

——— (1989) 'The Passing of the Golden Age', London School of Economics, Centre for Labour Economics, *Discussion Paper*, no. 347.

Nickell, S. (1987) 'Why is Wage Inflation in Britain So High?', *Oxford Bulletin of Economics and Statistics*, vol. 49, no. 11, pp. 103–28.

——— (1990) 'Inflation and the UK Labour Market', *Oxford Review of Economic Policy*, vol. 6, no. 4, pp. 26–35.

OECD (1988) *Employment Outlook*, September, Paris, OECD.

Oswald, A.J. and P.J. Turnbull (1985) 'Pay and Employment Determination in Britain: What are Labour "Contracts" Really Like?', *Oxford Review of Economic Policy*, vol. 1, no. 2, pp. 80–97.

Soskice, D. (1990) 'Wage Determination: the Changing Role of Institutions in Advanced Industrialised Countries', *Oxford Review of Economic Policy*, vol. 6, no. 4, pp. 36–61.

Winter-Ebmer, R. (1991) 'Some Micro Evidence on Unemployment Persistence', *Oxford Bulletin of Economics and Statistics*, vol. 53.

10 Organizational Form, Growth and Stability

USA

L11

L22

Jonathan S. Leonard

10.1 INTRODUCTION

Patterns of growth among establishments and firms are of central importance to questions of industrial organization and macroeconomics. Firms that gain efficiency or market power gain the opportunity to grow. The growth and decline of firms also means the creation and destruction of jobs, with consequent flows out of and into unemployment. Despite the important role establishment growth plays in both industrial organization and macroeconomic theories, it has rarely been subjected to systematic study. This chapter presents new empirical evidence of the nature and determinants of firm and establishment growth and stability.

This work has the advantage of examining national longitudinal samples of firms and of their constituent establishments, to explore the nature of agglomeration into firms. These results are compared to those from an earlier study of Wisconsin establishments (Leonard, 1987), so that the dependence of results on particular samples or on establishment size can be studied. These samples are not limited to the manufacturing sector.

This chapter focuses on the characteristics and causes of establishment and firm dynamics. An error-correction model is compared to models of both a random walk, and of persistent success and failure. The substantial diversity of growth patterns within industry across establishments, and more strikingly within establishments across time, is demonstrated. The relationship between growth and size, corporate structure, and skill intensity is also examined.

10.2 CHARACTERIZING ENTERPRISE DYNAMICS

Before attempting to develop economic models of enterprise dynamics, it is useful to characterize the patterns to be explained in a parsimonious but general fashion. Enterprise size can be modelled as the sum of transient and cumulative innovations.

$$S_{it} = W_{it} + \mu_{it} \tag{1}$$

and

$$W_{it} = W_{i, t-1} + \epsilon_{it} \tag{2}$$

where
S_{it} = logarithm of establishment i size in year t
μ_{it} = white noise, $E(\mu_{it} \cdot \epsilon_{it}) = 0$
W_{it} = random walk component.

The first difference $(S_{it} - S_{i-1})$ of the logarithm of size is the growth rate, and is expressed as:

$$D_{it} = \epsilon_{it} + \mu_{it} - \mu_{t-1} \tag{3}$$

where ϵ_{it} is the innovation in the random walk component of size, and the remaining expression is a moving average component. Positive autocorrelation of the ϵ_{it} indicates persistent shocks or adjustment lags. If the ϵ_{it} are serially uncorrelated, then this model predicts that growth rates more than two years apart are uncorrelated and follow a random walk. It also predicts that growth rates in adjoining years are negatively correlated:

$$\text{COR}(D_{it}, D_{1, t1}) = \frac{-\sigma_\mu^2}{\sigma_\epsilon^2 + 2\sigma_\mu^2} \tag{4}$$

$$= \frac{-1}{\dfrac{\sigma_\epsilon^2}{\sigma_\mu^2} + 2} \tag{5}$$

In this model the ratio of cumulative to transient errors is identified from the correlation of growth rates in adjoining years. The fit of this model can be determined from its prediction of negatively correlated growth rates in adjoining years, and uncorrelated growth rates in years further apart.

Consider two special cases. If only cumulative shocks occur, $\sigma_\mu^2 = 0$. This is equivalent to a model with no measurement error, or to a model with complete adjustment to optimum size within one period. This implies that growth rates are serially uncorrelated, and that size follows a random walk.

The other special case has only transient shocks, $\sigma_\epsilon^2 = 0$. This is equivalent to a pure measurement error model. This implies that the correlation of growth rates is $-1/2$ one year apart, and zero at further remove. As the ratio of cumulative to transient shocks increases, the first-order autocorrelation of growth rates moves from $-1/2$ to zero. As positive serial correlation of the cumulative shocks increases, higher-order autocorrelations are positive.

If firms may be characterized as chronic winners or losers (strong positive autocorrelation of the e_{it}), then growth rates will be autocorrelated at higher orders. This would be expected in models in which some firms enjoy persistent advantages from greater efficiency or market power.

If firm growth is unpredictable, size follows a random walk. Such behaviour seems to characterize a number of economic aggregates, and it is interesting to learn whether the aggregate behaviour follows directly from firm or establishment behaviour. A classical statistical theory of the firm, Gibrat's law, is a random walk in the logarithm of size. The autocorrelation matrices also offer a test of Gibrat's law.

10.3   EVIDENCE OF ENTERPRISE DYNAMICS

The behaviour over time of establishments and of firms is remarkably similar. The nature of such dynamics involves some of the fundamental facts for theories of industrial organization. This section presents some simple time-series characterizations of establishment and firm dynamics in four samples, presented in Tables 10.1 through 10.4. The samples are as follows: single establishment firms (Table 10.1); constituent establishments of multi-establishments firms (Table 10.2); firm-level data for multi-establishment firms (Table 10.3); and establishments (Table 10.4). The first three samples are drawn from EEO data that are required by US law to be filed by all firms with 100 or more employees, and for firms with 50 or more employees and a federal contract of $50,000 or more. Such firms must also separately report employment data for each of their constituent establishments with 25 or more employees (50 or more beginning in 1983). The EEO data severely undersamples the smallest (<25) establishments (see Leonard, 1985). The adequacy of such data for representing establishments can be judged by comparing it with the last sample, which represents the

Table 10.1   Single establishments: correlation matrix of the logarithm of establishment size (S_t) and growth rate ($D_t = S_t - S_{t-1}$)

	Mean	σ	S_{79}	S_{80}	S_{81}	S_{82}	S_{83}	S_{84}	D_{79}	D_{80}	D_{81}	D_{82}	D_{83}	D_{84}
S78	5.45	0.77	0.96	0.95	0.93	0.91	0.88	0.86	−0.13	−0.02	−0.01	0.02	−0.04	−0.07
S79	5.49	0.77		0.97	0.95	0.93	0.89	0.87	−0.14	−0.09	−0.02	0.02	−0.05	−0.07
S80	5.51	0.78			0.96	0.94	0.90	0.88	0.07	0.16	−0.08	0.03	−0.05	−0.08
S81	5.51	0.79				0.97	0.93	0.90	0.06	0.08	0.21	−0.01	−0.08	−0.08
S82	5.50	0.81					0.95	0.92	0.06	0.09	0.17	0.23	−0.11	−0.09
S83	5.48	0.83						0.97	0.04	0.08	0.14	0.17	0.23	−0.15
S84	5.51	0.83							0.04	0.08	0.13	0.15	0.17	0.15
D79	0.038	0.21								−0.27	−0.04	0.02	−0.05	−0.02
D80	0.019	0.19									−0.24	0.03	−0.02	−0.01
D81	0.004	0.23										−0.14	−0.08	−0.01
D82	−0.006	0.19											−0.15	−0.05
D83	−0.024	0.28												−0.19
D84	0.027	0.25												

Note:
$N = 11{,}739$ establishments with positive employment in all years.

Table 10.2   Constituent establishments: correlation matrix of the logarithm of establishment size (S_t) and growth rate ($D_t = S_t - S_{t-1}$)

	Mean	σ	S_{79}	S_{80}	S_{81}	S_{82}	S_{83}	S_{84}	D_{79}	D_{80}	D_{81}	D_{82}	D_{83}	D_{84}
S78	4.99	0.95	0.95	0.93	0.89	0.87	0.84	0.81	−0.19	−0.09	−0.14	−0.14	−0.12	−0.07
S79	5.02	0.94		0.96	0.92	0.90	0.86	0.83	0.13	−0.19	−0.14	−0.15	−0.14	−0.06
S80	5.04	0.93			0.94	0.91	0.87	0.84	0.05	0.10	−0.21	−0.14	−0.15	−0.06
S81	5.03	0.92				0.96	0.89	0.86	0.06	0.01	0.15	−0.21	−0.21	−0.07
S82	5.02	0.90					0.91	0.87	0.05	0.01	0.09	0.08	−0.27	−0.08
S83	5.01	0.88						0.94	0.04	0.00	0.03	−0.01	0.15	−0.14
S84	5.03	0.89							0.04	−0.00	0.02	−0.02	0.10	0.21
D79	0.033	0.31								−0.30	0.02	−0.02	−0.05	0.03
D80	0.015	0.27									−0.25	0.02	−0.03	−0.01
D81	−0.006	0.33										−.19	−0.16	−0.01
D82	−0.009	0.27											−0.21	−0.04
D83	−0.015	0.38												−0.14
D84	0.024	0.31												

Note:
$N = 38{,}154$ establishments with positive employment in all years.

population of establishments in the State of Wisconsin. The interpretation of results here must be viewed cautiously in light of the absence of controls other than through sampling, and of the longitudinal nature of the samples which eliminate entrants or exits. Related analyses indicate that sample selection due to exits does not greatly affect estimates of growth (Evans, 1987; Hall, 1987).

Neither the pure random walk model (Gibrat's law), nor models of

Table 10.3   Multi-establishment firms: correlation matrix of the logarithm of firm size (S_t) and growth rate ($D_t = S_t - S_{t-1}$)

	Mean	σ	S_{79}	S_{80}	S_{81}	S_{82}	S_{83}	S_{84}	D_{79}	D_{80}	D_{81}	D_{82}	D_{83}	D_{84}
$S78$	6.39	1.34	0.99	0.98	0.96	0.96	0.95	0.93	−0.07	−0.04	−0.07	−0.03	−0.03	−0.05
$S79$	6.44	1.34		0.99	0.97	0.96	0.95	0.94	0.10	−0.10	−0.07	−0.03	−0.03	−0.04
$S80$	6.47	1.34			0.98	0.97	0.96	0.95	0.05	0.07	−0.09	−0.02	−0.03	−0.05
$S81$	6.44	1.34				0.99	0.97	0.96	0.06	0.04	0.10	−0.07	−0.06	−0.05
$S82$	6.44	1.34					0.98	0.97	0.06	0.05	0.07	0.10	−0.07	−0.05
$S83$	6.42	1.35						0.99	0.06	0.05	0.03	0.10	0.12	−0.06
$S84$	6.45	1.36							0.06	0.05	0.03	0.10	0.11	0.11
$D79$	0.051	0.23								−0.30	0.03	0.01	−0.00	0.01
$D80$	0.028	0.23									−0.14	0.05	0.00	−0.03
$D81$	−0.022	0.26										−0.21	−0.19	−0.00
$D82$	−0.004	0.23											−0.04	−0.00
$D83$	−0.024	0.25												−0.05
$D84$	0.033	0.23												

Note:
N = 8353 firms with positive employment in all years.

Table 10.4   Correlation matrices of the logarithm of firm size (S_t) and of the first difference ($D_t = S_t - S_{t-1}$) of the logarithm of firm size, 1977–82

	Mean	σ	S_{78}	S_{79}	S_{80}	S_{81}	S_{82}	D_{78}	D_{79}	D_{80}	D_{81}	D_{82}
S_{77}	1.93	1.34	0.966	0.949	0.932	0.918	0.898	−0.118	−0.046	−0.051	−0.069	−0.076
S_{78}	1.99	1.35		0.967	0.950	0.935	0.914	0.142	−0.104	−0.055	−0.073	−0.078
S_{79}	2.02	1.35			0.966	0.951	0.930	0.084	0.150	−0.115	−0.076	−0.079
S_{80}	2.02	1.36				0.967	0.947	0.079	0.089	0.143	−0.142	−0.077
S_{81}	2.01	1.35					0.963	0.075	0.085	0.077	0.114	−0.138
S_{82}	1.97	1.35						0.073	0.085	0.079	0.049	0.132
D_{78}	0.058	0.349							−0.225	−0.017	−0.018	−0.008
D_{79}	0.033	0.344								−0.237	−0.015	−0.003
D_{80}	0.001	0.350									−0.258	0.006
D_{81}	−0.017	0.347										−0.239
D_{82}	−0.035	0.366										

Notes: All of these correlations are significant well beyond conventional levels, with the following exceptions: (D_{82}, D_{78}) at 0.06, (D_{82}, D_{79}) at 0.53, and (D_{82}, D_{80}) at 0.16.

chronic success or failure (including partial adjustment and persistent shock models) adequately characterize the time-series behaviour of any of these samples.

Enterprises are tremendously heterogeneous. In all samples, the cross-section variance of growth rates is very large, ranging from 0.19 to 0.37. In other words, it is not unusual to find a third of all enterprises shrinking or growing 25 percent or more than average. We shall return to the limited role that differences across industries play in accounting for this heterogeneity. It is not unusual for establishment-level employment to vary by 25 percent or more from year to year. This establishment instability exposes workers to considerable unemployment risk.

The half-life of a newly created job is very short. Marginal jobs are unstable. At the same time, many of the jobs in these enterprises are stable. Such a skewed distribution of job durations combining high persistence for some jobs with high job turnover rates is familiar from other contexts such as unemployment spell distributions.

The evidence that enterprises are stable is that in these samples the correlation of size (employment) five years apart ranges from 0.83 to 0.95. One can predict quite well enterprise size from knowledge of past size.

Growth is a different story. Growth neither persists (as in models of chronic success and failure, or of lagged adjustment), nor does it follow a random walk. Rather, in all samples, growth tends to a follow a mean-reverting and error-correcting process. Neither success nor failure appear to be chronic conditions. Not surprisingly, firms with above average growth tend to have been small, and to become large. Small enterprises tend to have had below average growth in the past, and to have above average growth in the future. This unsurprising regression to the mean is the statistical artifact that underlies the common belief that small enterprises are the source of most new job creation.

Enterprises with above average growth in one year tend to suffer below average growth the following year. This error-correction process is observed in all samples. The lower right hand quadrant of Tables 10.1 through 10.4 presents the relevant autocorrelations of growth rates. One year apart, these growth rates are negatively correlated. The correlations generally damp quickly down towards zero for growth rates more than two years apart. This indicates that enterprises do not generally suffer from persistent shocks nor from slow adjustment, and that it will be difficult to predict growth. The classic partial adjustment model appears to have little relevance to employment changes at the establishment or firm level. Rather than adjusting too slowly, enterprises appear to adjust too quickly, overshooting sustainable growth paths. This is consistent with models of lumpy adjustment as with fixed adjustment costs.

The autocorrelation matrices of growth rates can be interpreted in terms of equation (3). Growth rates one year apart are negatively correlated. Those more than two years apart are generally close to uncorrelated. That $E(e_{it}, E_{i, t + k})$ usually tends to zero for k > 1 suggests that enterprises quickly adjust and that growth shocks do not persist.

The one year apart correlations average about -0.21 for the EEO establishments. This corresponds to $\sigma_\epsilon^2 = 3\sigma_\mu^2$. The variance of the transient component of errors is one-third that of the cumulative component. About 60 percent of the variance of growth rates then represents real shocks having permanent effects on size, and the remaining 40 percent a moving average process of transient errors. Since a simple pure measurement error process is MA(1) in growth rates and implies a first-order correlation of growth rates equal to -0.5, this increases our confidence in the limited role played by measurement error in the results reported here. The role of measurement error may also be limited because of legal sanctions for misreporting.

There appears to be weak synchronization of growth. At the bottom of the business cycle, a substantial portion of establishments are growing. Between 1981 and 1982 the US unemployment rate rose from 7.5 to 9.5. Over the same period the average growth rate of employment in EEO firms was -0.4 percent – nearly stable. The small cyclical shifts in average growth rates, together with the substantial heterogeneity and transience of enterprise growth, suggests that frictional unemployment may be of great importance (Leonard, 1987).

10.4 CORPORATE STRUCTURE

To ask why the dynamics of single establishments are expected to differ from those of establishments that are part of multi-establishment firms is to ask why multi-establishment firms exist. In some cases, economies of scope or of integration may provide answers. The role of such factors is presumably limited in the case of conglomerates of unrelated businesses. Such conglomerates may offer advantages if capital markets are imperfect. Cross-subsidization within a conglomerate may overcome credit-rationing that lines of business might face on their own externally. Within industry, this implies slower growth and possibly greater instability at single than at constituent establishments.

Comparing Tables 10.1 and 10.2, single establishments are more stable and not clearly slower growing than are constituent establishments. They do appear more cyclically sensitive. Part of these differences may reflect other differing characteristics, such as industrial distribution or size. In a credit-rationing model, credit rationed establishments have an incentive to conglomerate with asynchronous establishments. While this may increase the stability of the constituent establishments, its effects may not be observable in a cross-section because of selection on the underlying heterogeneity. On its face, however, this comparison offers little evidence of cross-subsidization among constituent establishments.

There is some evidence of risk-pooling in multi-establishment firms, but it is evidence of the sort that is almost unavoidable. Unless the growth of constituent establishments were perfectly correlated, the variance of the growth rate of multi-establishment firms will be less than that of the constituent establishments. This condition may be violated because of mergers, acquisitions, or divestitures of establishments that are not always part of ongoing multi-establishment firms. Comparing Tables 10.2 and 10.3, the variance of growth rates of multi-establishment firms is less than that of constituent establishments. This is also demonstrated in the autocorrelation matrices of size. As expected from the law of large numbers, firms are more stable over time than are the constituent establishments. Finance theories typically assume that whatever risk reduction such corporate diversification achieves could be replicated by an investor holding a portfolio of the separate assets.

10.5 SIZE AND STABILITY

It is often assumed that stability increases with size. We have already seen the unsurprising evidence that firms are more stable than constituent establishments, in part because of diversification. This section shows that the relation between size and stability is more complex than would be expected simply from the law of large numbers.

Stability is a non-linear function of data. Across these four samples, as expected the greatest stability is observed in the sample with the largest average size: multi-establishment firms. More surprisingly, the sample with the smallest average size, Wisconsin enterprises, shows the second highest stability. This ignores high infant mortality among the small. One possible explanation is that small enterprises tend to occupy niches protected from market shocks.

Three major empirical regularities stand out from the above analysis. First, a stochastic process of mean reversion and error-correction typifies both firms and establishments of all sizes. Persistent growth or decline is rare. Second, no strong evidence emerges that firms cross-subsidize constituent establishments. Third, cyclical effects are more widely shared across large than small establishments. The cross-sectional variation in growth rates is substantial. As section 10.6 demonstrates, heterogeneity is also substantial within industries.

10.6   DETERMINANTS OF ESTABLISHMENT GROWTH

Certain factors would seem likely to be part of most deterministic economic models of establishment growth. Product demand, optimum technological scale, market power, factor costs, and macroeconomic conditions would seem to be fundamental elements of models of establishment growth. If such factors are important, then industry, region, and year should strongly account for a substantial part of the variation in establishment growth. Both the external and internal organization of an establishment may also affect its success within particular markets. With economies of scope, establishments that are part of larger firms may enjoy advantages over single establishments (although the statement verges on tautology). With technological change, establishments with human capital or skill intensive workforces may be favored over those employing predominantly unskilled labor. To date, studies of establishment dynamics are rare, often limited to manufacturing, and usually with little or no information on internal or external structure. This section presents basic empirical evidence of the relative importance of industry, region, macroeconomic, corporate structure, and skill intensity effects in determining establishment growth in a national sample.

Table 10.5 presents a regression of the logarithm of annual establishment growth on sets of dichotomous variables for two-digit SIC industry, geographical region, year and corporate structure. Controls are also included indicating whether the establishment is a contractor of the federal government, and for the skill intensity of its workforce. This regression is estimated for the sample of 49,893 EEO establishments, for each of which six annual growth rates are observed between 1978 and 1984.

Almost all of the substantial heterogeneity in this sample occurs within industries, within regions, and within years, the full set of controls of Table 10.5 can account for less than 1 percent of the variance in annual growth rates. This information is simply not of substantial use in predicting growth. Judging from the negative or negligible autocorrelations of establishment growth rates previously observed, establishment specific effects would offer little prospect of improvement.

Conditional on these controls, the standard deviation of growth rates is 0.295. Within a given industry, region and year, one must construct an interval of growth rates 60 percentage points wide in order to include at least two-thirds of the establishments. Part of this considerable within-industry heterogeneity may reflect life-cycle effects (Dunne, Roberts and Samuelson, 1987; Evans, 1987).

Table 10.5 Regression of logarithm of annual establishment growth rate on establishment characteristics, 1979–84

Variable	Parameter estimate	Standard error
Intercept	0.0039	0.0030
1980	−0.0176	0.0019
1981	−0.0379	0.0019
1982	−0.0425	0.0019
1983	−0.0507	0.0019
1984	−0.0095	0.0019
SIC1	0.0272	0.00
SIC2	0.0310	0.0044
SIC3	0.0207	0.0047
SIC20	0.0213	0.0030
SIC22	0.0130	0.004
SIC23	0.0294	0.0039
SIC24	0.0157	0.00
SIC25	0.0201	0.005
SIC26	0.0233	0.004
SIC27	0.0289	0.0038
SIC28	0.0204	0.0039
SIC29	−0.0568	0.0092
SIC30	0.0323	0.004
SIC31	0.0104	0.0076
SIC32	0.0139	0.0049
SIC33	−0.0026	0.0043
SIC34	0.0104	0.0035
SIC35	0.0030	0.0033
SIC36	0.0252	0.0035
SIC37	0.0121	0.0042
SIC38	0.0330	0.0052
SIC39	0.0214	0.0067
SIC40	0.0157	0.0032
SIC41	0.0317	0.0030
SIC50	0.0262	0.0028
SIC60	0.0380	0.0024
SIC70	0.0396	0.0019
Region2	−0.0124	0.0024
Region3	−0.0062	0.0029
Region4	0.0004	0.0024
Region5	−0.0021	0.0026
SINGLE	−0.0026	0.0014
Contracts in 1978	−0.0042	0.0012
% White-collar in 1978	0.0486	0.0022
Sample size	299,358	
SSE	26,022	
MSE	0.0869	

Industry effects range from +4 percentage points (services) to −0.5 percentage points (petroleum). The standard deviation of industry effects is small, particularly in relation to that of establishment growth rates. While the industry effects are tightly clustered, F-tests reject the hypothesis that they are jointly insignificant. The same holds true for region and year effects. The substantial within-industry diversity means that declining industries contain many growing establishments. Rather than being broadly spread over all the establishments within an industry, declines appear to be concentrated within a small proportion of establishments.

The small role played here by industry effects in accounting for establishment growth would seem to raise some interesting questions for theories of industrial organization. A number of responses are possible. First, the two-digit standard industrial classifications used here may simply be too broad or too inaccurate measures of true markets. Such problems may be compounded in the case of multi-product establishments. Establishments within industries so defined may face idiosyncratic demand shocks. However, similar heterogeneity is found within more detailed (three-digit SIC), and more self-defined product markets. A second alternative is that these patterns reveal divergent behaviour within well defined product markets. Indeed, it is possible to construct models of competitive markets that yield such divergent behaviour. For example, if establishments are subject to random technological shocks that yield temporary cost advantages, and jointly face inelastic industry demand, then growth rates within an industry that are not positively correlated across establishments may easily result. This may be a sign of a competitive rather than a managed market.

Macroeconomic conditions are not irrelevant. Of course, for total employment among the largest employer in the country, this approaches an identity. Average establishment growth rates fall significantly by 5.1 percentage points between 1979 and 1983. F-tests reject the joint insignificance of year effects, and individually each of the year effects is highly significant. This result for the EEO sample stands in sharp contrast to the insignificant year effects previously estimated in the sample of Wisconsin establishments (Leonard, 1987). This comparison suggests that small establishments tend to be in niches insulated from direct and multiplier cyclical effects. This in turn suggests the possibility of diversifying against cyclical risk by diversifying investment or employment into smaller establishments.

There are only slight differences across regions in growth rates. The industrial heartland of the mid-Atlantic and east–north central regions saw establishments grow 1.2 percentage points slower than in the South. Similar growth patterns across regions, along with the absence of significant difference in optimal scale across regions, suggests a national market in which the constraints of geography are of minor importance.

10.7 EXTERNAL AND INTERNAL CORPORATE STRUCTURE, AND MARKET ORIENTATION

Corporate structure has only a small and insignificant impact on establishment growth. Within industry and region, single establishments do not grow at substantially different rates than do their counterparts that are part of larger firms. The advantages of agglomeration are not apparent in trend growth rates. An alternative and untestable explanation of the same pattern is that constituent establishments select into larger firms because they would otherwise have slower growth.

The market towards which an establishment is oriented does affect its growth. Establishments that are contractors of the federal government grow slightly (0.4 percentage points) but significantly slower than their counterparts in the same two-digit SIC industries. Despite the growth in federal expenditures during this period, establishments oriented toward the private market grew faster than federal contractors.

The skill intensity of an establishment's workforce is one of the most significant predictors of its growth. Establishments with a higher proportion of white-collar workers grow faster than others in the same two-digit industries. A one standard deviation increase in the proportion of white-collar workers is associated with growth rates 1.5 percentage points faster. Either such establishments are located in faster growing market segments, or else they enjoy a competitive advantage over others in the same markets. In an era of rapid technological change, it appears that establishments with highly skilled workforces enjoy faster growth.

Small establishments are often cast as the fountainheads of growth. To the equation of Table 10.5, the logarithm of average size is added. The result is an estimate of the average association of growth and average size. The estimated coefficient is -0.007 and significant. Within industry, smaller establishments are associated with slightly higher growth rates. The effect is a small one. Establishments one standard deviation (0.89) above average size grow 0.6 percentage points slower.

10.8   IN THE CONTEXT OF JAPAN

How might the results of similar establishment-level studies differ in Japan? From studies of worker turnover, we know that Japanese workers have longer job tenures and far less mobility across employers than their US counterparts (Tachibanaki, 1984; Hasimoto and Raisian, 1985).

Complementary evidence indicates that one overlooked reason for the greater stability of Japanese workers is the greater stability of Japanese jobs. The evidence is contained in tabulations prepared by Kuwahara (1986) and reported by the OECD (1987). Among continuing establishments in the *Survey of Employment Trend* job creation was 4.1 percent, and job destruction 3.6 percent annual between 1982 and 1984. Between 1970 and 1981 the annual average birth rate of establishments (not employment in new establishments) was 6.4 percent, while the death rate was 3.6 percent. In all cases, these rates are among the lowest found in industrialized states.

It is not clear whether the *Survey of Employment Trend* sample is representative of the entire population of Japanese establishments. Our particular concern is that small establishments are underrepresented. The *Survey of Employment Trend* covers 15,000 private and public sector establishments regularly employing at least five dependent workers – defined as wage or salary earning employees on indefinite contract or on a fixed-term contract of more than one month (OECD, 1987, p. 208). Clearly the smallest establishments are excluded. Smaller establishments above the five employee cutoff may also be undersampled. It is likely that in Japan, as in other countries, job turnover rates are higher among smaller establishments. In combination, these two factors could lead to a systematic understatement of Japanese job turnover. Clearly the larger establishments in Japan are more stable than establishments of the same size in nearly all other OECD countries. What is not clear is whether or not the greater stability of the large has been bought at the expense of greater instability among the small – whether the Japanese economy concentrates the adjustment to shocks in small employees who serve as a buffer. The more challenging alternative is that Japanese jobs may be more stable throughout the size distribution.

While a great deal of thought has been devoted to explaining the greater stability of Japanese workers in terms of cultural, economic, or behavioural differences, the more dramatic difference in job stability has gone largely unnoticed. Clearly, it is not simply explained by any cultural or behavioural difference in the workers because the measure is distinct from worker turnover. It is, however, consistent with two other stories. The first says there is greater functional flexibility within Japanese firms so that demand shifts that would be accommodated by employment shifts across firms in other countries are accommodated within Japanese firms. The second says that there is greater vertical integration in practice between Japanese intermediate and final goods producers. The limited competition and long-term relations may stabilize employment. Such distinctions are of course difficult to measure with confidence.

If one accepts the characterization of the Japanese economy as undergoing one of the world's highest rates of technological advance, then these comparisons clearly call into question that allegation that technological change necessarily entails job turnover.

Variations in hours worked per employee is a substitute for variation in the number of employees. The greater stability of the latter in Japan may reflect greater instability in the former. On this matter, Hashimoto (1990) and Abraham and Houseman (1989) present differing results.

In some descriptions of the Japanese economy, subcontractors absorb most of the economic shocks, serving as buffers for the productive shocks of the primary employers. If so, we would expect to see a greater difference in the relative stability of jobs at small versus larger plants in Japan than elsewhere. This will depend upon the extent to which subcontractors serve a diversified set of primes, as well as on whether subcontractors are also expected to absorb the prime's excess labour.

10.9 CONCLUSIONS

This chapter has presented new empirical evidence on the dynamics of establishments and firms in a national sample between 1978 and 1984. These results have been compared to those from an earlier analysis of Wisconsin establishments (Leonard, 1987).

A major finding is the tremendous heterogeneity across establishments. The standard deviation of establishment annual growth rates is about 0.30. This substantial diversity is hardly reduced within industries, regions or years. This suggests that frictional unemployment arising from fluctuations in labour demand may be of great importance. Common industry shocks are of little importance in explaining establishment growth patterns. Models of transient and idiosyncratic cost advantage may be more useful.

Persistent growth or decline is rare among establishments. Growth rates are not positively autocorrelated. Growth rates appear to follow a pattern of error-correction and mean-reversion. The first-order autocorrelation of growth rates is negative. Rather than hoarding labour, or smoothing its fluctuation, establishments appear to make quick adjustments that overshoot. This does not appear to be all due to measurement error. This result is consistent with lumpy adjustment in the face of fixed adjustment costs.

Corporate structure is of little importance. Firms show no strong evidence of cross-subsidizing their constituent establishments. Single establishments show growth rates similar to those of similar establishments that are part of larger firms. The greater stability of firms than of establishments follows from the law of large numbers.

Smaller establishments appear surprisingly stable and insulated from cyclical pressures. This may reflect their location in less competitive market niches. Smaller establishments are associated with slightly faster growth, although much of the growth attributed to small establishments may be an artifact of regression to the mean.

The level of technology in the production process is important in determining growth. One of the most significant predictors of establishment growth is the skill intensity of the workforce. Within industries, establishments with higher proportions of white-collar workers enjoy faster rates of growth. Presumably, investment in a skilled workforce offers competitive advantages during a period of rapid technological change.

References

Abraham, Katharine G. and Susan N. Houseman (1989) 'Job Security and Work Force Adjustment: How Different are U.S. and Japanese Practices?' *Journal of the Japanese and International Economy*, vol. 3, no. 4, pp. 500–21.

Davis, Steve (1987) 'Allocative Disturbances and Specific Capital in Real Business Cycle Theories', *American Economic Review*, vol. 77, no. 2, May, pp. 326–32.

Dunne, Timothy, Mark Roberts and Larry Samuelson (1987) 'Plant Failure and Employment Growth in the U.S. Manufacturing Sector', Pennsylvania State University, unpublished.

Evans, David S. (1987) 'Tests of Alternative Theories of Firm Growth',

Journal of Political Economy, vol. 95, no. 4, August, pp. 657–74.

Hall, Bronwyn (1987) 'The Relationship between Firm Size and Firm Growth in the U.S. Manufacturing Sector', *Journal of Industrial Organization*, June.

Hashimoto, Masanori (1990) *The Japanese Labor Market in a Comparative Perspective with the United States*, Kalamazoo, MI, W.E. Upjohn Institute.

Hashimoto, Masanori and John Raisian (1985) 'Employment, Tenure, and Earnings Profiles in Japan and the United States', *American Economic Review*, vol. 75, September, pp. 721–35.

Kumar, M.S. (1985) 'Growth, Acquisition Activity and Firm Size: Evidence from the United Kingdom,' *Journal of Industrial Economics*, vol. 33, pp. 327–38.

Kuwahara, Y. (1986) 'Job Creation and Job Destruction Process in Japan', unpublished paper.

Leonard, Jonathan S. (1985) 'On the Size Distribution of Establishments and Employment,' University of California at Berkeley, unpublished.

———— 'Employment Variation and Wage Rigidity: A Comparison of Union and Non-Union Plants', unpublished paper.

———— 'In the Wrong Place at the Wrong Time: The Extent of Frictional and Structural Employment', in K. Lang and J. Leonard (eds), *Unemployment and the Structure of Labor Markets* Oxford: Basil Blackwell.

———— 'Firm and Establishment Growth and Stability', unpublished paper.

Leonard, Jonathan and R. Schettkat (1991) 'A Comparison of Job Stability in Germany and the USA', *Labour*, vol. 5, no. 2, pp. 143–57.

Mincer, Jacob and Yoshio Higuchi (1988) 'Wage Structures and Labor Turnover in the United States and Japan', *Journal of the Japanese and Institutional Economies*, vol. 2, June, pp. 97–133.

Oi, Walter (1962) 'Labor as a Quasi-Fixed Factor', *Journal of Political Economy*, vol. 70, no. 6, pp. 538–55.

Organization for Economic Cooperation and Development (OECD) (1987) *Employment Outlook*, chapter 4, September.

Shimado, Haruo (1984) 'Employment Adjustment and Employment Policies: Japanese Experience', Keio University, unpublished, October.

Tachibanaki, Toshiaki (1984) 'Labor Mobility and Job Tenure', in M. Aoki, (ed.), *The Economic Analysis of the Japanese Firm*, Amsterdam, North-Holland.

———— (1987) 'Labour Market Flexibility in Japan in Comparison with Europe and the U.S.', *European Economic Review*, vol. 31, pp. 647–84; reprinted (1992) in G. de Mérul and R.J. Gordon (eds), *International Volatility and Economic Growth*, Amsterdam, North-Holland.

11 'Main' Bank System, Implicit Contracts and Trust in Deferred Payment Arrangements

Hiroshi Osano and Toshio Serita*

11.1 INTRODUCTION

In his theoretical and survey papers, Aoki (1989, 1990) has examined the nature of Japanese firms as a nexus of employment and financial contracts.[1] He has suggested the 'institutional complementarity' for Japanese firms by which the combination of life-time employment contracts (with deferred compensation plans) and 'main' bank relations (with corporate cross-holdings) can provide an efficient mechanism through which individual wealth-risk is diversified and thereby reduced. The 'main' bank is conventionally defined as the bank which sustains the largest lending share among private financial institutions that make loans to the firm. Most large Japanese firms have close financial, shareholding and managerial ties with the main bank. The object of this chapter is to explore empirically how financial customer relations (between firms and banks) affect the profile of long-term employment contracts (with deferred compensation plans) in Japanese firms. The research can also shed light on the question of whether the combination of life-time employment contracts and 'main' bank relations contribute to good economic performance in Japan.

To accomplish this purpose we present theoretical hypotheses that illustrate the effects of the main bank relation on deferred compensation schemes determined from the optimal contracting arrangements between the firm and workers. Testing our hypotheses with microdata from Japanese firms, we can discuss whether in the labour contract arrangements the main bank relation is expected to reduce the probability that the firm is bankrupt or taken over. This test also enables us to examine the question of whether deferred compensation plans are used to give incentives to greater effort by workers (as predicted by Lazear, 1979) and to greater investment in the specific human capital of workers (as predicted by Becker, 1975 and Hashimoto, 1979) or to provide insurance for workers against uncertain future events (as predicted by Harris and Holmstrom, 1982 and Merton, 1985).

Our empirical results give some broad evidence (1) that in the labour contract arrangements the main bank relation is expected to decrease the probability of the firm becoming bankrupt or being taken over, (2) that retirement compensation for male workers is used as an insurance instrument, and (3) that the combination of life-time employment contracts and main bank relations in Japanese firms provides an efficient mechanism through which individual wealth-risk is diversified and thereby reduced. However, the results are not robust enough to conclude that retirement compensation for female workers is used as an incentive-inducing device, or that employee stock ownership plans are used as an insurance device. Furthermore, our estimates are inconsistent with the hypothesis that bonus payments for male workers are used as an incentive-inducing or an insurance device.

This chapter is organized as follows. Section 11.2 gives an overview of the characteristics of employment and financial contracts in Japanese firms. Section 11.3 specifies two competing hypotheses about the role of the main bank in reducing the breach costs of deferred compensation contracts. Section 11.4 examines the empirical procedure for testing the hypotheses. Section 11.5 describes the estimation results, and section 11.6 summarizes our conclusions.

11.2 AN OVERVIEW OF EMPLOYMENT AND FINANCIAL CONTRACTS IN JAPANESE FIRMS

In Japanese industrial relations a worker is usually employed by a firm immediately after graduating from school, and remains with the same firm until his retirement. This system commonly involves deferred compensation programmes such as the 'Nenko' wage (length-of-service reward), bonus compensation scheme, employee stock ownership, and payment of lump sum amounts at the time of retirement or private pensions. The deferred compensation schemes prevailing in Japanese industrial relations can be explained as a device to give incentives for greater effort to workers (as predicted by Lazear, 1979) and for greater investment in the specific human capital of workers (as predicted by

Becker, 1975 and Hashimoto, 1979) or to provide insurance for workers against uncertain future events (as predicted by Harris and Holmstrom, 1982 and Merton, 1985). However, in order to implement these deferred compensation programmes for incentive-inducing or insurance purposes, firms are required to commit themselves to honouring their implicit or explicit contract arrangements even though they have an incentive to violate their promises *ex post*.[2]

The so-called 'main' bank system is characterized as long-term, stable relations between firms and banks in the Japanese financial market, corresponding to the life-time employment system in industrial relations. The 'main' bank is defined as the bank which maintains the largest lending share among private financial institutions that make loans to the firm. The main bank usually owns some of the equities of the firm, and may even send bank executives to top management positions in the firm. As a result most large Japanese firms have close financial, shareholding and managerial ties with the main bank. The key role of the main bank system is conventionally thought to be a risk-shifting mechanism whereby the main bank gives financial support to the firm in times of financial distress while the firm pays insurance premiums to the main bank in normal times. It is also recognized that the main bank relation, together with corporate cross-holdings, is so effective that external takeovers through open bids are almost impossible. Thus, the main bank system serves to lessen the risks that firms become bankrupt or are taken over.[3]

This combination of employment and financial contracts observed in Japanese firms is not coincidental. Under long-term employment contracts workers tend to be obliged to stake their life-time wealth on the employing firms, in the form of implicit future claims for seniority payments and retirement compensation. However, the deferred compensation plans force workers to bear additional risks if there exists some possibility that the firms become bankrupt or are taken over. This is because bondholders or raiders are not committed to upholding the implicit deferred compensation contracts in the event of bankruptcy or takeover (see Figure 11.1). Long-term employment contracts with deferred compensation plans are thus less likely to hold as firms are more likely to face the threat of bankruptcy or takeover. Due to the risks of deferred compensation plans, risk-averse workers usually prefer current wage compensation to the same amount of deferred risky compensation. Hence, firms must trade off incentive benefits against extra risk-sharing costs under deferred compensation plans. The main bank system can reduce the extent of this tradeoff because the bank-

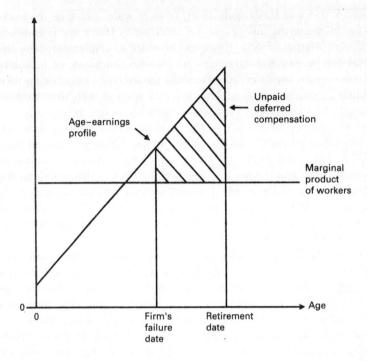

Figure 11.1   Unpaid deferred compensation in the event of firm's failure

ruptcy (takeover) of corporate firms is expected to be rather rare (almost impossible) under long-term customer relations between firms and banks associated with intercorporate shareholdings. Long-term contracts with deferred compensation plans are, therefore, more likely to be observed as firms have closer financial, shareholding and managerial ties with their main banks.

11.3   THE WORKER-INCENTIVE MODEL VERSUS THE RISK-SHARING MODEL

In this section, we derive two competing hypotheses from incorporating the worker-incentive or the risk-sharing model into the main bank model. We first attempt to combine the worker–incentive model with the main bank model.

Let us describe the worker-incentive model. The worker-incentive model studied here is based on the model of Curme and Kahn (1990) in which deferred compensation plans are used to provide incentives for no shirking of workers.

Workers, taken to be identical, live two periods. Workers work only in the first period, but they may receive a wage payment not only in the first period but also in the second period. We also assume that workers choose either to shirk or not to shirk and derive utility from shirking. The representative worker's preferences are then given by

$$V = U(W_1 + W_2) + sI,$$

where W_1 is a wage payment in the first period, W_2 a wage payment in the second period, s the utility of shirking, and I an indicator variable that takes on the value one when the worker shirks and the value zero when the worker does not shirk. Note that if a wage is not paid in the second period, then $W_2 = 0$.

In the subsequent analysis, we assume (1) that workers cannot post performance bonds at the beginning of the first period, and (2) that the firm cannot make the wage payment conditional on the level of output. The first assumption is justified if workers do not have enough wealth to post bonds (see Shapiro and Stiglitz, 1984). The second assumption is also justified if the firm cannot distinguish the contribution of any worker to the firm's total output or if an outside court cannot observe the level of output produced by any worker (see Hart and Moore, 1988). Under these assumptions the firm must make do with using the deferred compensation scheme to elicit effort from workers.

We now develop an optimal deferred compensation contract between the firm and the worker. For this purpose we must discuss several constraints to be satisfied by feasible deferred compensation contracts.

We first introduce the constraint which gives the worker no incentive to shirk. Let us examine the worker's expected utility level under a deferred compensation contract when the firm's survival probability is q. If a worker does not shirk, his expected utility is expressed by

$$V(NS) = qU(W_1 + W_2) + (1-q)U(W_1). \tag{1}$$

Note that deferred compensation is not paid to the worker if bondholders or raiders obtain control of the firm in the event of bankruptcy or takeovers. Since bondholders or raiders are not committed to upholding the deferred compensation contract, they do not have to pay W_2 to the worker. If a worker shirks, he is caught shirking with probability p. If he is caught shirking, he cannot receive any wage payments W_2 in the second period. However, shirking is detected with a lag, so that the worker can collect W_1 even if he is caught shirking. Then, the expected utility of the shirking worker is

$$V(S) = (1 - p)qU(W_1 + W_2) + [1 - (1 - p)q]U(W_1) + s. \quad (2)$$

Note that $(1-p)q$ is the probability that neither the worker is caught shirking nor the firm bankrupted or taken over. Comparing (1) and (2), the worker decides whether or not to shirk: the worker does not shirk if $V(NS) \geq V(S)$. Thus, the firm can induce the worker not to shirk if

$$U(W_1 + W_2) - U(W_1) \geq \frac{s}{pq}. \quad (3)$$

As long as (3) holds, the worker never shirks under the deferred compensation contract.

The other requirements to be satisfied by feasible deferred compensation contracts are the *ex ante* individual rationality constraints which give the firm and the worker an incentive to participate in the deferred compensation contracts. Let us suppose that the worker obtains ω from the alternative employment at the end of the first period if he is not employed by the firm. Since the firm must offer the worker a utility level at least as large as the exogenous reservation level $U(\omega)$, the individual rationality constraint of the worker is described by

$$qU(W_1 + W_2) + (1 - q)U(W_1) \geq U(\omega), \quad (4)$$

where the left hand side of (4) represents the expected utility level of the worker if he enters into a deferred compensation contract and does not shirk. Note that we focus on the no-shirking case because the worker never shirks under the optimal deferred compensation contract.

Similarly, deferred compensation contracts must give the firm more profits than any alternative contract. In the subsequent analysis, we assume that the worker always shirks and produces no output unless the firm monitors the worker with the imperfect monitoring technology discussed above. With this assumption, the firm always offers a deferred compensation contract as long as the profit is larger than zero. We also restrict our attention to the case that the profit of the firm under the optimal deferred compensation contract is greater than zero.

Given (3) and (4), an optimal deferred compensation contract is derived from the following maximization problem:

$$\max_{\{W_1, W_2\}} \{qR - W_1 - qW_2\}, \tag{5}$$

subject to (3) and (4),

where R is the productivity of the worker when he does not shirk. Note that the firm need not pay W_2 if the firm is bankrupt or taken over in the second period. To simplify the analysis, we do not specify the process whereby the firm becomes bankrupt or is taken over due to the various activities such as financing, investment, and litigation involved. In this sense, the failure probability q is regarded as exogenous although the subsequent analysis will consider how the level of q depends on the strength of ties generated by the main bank relation.

Solving (5) and totally differentiating the first-order conditions with respect to W_1, W_2, q and p, we can characterize the main predictions of the worker-incentive model: a rise in the firm's survival probability, q, *decreases* the level of deferred compensation, W_2 (and the ratio of deferred compensation to current compensation, W_2/W_1).[4]

The intuition for this result is explained as follows. In the worker-incentive model, the firm can motivate the worker only by designing deferred compensation plans. Although a deferred compensation contract gives the worker an incentive not to shirk, the contract forces the worker to bear additional risks because the worker cannot recover the unpaid part of deferred compensation in the event of the firm's failure. If he is risk-averse the worker prefers current compensation to the same amount of risk-adjusted deferred risky compensation. As the firm's survival probability increases, the worker is more willing to trust the promise that the firm pays wage compensation in the later period. In other words, a rise in the firm's survival probability makes a given deferred payment more attractive to the worker. Thus, an increase in the firm's survival probability induces the worker to be less likely to shirk for a given level of deferred compensation (or a given ratio of deferred compensation to current compensation). This implies that, as the firm's survival probability increases, the firm can reduce the level of deferred compensation (or the ratio of deferred compensation to current compensation) used to prevent the worker from shirking.

From the above argument, the main predictions of the worker-incentive model can be represented by

$$W_2 = \alpha_0 + \alpha_1 q + \alpha_2 p + \alpha'_3 X_D, \tag{6a}$$
$$ (-) \quad (-)$$

$$W_2/W_1 = \beta_0 + \beta_1 q + \beta_2 p + \beta'_3 X_D, \tag{6b}$$
$$ (-) \quad (-)$$

where W_2 is the amount of deferred compensation, W_1 the amount of current compensation, q the firm's survival probability, p the firm's monitoring ability, and X_D a vector of other control variables which may be related to the level of deferred compensation or the ratio of deferred compensation to current compensation. The effect of a change in p on W_2 or W_2/W_1 in (6) is not surprising. A rise in p leads the worker to be less likely to shirk for a given W_2 or W_2/W_1. Thus, as p increases, the firm can reduce W_2 or W_2/W_1 used to prevent the worker from shirking.[5]

We next present how the firm's survival probability depends upon the strength of ties generated by the main bank relation. The firm's survival is ordinarily threatened by the possibility of bankruptcy or takeover. In the Japanese financial and industrial structure, a number of researchers suggest that the main bank system together with corporate cross-holdings reduces the threat of bankruptcy or takeover.[6] Thus, if this is true, the firm's survival probability q is expressed as an increasing function of the strength of ties generated by the main bank relation:

$$q = \gamma_0 + \gamma_1 MB + \gamma'_2 X_S, \tag{7}$$
$$ (+)$$

where MB represents the index of strength of the firm's relationship to the main bank; and X_S is a vector of other control variables that may be related to the firm's survival probability.

Substituting (7) into (6a) and (6b), we have the regression equations that show how the strength of ties generated by the main bank relation affects the profile of deferred compensation within the worker-incentive and main bank model:

$$W_2 = \zeta_0 + \zeta_1 MB + \zeta_2 p + \zeta'_3 X_S + \zeta'_4 X_D, \tag{8a}$$
$$ (-) \quad\quad (-)$$

$$W_2/W_1 = \theta_0 + \theta_1 MB + \theta_2 p + \theta'_3 X_S + \theta'_4 X_D, \tag{8b}$$
$$ (-) \quad\quad (-)$$

The key hypothesis to be tested is that ζ_1 and θ_1 are negative: W_2 (or W_2/W_1) decreases as the firm has closer financial, shareholding and managerial ties with the main bank.

We now proceed to consider the risk-sharing and main bank model. As an alternative to the worker-incentive model, Curme and Kahn (1990) suggest the risk-sharing hypothesis that a rise in the firm's survival probability *increases* the level of deferred compensation (and the ratio of deferred compensation to current compensation). In this view, workers may rely on a deferred compensation scheme to insure their wage income against uncertain future events under an imperfect capital market. If the firm becomes bankrupt or is taken over, then workers who enter into an implicit contract involving deferred payments suffer a transfer of resources to the debtholders or the stockholders of the firm. To limit the exposure to such a loss, workers desire to reduce the amount of deferred compensation as the probability of bankruptcy or takeover increases. Combining this argument with the main bank model, we can show that if deferred compensation is used for insurance purposes, ζ_1 and θ_1 in (8a) and (8b) are positive: closer ties between the firm and its main bank increase the firm's survival probability, thereby strengthening the reliance of workers on deferred compensation.

Several comments about these two competing hypotheses are in order. First, the specific human capital model yields the same prediction as the worker-incentive model.[7] Thus within the present framework we cannot distinguish between these two hypotheses. Second, if workers have a wide choice of effort levels in the worker-incentive model, an increase in the firm's survival probability may not necessarily lead to a decrease in the level of deferred compensation (and the ratio of deferred compensation to current compensation). This is because an increase in the firm's survival probability may induce workers to choose a higher effort level. If this is the case, the firm needs to pay a higher amount of deferred compensation to prevent workers from shirking. Hence, even if the estimated sign of the coefficient on *MB* is positive, this finding may not determine whether deferred compensation plans are used for incentive-inducing or insurance purposes.

To summarize, we estimate equations (8) and test whether the estimated coefficients on *MB* are negative or positive. If they are significantly negative, the joint hypothesis of the worker-incentive (or specific human capital) and main bank model is supported. If the estimated coefficients are significantly positive, the joint hypothesis of the risk-sharing and main bank model will be consistent with the data although there remains the possibility that the results are evidence for the worker-incentive (or specific human capital) and main bank model. If the estimated coefficients are insignificantly different from zero, we have two possibilities: (1) the main bank hypothesis is rejected or (2) both the worker-incentive (the specific human capital) and the risk-sharing hypotheses are rejected. In this case, we cannot distinguish between these two possibilities.

11.4 EMPIRICAL METHOD

In this section, on the basis of microdata for both manufacturing and non-manufacturing firms in Japan, we develop the empirical procedure for testing the hypotheses presented in section 11.3. The precise definition and sources of the data are summarized in the Appendix.[8]

Our hypotheses are tested in three ways that correspond to which proxy we choose for the dependent variable.[9] We first discuss the cross-section regression test where the notional payments of retirement compensation are used to measure the dependent variable. In this test, we estimate only (8a). We do not employ (8b) because we cannot collect data on W_1 which are consistent with the data on W_2 presented below. To test the joint hypothesis of the worker-incentive and main bank model, we take the following cross-section regression:

$$W_{2i} = \zeta_0 + \zeta_1 MB_i + \zeta_2 p_i + \zeta'_3 X_{si} + \zeta'_4 X_{Di} + \epsilon_i, \qquad (9)$$
$$\quad\;\; (-) \qquad\;\; (-)$$

where the subscript i indicates firm i and ϵ_i is an error term. To test the joint hypothesis of the risk-sharing and main bank model, we employ the following cross-section regression form:

$$W_{2i} = \zeta_0 + \zeta_1 MB_i + \zeta_2 p_i + \zeta'_3 X_{si} + \zeta'_4 X_{Di} + \epsilon_i. \qquad (9')$$
$$\quad\;\; (+) \qquad\;\; (?)$$

Note that the risk-sharing and main bank model does not give any unambiguous sign of the coefficient on the firm's monitoring ability p_i because the risk-sharing model does not depend upon the firm's monitoring activity.

The dependent variable of equations (9) and (9') in this estimation is measured by the notional payments of retirement compensation, computed from the lump-sum compensation plus the present value of private pensions at the time of workers' retirement in each firm. These notional payments, $NPRC_i$, depend upon sex, educational attainment, job category, retirement age, rank and voluntary or involuntary retirement. Thus in subsequent estimation we use two kinds of cross-section data obtained from $NPRC_i$ for male workers who are retired at the mandatory age,[10] and two kinds of cross-section data taken from $NPRC_i$ for female workers who are voluntarily retired at age 25 or 27.[11]

However, these cross-section data of $NPRC_i$ are affected by wage differentials across firms. Although we could control for this effect by including as an explanatory variable the average monthly contract cash earnings of regular male (or female) workers in each firm, $AMCCEM_i$ (or $AMCCEF_i$), our estimation results would then have simultaneous biases because $AMCCEM_i$ (or $AMCCEF_i$) contains some elements of W_1. To avoid these simultaneity biases we take the ratio of $NPRC_i$ to $AMCCEM_i$ (or $AMCCEF_i$) – that is, $[NPRC/AMCCEM]_i$ (or $[NPRC/AMCCEF]_i$) – as a proxy of W_2 in our actual estimation. In fact, our main estimation results are not modified whichever procedure we choose to compensate for wage differentials across firms.

The key explanatory variable of equations (9) and (9′) is MB_i, which captures the effect on the implicit deferred payment due to the relation between firm i and its main bank. If the main bank relation is expected to increase the probability of survival of the firm, the arguments in the previous section suggest that the coefficient on MB_i is negative if retirement compensation is mainly used for incentive-inducing purposes. On the other hand, the coefficient on MB_i is predicted to be positive if retirement compensation is mainly used for risk-sharing purposes. We use two proxy variables for measuring MB_i:[12] (1) (the outstanding loans of the main bank to firm i)/(the total liabilities of firm i), $[LMB/L]_i$, and (2) the main bank dummy variable equalling unity for the firms which had not changed their main bank for the last three years, $MBDUM_i$.

The main bank is conventionally defined as the bank which has the largest lending share among private financial institutions that make loans to the firm. However, the major industrial groups in Japan – in particular, the nine largest industrial groups (Mitsubishi, Mitsui, Sumitomo, Fuyo, Dai-ichi Kangyo, Sanwa, Tokai, Daiwa, and Taiyo-Kobe) – each contain several financial institutions.[13] For example, the Mitsubishi group has the Mitsubishi Bank, Mitsubishi Trust Bank, Meiji Life Insurance, and Tokyo Fire and Marine Insurance. It is commonly believed that if a financial institution in an industrial group is viewed to be the main bank of a group firm, that financial institution can count on the help of the other financial institutions in the same group when performing its role as the main bank of the group firm. Thus, for each of the firms belonging to the nine largest industrial groups, we calculate $[LMB/L]_i$ by summing up the corresponding figure for each financial institution in the industrial group of which firm i is a member.

The monitoring ability of the firm, p_i, is measured by two proxy variables. One is the dummy variable equalling unity for the firms belonging to service industries, $[Service\ industry]_i$,[14] which reflects the intuition that if a worker shirks, the probability that he is caught is smaller in service industries than in non-service industries. The other is the number of regular employed workers of firm i, $[Employment\ size]_i$, which implies that an increase in the number of regular employed workers decreases the probability of the worker being caught shirking. The coefficients on both these two variables are expected to be positive in the worker-incentive and main bank model because an increase in $[Service\ industry]_i$ or $[Employment\ size]_i$ decreases p_i.[15] On the other hand, the predicted signs of the coefficients on these two variables are ambiguous in the risk–sharing and main bank model.

The term X_{si} is a vector of those control variables apart from MB_i which may be related to the firm's survival probability. In this research, X_{si} consists of two variables: (1) the ratio of the market value of equity to the sum of the total liabilities and the market value of equity of firm i, $[Equity/assets]_i$, and (2) the operating risk of firm i defined by the standard deviation of the ratio of the operating income to the net sales of firm i, $[Operating\ risk]_i$. The intuitive argument suggests that an increase in $[Equity/assets]_i$ raises the firm's survival probability because the firm is less likely to go bankrupt. However, the tax shields-bankruptcy costs hypothesis shows that there does not necessarily exist a positive relation between $[Equity/assets]_i$ and the firm's survival probability if firms select their capital structure by considering the attributes that determine various costs and benefits associated with debt and equity financing (see Castanias, 1983; Titman and Wessels, 1988; Kale, Noe and Ramirez, 1991). Thus, we cannot predict the effect of $[Equity/assets]_i$ on $[W_2/W_1]_i$ unambiguously. On the other hand, an increase in $[Operating\ risk]_i$ decreases the firm's survival probability. Hence, if deferred compensation plans are used for incentive-inducing purposes, it is immediate from (6) and (7) that the coefficient on $[Operating\ risk]_i$ is expected to be positive. If deferred compensation plans are used for risk-sharing purposes, the coefficient on $[Operating\ risk]_i$ is expected to be negative.

Clearly, the index of operating risk adopted here is an imperfect indicator of complexity of the environment in which the firm operates. It would be possible to construct more sophisticated measures of riskiness, using the theory of efficient markets. However, given that the reliability and robustness of such measures are open to question, it does not seem worthwhile to construct more sophisticated measures of riskiness.

The term X_{Di} is a vector of other control variables that may be related to differences of W_2 observed among firms. For $NPRC_i$ of male workers, X_{Di} consists of the retirement age of regular employees of firm i, $[Retirement\ age]_i$,[16] and the average length of service of regular male employees of firm i, $[LengthM]_i$. The variable $[Retirement\ age]_i$ is contained in the set of X_{Di} because an increase in $[Retirement\ age]_i$ results in a rise in $NPRC_i$. The variable $[LengthM]_i$ is included in the set of X_{Di}, since an increase in $[LengthM]_i$ raises $AMCCEM_i$, which is used to compensate for wage differentials among firms. The expected sign of the coefficient on $[Retirement\ age]_i$ is positive, whereas the expected sign of the coefficient on $[LengthM]_i$ is negative. For $NPRC_i$ of female workers, X_{Di} comprises only the average length of service of regular female employees of firm i, $[LengthF]_i$. The coefficient on $[LengthF]_i$ is expected to be negative.

We next proceed to consider the estimation of (9) and (9$'$) in which a proxy for the dependent variable is constructed from data on employee stock ownership plans of the firms belonging to the chemicals or the electrical machinery industry.[17] In this case, the dependent variable of equations (9) and (9$'$) is captured by the market value of the firm's shares per regular employee that are owned by the 'mochikabukai' (employee stock ownership association), $ESOP_i$.[18] Again, to control for wage differentials across firms, we divide $ESOP_i$ by the labour expenses per regular employee of firm i, LE_i. The explanatory variables in this estimation are the same as those in the estimation of (9) and (9$'$) for $NPRC_i$ of male workers except that $[Service\ industry]_i$ is dropped and that only the average length of service of regular employees of firm i, $[Length]_i$, is included in X_{Di}.

We finally discuss the estimation of (8) in which annual notional bonus payments are used as a proxy for the dependent variable. Since data on W_1 consistent with the data on W_2 are available in this case, we can use (8b) and rewrite it in the following form. To test the joint hypothesis of the worker-incentive and main bank model, we have

$$[W_2/W_1]_i = \theta_0 + \theta_1 MB_i + \theta_2 p_i + \theta'_3 X_{Si} + \theta_4 PROF_i + \epsilon_i, \quad (10)$$
$$\quad\quad\quad (-)\quad\quad (-)$$

where the subscript i indicates firm i, $PROF_i$ is the current profit per employee of firm i, and ϵ_i is an error term. To test the joint hypothesis of the risk-sharing and main bank model, we obtain

$$[W_2/W_1]_i = \theta_0 + \theta_1 MB_i + \theta_2 p_i + \theta'_3 X_{Si} + \theta_4 PROF_i + \epsilon_i. \quad (10')$$
$${(+)} \quad\quad {(?)}$$

Note that the risk-sharing and main bank model does not predict any unambiguous sign of the coefficient on p_i.

Several comments about equations (10) and $(10')$ are in order. First, to measure the dependent variable of equations (10) and $(10')$, we take the ratio of annual notional bonus compensation to annual notional wage compensation at age 35, $[ANBC/ANWC]_i$, multiplied by 10^2. Since the ratio of notional payment $[ANBC/ANWC]_i$ depends upon sex, educational attainment, job category, and rank, we use two kinds of cross-section data for male workers as defined in the Appendix. Second, the proxy variables for MB_i, p_i and X_{Si} in the estimation of (10) and $(10')$ are the same as those in the estimation of (9) and (9') for $NPRC_i$ of male workers. Thus, the predicted signs of the coefficients on these variables in (10) and $(10')$ are identical to those in (9) and (9'). Third instead of X_{Di}, the profit variable, $PROF_i$, is included as an explanatory variable to control for the effect of the firm's profit on the dependent variable. A number of studies have explored the role of the bonus system. In particular, Hashimoto (1979) and Freeman and Weitzman (1987) have supported the profit-sharing hypothesis that implies a positive correlation between profits and bonuses. These authors have suggested that the bonus system plays a key role in explaining wage flexibility and employment stability in the Japanese labour market. If the profit-sharing hypothesis is consistent with our data set, the coefficient on $PROF_i$ is expected to be positive.

11.5 EMPIRICAL RESULTS

Tables 11.1–11.6 provide the OLS regression estimates of (9) and (9') using cross-section data on the notional payments of retirement compensation, $NPRC/AMCCEM$ or $NPRC/AMCCEF$. Tables 11.7 and 11.8 list the OLS estimation results of (9) and (9') using cross-section data on employee stock ownership plans, $ESOP/LE$. Finally, Tables 11.9–11.11 give the OLS regression estimates of (10) and $(10')$ using cross-section data on the ratio of annual notional bonus compensation to annual notional wage compensation, $ANBC/ANWC$. All the data on the variables in Tables 11.1–11.6 and Tables 11.9–11.11 are taken from data for the fiscal year 1988 except that data on [*Operating risk*] are calculated over the 10 years, 1978–1987. Similarly, all the data on the variables in Tables 11.7 and 11.8 are obtained from data for the fiscal year 1987 except that data on [*Operating risk*] are calculated over the 10 years, 1977–1986.

We first discuss the regression results in Tables 11.1–11.3 for the notional payments of retirement compensation of male, white-collar workers. Table 11.1 reports the OLS regression estimates for *NPRC/ AMCCEM* of male, white-collar workers who are *college* graduates and are promoted to *senior* middle-ranking management level before retirement age. Table 11.2 gives the regression estimates for *NPRC/AMCCEM* of male, white-collar workers who are *senior high school* graduates and are promoted to *junior* middle-ranking management level before retirement age. We also provide the estimation results in Table 11.3 by combining the data used in Tables 11.1 and 11.2 with the dummy variable equalling unity for the data of senior high school graduates.

In these estimations, the estimated coefficients on the two main bank variables (*LMB/L* and *MBDUM*) – the key explanatory variables in our analysis – are broadly consistent with the risk-sharing and main bank model: (1) the estimated effects of *LMB/L* are positive and are significant at the 5 percent level in Tables 11.1 and 11.2 and at the 1 percent level in Table 11.3; and (2) the estimated effects of *MBDUM* are positive and are significant at the 10 percent level in Table 11.2 and at the 5 percent level in Table 11.3. Although some of the estimated coefficients on [*Operating risk*] and [*Retirement age*] are inconsistent with the risk-sharing and main bank model, these estimates are insignificant except for the coefficient on [*Operating risk*] estimated with *LMB/L* in Table 11.3. Since the index of [*Operating risk*] is not necessarily a reliable indicator of complexity of the environment in which the firm operates, the findings in Tables 11.1–11.3 can give some evidence for the risk-sharing and main bank model.

We next examine the regression estimates in Tables 11.4–11.6 for the notional payments of retirement compensation for female, white-collar workers. Table 11.4 lists the OLS regression estimates for *NPRC/ AMCCEF* of female, white-collar workers who are *junior college* graduates and are voluntarily retired at age 27. Table 11.5 indicates the estimation results for *NPRC/AMCCEF* of female, white-collar workers who are *senior high school* graduates and are voluntarily retired at age 25. We also provide the regression results in Table 11.6 by combining the data used in Tables 11.4 and 11.5 with the dummy variable equal-

Table 11.1   Estimation results for [*NPRC/AMCCEM*] of male, white-collar workers who are College graduates and are promoted to senior middle-ranking management level

Independent variable	Coefficient estimates (t-values in parentheses)	
Intercept	−40.86	−62.36
	(−0.6098)	(−0.8725)
LMB/L	1.326**	
	(2.370)	
MBDUM		8.342
		(1.251)
Service	3.535	4.964
industry	(0.4929)	(0.6617)
Employment	−0.000738	−0.002345
size	(−0.4920)	(−1.551)
Equity/	0.6563***	0.3401*
assets	(2.909)	(1.787)
Operating	−86.31	53.84
risk	(−0.2695)	(0.1640)
Retirement	1.719	2.333*
age	(1.418)	(1.839)
LengthM	−1.397**	−0.8188
	(−2.251)	(−1.387)
R^2	0.3098	0.2373
Number of samples	45	45

Notes:
***: 1% significant.
**: 5% significant.
*: 10% significant.

Table 11.2   Estimation results for [*NPRC/AMCCEM*] of male, white-collar workers who are Senior High School graduates and are promoted to junior middle-ranking management level

Independent variables	Coefficient estimates (t-values in parentheses)	
Intercept	88.96	70.98
	(1.241)	(0.9569)
LMB/L	1.387**	
	(2.288)	
MBDUM		11.77*
		(1.788)
Service	−7.868	−5.081

Table continued on page 328

328   *Deferred Payment Arrangements: the 'Main' Bank System*

Table 11.2   continued

Independent variables	Coefficient estimates (t-values in parentheses)	
industry	(−1.110)	(−0.7094)
Employment	−0.000638	−0.002386
size	(−0.4194)	(−1.553)
Equity/	0.3950*	0.07115
assets	(1.749)	(0.3968)
Operating	−728.1**	−624.2*
risk	(−2.274)	(−1.947)
Retirement	−0.04220	0.4843
age	(−0.03286)	(0.3691)
LengthM	−1.644***	−1.051*
	(−2.729)	(−1.910)
R^2	0.2821	0.2448
Number of samples	44	44

Notes:
***: 1% significant.
**: 5% significant.
*: 10% significant.

Table 11.3 Estimation results for [*NPRC/AMCCEM*] of male, white-collar workers who are College or Senior High School graduates and are promoted to senior middle-ranking or junior middle-ranking management level

Independent variable	Coefficient estimates (t-values in parentheses)	
Intercept	20.17	−0.09008
	(0.4175)	(0.001776)
LMB/L	1.365***	
	(3.359)	
MBDUM		10.03**
		(2.164)
Service	−2.603	−0.5572
industry	(−0.5242)	(−0.1092)
Employment	−0.000643	−0.002314**
size	(−0.6097)	(−2.175)
Equity/	0.5115***	0.1895
assets	(3.249)	(1.471)
Operating	412.2*	−286.2
risk	(1.845)	(−1.266)
Retirement	0.9786	1.560*
age	(1.126)	(1.736)

Table 11.3 continued

Independent variable	Coefficient estimates (t-values in parentheses)	
LengthM	−1.546***	−0.9593**
	(−3.626)	(−2.413)
Schooling	−6.085**	−6.124**
	(−2.066)	(−2.002)
R^2	0.2728	0.2161
Number of samples	89	89

Notes:
***: 1% significant.
**: 5% significant.
*: 10% significant.

Table 11.4   Estimation results for [*NPRC/AMCCEF*] of female, white-collar workers who are Junior College graduates

Independent variable	Coefficient estimates (t-values in parentheses)	
Intercept	5.202**	4.328**
	(2.689)	(2.366)
LMB/L	−0.08567	
	(−1.694)	
MBDUM		−0.9079
		(−1.215)
Service industry	0.5554	0.5093
	(0.7228)	(0.6441)
Employment size	−0.0000950	−0.0000195
	(−1.059)	(−0.2280)
Equity/ assets	−0.007443	0.01181
	(−0.3445)	(0.6582)
Operating risk	−5.057	−31.73
	(−0.1449)	(−1.016)
LengthF	−0.08167	−0.08887
	(−0.8595)	(−0.8979)
R^2	0.3003	0.2587
Number of samples	29	29

Note:
**: 5% significant.

Table 11.5   Estimation results for [*NPRC/AMCCEF*] of female, white-collar workers who are Senior High School graduates

Independent variable	Coefficient estimates (t-values in parentheses)	
Intercept	3.872**	2.592*
	(2.309)	(1.913)
LMB/L	−0.05743	
	(−1.331)	
MBDUM		−0.2766
		(−0.4625)
Service	0.4716	0.4827
industry	(0.6439)	(0.6469)
Employment	−0.0000358	−0.0000223
size	(−0.8803)	(−0.5497)
Equity/	−0.001208	0.01511
assets	(−0.06274)	(0.9510)
Operating	−27.62	−34.27
risk	(−1.193)	(−1.493)
LengthF	−0.008353	0.006814
	(−0.1363)	(0.1095)
R^2	0.1446	0.1131
Number of samples	49	49

Notes:
**: 5% significant.
*: 10% significant.

Table 11.6   Estimation results for [*NPRC/AMCCEF*] of female, white-collar workers who are Junior College or Senior High School graduates

Independent variable	Coefficient estimates (t-values in parentheses)	
Intercept	4.536***	3.240***
	(3.714)	(3.247)
LMB/L	−0.06296**	
	(−2.014)	
MBDUM		−0.4369
		(−0.9863)
Service	0.4437	0.4483
industry	(0.8641)	(0.8544)
Employment	−0.0000462	−0.0000265
size	(−1.360)	(−0.7872)
Equity/	−0.002804	0.01502
assets	(−0.2007)	(1.326)

Table 11.6 continued

Independent variable	Coefficient estimates (t-values in parentheses)	
Operating	−24.26	−33.63*
risk	(−1.385)	(−1.973)
LengthF	−0.03322	−0.01556
	(−0.6861)	(−0.3184)
Schooling	−0.3456	−0.3253
	(−1.210)	(−1.116)
R^2	0.1930	0.1579
Number of	78	78
samples		

Notes:
***: 1% significant.
**: 5% significant.
*: 10% significant.

ling unity for the data of senior high school graduates.

In these tables, the estimates of the coefficients on the two main bank variables (*LMB/L* and *MBDUM*) show less clear results than those in Tables 11.1–11.3: All of the estimated coefficients on the main bank variables are negative, but only the coefficient on *LMB/L* in Table 11.6 is significant. Furthermore, all of the estimated coefficients on [*Operating risk*] are negative, thus being inconsistent with the worker-incentive and main bank model.

Given the results in Tables 11.1–11.6, we summarize our evidence as follows: (1) an increase in the strength of ties generated by the main bank relation is expected to reduce the probability that the firm goes bankrupt or is taken over, and (2) retirement compensation for male workers is used for risk-sharing purposes. However, our findings are not robust enough to state that retirement compensation for female workers is used for incentive-inducing purposes.

Our conclusions should not be regarded as definitive because there are several caveats in order. First, we cannot generally succeed in controlling for the effect on the notional payments of retirement compensation of differences in ranking hierarchies across firms. Second, to control for wage differentials across firms, we divide the notional payments of retirement compensation of male (female) workers by the average monthly contract cash earnings of regular male (female) workers. In fact, data on the average monthly contract cash earnings of regular male (female) workers are not necessarily consistent with data on the notional payments of retirement compensation of male (female), white-collar workers who are college (junior college) or senior high school graduates.

We now proceed to explore the estimation results given in Tables 11.7 and 11.8. Table 11.7 presents the regression estimates for *ESOP/LE* of those firms of the chemicals industry whose shares are traded in the First Section of the Tokyo Stock Market. Table 11.8 provides the regression results for *ESOP/LE* of those firms of the electrical machinery industry whose shares are traded in the First Section of the Tokyo Stock Market. The estimated values in these two tables do not give enough evidence to conclude that employee stock ownership plans are used for insurance purposes. Although the estimates of the coefficients on the two main bank variables are positive, they are all insignificant.

One reason for this weak evidence may arise from the data restriction that, to control for the size of the employee stock ownership association, we must make do with using the number of regular employees instead of the number of members belonging to the employee stock ownership association. Another reason may be that we cannot necessarily succeed in controlling for the effect on employee stock ownership plans of wage differentials across firms.

Finally we examine the regression results in Tables 11.9–11.11. Table 11.9 reports the OLS regression estimates for *ANBC/ANWC* of male, white-collar workers who are *college* graduates. Table 11.10 presents the regression estimates for *ANBC/ANWC* of male, white-collar workers who are *senior high school* graduates. We also give the regression results in Table 11.11 by combining the data used in Tables 11.9 and 11.10 with the dummy variable equalling unity for the data of senior high school graduates. In these regressions, none of the estimated coefficients on the two main bank variables are significant except that the coefficient on *LMB/L* in Table 11.10 is negative and significant at the 10 percent level. Furthermore, the estimation results on the two main bank variables are mixed: the estimated effects of *LMB/L* are positive, whereas the estimated effects of *MBDUM* are negative. The estimates of the coefficients on the other explanatory variables also indicate ambiguous results. Given the empirical evidence in Tables 11.9–11.11, we can state that our dataset on bonus compensation is inconsistent with both the worker-incentive and the risk-sharing model.

One explanation for the insignificant estimated effects of the main bank variables on bonus compensation is that the lag of bonus compensation is at most seven months because bonus compensation is usually

Table 11.7 Estimation results for [*ESOP/LE*] of the chemicals industry

Independent variable	Coefficient estimates (t-values in parentheses)	
Intercept	17.75**	17.28**
	(2.040)	(2.059)
LMB/L	0.2090	
	(1.032)	
MBDUM		4.119
		(1.634)
Employment size	0.001322***	0.001328***
	(3.303)	(3.349)
Equity/ assets	0.1935**	0.1798**
	(2.038)	(2.329)
Operating risk	−121.2	−86.12
	(−1.490)	(−1.092)
Length	−0.09678**	−0.1039**
	(−2.362)	(−2.537)
R^2	0.2977	0.3104
Number of samples	92	92

Notes:
***: 1% significant.
**: 5% significant.

Table 11.8 Estimation results for [*ESOP/LE*] of the electrical machinery industry

Independent variable	Coefficient estimates (t-values in parentheses)	
Intercept	1.957	8.729
	(0.1618)	(0.8102)
LMB/L	0.4178	
	(1.268)	
MBDUM		1.743
		(0.4348)
Employment size	0.0000638	0.0000214
	(0.5293)	(0.1837)
Equity/ assets	0.3286***	0.2371**
	(2.650)	(2.365)
Operating risk	−131.7	−108.6
	(−1.193)	(−0.9898)
Length	−0.04153	−0.05374
	(−0.8286)	(−1.046)

Table continued on page 334

Table 11.8   Continued

Independent variable	Coefficient estimates (t-values in parentheses)	
R^2	0.1223	0.1096
Number of samples	104	104

Notes:
***: 1% significant.
**: 5% significant.

Table 11.9   Estimation results for [*ANBC/ANWC*] of male, white-collar workers who are College Graduates

Independent variable	Coefficient estimates (t-values in parentheses)	
Intercept	71.48**	66.19**
	(2.605)	(2.356)
LMB/L	−0.1178	
	(−0.1546)	
MBDUM		3.283
		(0.3092)
Service industry	−7.069	−7.662
	(−0.7557)	(−0.8314)
Employment size	−0.000581	−0.000567
	(−0.3565)	(−0.3570)
Equity/ assets	−0.5243	−0.4963
	(−1.231)	(−1.162)
Operating risk	−47.47	−54.89
	(−0.2352)	(−0.2779)
PROF	1.279	1.306
	(0.5532)	(0.5854)
R^2	0.05850	0.06010
Number of samples	49	49

Note:
**: 5% significant.

Table 11.10 Estimation results for [*ANBC/ANWC*] of male, white-collar workers who are Senior High School graduates

Independent variable	Coefficient estimates (t-values in parentheses)	
Intercept	26.17***	22.60***
	(9.077)	(8.097)
LMB/L	−0.1202*	
	(−1.689)	
MBDUM		0.9201
		(0.8984)
Service	0.5993	−0.01517
industry	(0.5539)	(−0.01393)
Employment	0.0000645	0.0000911
size	(0.7654)	(1.070)
Equity/	0.05728	0.08728**
assets	(1.363)	(2.172)
Operating	−17.82	−27.71
risk	(−0.9594)	(−1.556)
PROF	0.3110*	0.3313*
	(1.872)	(1.957)
R^2	0.3364	0.3086
Number of samples	55	55

Notes:
***: 1% significant.
**: 5% significant.
*: 10% significant.

Table 11.11 Estimation results for [*ANBC/ANWC*] of male, white-collar workers who are College or Senior High School graduates

Independent variable	Coefficient estimates (t-values in parentheses)	
Intercept	49.81***	44.99***
	(3.731)	(3.416)
LMB/L	−0.1528	
	(−0.4382)	
MBDUM		2.040
		(0.4138)
Service	−2.685	−3.387
industry	(−0.5639)	(−0.7201)
Employment	−0.0000901	−0.0000494
size	(−0.1771)	(−0.09862)

Table continued on page 336

Table 11.11   continued

Independent variable	Coefficient estimates (t-values in parentheses)	
Equity/ assets	−0.2193 (−1.104)	−0.1871 (−0.9720)
Operating risk	−32.36 (−0.3521)	−42.87 (−0.4885)
PROF	0.6322 (0.6968)	0.6835 (0.7614)
Schooling	−3.862 (−1.053)	−4.042 (−1.106)
R^2	0.03711	0.03690
Number of samples	104	104

Note:
***: 1% significant.

paid in July and December in Japanese firms. Since workers have little concern about the possibility of the firm being bankrupted or taken over seven months later, it is not surprising that bonus compensation does not necessarily depend upon the main bank variables.

Several recent studies have explored the role of the bonus system. Hashimoto (1979) and Freeman and Weitzman (1987) have supported the profit-sharing hypothesis (1) that there exists a positive correlation between profits and bonuses, and (2) that the bonus system plays a key role in explaining wage flexibility and employment stability in the Japanese labour market. On the other hand, Ohashi (1989) has obtained some evidence for the efficiency wage hypothesis that bonuses are paid by firms to compensate employees for the intensity of work experienced during the last period. Since we have discussed the role of deferred compensation plans in a variant of the efficiency-wage model, our empirical findings seem to be inconsistent with the efficiency-wage hypothesis for the role of bonus payments. Nevertheless, these findings should not be regarded as definitive because our model is considerably different from the model of Ohashi (1989).

11.6   CONCLUSION

On the basis of Japanese microdata, we have examined how deferred compensation plans of the firm are affected by the relation of the firm to the main bank. Our empirical results have given some evidence (1) that in labour contract arrangements, the main bank relation is expected to reduce the probability of the firm becoming bankrupt or being taken over, and (2) that retirement compensation for male workers is used for insurance purposes. These empirical findings have supported the 'institutional complementarity' suggested by Aoki (1989, 1990) that the combination of life-time employment contracts (with deferred compensation plans) and main bank relations (with intercorporate shareholdings) provides an efficient mechanism through which individual wealth-risk is diversified and thereby reduced. However, our estimation results have not been robust enough to conclude that retirement compensation for female workers is used for incentive-inducing purposes, or that employee stock ownership plans are used for insurance purposes. Furthermore, our empirical evidence has been inconsistent with the hypothesis that bonus compensation is used for incentive-inducing or insurance purposes.

Our research can shed new light on the role of the main bank system in Japan. Recently a number of studies have dealt with the effects of the financial relationship of the firm with its main bank on capital structure and corporate investment (See Hoshi, Kashyap, and Scharfstein, 1990, 1991; Ikeo and Hirota, 1991; Okazaki and Horiuchi, 1991). Our empirical findings show that the main bank relation has a significant effect not only on capital structure and corporate investment but also on long-term labour contract arrangements.

Data Appendix

In this Appendix we first provide precise definitions and sources of the data. Then we list the firms upon which our empirical work is based.

Definitions and Data Sources of the Variables

(1) [*NPRC*]: The notional payments of retirement compensation defined by the total amount of lump-sum compensation plus the present value of private pensions at the time of workers' retirement from the firm.[19] Four kinds of cross-section data for NPRC are taken from the *Taishokukin Nenkin Jijyo* (Current Report on Retirement Compensation), Romu Gyosei Kenkyudyo (Institute of Labor Administration), 1989. (1) NPRC for male, white-collar workers who are college graduates and are promoted to senior middle-ranking management level before retirement age. (2) NPRC for male, white-collar workers who are senior high school graduates and are promoted to junior middle-ranking management level before retirement age. (3) NPRC for female, white-collar workers who are junior college graduates and are voluntarily retired at age 27. (4) NPRC for female, white-collar workers who are senior high school graduates and are voluntarily retired at age 25.

(2) [*AMCCEM*]: The average monthly contract cash earnings of regular male workers of the firm taken from the *Current Report on Retirement Compensation*, Institute of Labor Administration, 1989.

(3) [*AMCCEF*]: The average monthly contract cash earnings of regular female workers of the firm taken from the *Current Report on Retirement Compensation*, Institute of Labor Administration, 1989.

(4) [*MB*]: The strength of ties of the firm to its main bank. This index is measured in the following two ways. (1) [LMB/L]: (The outstanding loans of the main bank to the firm)/(The total liabilities of the firm). The numerator is reported in the *Kigyo Keiretsu Soran*, Toyokeizai Shinposha, 1988 (for Tables 11.7 and 11.8) and 1989 (for Tables 11.1–11.6, 11.9–11.11). The denominator is collected from the *Yuka Shoken Hokokusho* (Report on Securities), 1988 (for Tables 11.7 and 11.8) and 1989 (for Tables 11.1–11.6, 11.9–11.11). (2) [MBDUM]: The dummy variable is equal to unity for the firms which had a main bank and had not changed the main bank for the last three years.

In the index of LMB/L, the main bank is defined as the bank which has the largest lending share among private financial institutions that make loans to the firm. In fact, for each of the firms belonging to the nine largest industrial groups (Mitsubishi, Mitsui, Sumitomo, Fuyo, Dai-ichi Kangyo, Sanwa, Tokai, Daiwa, and Taiyo–Kobe), the index of LMB/L is measured by summing the corresponding figure for each financial institution in the industrial group of which the firm is a member. In the index of MBDUM, the main bank is defined according to the criteria of

338

Kigyo Keiretsu Soran, so that some of our sampling firms are classified as firms which do not have a main bank.

(5) [*Service industry*]: The dummy variable is equal to unity for the firms belonging to commerce, real estate, warehouse, and other service industries excluding the transportation, communication, and electric and gas industries.

(6) [*Employment size*]: The number of regular employees of the firm taken from the *Report on Securities*, 1988 (for Tables 11.7 and 11.8) and 1989 (for Tables 11.1–11.6, 11.9–11.11).

(7) [*Equity/assets*]: (The outstanding shares of the firm)×(The market value of the firm's shares on 31 March)/[(The total liabilities of the firm) + (The outstanding shares of the firm)×(The market value of the firm's shares on 31 March)]. These data are taken from the *Report on Securities*, 1988 (for Tables 11.7 and 11.8) and 1989 (for Tables 11.1–11.6, 11.9–11.11).

(8) [*Operating risk*]: The standard deviation of the ratio of the operating income to the net sales of the firm obtained from the *Report on Securities*, 1979–88 (for Tables 11.7 and 11.8) and 1980–89 (for Tables 11.1–11.6, 11.9–11.11).

(9) [*Retirement age*]: The retirement age of regular employees of the firm obtained from the *Current Report on Retirement Compensation*, Institute of Labor Administration, 1989.[20]

(10) [*LengthM*]: The average length of service of regular male employees of the firm taken from the *Current Report on Retirement Compensation*, Institute of Labor Administration, 1989.

(11) [*LengthF*]: The average length of service of regular female employees of the firm taken from the *Current Report on Retirement Compensation*, Institute of Labor Administration, 1989.

(12) [*Schooling*]: The dummy variable is equal to unity for the data for senior high school graduates.

(13) [*ESOP*]: [The holding ratio of the firm's shares that are owned by the mochikabukai (employee stock ownership association)]×[The market value of the firm's shares on 31 March 1988]/[Employment size]. Data on the first variable are collected from the *Okabunushi Soran*, Toyokeizai Shinposha, 1992.

(14) [*LE*]: The labour expenses per regular employee taken from the *Report on Securities*, 1988.

(15) [*Length*]: The average length of service of regular employees of the firm taken from the *Report on Securities*, 1988.

(16) [*ANBC/ANWC*]: The ratio of annual notional bonus compensation to annual notional wage compensation at age 35, which is multiplied by 10^2. The annual notional wage compensation consists of annual notional contract cash earnings and annual notional bonus payments. Two kinds of cross-section data for [ANBC/ANWC] are taken from the *Nenkan Chingin Syoyo no Jittai* (Actual State of Annual Wages and Business), Institute of Labor Administration, 1989. (1) [ANBC/ANWC] for male, white-collar workers who are college graduates. (2) [ANBC/ANWC] for male, white-collar workers who are senior high school graduates.

(17) [*PROF*]: The current profit of the firm taken from the *Report on Securities*, 1989.

Lists of the Firms

(1) List of the firms upon which the empirical analysis in Tables 11.1–11.6 is based.

Note that we do not use all the sampling firms in any table because the sampling firms do not necessarily have data available for the test of our estimating equations in every table.

Nichiro[34] Gyogyo Kaisha	Taiyo Fishery[2]	Fujita[1234]	Nishimatsu[1234] Construction
Nippon[134] Koei	Nitto Flour[134] Milling	Meito[12] Sangyo	Fujiya[12]
Morozoff[1234]	Nippon Meat[124] Packers	Itoham[2] Foods	Toyo Jozo[1234]
Kikkoman[14]	Daiwabo[1234]	Kureha[124] Chemical Industry	Daido Sanso[124]
Nippon[1234] Chemical Industrial	Daisel[1234] Chemical Industries	Sekisui[1234] Chemical	Nippon Zeon[12]
Nichiban[1234]	Nippon[124] Kayaku	Nippon[1234] Paint	Lion[4]
NGK[1234] Insulators	Nichias[1234]	Aichi[4] Steel Works	Showa[124] Electric Wire & Cable
Toshiba[124] Tungaloy	Howa[1234] Machinery	Komori[234] Printing Machinery	Daikin[34] Industries
Tsubakimoto[124] Chain	Daifuku[124]	Copyer[1234]	Toyo Denki[1234] Seizo
Kyosan[4] Electric Mfg	TEAC[12]	Yokogawa[124] Electric	Shindengen[124] Electric
Yamatake[124] Honeywell	Honda[4] Motor	Shimano[124] Industrial	Tokyo[124] Keiki
Sankyo[1234] Seiki Mfg	Shin-Etsu[12] Polymer	Tsukamoto[13] Syoji	Tokyu[124] Department Store

The[1234] Daimaru	Sogo[12]	Yunido Daiei[124]	Mitsubishi[1234] Warehouse & Transportation
The Sumitomo[12] Warehouse	Ajinomoto[4]	Terumo[34]	Kawasaki[34] Steel
Sumitomo[34] Light Metal Industries	Toyota[34] Automatic Loom works	Kyokuyo[1234]	

Notes
1. Data on these firms are used in Tables 11.1 and 11.3.
2. Data on these firms are used in Tables 11.2 and 11.3.
3. Data on these firms are used in Tables 11.4 and 11.6.
4. Data on these firms are used in Tables 11.5 and 11.6.

(2) List of the firms upon which the empirical analysis in Tables 11.9–11.11 is based.

Note that we do not use all the sampling firms in any table because the sampling firms do not necessarily have data available for the test of our estimating equations in every table.

Kanto[12] Natural Gas Development	Kajima[12]	Tekken[1] Construction	Nissan[1] Construction
Nishimatsu[12] Construction	Toyo[12] Construction	Raito Kogyo[12]	Nitto Flour[1] Milling
Fujiya[12]	Asahi[1] Breweries	Toyo Jozo[1]	Sanyo Coca-cola[12] Bottling
Ajinomoto[12]	Daido[12] Worsted Mills	Toho Rayon[2]	Kanzaki Paper[2] Mfg.
Rengo[1]	Mitsui[2] Toatsu Chemical	Kureha[12] Chemical Industry	Nippon Soda[2]
Nippon[12] Sanso	Nippon[12] Chemical Industrial	Daisel[12] Chemical Industries	Sumitomo[2] Bakelite
Sekisui[2] Chemical	Nippon Zeon[2]	Nippon[2] Kayaku	Asahi Denka[2] Kogyo
Dai-chi[2] Kogyo	Sanyo[2] Chemical	Kaken[12] Pharmaceutical	Nippon Paint[12]

Seiyaku	Industries		
Toyo Ink[1] Mfg	Fuji Photo[2] Film	Konica[2]	Cemedine[12]
INAX[1]	Toho[12] Titanium	Niigata[2] Engineering	Takuma[1]
Toshiba[2] Tungaloy	Toyota[1] Automatic Loom works	Howa[12] Machinery	Komori[12] Printing Machinery
Daikin[2] Industries	Juki[12]	Yamatake[2] Honeywell	Daihatsu[1] Motor
Aichi[2] Machine Industry	Honda[2] Motor	Tokyo Keiki[2]	Canon[2] Electronics
Copal[12]	Sankyo[12] Seiki Mfg.	Naigai[1]	Tsukamoto[1] Syoji
Nomura[1]	Tokyu[12] Department Store	The Daimaru[12]	Matsuzakaya[12]
Sogo[12]	Meitetsu[12] Hyakkaten	Tobu[2] Railway	Sagami[2] Railway
Hankyu[12]	Senko[12]	Shinki[1] Bus	Mitsui O.S.K.[1] Lines
Mitsubishi[12] Warehouse & Transportation	Yokkaichi[1] Warehouse	Tokyo[12] Broadcasting System	Tokyo[12] Theatres

Notes
1. Data on these firms are used in Tables 11.9 and 11.11.
2. Data on these firms are used in Tables 11.10 and 11.11.

Notes

*   An earlier version of this chapter was presented at the Biwako Conference, Osaka (July 1992). We thank Hiroyuki Chuma, Yoshifumi Nakata, Stephen Nickell, Fumio Ohtake, Masahiro Okuno, Toshiaki Tachibanaki, Robert Topel, Kotaro Tsuru, and Hiroshi Yoshikawa for their helpful comments and suggestions. We are also grateful to Randal Watson for editing the English of our manuscript.

1. For the related literature, see Sheard (1992).
2. Using US firms data, a number of researchers have examined the empirical issues of an increase in labour costs caused by the breach of trust of implicit long-term contracts or pension plans in the event of takeovers. See Brown and Medoff (1988), Shleifer and Summers (1988), Bhagat, Shleifer, and Vishny (1990), Pontiff, Shleifer, and Weisbach (1990), Rosett (1990), and Ippolito and James (1992).
3. See Nakatani (1984), Suzuki and Wright (1985), Osano and Tsutsui (1985), Sheard (1986), Hoshi, Kashyap and Scharfstein (1990), and Fujiwara (1991) for empirical studies. For the theoretical mechanism see Osano (1991).
4. See Curme and Kahn (1990). For the detailed theoretical analysis, see Osano and Serita (1992).
5. For the detailed theoretical analysis, see Osano and Serita (1992).
6. See Nakatani (1984), Suzuki and Wright (1985), Osano and Tsutsui (1985), Sheard (1986), Hoshi, Kashyap and Scharfstein (1990), and Fujiwara (1991) for the empirical study. For the theoretical mechanism, see Osano (1991).
7. Even though we assume that workers decide whether or not to invest in specific human capital instead of choosing whether or not to work, we can derive the same implications suggested by the worker-incentive model presented here.
8. Since our data sources include only a small number of sampling firms, we select all the sampling firms whose data are available for the estimation of our equations. Thus, our choice of sampling firms may not be random.
9. Note that not only the set of sampling firms but also the source of the data depends upon the proxy variables which we adopt for the dependent variable.
10. Since a number of firms force their workers to retire before the mandatory retirement age, the firms have no workers who are retired at the mandatory retirement age. In this early retirement case, we take the maximal retirement age of the retired workers instead of the stipulated mandatory retirement age.
11. In Japan, most female workers who are employed by firms immediately after graduating from school are voluntarily retired around age 26 because of marriage or other reasons.
12. Ikeo and Hirota (1991) and Okazaki and Horiuchi (1991) use a similar proxy variable.
13. In our sampling period, the Taiyo-Kobe group did not merge with the Mitsui group.
14. More precisely, the dummy variable is equal to unity for the firms belonging to commerce, real estate, warehouse, and the other service industries excluding transportation, communication, and electric and gas industries.
15. In fact, the effect of [*Employment size*]$_i$ on deferred compensation may be caused through the mechanism in which [Employment size]$_i$ is expected to raise the firm's survival probability. If this effect dominates the effect of [Employment size]$_i$ on deferred compensation through monitoring ability, the estimated coefficient on [Employment size]$_i$ may be negative under the worker-incentive and main bank model.

16. As mentioned in n. 10 above, we need to use as [Retirement age], the maximal retirement age of retired workers instead of their mandatory retirement age.
17. The chemicals industry defined here excludes the firms belonging to the medicines industry.
18. Since we do not have data on the number of 'mochikabukai' (employee stock ownership association) members, we must make do with using the number of regular employees to control for the size of the mochikabukai.
19. See n. 16 above.
20. See n. 16 above.

References

Aoki, M. (1989) 'The Nature of the Japanese Firm as a Nexus of Employment and Financial Contracts: An Overview', *Journal of the Japanese and International Economies*, vol. 3, pp. 345–66.

———— (1990) 'Toward an Economic Model of the Japanese Firm', *Journal of Economic Literature*, vol. 28, p. 1–27.

Becker, G. (1975) *Human Capital*, Chicago, University of Chicago Press.

Bhagat, S., A. Shleifer and R.W. Vishny (1990) 'Hostile Takeovers in the 1980s: The Return to Corporate Specialization', *Brooking Papers on Economic Activity: Microeconomics*, vol. 2, pp. 1–84.

Brown, C. and J.L. Medoff (1988) 'The Impact of Firm Acquisitions on Labor', in A.J. Auerbach (ed.), *Corporate Takeovers: Causes and Consequences* Chicago, University of Chicago Press.

Castanias, R. (1983) 'Bankruptcy Risk and Optimal Capital Structure', *Journal of Finance*, vol. 38, pp. 1617–35.

Curme, M. and L.M. Kahn (1990) 'The Impact of the Threat of Bankruptcy on the Structure of Compensation', *Journal of Labor Economics*, vol. 8, pp. 419–47.

Freeman, R.F. and M.L. Weitzman (1987) 'Bonuses and Employment in Japan', *Journal of the Japanese and International Economies*, vol. 1, June, pp. 168–94.

Fujiwara, K. (1991) 'Kigyo Tousan to Mein Banku sei: Mein Banku no Hoken Teikyo Kinou ni Tsuite' (Firm Bankruptcy and the Main Bank System: The Insurance Role of the Main Bank), Hiroshima University, mimeo.

Harris, M. and B. Holmstrom (1982) 'A Theory of Wage Dynamics', *Review of Economic Studies*, vol. 49, pp. 315–53.

Hart, O. and J. Moore (1988) 'Incomplete Contracts and Renegotiation', *Econometrica*, vol. 56, pp. 755–85.

Hashimoto, M. (1979) 'Bonus Payments, On-the-job Training and Lifetime Employment in Japan', *Journal of Political Economy*, vol. 87, pp. 1086–104.

Hoshi, T., A. Kashyap, and D. Scharfstein (1990) 'The Role of Banks in Reducing the Costs of Financial Distress in Japan?', *Journal of Financial Economics*, vol. 27, pp. 67–88.

———— (1991) 'Corporate Structure Liquidity and Investment: Evidence from Japanese Industrial Groups', *Quarterly Journal of Economics*, vol. 106, pp. 33–60.

Ikeo, K. and S. Hirota (1991) 'Nihon Kigyo no Shihon Kosei: Eijansi – cosuto to Ginko' (Capital Structure of the Japanese Firm: Agency Costs and Banks), in A. Horiuchi and N. Yoshino (eds), *Gendai Nihon no Kinyu Bunseki* (Structural Analysis of the Japanese Financial System) Tokyo, University of Tokyo Press.

Ippolito, R.A. and W.H. James (1992) 'LBOs, Reversions and Implicit Contracts', *Journal of Finance*, vol. 47, pp. 139–67.

Kale, J.R., T.H. Noe and G. Ramirez (1991) 'The Effect of Business Risk on Corporate Capital Structure: Theory and Evidence', *Journal of Finance*, vol. 46, pp. 1693–715.

Lazear, E.P. (1979) 'Why Is There Mandatory Retirement?', *Journal of Political Economy*, vol. 87, pp. 1261–84.

Merton, R.C. (1985) Comment (on Diamond and Mirrlees), in D. Weiss (ed.), *Pensions, Labor, and Individual Choice*, Chicago, University of Chicago Press.

Nakatani, I. (1984) 'The Economic Role of Financial Corporate Grouping', in M. Aoki (ed.), *The Economic Analysis of the Japanese Firm*, Amsterdam, North-Holland, pp. 227–58.

Ohashi, I. (1989) 'On the Determinants of Bonuses and Basic Wages in Large Japanese Firms', *Journal of the Japanese and International Economies*, vol. 3, pp. 451–79.

Okazaki, R. and A. Horiuchi (1991) 'Kigyo no Setubi Toshi to Mein Banku Kankei' (Plant and Equipment Investment of the Firm and the Main Bank Relation), in A. Horiuchi and N. Yoshino (eds), *Gendai Nihon no Kinyu Bunseki* (Structural Analysis of the Japanese Financial System), Tokyo, University of Tokyo Press.

Osano, H. (1991) 'Default and Renegotiation in Financial Distress with Multiple Banks Model: The Analysis for the Japanese Main Bank System', Osaka University, mimeo.

Osano, H. and T. Serita (1992) 'Deferred Compensation Programs and the Banking System in Japan', Osaka University, mimeo.

Osano, H. and Y. Tsutsui (1986) Credit Rationing and Implicit Contract Theory, *International Journal of Industrial Organization*, vol. 4, pp. 419–38.

Pontiff, J., A. Shleifer and M.S. Weisbach (1990) 'Reversions of Excess Pension Assets After Takeovers', *RAND Journal of Economics*, vol. 21, pp. 600–13.

Rosett, J.G. (1990) 'Do Union Wealth Concessions Explain Takeover Premiums?' *Journal of Financial Economics*, vol. 27, pp. 263–82.

Shapiro, C. and J.E. Stiglitz (1984) 'Equilibrium Unemployment as a Worker–Discipline Device', *American Economic Review*, vol. 74, pp. 433–44.

Sheard, P. (1986) 'Main Banks and Internal Capital Markets in Japan', *Shoken Keizai*, vol. 157, pp. 255–85.

—— (1992) 'Interlocking Shareholding, Corporate Governance, and the Japanese Firm', *Richerche Economiche*, vol. 45, pp. 421–48.

Shleifer, A. and L.H. Summers (1988) 'Breach of Trust in Hostile Takeovers', in A.J. Auerbach (ed.), *Corporate Takeovers: Causes and Consequences*, Chicago, University of Chicago Press.

Suzuki, S. and R. Wright (1985) 'Financial Structure and Bankruptcy Risk in Japanese Companies', *Journal of International Business Studies*, pp. 97–110.

Titman, S. and R. Wessels (1988) 'The Determinants of Capital Structure Choice', *Journal of Finance*, vol. 43, pp. 1–19.

Part IV

Unions

12 The Determinants of Labour Disputes in Japan: A Comparison with the US

Fumio Ohtake and Joseph S. Tracy*

An important issue in the study of labour unions is the design of the mechanism for setting the terms and conditions of employment for the workers in the bargaining unit. Comparing the structure of bargaining between Japan and the US is of particular interest given the common legal roots and the different evolution of unionism in each country. Postwar labour law in Japan was modelled closely after the Wagner Act. However, Japan did not follow the US movement toward long-term contracts in the 1950s, nor did industrial unions evolve as an important bargaining structure. A cooperative model for unionism has prevailed in Japan, with confrontation replaced largely by consultation.

In this chapter we compare the mechanism for collective bargaining in Japan and the US. We present empirical results on the determinants of strikes and disputes in Japan. Our primary findings are that difficulties in reaching a settlement increase during periods of low unemployment and uncertainty over inflation. In comparison to the US, there is some evidence that strike activity in Japan depends less on firm specific uncertainty and more on general macro uncertainty.

12.1 DISPUTE INCIDENCE IN THE US AND JAPAN

Collective bargaining in Japan is known for its relative absence of strike activity. Figure 12.1 shows that the number of working days lost due to strike activity per 10 employees in Japan is much less than that in the US, especially after the first oil shock. The decrease in strike activity in Japan is one of the causes of the improvement in productivity in Japan. There are many theories as to why unions and

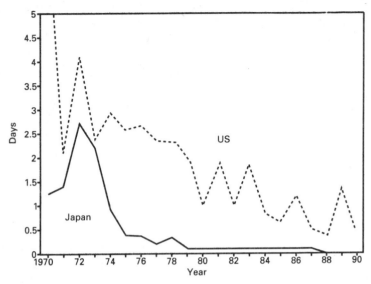

Figure 12.1   Working days lost per 10 employees in Japan and US, 1970–90

firms in Japan are able to conduct negotiations without resorting to strikes. We will evaluate these later in the chapter. However, even in the US, strikes represent only 18 percent of the total number of contract disputes. Cramton and Tracy (1992) show that a prominent feature of collective bargaining in the US is the holdout: negotiations often continue without a strike after the contract has expired. Dispute incidence defined to include both strikes and holdouts has averaged around 58 percent in the US over the last two decades. A more complete view of collective bargaining in Japan requires a comparison of overall dispute rates in addition to strike rates.

Table 12.1 compares the strike and dispute rates in each country. The figures for the US include bargaining units with at least 1000 workers.[1] The figures for Japan include bargaining units of all size categories. Column (1) shows the published data on dispute incidence in Japan. According to these data, the dispute rate in Japan has been declining from 5.3 percent in the early 1970s to 1.6 percent in the late 1980s. The level of dispute activity is very low in comparison to the US.

This order of magnitude difference in dispute rates in fact reflects non-comparable definitions of what constitutes a dispute. In the *Survey on Labour Dispute Statistics*, which is the official survey on labour disputes conducted by Japan's Ministry of Labour, a dispute is

Table 12.1 Strike and dispute rates for Japan and the US

Year	Dispute incidence (%) (1)			Strike incidence (%) (2)		Dispute duration (days) (3)		Strike duration (days) (4)	
	JPN-1	JPN-2	US	JPN	US	JPN	US	JPN	US
70–74	5.3	70.0	54.3	2.9	12.1	39.8	102.2	2.7	41.1
75–79	4.8	80.3	53.3	1.7	12.6	32.7	74.1	2.1	47.8
80–84	2.7	67.3	93.4	0.7	7.8	29.2	93.4	1.9	41.9
85–89	1.5	61.9	71.4	0.4	9.1	31.0	70.5	1.9	36.3
70–89	3.6	69.9	58.9	1.4	10.2	33.2	83.0	2.2	42.5

Note: Strike rates for the US are based on strike data provided by the Bureau of Labor Statistics and the Bureau of National Affairs. The bargaining dates used to construct the dispute rates are provided by the Bureau of Labour Statistics. All US data refer to bargaining units with at least 1000 workers. Strike and dispute frequencies for Japan are taken from the *Survey on Labour Disputes Statistics* published by the Ministry of Labour. Strike and dispute rates are calculated by dividing the relevant frequency by the number of unions. Data on the number of unions is reported in the *Basic Survey on Labour Unions* published every June by the Ministry of Labour.

defined to be any negotiation involving 'acts of dispute' or settled by third-party intervention. As such, the measured dispute rate does not include all holdouts. However, holdouts are a common occurrence during the Shunto (Spring Wage Offensive) in Japan. A common form of holdout is refusal of overtime or holiday work.

In order to make the dispute rates more comparable, we construct a broader measure of disputes for Japan. Most labour contracts in Japan are annual with expirations in the end of March. Wage increases negotiated in the spring are typically made effective during the period from 20–25 April. Settlements between the end of March and the first wage payment in April result in no loss or deferment of wages to workers. Consequently, we define a holdout as a settlement which takes place after 21 April (and which does not involve a strike).

Our broader definition of disputes during the Spring Wage Offensive includes all strikes and holdouts as defined above. Column (2) of Table 12.1 gives the dispute rates for Japan disaggregated by five year intervals. Over the last two decades the dispute incidence in Japan has averaged nearly 70 percent, higher than the US average. In contrast with the US, the dispute rate for Japan was lower in the 1980s than in the 1970s. Figures 12.2–12.3 present the annual time series on strikes

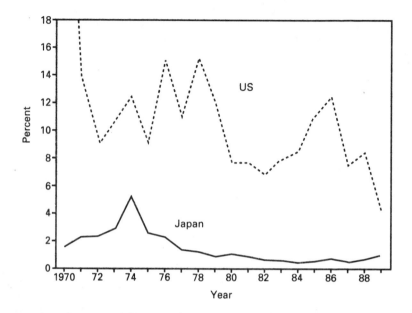

Figure 12.2   Strike incidence in Japan and US, 1970–90

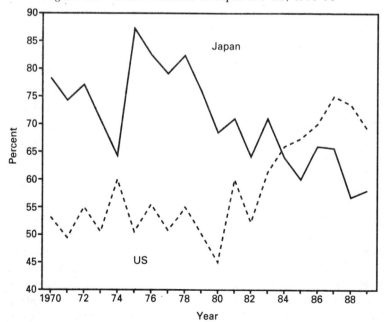

Figure 12.3   Dispute incidence in Japan and US, 1970–90

and disputes rates for each country over the past two decades. While dispute rates are higher in Japan, dispute durations are on average shorter by 50 days. Similarly, strike durations in Japan are quite short as compared to the US.

Several important features of collective bargaining in Japan relative to the US emerge from these comparisons. Overall dispute rates are more comparable between the two countries than the official statistics would suggest. However, the composition of disputes in Japan is strongly shifted toward holdouts and away from strikes. Finally, disputes are resolved more quickly in Japan, resulting in significantly lower dispute durations.

12.2   COMPARISON OF COLLECTIVE BARGAINING IN THE US AND JAPAN

The sharp contrast in strike activity between the US and Japan has generated considerable discussion of the reasons why collective bargaining appears to be more harmonious in Japan. This is part of a larger debate on the differences between the two countries in the structure of unions, work environments, and labour markets. We will use an asymmetric information model of bargaining to evaluate these explanations, as well as to suggest some new factors for consideration. This class of model is useful in that it provides a unified framework for evaluating each hypothesis.

The basic idea behind the asymmetric information bargaining literature is that contract negotiations are an attempt to arrive at a division of the rents to the firm and the bargaining unit. These rents represent the difference between the joint value of a settlement to the firm and union and the joint value of a disagreement. We assume in our discussion that it is efficient for the bargaining unit to continue operations, implying that rents exist.

This class of model suggests that uncertainty over rents is the critical determinant of disputes. If the magnitude of the rents were known to both the union and the firm, then rational bargaining would probably lead to an immediate settlement without costly disputes. In contrast, when there are informational asymmetries concerning the size of this surplus, then disputes can serve as signalling or screening mechanisms which convey information between the parties to the negotiation. In particular, when the firm is fully informed and the union lacks information on the magnitude of the rents, disputes provide a way in 'bad' times for the firm to convince the union that rents are small, and therefore that the union should settle for a low wage. The model predicts that greater uncertainty over rents will result in higher dispute rates and longer dispute durations.

Cramton and Tracy (1992) extend the basic bargaining model by allowing the union a choice between striking or holding out by negotiating under an expired contract. The tradeoff facing the union when making this threat decision is that strikes generally result in higher wage gains, but involve on average a higher bargaining cost to the union. Strikes will tend to be the preferred threat when the wage under the prior contract is relatively low.

With this basic bargaining model in mind, we would like to evaluate the arguments in the literature on why strikes are infrequent in Japan. Two traditional explanations focus on the structure of unionism and the long-term attachments between workers and firms.

Unions in Japan are typically 'enterprise' unions, meaning that the union's membership is confined within the boundaries of the firm. In addition, both blue- and white-collar workers are organized by the same union. While there are national federations, union business, including contract negotiations, is handled within the union by leaders elected from its membership. The end result is that the union leaders are often drawn from the firm's mid-level managers. This promotes a greater understanding by the union leaders of the firm's structure and its product markets. Moreover, corporate executives for personnel management are often drawn from workers who have previously served as union leaders. From the perspective of bargaining theory, this structural feature of Japan's unions should reduce overall dispute activity.[2]

In contrast to US industrial unions, enterprise unions cannot diversify the financial cost of a strike across members of bargaining units at other firms. This financial weakness has been advanced as one reason for the reluctance to call strikes (Hanami, 1979, 1984). While the direction of this effect is consistent with the prediction from a bargaining model, we are reluctant to conclude that this is a primary explanation. First, an enterprise union can still intertemporally diversify the financial cost of the strike. Second, there is a lack of empirical evidence supporting the importance of strike funds as a determinant of US strikes.[3]

The second traditional argument is that Japanese workers are reluctant to engage in strikes because of their long-term attachment to the firm. The life-time employment system creates a strong loyalty to the firm. The future prosperity of the workers is seen as dependent on the future prosperity of the firm (Shirai, 1984a). This explanation seems to fall short, for two reasons. First, Hall (1982) and Koike (1988) both point out that average tenure is quite high in the US, especially in the unionized sector. Second, initiating a strike is not inconsistent with a long-term interest by the union in the firm's prosperity. The risk of significant losses due to a protracted strike are the incentive for a firm to reach a settlement early in the negotiations.

Some alternative explanations have appeared in the literature in recent years. Freeman & Weitzman (1987) argue that the semi-annual bonus system in Japan constitutes a source of profit-sharing between firms and workers. If bonuses were explicitly indexed to firm profits, then they might serve as an alternative mechanism to disputes for raising union wages in 'good times'. However, bonuses are sometimes specified at the time of negotiations as a fixed number of months of pay.[4] In the context of a bargaining model, pre-specified bonuses are similar to deferred lump-sum payments. Viewed this way, the bonus system in Japan may in fact encourage strikes by keeping the base wage low.[5]

Morishima (1991) argues that information sharing through the Joint Consultation System (JCS) has resulted in lower dispute rates in Japan. The JCS represents an ongoing dialogue between the firm and the union through which the firm can inform the union on current business conditions, problems with productivity, and management plans for future investment. It is an established practice that as long as issues are being discussed in joint consultation unions will not exercise their right to strike over these issues (Shirai, 1984b, p. 120).

Morishima studies the effect of information sharing between workers and managers through joint consultation on collective bargaining outcomes during the 1980 Spring Wage Offensive. The data on information sharing consists of responses from 97 unions regarding whether the firm provided confidential information on profitability, employee productivity, plans for staffing adjustments, and labour costs. The union responses were coded into a summary variable which ranged from 0 for firms that provided no confidential information to 4 for firms that provided confidential information on each topic. Morishima finds that, controlling for other factors which may affect bargaining, firms which provide unions with more information experience on average shorter wage negotiations. Morishima interprets this result as supportive of the asymmetric information bargaining model.

In the case of a dispute, the cost of the dispute serves to convince the union of the veracity of the firm's claim as to the size of the surplus. With joint consultation, the issue is what insures the union that the information provided by the firm is accurate. Two factors seem to be important. First, one function of union federations is to gather and disseminate information to the member unions (Shimada, 1983). This information provides the union with a rough consistency check on the firm's information. Second, much of the confidential information provided through JCS is later made public through financial disclosure required of publicly held firms. Serious discrepancies, then, will be quickly detected and could result in difficult spring negotiations the following year.[6]

The potential role for JCS to reduce aggregate dispute activity in Japan also depends on the prevalence of JCS in Japanese firms. Table 12.2 shows the percentage of establishments which have JCS disaggregated by firm size, union status, and time period. The overall use of JCS increased from 63 percent in 1977 to 69 percent in 1989. The likelihood of a JCS increases with firm size. Similarly, unionized firms are more likely to have a JCS. Among unionized firms, the use of JCS increased from 72 percent in 1977 to 84 percent in 1989. This may be a part of the explanation for the decrease in the Japanese dispute rate in the 1980s.[7]

At this point, we would like to suggest some additional factors that may be important to understanding both the shift in composition of Japanese disputes away from strikes and the short dispute duration. The legal structure in Japan may contribute to the reluctance by unions to initiate strikes. This may at first seem paradoxical since the right to strike is more protected in Japan than in the US. In particular, the right to strike is guaranteed by the Japanese Constitution.

While much of the labour law in Japan was derivative from the Wagner Act, there are important exceptions. Once a union in the US is recognized as the official bargaining agent for a bargaining unit, that union has 'exclusive bargaining rights'. This implies that it is an unfair labour practice for the firm to negotiate either with another union claiming to represent some of the workers in the bargaining unit, or directly with the workers themselves. In return, the union is obligated to represent all workers in the bargaining unit, regardless of their union status.

In Japan, unions are not granted exclusive bargaining rights. This may have important implications for the union's choice of threats during negotiations. Kōshiro (1984, p. 206) explains this as follows:

> The system of exclusive representation has not been adopted in Japan, although the employee's right to collective negotiations is protected

Table 12.2   Percentage of establishments with Joint Consultation System

Year	1977	1984	1989
All	**62.6**	**65.2**	**69.4**
Firm size			
5000 +	70.3	81.0	83.4
1000 – 4999	75.7	74.0	76.1
300 – 999	65.8	64.4	66.6
100 – 299	52.1	56.1	57.2
With union	72.4	78.5	84.1
Without union	37.5	39.1	44.2

Source: *Survey on Labour–Management Communication* (1977, 1984, 1989), Ministry of Labour.

by the same articles in the law that sustain their right to organize. Therefore, if any group of two or more workers chooses to organize its own union and wishes to negotiate with its employer on behalf of its members, the employer is obligated to bargain with them.

A consequence is that unions may be reluctant to call a strike and risk having factions of its membership form breakaway unions. This would still be a concern even though a majority vote through secret ballot is required to initiate a strike (Articles 5, § 2 of the Trade Union Law).[8] This difference in union security would be consistent with a shift in the composition of disputes in Japan toward holdouts.

Recall from Table 12.1 that Japanese disputes tend to be resolved quickly. The average dispute duration over the past two decades was 33 days in Japan as compared to 83 days in the US. Cramton and Tracy (1992) show that the dispute duration necessary for the firm to signal its private information on the size of the surplus is expressed as a fraction (using discounted time) of the contract period. Negotiations in Japan take place on an annual basis. In contrast, long-term contracts in the US have become the norm since the 1950s. Borland and Tracy (1991) report that the *ex ante* contract duration for large bargaining units in the US is approximately 32 months. Ignoring discounting, this difference in contract duration alone would imply that dispute durations in Japan should on average be only 37 percent as long as in the US. This translates into an average dispute duration of 31 days, which is quite close to the observed duration of 33 days.

Before turning to our empirical findings, we would like to present the results of a Ministry of Labor survey which asked labour unions

Table 12.3　Union responses for reason for no disputes

Reason	Total	Firm size						JCS	
		30–99	100–299	300–499	500–999	1000–4999	5000+	with JCS	without JCS
Peace obligation in contract	6.2	1.1	0.0	14.0	2.7	22.7	6.1	8.1	0.0
Participation of Labour Relations Council	1.9	1.2	0.0	0.0	10.3	2.5	0.0	1.1	4.4
Desire to negotiate contract themselves	84.3	89.1	63.9	95.1	63.0	91.6	98.2	88.6	69.5
Concern over effect on firm's profitability	6.2	22.3	0.0	0.0	0.0	0.0	4.8	1.4	22.3
View disputes as ineffective	24.0	36.2	45.9	5.3	28.1	7.0	10.2	25.8	18.1
No important issues to dispute over	6.6	7.3	11.6	0.0	12.1	11.8	0.0	8.5	0.0
No direction or consent from upper organization	0.1	0.0	0.0	0.0	0.0	0.0	0.4	0.1	0.0
Loss of wages for members	4.3	0.0	2.9	1.2	4.2	29.7	0.0	4.8	2.4
Union finances	7.3	8.6	2.9	1.2	12.0	29.7	0.0	4.8	15.5
Too few members	0.7	0.0	0.0	1.3	4.2	0.0	0.0	0.2	2.4
Union security	1.0	0.0	0.0	1.3	4.2	3.1	0.0	0.6	2.4
No agreement by membership	5.3	7.3	0.0	0.0	0.0	34.7	0.4	4.7	7.4
Other	11.5	17.2	22.2	0.0	23.6	0.0	1.8	6.5	28.2

Source: Ministry of Labour (1987). Figures represent the percentage of union responses (where multiple responses were allowed) corresponding to the stated reason. The sample of unions was restricted to those which had not engaged in a labour dispute for the past three years.

their reasons for not engaging in labour disputes. The 1987 survey was administered to unions which had not been involved in a dispute for at least three years. Unions were allowed to give multiple responses. Table 12.3 provides the results of the survey. Each figure in Table 12.3 represents the percentage of unions indicating that response as a reason for not engaging in a dispute. A large percentage of unions felt generally that disputes were ineffective. In comparing specific reasons cited, union finances and concern for firm profits appear to be more important in the thinking of union leaders than union security – that is, the lack of exclusive bargaining rights.

12.3 EMPIRICAL ANALYSIS OF DISPUTES AND STRIKES IN JAPAN

In this section, we present our empirical results on the determinants of dispute and strike rates in Japan based on the industry aggregate data for the manufacturing industry. We begin the section with a discussion of the construction of the variables we use in our analysis. We then present our findings and compare them to the existing empirical literature on strikes in the US.

We use stock price data to construct measures of industry profitability and profit uncertainty. We control for industry profitability using the rate of return on the industry portfolio for the year preceding the Spring Wage Offensive.[9] To measure the degree of uncertainty over industry profits, we estimate the following market model for each industry.

$$R_{it} = \alpha + \beta R_{mt} + \epsilon_{it} ,$$

where R_{mt} is the market return at time t, R_{it} is the industry return at time t, and ϵ_{it} is the 'excess return' at time t. By netting out the effect of market conditions, the excess return reflects conditions specific to the industry.

To capture industry specific profit uncertainty, we control for the standard deviation of the industry's excess returns over the five month period ending on 31 December. To capture general market uncertainty, we control for the estimated industry beta times the standard deviation of the market returns over the same five month period.

We include controls for both the level of and uncertainty over inflation. The inflation rate is measured by the rate of increase in the quarterly GDP deflator for the Spring quarter. To measure inflation uncertainty, we estimate the following GARCH(1,1) model using the quarterly GDP deflator time series, π_t, for the period 1956:1 to 1989:1:

$$\pi_t = \alpha_0 + \alpha_1 \pi_{t-1} + \alpha_2 \pi_{t-2} + \epsilon_t , \quad where \; \epsilon_t \sim N(0, h_t)$$

$$h_t = \beta_0 + \beta_1 \epsilon_{t-1}^2 + \gamma h_{t-1} .$$

We use the square root of the conditional variance, h_t, as our measure of inflation uncertainty.

We characterize differences in labour market conditions using both level of the national unemployment rate and the uncertainty over unemployment. To measure unemployment uncertainty, we estimate the following GARCH(1,1) model using the quarterly national unemployment rate time series, u_t, for the period 1956.:1 to 1991:1:

$$u_t = \alpha_0 + \sum_{i=1}^{8} \alpha_i\, u_{t-i} + \epsilon_t\,, \quad where \ \epsilon_t \sim N(0,\, uh_t)$$

$$uh_t = \beta_0 + \beta_1\, \epsilon_{t-1}^2 + \gamma\, uh_{t-1}\,.$$

We use the square root of the conditional variance, uh_t, as our measure of unemployment uncertainty.

To test the effect of the profit-sharing on bargaining, we include a variable measuring the percentage of firms with a profit-sharing bonus system. This variable is obtained from the *1983 General Survey on Wages and Working Hours System* (GSWHS) conducted by Japan's Ministry of Labor. GSWHS gives the percentage of firms with a profit-sharing bonus system by five year intervals. We use linear interpolation to get yearly data. We also include a variable measuring the percentage of firms in an industry which negotiate both semi-annual bonus payments at the same time. This variable is also obtained from the 1983 GSWHS. Although most of small firms in Japan separately negotiate each bonus payment, some large firms negotiate both bonus payments either before the Winter or the Summer bonus season. Separate bonus negotiations allows each bonus payment to reflect more current information on the firm's performance. This should help to limit labour disputes during the Spring Wage Offensive.

The next set of variables attempts to control for the characteristics of the workers in each industry. We constructed industry averages for the years of job tenure, percentage male, and percentage university graduates using the data from the *Basic on Wage Structure Survey*. We can use the average tenure variable to test the effect of the long-term employment relationships on labour disputes.

Our empirical specification is completed with the following three variables. To control for possible firm size effects, we include the percentage of firms in the industry with less than 1000 workers. We also use this firm size variable to help control for the presence of JCS in the industry. Recall from Table 12.2 that there is a positive correlation between firm size and the likelihood that a firm has a JCS. We must resort to using firm size as a proxy for JCS since we do not have disaggregated industry time-series data on the prevalence of JCS. We control for the export intensity of each industry using the ratio of exports to total production. Firms in industries heavily involved in exports may face added pressure to keep their labour costs down. In addition, firms in export intensive industries must contend with uncertainties over changes in trade restrictions in the importing countries. Finally, we include the sales concentration ratio (Herfindahl Index) taken from the survey conducted by the Fair Trade Commission of Japan, because it is possible that the presence of monopoly rents in an industry may significantly affect the bargaining process.

For each industry and year in our sample, we observe the number of strikes (disputes), s_{it} (d_{it}), and the number of unions in the industry, n_{it}. To estimate the coefficients for the independent variables, we use the minimum logit chi-square method suggested by Berkson (1953).[10] Let p_{it} denote the observed strike (dispute) frequency for industry i in year t. Berkson's method of estimation is to use weighted least squares on the logistic transformation of p_{it}:

$$\ln\left(\frac{p_{it}}{1 - p_{it}}\right) = X_{it}\,\beta + u_{it}\,, \tag{1}$$

where,

$$V(u_{it}) = \frac{1}{n_{it}\,\theta_{it}(1 - \theta_{it})}\,, \tag{2}$$

and θ_{it} is the true strike (dispute) probability for each negotiation in industry i and year t.

For some industries p_{it} equals zero in certain years. The standard logistic transformation is undefined in these cases. We follow Cox (1970, p. 33) and use the following modified transformation:

$$\ln\left(\frac{p_{it} + \frac{1}{2n_{it}}}{1 - p_{it} + \frac{1}{2n_{it}}}\right) = X_{it}\,\mathbf{B} + u_{it}\,. \tag{3}$$

We use a two-step estimation procedure to generate our coefficient estimates. In the first step, we substitute $p_{it} + 1/2n_{it}$ for θ_{it} in the estimate of the variance in (2). We then estimate (3) using weighted least squares (WLS), where the weight is the reciprocal of the square root of the estimated variance. Using the estimates for β from the first-stage regression, we calculate predicted strike (dispute) probabilities for each observation in the sample, $\hat{p}_{it}$. We substitute $\hat{p}_{it}$ for θ_{it} in (2) and recalculate the weights for each observation. These new weights are used in a second-stage WLS estimation of (3) to obtain the final estimates for β.

Summary statistics for the variables used in the analysis are provided in Appendix Table A1. Prior to estimation, we standardized all continuous variables to have zero mean and unit standard deviation. For ease of interpretation and to facilitate comparisons across variables, we report 'standardized' marginal effects in addition to the logistic coefficients. Each marginal effect measures the change in the probability of a strike (dispute) associated with a one standard deviation change in the underlying variable.

We estimated logistic models for the strike incidence, dispute incidence, and dispute composition, the latter being defined as the percentage of disputes involving a strike. The findings are presented in Tables 12.4–12.6. Rather than discuss each table separately, we will discuss related results from each specification.

We find that difficulties in wage bargaining in Japan are more likely in periods of increased uncertainty. In particular, we find that in comparison with the US dispute and strike activity in Japan depends less on industry specific profit uncertainty, and more on general macro uncertainty. Inflation uncertainty has positive marginal effects on the incidence of strikes. The composition of disputes also shift toward strikes during periods of increased uncertainty over inflation.[11] In contrast, unemployment uncertainty has no effect on strike incidence but is associated with a higher overall level of dispute activity. This reflects the fact that the composition of disputes shifts toward holdouts during periods of increased uncertainty over unemployment.

The standard deviation in industry excess returns captures industry specific sources of uncertainty. To the extent that industry specific uncertainty is more likely than the macro uncertainty to reflect asymmetries in the information available to the firm and the union, bargaining models would suggest that the variability of the industry excess returns would have the strongest association with strikes and disputes. Tracy (1987), using firm specific excess return variances, finds this to be true for strikes in the US. In contrast, we find that increased industry uncertainty is associated with *less* strike and dispute activity. Industry specific uncertainty also shifts the composition of disputes away from strikes.

While the uncertainty over profitability and inflation are strongly associated with strikes and disputes, the industry rate of return on

Table 12.4   Strike incidence: logistic regression results

Variable	(1)		(2)	
	Logistic coeff.	Marginal effect	Logistic coeff.	Marginal effect
Constant	−3.37		−3.366	
	(0.032)		(0.032)	
Indus. stock	0.012	0.040	−0.005	−0.018
return	(0.029)	(0.096)	(0.030)	(0.097)
Std dev. of excess	−0.102	−0.327	−0.065	−0.211
rets	(0.033)	(0.108)	(0.035)	(0.114)
Std dev. of excess			0.059	
rets · % firms <			(0.0201)	
1000				
ß·Std dev. of mkt	0.033	0.106	0.021	0.067
rets	(0.023)	(0.074)	(0.023)	(0.075)
Inflation	0.127	0.409	0.123	0.396
rate	(0.0343)	(0.112)	(0.034)	(0.110)
Inflation	0.338	1.081	0.327	1.055
uncertainty	(0.030)	(0.105)	(0.029)	(0.104)
Unemployment	−0.352	−1.128	−0.318	−1.028
rate	(0.075)	(0.247)	(0.074)	(0.246)
Unemployment	0.003	0.009	0.001	0.004
uncertainty	(0.030)	(0.095)	(0.029)	(0.094)
Indus. export	−0.114	−0.364	−0.145	−0.466
intensity	(0.043)	(0.139)	(0.044)	(0.142)
Sales	0.085	0.273	0.063	0.201
concentration index	(0.045)	(0.146)	(0.045)	(0.146)
% firms <	−0.094	−0.300	−0.134	−0.433
1000	(0.037)	(0.117)	(0.037)	(0.123)
% change in real	−0.094	−0.301	−0.087	−0.280
wage	(0.036)	(0.116)	(0.035)	(0.115)
Profit-sharing	−0.133	−0.425	−0.102	−0.329
bonus system	(0.058)	(0.189)	(0.059)	(0.190)
Annual contract	0.036	0.116	0.096	0.310
bonus system	(0.044)	(0.140)	(0.047)	(0.153)
Job tenure	−0.456	−1.459	−0.513	−1.657
	(0.064)	(0.213)	(0.065)	(0.220)
Percentage male	0.191	0.612	0.234	0.757
	(0.053)	(0.171)	(0.054)	(0.174)
Percentage University	0.348	1.114	0.336	1.083
graduates	(0.036)	(0.126)	(0.036)	(0.125)
R^2	0.815		0.822	

Note: N=266 for all specifications. Standard errors are given in parentheses. Marginal effects represent the percentage point change in the strike incidence associated with a one standard deviation change in the underlying variable.

Table 12.5   Dispute incidence: logistic regression results

Variable	(1)		(2)	
	Logistic coeff.	Marginal effect	Logistic coeff.	Marginal effect
Constant	0.627		0.630	
	(0.022)		(0.021)	
Indus. stock	0.048	1.09	0.043	0.973
return	(0.027)	(0.613)	(0.027)	(0.623)
Std dev. of excess	−0.119	−2.70	−0.110	−2.492
rets	(0.027)	(0.615)	(0.029)	(0.650)
Std dev. of excess			0.017	
rets · % firms < 1000			(0.018)	
ß·Std dev. of mkt	0.009	0.199	0.006	0.132
rets	(0.016)	(0.362)	(0.016)	(0.369)
Inflation	0.024	0.537	0.0225	0.510
rate	(0.024)	(0.546)	(0.024)	(0.545)
Inflation	0.047	1.070	0.044	0.990
uncertainty	(0.031)	(0.702)	(0.031)	(0.706)
Unemployment	−0.143	−3.258	−0.137	−3.102
rate	(0.052)	(0.195)	(0.053)	(1.204)
Unemployment	0.109	2.474	0.108	2.461
uncertainty	(0.025)	(0.574)	(0.025)	(0.573)
Indus. export	−0.075	−1.706	−0.081	−1.83
intensity	(0.035)	(0.797)	(0.036)	(0.806)
Sales	0.026	0.592	0.022	0.498
concentration index	(0.037)	(0.840)	(0.037)	(0.844)
% firms <	−0.117	−2.660	−0.125	−2.843
1000	(0.032)	(0.723)	(0.033)	(0.750)
% change in real	−0.191	−4.323	−0.190	−4.298
wage	(0.032)	(0.736)	(0.032)	(0.736)
Profit-sharing	−0.154	−3.499	−0.149	−3.370
bonus system	(0.042)	(0.951)	(0.042)	(0.959)
Annual contract	0.018	0.408	0.030	0.682
bonus system	(0.034)	(0.763)	(0.036)	(0.816)
Job tenure	−0.391	−8.865	−0.402	−9.117
	(0.048)	(1.093)	(0.050)	(1.128)
Percentage male	0.323	7.333	0.330	7.482
	(0.044)	(0.999)	(0.044)	(1.012)
Percentage University	0.084	1.906	0.082	1.857
graduates	(0.029)	(0.651)	(0.028)	(0.652)
R^2	0.646		0.648	

Note: $N=266$ for all specifications. Standard errors are given in parentheses. Marginal effects represent the percentage point change in the dispute incidence associated with a one standard deviation change in the underlying variable.

Table 12.6 Dispute composition: logistic regression results

Variable	(1) Logistic coeff.	(1) Marginal effect	(2) Logistic coeff.	(2) Marginal effect
Constant	−2.90 (0.032)		−2.898 (0.032)	
Indus. stock return	−0.006 (0.032)	−0.029 (0.159)	−0.025 (0.033)	−0.122 (0.161)
Std dev. of excess rets	−0.071 (0.036)	−0.348 (0.175)	−0.035 (0.038)	−0.172 (0.186)
Std dev. of excess rets · % firms < 1000			0.058 (0.022)	
ß·Std dev. of mkt rets	0.038 (0.024)	0.189 (0.119)	0.026 (0.024)	0.130 (0.120)
Inflation rate	0.115 (0.036)	0.567 (0.179)	0.110 (0.035)	0.547 (0.172)
Inflation uncertainty	0.372 (0.032)	1.832 (0.173)	0.361 (0.032)	1.789 (0.172)
Unemployment rate	−0.268 (0.078)	−1.318 (0.391)	−0.238 (0.077)	−1.176 (0.390)
Unemployment uncertainty	−0.074 (0.032)	−0.363 (0.160)	−0.076 (0.032)	−0.374 (0.157)
Indus. export intensity	−0.101 (0.046)	−4.983 (0.229)	−0.129 (0.047)	−0.639 (0.233)
Sales concentration index	0.051 (0.048)	0.251 (0.239)	0.031 (0.048)	0.152 (0.240)
% firms < 1000	−0.061 (0.039)	−0.302 (0.193)	−0.100 (0.041)	−0.495 (0.203)
% change in real wage	−0.012 (0.039)	−0.062 (0.191)	−0.007 (0.038)	−0.033 (0.189)
Profit-sharing bonus system	−0.085 (0.061)	−0.420 (0.303)	−0.058 (0.062)	−0.285 (0.305)
Annual contract bonus system	0.066 (0.046)	0.323 (0.225)	0.120 (0.049)	0.595 (0.246)
Job tenure	−0.370 (0.0666)	−1.819 (0.334)	−0.423 (0.068)	−2.094 (0.345)
Percentage male	0.125 (0.056)	0.616 (0.276)	0.163 (0.057)	0.810 (0.281)
Percentage University graduates	0.316 (0.038)	1.552 (0.201)	0.304 (0.037)	1.508 (0.200)
R^2	0.785		0.793	

Note: $N=266$ for all specifications. Standard errors are given in parentheses. Marginal effects represent the percentage point change in the dispute composition associated with a one standard deviation change in the underlying variable.

equity and the rate of inflation have less important effects. For strike incidence, the marginal effect of the inflation rate is only 40 percent of the magnitude of the marginal effect of uncertainty over inflation. For dispute incidence, the marginal effect of industry profitability is only 50 percent of the magnitude of the marginal effect of uncertainty over profitability. The evidence of these effects on bargaining in the US is mixed. Tracy (1986) and Gramm, Hendricks and Kahn (1988) find no relationship between the rate of return on equity and the strike incidence. In contrast, McConnell (1990) finds strike incidence to have a significant negative relationship with an industry profitability index. Vroman (1989) finds a positive but imprecisely measured effect of the expected inflation rate on strike incidence.

The structure of bargaining in Japan may explain why industry specific uncertainty is less likely to generate disputes (but not why it has a negative effect). As we noted above, union leaders typically have experience as managers for the firm. This should increase the union's awareness of the impact of changing industry conditions on the firm's competitive position. In addition, JCS provide an ongoing conduit of information between the firm and the union, which in conjunction with annual contracts should minimize informational asymmetries at the outset of negotiations.

As a proxy for the prevalence of JCS, the bargaining model would suggest that our measure of firm size should have a positive effect on dispute and strike incidence, and a positive interaction with the variability of industry excess returns. What we find is that smaller firms in Japan are less likely to be involved in a dispute and a strike. The magnitudes of these effects are roughly proportionate so that firm size has no net effect on the composition of disputes. The interaction effect is positive for both strike and dispute, and significant for strikes.

Firm size may also affect bargaining for reasons independent of its relationship with JCS. In Japan, the prevalence of enterprise unionism implies that firm size and bargaining unit size are essentially the same. In the US, these size measures typically differ and researchers have estimated the role of each on strike activity. Gramm, Hendricks and Kahn (1988) and McConnell (1990) both find that the likelihood of a strike increases with the size of the bargaining unit. In contrast, Tracy (1986) finds that strike incidence is decreasing with firm size as measured by firm sales. These contrasting findings for bargaining unit and firm size make it difficult to infer what the pure size effect would be in Japan.

A common finding in studies of US bargaining is that strike incidence is procyclic as measured by the unemployment rate. McConnell

(1990) provides the most detailed study of this relationship by reporting specifications with aggregate, regional, and industry unemployment rate.[12] All three measures of unemployment have a negative effect on strike activity, with the regional measure being the most robust.

Consistent with the US findings, we find that dispute and strike activity in Japan are strongly procyclic with respect to the unemployment rate. In addition, we find that in periods of higher unemployment the composition of disputes shifts away from strikes. This is consistent with the predictions of a bargaining model with a threat choice between holdout and strike.[13]

A second consistent finding in US studies is the negative impact of real wage growth over the prior contract on strike activity. We find similar negative effects on both the dispute and strike incidence in Japan. A bargaining model would suggest that real wage growth would lower strike rates through shifts in the composition of disputes away from strikes. We find no confirmation of this prediction in our data. Changes in the real wage have no effect on the composition of disputes.

Our data indicate that the structure of compensation affects the level of dispute activity in the industry. Firms with profit-sharing bonus systems appear to be less likely to experience either a strike or a holdout during their contract negotiation. This suggests that profit-sharing plans may act as a substitute mechanism for the screening or signalling role of costly negotiations as a way of linking compensation to the future performance on the firm. Firms that negotiate bonus payments once a year instead of twice a year appear to experience more disputes, but this effect is imprecisely measured.

The data also indicate that the structure of the product market has important implications for bargaining outcomes. Firms in export intensive industries face less difficulty negotiating contracts. Both dispute incidence and strike incidence are significantly lower in these industries. In addition, increasing the importance of exports in an industry is associated with a shift in the composition of disputes towards holdouts. Industries with higher sales concentrations have higher levels of strike activity. While the effect of sales concentration on dispute activity is positive as well, it is imprecisely measured. Studies using US negotiations have found negative but insignificant effects of sales concentrations on strike activity (Gramm, Hendricks and Kahn, 1988; Abowd and Tracy, 1989).

The personal characteristics of the workforce are important determinants of strike and dispute activity. We find strong support for the claim that long-term employment relationships are associated with fewer

labour disputes. Increasing the average job tenure of the workers by 2.1 years is associated with roughly a 1.5 percent decline in the likelihood of a strike and roughly a 7.5 percent decline in the likelihood of a dispute. Firms with a higher percentage of male worker are more likely to experience both strikes and disputes. The more educated the workforce, the greater the risk of strikes and labour disputes. The composition of disputes shifts toward strikes as both the percentage of males and the percentage of college graduates increases. This could reflect a lower relative cost of strikes to holdouts due to a greater ability of these workers to secure part-time employment during a strike.

12.4   CONCLUSION

In this chapter we present time-series evidence on the prevalence of disputes and strikes in Japan and the US. We use the asymmetric information bargaining framework to evaluate the many hypotheses on why the mechanism for negotiating labour contracts in Japan produces fewer strikes. To further understand how this mechanism works, we present estimates of the empirical determinants of disputes and strikes and compare them to findings for collective bargaining in the US.

A robust finding for US negotiations is that strike activity is procyclic with respect to the aggregate unemployment rate. We find a similar pattern in Japan. In contrast, we find that in Japan macro uncertainty rather than industry specific uncertainty is an important reason for protracted negotiations.

This raises some challenges for the asymmetric information bargaining framework, and suggests that JCS may play an important role in reducing the difficulty in reaching a settlement.

We also find that the facts are consistent with the traditional argument that long-term employment system and the profit sharing system reduce dispute activity.

Appendix

Table 12.A.1 Summary statistics

Variable	Mean	Std. dev.	Minimum	Maximum
Indus. stock return	0.0138	0.12	−0.32	0.45
Std dev. of excess rets	0.72	0.29	0.24	3.00
ß·Std Dev. of Mkt rets	0.72	0.51	0.02	3.01
Inflation rate	1.50	0.94	−0.61	2.84
Inflation uncertainty	0.72	0.20	0.53	1.30
Unemployment rate	2.20	0.46	1.26	2.84
Unemployment uncertainty	0.015	0.002	0.013	0.020
Indus. export intensity	11.7	8.37	1.13	35.3
Concentration index (HI)	1238.4	499.2	145	2537
% Firms < 1000	81.0	9.39	45.6	97.74
Profit-sharing bonus system	22.4	6.57	6.77	39.5
Annual contract bonus system	11.6	4.63	2.49	39.6
Job tenure	10.7	2.07	6.48	17.6
Percentage of male worker	73.1	13.4	36.2	91.6
Percentage of University graduate worker	11.0	5.62	2.42	24.7
% change in real wage	1.45	1.67	−2.13	7.32

Note: Variables are defined in its text.

370 *Labour Disputes in Japan and the US*

Notes

* This chapter was presented at the Biwako conference, Osaka (July 1992), and the NBER University Research Conference, 'The Labor Market in International Perspective.' We would like to thank Thomas Kneisner, Motohiro Morishima, Mari Sako and David Weinstein for their helpful comments. Ohtake acknowledges financial assistance from the Nomura Foundation for Social Science.

1. A detailed description of this data can be found in Tracy (1987).
2. Reder and Neumann (1980) stress the importance of bargaining 'protocols' as a mechanism for peaceful negotiations. Enterprise unionism fosters the development of these protocols by ensuring that the union leadership and management have a solid working relationship that they bring to the bargaining table.
3. However, there are many examples in the press where the decision by a union to either continue or discontinue subsidizing a strike by a particular bargaining unit is seen as pivotal to the timing of a settlement. An example is the series of votes by the pilots' union over the surtax placed on its membership to finance the pilots' strike at Eastern Airlines (see the *New York Times*, 13 September 1989, and the *Wall Street Journal*, 11 October 1989 (Bvadshen, 1989a, 1989b).
4. For large corporations, recent bonuses have averaged seven months of base pay – three months paid in the summer bonus and four months paid in the winter bonus.
5. This argument applies even though Freeman and Weitzman find that bonuses show more sensitivity to firm profits than the base wage.
6. More generally, if the union observes *ex post* an imperfect signal of the true surplus, then strikes may be viewed as a punishment scheme when the firm's report appears to be an outlier. This argument is formalized in papers by Bayer (1991) and Robinson (1991).
7. Unfortunately, we do not have similar time-series information on the amount of information provided to unions through JCS.
8. The Nihon steel strike of 1954 is one example where the union organization split as a result of a long strike.
9. The industry portfolio is a value weighted index.
10. See also Maddala (1983, pp. 28–32).
11. Gramm, Hendricks and Kahn (1988) find that inflation uncertainty as measured by the dispersion in CPI forecasts in the Livingston Surveys has a significant positive relation to strike incidence in the US. However, this study did not include any industry or firm specific uncertainty measures.
12. McConnell also estimates a specification that replaces the unemployment rates with a measure of the business cycle. She finds a negative and significant coefficient for the business cycle index.
13. See the discussion in Cramton and Tracy (1992).

References

Abowd, John and Joseph Tracy (1989) 'Market Structure, Strike Activity, and Union Wage Settlements', *Industrial Relations*, vol. 28, no. 2, Spring, pp. 227–50.

Bayer, Amanda (1991) 'The Effect of Past, Present and Future on Strike Activity: Supergame Play Within a Bargaining Unit'. *Working Paper*, Yale University.

Berkson, J. (1953) 'A Statistically Precise and Relatively Simple Method of Estimating the Bio-Assay with Quantal Response, Based on the Logistic Function'. *Journal of the American Statistical Association*, vol. 48, pp. 565–99.

Borland, Jeff, and Joseph S. Tracy (1991) 'The Determinants of Labor Contract Duration and Early Renegotiation: Empirical Analysis', *Working Paper*, Yale University.

Bradsher, Keith (1989b) 'Strike Pay At Eastern Continuing'. *Wall Street Journal*, 11 October.

————— (1989a) 'Pilots' Union is Divided by Walkout at Eastern'. *New York Times*, 13 September.

Cox, D.R. (1970) *Analysis of Binary Data*. London, Methuen.

Cramton, Peter C. and Joseph S. Tracy (1992) 'Strikes and Holdouts in Wage Bargaining: Theory and Data'. *American Economic Review*, vol. 82, March, pp. 100–21.

Freeman, Richard and Martin L. Weitzman (1987) 'Bonuses and Employment in Japan'. *Journal of the Japanese and International Economies*, vol. 1, June, pp. 168–94.

Gramm, Cynthia L., Wallace E. Hendricks and Lawrence M. Kahn (1988) 'Inflation Uncertainty and Strike Activity'. *Industrial Relations*, vol. 27, Winter, pp. 114–29.

Hall, Robert E. (1982) 'The Importance of Lifetime Jobs in the U.S. Economy'. *American Economic Review*, vol. 72, September, pp. 716–24.

Hanami, Tadashi (1979) *Labor Relations in Japan Today*, Tokyo, Kodansha International.

————— (1984) 'The Function of the Law in Japanese Industrial Relations', In Taishiro Shirai (ed.), *Contemporary Industrial Relations in Japan*, Madison, WI, University of Wisconsin Press, pp. 161-77.

Koike, Kazuo (1988) *Understanding Industrial Relations in Modern Japan*, London, Macmillan.

Kōshiro, Kazutoshi (1984) 'Development of Collective Bargaining in Postwar Japan', in Taishiro Shirai (ed.), *Contemporary Industrial Relations in Japan*, Madison, WI, University of Wisconsin Press, pp. 205–57.

Maddala, G.S. (1983) *Limited-Dependent and Qualitative Variables in Econometrics, Cambridge*, Cambridge University Press.

McConnell, Sheena (1990) 'Cyclical Fluctuations in Strike Activity'. *Industrial & Labor Relations Review*, vol. 44, no. 1, October, pp. 130–43.

Morishima, Motohiro (1991) 'Information Sharing and Collective Bargaining in Japan: Effects on Wage Negotiation'. *Industrial & Labor Relations Review*, vol. 44, no. 3, pp. 469–85.

Reder, Melvin and George Neumann (1980) 'Conflict and Contract: The

Case of Strikes', *Journal of Political Economy*, vol. 88, October, pp. 867–86.

Robinson, James (1991) 'Theory of Strike Behavior', *Working Paper,* Yale University.

Shimada, Haruo (1983) 'Wage Determination and Information Sharing: An Alternative Approach to Incomes Policy?', *Journal of Industrial Relations*, vol. 25, June, pp. 177–200.

Shirai, Taishiro (1984a) 'Characteristics of Japanese Managements', in Taishiro Shirai (ed.), *Contemporary Industrial Relations in Japan*, Madison, WI, University of Wisconsin Press, pp. 369–82.

————— (1984b) 'A Theory of Enterprise Unionism', in Taishiro Shirai (ed.), *Contemporary Industrial Relations in Japan*, Madison, WI, University of Wisconsin Press, pp. 117–43.

Tracy, Joseph S. (1986) 'An Investigation into the Determinants of U.S. Strike Activity'. *American Economic Review*, vol. 76, no. 3, pp. 423–36.

————— (1987) 'An Empirical Test of an Asymmetric Information Model of Strikes'. *Journal of Labor Economics*, vol. 5, April, pp. 149–73.

Vroman, Susan (1989) 'A Longitudinal Analysis of Strike Activity in U.S. Manufacturing: 1957–1984', *American Economic Review*, vol. 79, September, pp. 816–26.

Index of Authors

Note: **bold type** indicates contributions to this volume.

Index of Subjects

rank order contest wage
    determination 222
real wage resistance 266, 271, 272–3,
    279–80
real wages
    and economic shocks 273–5
    and incidence of disputes 367
    international differences 2
    see also wages
regional effects
    growth of firms, USA 306–7
    Swedish labour market
        programmes 36, 37–8, 39, 46
    wage differentials: Japan 60, 61,
        62–4; USA 14, 93–126
regulation, and wage differentials
    74–7, 79–80
relative performance evaluation wage
    determination 221–2, 223
relief jobs 40, 47, 48
    see also labour market programmes
Report on Securities, Japan 147,
    148
risk
    and corporate diversification 303
    and deferred payment
        arrangements 314, 320–1
    Japanese aversion to 6–7
    and main bank system 314, 323–4
    see also uncertainty

Sanwa 322
seniority wage system
    and age of employees 131–4, 135,
        147, 148
    in Japan 3–4, 131–53
    and job tenure 131–4, 146–51
    promotion in 3–4, 51, 131, 135,
        137–46, 228–30
    in USA 226, 228–9
sex of employee
    and incidence of disputes 360, 368
    as labour market programmes
        variable 40, 47
    as wage differential variable 62–4,
        67–8, 70–2, 74–7, 84–5
share economy and profit-sharing 16,
    140–1, 324, 355, 360, 367
shirking 146, 224, 315–20
size of establishment
    and performance-related pay 225,
        234, 235, 238, 243
    as wage differential variable 60,
        62–4, 70

size of firm
    and corporate structure 298–302
    and growth of firm 297–302, 307,
        310
    and Japanese labour market 8, 26
    and job creation 301
    and job satisfaction 186, 198, 201,
        203–7, 208–9
    and joint consultation system
        (JCS) 356, 357, 360, 363–6
    and labour market programmes 49
    and labour turnover 301
    as promotion variable 143–6
    and stability 303
    as wage differential variable
        62–4, 67–8, 70–2, 74–7, 81–8
        passim
    and wage dispersion 85–6
skills
    and educational levels 108–9, 114,
        125
    and employment 109
    supply and demand 108–9, 110–13,
        114, 123, 125
    and wage differentials 104–6,
        108–13, 118–21, 122
    see also human capital;
        qualifications; training
Spain, unemployment 254, 277, 281,
    282–3
specialization
    and job satisfaction 209–10
    and wage differentials 14, 103–4,
        117
Spring Wage Offensive 136, 137,
    147–8, 351
strikes
    comparative incidence in USA and
        Japan 349–53
    Japan 359–68
    see also disputes
substitution effects
    high and low skilled men 110–13
    male by female workers 15, 105,
        106–7, 110–13
Sumitomo 322
supply of labour *see* labour market
*Survey on the Accumulation of Assets
    and on Worker Life in Major
    Metropolitan Areas*, Japan
    18–183
*Survey on Labor Management of
    Female Workers*, Japan 158,
    176, 179

working conditions *cont.*
  and wage differentials 58–9, 74–7,
    79, 87
working hours
  flexible 17, 176, 178, 179
  and growth of firm 309

international differences 2
and job retention 156, 176–8
as job satisfaction variable 209,
  210
as variable of wage differentials
  60–1, 62–4, 70, 71